Higher Education
India and Abroad

Volume 1

University: The Seat of Higher Learning

Higher Education
India and Abroad

Volume 1

University: The Seat of Higher Learning

Rashmi Soni

Published by

ATLANTIC

PUBLISHERS & DISTRIBUTORS (P) LTD

7/22, Ansari Road, Darya Ganj, New Delhi-110002
Phones : +91-11-40775252, 23273880, 23275880, 23280451
Fax : +91-11-23285873
Web : www.atlanticbooks.com
E-mail : orders@atlanticbooks.com

Branch Office
5, Nallathambi Street, Wallajah Road, Chennai-600002
Phones : +91-44-64611085, 32413319
E-mail : chennai@atlanticbooks.com

ISBN 978-81-269-1877-5
ISBN 978-81-269-1879-9 (Set)

Printed in India at Glorious Printers, A-13, D.S.I.D.C., Jhilmil Industrial Area, Delhi-110095

Foreword

Unlike other professional fields, leaders and managers in higher education are not well conversant with systems, practices, experience, innovations and thinking in this area, considered as an engine of leadership, growth and development. Hence, the decisions at micro to macro level are made without adequate knowledge base and are in many cases not quality decisions. Further, the non-availability of scholars and experts in the area has worsened the situation; in fact the schools of education in the country devote their attention and efforts, to a very large extent, to secondary education; some academic efforts are also being made in the field of primary education. On the whole, little if any, importance is attached to higher education and its management in the academic activities of the schools of education. This is another reason for dearth of professional expertise in the field.

Very few books which consider the multifarious facets of higher education in reasonable depth are available, and in the absence of an adequate knowledge base, the decision makers have to be content with some stray articles and intuition or advice, based on experience. The state of affairs is also a handicap for the few researchers in this rather unpopular area.

The present book by Dr. Rashmi Soni, in two volumes, is an admirable attempt, which provides a knowledge base for graduate students and researchers. It fulfills the awareness-cum-referral needs of managers and decision makers in this crucial area. Many new areas of contemporary importance have been introduced in the book.

A novel feature of the book is its brief discussion of the higher education system around the world. In addition to providing a knowledge base, it is also a source of innovation and identification of opportunities for mutually profitable collaboration. Acquisition of such knowledge is necessary for rational participation in higher education at the global scale.

Some exercises at the end of the chapters would have considerably enhanced the tutorial value of the book; the author may take up this suggestion in the next edition. I congratulate Rashmi on a job, exceedingly well done.

Mahendra Singh Sodha
Lucknow University
Lucknow, India

Preface

> Beyond its traditional functions of teaching, training, research and study, all of which remain fundamentally the educational mission of higher education, its responsibility also includes promoting development of the whole person and training responsible, informed citizens committed to a better society in the future.
>
> —*UNESCO, 2009*

Education is the most critical input in shaping human destinies. The natural potential of any person requires educational inputs to provide a framework for maximum development. The goal of education is to empower human beings for improving the quality of life of the society. While basic education provides a framework for skill development, it is higher education which empowers individuals and nations to compete and prosper in this world.

People from all ages and backgrounds decide to enter higher education for a variety of reasons. Although the decision to enter higher education is a very individual one, yet most students enter the university to experience the lifestyle, meeting new people and qualifying for employment. In the school, it is normal for the students to wonder about the nature of university and higher education, the difference between the universities in India and those abroad, and whether the university functions the same way as a school. They also ponder over different types of universities and the difference between a university and a professional institute. They also wonder as to how the university teaching differs from school teaching.

The importance of higher education in society changes according to the country. For example, in many countries, a student goes to a university to obtain a diploma for work, but university also provides an opportunity to be independent. Students also learn to interact with people of different origins, and to grow as one entity. University is about more than what is taught within the walls of a classroom. It is about getting involved with and becoming a part of the campus life. Joining student organizations and volunteering to work in the community develops leadership skills. The personal development and growth that a student experiences will make him/her more organized, confident, and capable of handling the responsibilities in life. He/she will greatly enhance the ability to work in a more effective and efficient manner along with a variety of people.

Higher education has given ample proof of its viability over the centuries and of its ability to bring change and progress in society. Owing to the scope and pace of change, society has become increasingly knowledge-based so that higher learning and research now act as essential components of cultural, socio-economic and environmentally sustainable development of individuals, communities and nations. The place of a country in the comity of nations is determined much more by its knowledge base and intellectual potential than by material resources. Higher education itself is confronted therefore with formidable challenges and must proceed to the most radical change and renewal it has ever been required to undertake, so that our society, which is currently undergoing a crisis of values, can transcend mere economic considerations and incorporate deeper dimensions of morality and spirituality.

The book *Higher Education: India and Abroad* is an effort to provide an introduction to the essential topics of higher education. The book is important because we are living in an age of knowledge and globalization. Higher education is an important dimension in the economic development of the nation and the world at large. It has become important for the teachers and the students to understand the nature and potential of the institution of university and be aware of its history. This book provides ways and means to achieve this end. Research scholars and graduate level students in higher education and related fields will find the book useful for expanding the domains and exploring these central issues, while policymakers and academic administrators will find the thoughtful ideas on a particular issue useful for decision-making. It is unfortunate that higher education is hardly mentioned in the current programmes of faculty of education in universities, viz. B.Ed., M.Ed. M.Phil., M.A. (Edu) in India. There are very few professionals available in the area of higher education. Stakeholders, namely vice chancellors, deans, heads, professors, administrators, government officials, parents, students and general public are not conversant with the issues and options in the field. Further, there is dearth of research on higher education and related aspects, especially with reference to India. Higher education is gradually entering the curriculum of universities all over India, but unfortunately there is no textbook available which covers salient aspects and issues. The book attempts to fill this gap.

The book is presented in two volumes for focused study of different issues separately, and convenience in reading. Chapters in the first volume cover central themes in the study of higher education, viz. idea and concept of a university institution; history of university in India and around the world; aims and philosophy of higher education around the world in the present changing environment; governance, management and administration of a university system; and structure and organization of universities around the world. Chapters in the second volume focus on contemporary issues related to higher education, especially with reference to India, viz. university autonomy and accountability, financing higher education, globalization and privatization in higher education, collaboration of university and industry, research and innovation, value education, and quality management in higher education. The book will help the students and teachers understand that higher education is not just academics but an education for life—something beyond the walls of the university.

Together, these volumes provide an easily accessible and reliable source of concepts and information. It also provides "A Case Study in Institution Building: Devi Ahilya Vishwavidyalaya (1988-1992)", by Prof. Sodha and Prof. Pathak, which will help in learning that structure and conventions of an institution can be changed for the better through lateral thinking and innovations.

The book is neither a guide nor an encyclopedia; it provides a discussion of central and key concepts related to a university institution and higher education in general. The purpose of this book is to help the students, teachers, parents, government, and the community in general to appreciate the concept of higher education and university, since it is meant to serve a public cause. It is well known that high expectations inspire a university to maintain higher standards and that high expectations can only result from knowledge of the best university practices.

The book will create a desire in general and educationally aware readers to learn about the history, purpose and activities of this age-old institution. It provides concise, brief and consolidated information regarding important elements and dimensions of higher education. People, who wish to know about the contributions of the university and its futurology will find the book useful.

I hope that the book will convey a sense of dynamism, innovation and dialogue in this area to the readers. Although I am well aware of the omissions, it is really difficult to include details. I would be obliged if the readers share their comments and suggestions for upgrading the text in the next edition and thereby help me to be closer to their requirements.

Rashmi Soni

Contents

VOLUME 2: CONCEPTS RELATED WITH HIGHER EDUCATION

VOLUME 1
University: The Seat of Higher Learning

Understanding University Institution

1

A university is an organized and degree-giving institution, intended for the study and advancement of the different branches of higher learning and be self-governing in its nature, and, to some extent, national in scope.

—*Ernest Barker (1931)*

A university is an institution of higher education and learning, usually with a high reputation in teaching and research. It is a corporate body empowered to award its own degrees. It usually has post-graduate and professional schools that offer master's and doctoral degrees and an undergraduate division, which awards bachelor's degrees. It carries out research, consultancy and extension activities as well as teaching or empowerment for learning.

Higher education requires as a minimum condition of admission, the successful completion of secondary education or evidence of the attainment of an equivalent level of knowledge. Higher education is a segment of tertiary education, which usually refers to education being offered in institutions leading to graduate and post-graduate degrees and institutions training people in higher-level skills, knowledge and competencies. In a more restricted sense, the term "higher education" is used to mean regular education in colleges and universities. All institutions imparting instruction leading to a university degree or an equivalent may be termed as institutions (including colleges) of higher education. Institutions in this category include undergraduate degree colleges, and university departments in medicine, law, veterinary sciences, agriculture, engineering, nursing, secondary teacher training, etc. and post-graduate departments in university/college campuses and post-graduate institutions in management, agriculture, engineering, medicine, etc.; centers of advanced study and research are also components of higher education. Thus, higher education provides instruction in many branches of knowledge, to be acquired by concentrated effort.

A university is not an institution, as many suppose, where 'all' subjects are taught. The university, as the name suggests is a 'universe'. 'University' is derived from the Latin word *Universitas,* meaning an organized body or a corporation of individuals (community). In the past, scholars from various parts of the country formed themselves in the past into guilds for protection and security. So the word university means a meeting place of scholars, a place where knowledge-seeking people come, and take time off other activities to widen their intellectual horizons. In this sense, the university is a sanctuary—a unitary entity of space and time, quite separate from the hustle-bustle of the world surrounding it and thus it tends to be an island or an ivory tower onto itself. It is a self-governing community of scholars comprising teachers, students and administrators; who must guard, expand, and perpetuate knowledge. The purpose of this congregation is scholarship that is generating, acquiring and sharing knowledge. The university constitutes a community in the sense that it has a certain physical manifestation, similar to that of a community. Thus, scholars share a community life; they work in a single physical campus and constantly interact with each other. This community, which comprises the university, is self-governing. They govern themselves within the framework decided by the society or the State.

Within this broad framework of the societal mandate, the university community determines the specific directions it takes and the manner in which it discharges its social responsibilities. For the teachers, a university is a place where they generate new knowledge and share it with their professional peers and students. For the students, it is a place where they acquire knowledge. The relationship between these two categories of scholars is symbiotic.

In its modern sense, it means a body devoted to learning and education. It is a very special entity, where a community of scholars and students are ideally engaged in the eternal task of seeking the truth. It brings people together, who are professionally dedicated to the quest and transmission of truth in scientific terms. It is not merely a place for instruction but also provides a platform where the student can participate actively in research and innovative activities. This experience of research, innovation and experimentation helps him to acquire the intellectual discipline associated with education, which remains with him throughout his life.

Richard Livingstone (1974) in one of his well-known essays points out that the universities are nerve centers of modern civilization. Abolish the universities, abolish the mind. That is why Newman (1976) writes in *The Idea of a University* that the metropolis of a country is a university. A university is no doubt a seat of learning; the terminal state should be the completion and fulfillment of the initial state. It should be a spectrum of possibilities, not a church. It should be a laboratory of character-training and soul-making. Education does not only mean teaching people to know what they do not know; it means teaching them to behave as members of the family, of the community, of the nation and of the world at large. And it is by practicing greatness that one becomes great just as one becomes a swimmer by swimming or knows food by eating it. To practice greatness, the university should have a vision of greatness.

Thinking on these very lines, Kulandaiswamy (1999) in his article "Higher Education Leads towards Leadership" states that a university is a nursery for the creative talent to sprout; it is the farm that provides fertile soil and favourable climate for one's talent to find the fullest manifestation. It is the environment where leadership develops and a place where expeditions into the unknown are initiated and encouraged. It is also the place where inventions and innovations germinate and blossom. No developing nation can allow its university soil to become arid without endangering the future of its youth and therefore its own future. Thus, higher education should make the student an independent thinker, a critical listener and a human being, responsible to himself/herself who can explore and work out his/her own values, in particular those concerned with religion, politics and personal relationships. For many students, the most important thing they get from higher education is a clearer understanding of themselves and the principles by which they should live. The spirit of enquiry that drives research makes higher education different from the education provided at a school. It is characterized by an attitude of challenging, testing and criticizing the accepted truth of the day.

Many years after Kulandaiswamy opined his vision of university, the Yashpal Committee, 2008, in its report on "Renovation and Rejuvenation of Higher Education", expressed somewhat the same ideas on this institution. It idealized a university as a place where new ideas germinate, strike roots and grow tall and sturdy. It is a unique space, which covers the entire universe of knowledge. It is a place where creative minds converge, interact with each other and construct visions of new realities. Established notions of truth are challenged in the pursuit of knowledge. Prof. Yashpal opined that universities are diverse in their design and organization, reflecting the unique historical and socio-cultural settings in which they have grown.

Universities are centers of learning and have always been places where the skills and knowledge of students are chiseled to suit the requirements of the workplace. Often it is said, that in India the problem is more of employability, than that of unemployment, which means that the skills that the students have, are not appropriate for securing employment. Therefore, it is imperative that our universities assess the requirements of the job market well in advance, and structure courses in a manner that will help their students enter the employment market and to be rightly skilled for jobs that are available. Higher education should also encourage our youth to set up their own enterprises. In this context, interaction of the students of the university with local business/industry and socio-economic organizations would be useful for an understanding of the dynamics of business, particularly about sectors that have a growth potential.

In a rapidly changing world, graduates need to be lifelong *learners*. The primary role of higher education is increasingly to transform students by *enhancing* their knowledge, skills, attitudes and abilities while simultaneously *empowering* them as lifelong critical and reflective learners. Therefore, 'employability' of graduates should not be seen as the only focus of higher education. Rather, employability is a subset of, and fundamentally contingent on, transformative lifelong learning. In many countries, since the 1980s, there has been increasing pressure on higher education to contribute directly to national economic regeneration and growth. Increasingly, national and international assessments of the role and purposes of education indicate a need for higher education to contribute significantly to 'meeting the needs of the economy', to ensure future competitiveness (Ball, 1990; EC, 1991; IRDAC, 1990).

The ability of a nation to use and create knowledge capital determines its capacity to empower its citizens by increasing human capabilities. In the words of Dr. Manmohan Singh, "The time has come to create a second wave of institution building and of excellence in the field of education, research and capability building so that we are better prepared for the 21st century." With this broad framework in mind, the National Knowledge Commission (NKC), 2005 focussed on creating a world-class environment for creation of knowledge, promoting applications of knowledge for sustained and inclusive growth and using knowledge applications in efficient delivery of public places. It emphasized that the universities perform a critical role in economy and society. They create, assimilate and disseminate knowledge. Therefore, they must be flexible, innovative and creative and of course accountable to the society.

While institutions of higher education have their responsibilities of imparting good education to their students, students should also contribute to improved societal conditions. Undoubtedly, universities are public institutions meant to serve the public cause and not just ivory towers unconcerned with what takes place in the larger community. The universities have to equip our youths to contribute to the nation building. They are like a lighthouse showing direction to our students to help the country tread the path of success. University education is meant to make the life more meaningful that gives greater fulfillment. Advances in Science and Technology have opened new areas of activities and new fields of knowledge; the youths have to be equipped with knowledge and skills to grasp these opportunities.

Dr. Manmohan Singh, honourable Prime Minister of India in his inaugural address at the 98th Indian Science Congress (January 2011), on "Quality Education and Excellence in Science Research in Indian Universities", said "University is a vital link in the chain of science teaching and research. Unless we strengthen the base of our educational system, we can never hope to extend the height of the pyramid of excellence. We need to create an innovation eco-system so that innovation becomes a way of life in our knowledge institutions." He believes that university education is both the search for truth and adventure of ideas. Universities have to be more hospitable to creativity and genius, and less captive to bureaucracy and procedure. They should be completely open to talent and meeting the challenge of established ideas.

The Radhakrishnan Commission on University Education (1948) had set up goals for development of higher education. While articulating these goals, the Commission has said:

> The most important and urgent reform needed in education is to transform it and to endeavour to relate it to the life, needs and aspirations of the people and thereby make it the powerful instrument of social, economic and cultural transformation necessary for the realization of the national goals. For this purpose, education should be developed so as to increase productivity, achieve social and national integration, accelerate the process of modernization and cultivate social, moral and spiritual values.

Kothari Commission (1966) reiterated in its report: "While the fundamental values to which the universities owe their allegiances are largely unrelated to time and circumstances, their functions change from time to time. Their tasks are no longer confined to the two traditional functions of teaching and advancement of knowledge. They are assuming new functions and the older ones are increasing in range, depth and complexity." The National Policy on Higher Education (1986) translated the vision of Radhakrishnan Commission and Kothari Commission in five main goals for higher education, which include greater access, equal access (or equity), quality and excellence, relevance and value-based education.

University institutions are thus the national resources of knowledge; the knowledge, ideas and thinking skills bestowed by higher education can definitely be used for the socio-economic and political development of the country as a whole. These have the task of producing skilled human resources by youth empowerment, productivity, and efficiency in society that lies on skilled trainers and the quality of the training institutions. The rapid development of any nation depends largely on the caliber of its youth, since every sector of a nation's economy is managed by competent personnel who are mostly young people. The Introduction of microelectronics, telecommunication, Internet and computers in modern offices calls for training and development of competent youth, who are equipped with the various skills needed by the market. Thus, the goal of tertiary education is the acquisition of both physical and intellectual skills which will enable individuals to become self-reliant and useful members of the society. Higher learning should focus on making students' productive workers, self-reliant entrepreneurs, responsible parents, good citizens, selfless leaders, and thus, living healthy lives.

Meaning of University According to the Act

Section 2(f) of the University Grants Commission Act, 1956 defines *"a university"* to mean: "a university established or incorporated by or under a Central Act, a Provincial Act, or a State Act, and includes any such institution, as may in consultation with the university concerned, be recognized by the Commission in accordance with the regulations made in this behalf under this Act".

The definition of the university and the provisions in Section 23 of the Act refer to Acts of the Central, Provincial or the State Legislatures by which one or more universities are established or incorporated and not to institutions incorporated under a general statute providing for incorporation. The words "established" or "incorporated" refer to Act under which the universities are established or incorporated. Several universities in this country have been either established or incorporated under special statutes such as the Delhi University Act, the Banaras Hindu University Act, and the Allahabad University Act, etc. In these cases, there is a special Act either of the Central or the Provincial or the State Legislatures establishing and incorporating the particular universities. There is also another pattern—where under one compendious Act several universities are either established or incorporated—for instance, the Madhya Pradesh Universities Act, 1973.

It, therefore, becomes important to understand the meaning and concept of a University Act along with its objectives.

What is a University Act?

The objectives of the universities are specified in the Acts. The basic outline and general demarcation of University Authorities are pronounced in the Acts passed by the Legislature or the Parliament. Any change in the role and powers of the university authorities can be brought about only by appropriate amendments of the Acts. The Statutes are usually the elaboration of the Acts. The changes in the Statutes can be made only with the approval of a government level body/authority like the Chancellor/Visitor.

The Acts and Statutes are strikingly similar though not identical for different universities in most of the major respects. There are very few substantial variations among the State University Acts or among the Central University Acts. In many instances (such as the Uttar Pradesh Universities Act, Karnataka State Universities Act, M.P. State Universities Act), a common piece of legislation governing all the universities within a State has been enacted. Even in those States where there are differences between different University Acts due to historical reasons, there has been a constant attempt to bring about a uniform character among various universities.

There have been several instances of numerous amendments to the University Acts (e.g. Madras University Act was amended eleven times upto the latest amendment in 1983; Delhi University Act got amended six times upto 1981. The amendments were incorporated in the Aligarh Muslim University Act for as many as 15 times). This has been generally done to update and revise the older Acts at par with those of recent origin. In this process of 'homogenization', the State and the Central Universities, which traditionally enjoyed better autonomy and independence, were the ones to be adversely affected.

A cursory glance into the format and content of various University Acts across the country gives an impression that there are differences only in degree and not in kind. The objectives, chapter scheme, the sequence of sections in the Act and the phrases and the terminologies have remained almost the same over the period and among the various regions. There are only slight variations in length, in detail, in nomenclature; but the base is the same; corresponding authorities and similar officers with like functions. Though the same general description is filled into each enactment, each university shapes itself according to its own leadership and situation, uses its own constitution in a different way.

It is felt that an almost common Act for all universities is a major deterrent for experiments and innovations and thus for overall improvement of quality through better governance, with features which are specific to an individual university. It also limits the capacity of the university to meet the challenge of opportunities, emergencies and unforeseen changes.

Views of Some Great Thinkers and Philosophers on University Education

Cardinal John Henry Newman, the founder of the Catholic University of Dublin, presented the then modern concept of a university in 1852, in a series of discourses on the "Scope and Nature of University Education". These were later published under the title *The Idea of a University* (Kerr, 1976). The idea of a university means that a great university places high priority on teaching and gives importance to close interaction between a teacher and a student. The university is not just meant for professional competence, but as Newman believed, it is meant to develop "a habit of mind, which lasts through life". This habit of mind is embodied by the faculty, supported by the administration, and acquired by the students. "The intellect," said Newman, "instead of being formed or sacrificed to some particular or accidental purpose, some specific trade or profession, or study or science, is disciplined for its own sake, for the perception of its own proper objective, and for its own highest culture."

John Henry Newman

Newman opined, "A university is not a birthplace of poets or of immortal authors, of founders of schools, leaders of colonies or conquerors of nations". Nor should its purposes be limited to the training of professional men, though this too falls within its scope. "A university education" he urged, "gives a man a clear conscious view of his own opinions and judgments, a truth in developing them, eloquence in expressing them and a force in urging them." He visualized the university to be the high protecting power of all knowledge and science, of fact and principle, of inquiry and discovery, of experiment and speculation. Newman believed that the universities should be ivory towers, far separated from the cares and the influence of society, where scholars could indulge in the pursuit of knowledge in whatever area they chose, without being accountable to anyone. He believed that the university education had broader effects in civil society, beyond the benefits to individuals. It raises the 'intellectual tone of society', cultivates the public mind, purifies the national taste, provides fixed aims to popular aspiration and facilitates the exercise of political power while bringing refinement to private life.

Newman believed that liberal knowledge is lifelong in its benefits, "an acquired illumination, a habit, a personal possession and an inward endowment". He considered education to be a higher word. It implies an action upon our mental nature and the formation of character. It is something independent and permanent. He acknowledged that higher education should have practical benefits but saw these as flowing indirectly from the pursuit of knowledge for its own sake because it was necessary to separate the search of knowledge from the cares of mankind.

Thus, the basic idea of a university is that it is a place meant for comfort, freedom, and retreat. It means that a university is a place of spiritual well-being and rest. It provides a safe place for teachers, students, and graduates, where great issues may be explored and discussed without fear of criticism and with a sense of belonging. It is where one's hunger to learn and get prepared to bring the truth of life and culture is valued. Finally, the university is a place for deep exploration at many levels and for providing a platform for many different worldviews.

Wilhelm von Humboldt instigated university reform in Germany. He sought to combine received wisdom and the formation of individual intellect with objective scientific and scholarly knowledge, including scientific inquiry designed to push forward the frontiers of knowledge. Humboldt like Newman argued that knowledge should be cultivated for its own sake and not only its uses, but his idea of a university was a teaching/research institution in which each function supported the other; professors were free to teach and inquire as they wished while students were mature self-motivated persons.

Humboldt emphasized both science and scholarship in equal measure and sought to reconcile specialized science with intellectual breadth as well as depth. The university that he founded in Berlin and which opened as Friedrich Wilhelm University in 1810 was dedicated to the spirit of enlightenment. Humboldt was especially interested in creating the conditions necessary for science and scholarship. They rested on independent thought and stimulation; so the dominant principles of universities must be freedom and the absence of distraction. Intellectual work was essentially 'ungovernable' and he said that the State should respect this.

Humboldt University—Established in 1810

After Humboldt emphasizing on the importance of research, Karl Jaspers (1960), in his remarkable testament, *The Idea of the University* voiced that the objectives of the university are identified as research, education and instruction; to reach these objectives scholars must communicate with each other. Among the university's requirements for continued existence, "certain realities" impose restrictions on the university's well-being. These realities are the varying abilities and attitudes of human beings and the different needs and interest of the State and society that influence their efforts to sustain the university. The only motive that is at play in scientific and scholarly research is the quest for knowledge and recognition that work is required. The scientist and the scholar must learn and practice, thereby mastering methods of obtaining broader knowledge. Both the scholar and the scientist must have an intellectual conscience and strive for conscious and honest control over their creative impulses.

India has also given birth to great intellectuals and philosophers who have voiced their ideas on university and higher education from time to time depending on the situation in which they found themselves. While struggling for the independence of India from the British rule, Mahatma Gandhi (1915), the father of the nation, opined that the purpose of university education was to develop the capacity of self-rule that is *Swaraj* in Indian youth who may fulfill the responsibilities and duties as good citizens when India attained freedom. To him, *Swaraj* was not a final destination but an ongoing process in self-refinement, enrichment and enculturation in the values and culture, required for self-rule. This has a deep implication for the present university education where inculcation of national values and culture rarely find an honourable place in the curricula.

To learn for the sake of knowledge, to study in order to know the secrets of Nature and life, to educate oneself in order to grow in consciousness, to discipline oneself in order to become master of oneself, to overcome one's weaknesses, incapacities and ignorance, to prepare oneself to advance in life towards a goal that is nobler and vaster, more generous and true was the idea of a university or higher education for the noble laureate Rabindranath Tagore. In Tagore's view, the higher aim of education was the same as that of a person's life, that is, to achieve fulfillment and completeness. There was a lesser aim of providing the individual with a satisfactory means of livelihood, without which a person would not be able to satisfy his/her basic requirement and thus fail to achieve either of these two aims. Education was not intellectual development alone. It should develop a student's aesthetic nature and creativity. The quest for knowledge and physical activity in an agreeable environment were integral parts of the process.

In Tagore's philosophy of education, the aesthetic development of the senses was as important as the intellectual one and so music, literature, art, dance and drama were given great importance in the daily life of the school. This was particularly so after the first decade of the school. Drawing on his home life at Jorasanko, Tagore tried to create an atmosphere in which the arts would become instinctive. One of the first areas to be emphasized was music (Rabindranath Tagore, *My Reminiscences*, 1917: 141). The aim of education for Tagore was not to prepare the individual student to "succeed" in life and society but to strive for perfection.

Undoubtedly, Gurudev had an high ideal regarding higher education—an education that aims high in every aspect of the term, but the predicament is that looking at the present scenario, how much these ideals can be achieved. Instead of reaching nearer to the ideal of perfection as visualized by Tagore, we need to ask ourselves, are we not moving far from perfection with this higher education?

Mahatma Gandhi and Rabindranath Tagore both are brilliant personalities and they influenced the society by their educational ideals. Tagore's vision on education was based on the concept of religion of man and Mahatma Gandhi's educational principle was based on basic education system. But within 63 years of Indian independence, we lost Mahatma Gandhi's vision on education and value as well as Tagore's vision. Tagore's special contribution was his emphasis on harmony, the emphasis on balance, on all-sided development of personality so that no one aspect was submerged, no one aspect was sacrificed to develop any other aspect. For him beauty must be moral, and morality must be imbibed with the spirit of beauty, and in this way, truth, beauty and goodness these three values which he sought to fuse in the educational system still survive in the form of Path Bhawan at Shantiniketan. Viswa-Bharati is now a Central University where students from other countries attend and scholars from foreign universities participate in seminars and give lectures on international cultures and issues.

Mahatma Gandhi's ideas based on truth, non-violence and for the socio-economic and cultural reconstruction, all round harmonious development, constructive and productive manual labour, taken on a community basis and practiced as the chief medium of education. Thus, the basic philosophy of education of Gandhi and Tagore is same in the broader perspective. Both of them perceive education as the tools of overall development and manifestation of the man. To make universal man or a complete man was the aim of education for both of them. Only difference was the way of processing the same that is the pedagogy of education. Pedagogically, the two experiments are different and it's the way of implementation that is different otherwise it leads to the same aim and purpose.

Jawaharlal Nehru (1947), in his convocation address to the University of Allahabad, asked the universities to lay stress on "those standards of thoughts and action which make an individual and a nation." Nehru's exhortations were in keeping with his idealism but did not have much to offer as regards the mundane expectation of the multitude who were more concerned with the wherewithal for a better standard of living. "A university stands for humanism, for tolerance, for reason, for progress, for the adventure of ideas and for the search for truth. It stands for the onward march of the human race towards even higher objectives."

Sri Aurobindo believed that the idea of higher education is true progress, a step towards a complete evolution of the entire being and consciousness, so that a person can transcend all limitations to which a man as an evolutionary being is at present subject to. This evolution can only be achieved by man's continuous interaction with and understanding of his true self, his soul. All education should aim at the progress of the individual. Progress was considered as essentially the growth of consciousness, discovery and increasing awareness of an inner power and principle of guidance, which holds in it the

light and truth of the development, harmony and perfection of our body, life and mind. Thus, Aurobindo talked about consciousness and developing the psychological and intellectual skills through which a person can be made aware of his true self.

For Aurobindo, an institution of higher education should aim at helping learners develop the psychological and intellectual faculties and skills required for them to know clearly, and to manifest their highest ideals. The idea of higher education for Aurobindo was the synthesis of the best of Eastern and Western intellectual and spiritual traditions and philosophy, which is extremely relevant to the modern world, as it struggles to find its future and its new form and spirit.

Swami Vivekananda believed that education plays a vital role in curing the evils in society and it is critical in shaping the future of humanity. For him education is the manifestation of the perfection already in man. The word 'manifestation' implies that something already exists and is waiting to be expressed thus the main focus in learning is to make the hidden ability of a learner manifest itself. As Vivekananda said, "what a man learns is really what he 'discovers' by taking the cover off his own soul, which is a mine of infinite knowledge".

Expression 'already in man' refers to a human being's potential, which is the range of his abilities and talents known and unknown, with which he was born. Potential speaks of the possibility of awakening something that is lying dormant. Perfection in educational parlance is the goal of actualizing the highest human potential. Education must provide "life-building, man-making, character-making assimilation of ideas". The idea of this type of education would be to produce an integrated person—one who has learned how to improve his intellect, purify his emotions and stand firm on moral virtues and unselfishness. Vivekananda observed that if education were to serve the entire human being, in all his/her dimensions, the pursuit of knowledge would be a life-long process. Training the mind should be a student's highest priority, and not simply the accumulation, memorizing and the repeating of facts. "To me the very essence of education is concentration of mind, not the collection of facts." In order to be worthwhile and effective, education must be rooted in religion, in the science of spirituality and evidently not in dogma.

An analysis of the views of great thinkers ultimately leads to a conclusion that we should aim to provide a university climate that is learner-centered, emphasize academic rigor and high expectations of students, faculty, and staff, encourage involvement in the life of the institution beyond the classroom; we should also foster an environment of caring and concern and promote success and leadership development for all students providing a positive environment to help the students become conscious of his/her inner self and potential.

The education system in India is inadequate in either the utilitarian or holistic terms. The unbridled pursuits of modern-day perceived needs and even rising expectations in this high-tech and knowledge thirsty world often makes man believe in what one sees the most in print and electronic media—corruption, dishonesty and violence in familial, corporate world and national and international politics. It appears as if there is well-established network of all these in human tendencies. In addition to such apparent pejorative tends, requirements of modern education also go simultaneously more in the direction of obtaining technological training and competence in the emerging scenario of globalization, good governance and civil society. But education does not mean merely obtaining various Bachelor's and Master's degrees, certificates and diplomas. Education prepares a man for a life—truly human, full of an independent, interdependent, self-sufficient, fearless, mutually cooperating and highly cultured existence with a deep sense of social commitment and urge for public welfare. This type of education is possible in 21st century only when individuals and nations alike keep away from absolute personal aggrandizement of political and economic power in the inherent of public welfare-oriented political will, proper intention and societal commitment. All this is in addition to excellence and relevance in learning, research, development, consultancy, extension and service to society.

According to Dr. William James of Harvard University, the greatest discovery of this generation is that human beings can alter their lives by altering their attitudes of mind. Most of our attitude is established during our formative years. It is the responsibility of the universities to suitably mould the attitudes of the students so that the quality of the society is improved. Surprisingly, almost 100% of money in education go to teach facts and figures which account for only 15% of success in work. Knowledge strategically applied translates into wisdom, ensuring success. We are drowning in information but starving for knowledge and wisdom. Education, especially higher education ought to teach the youths not only to make a living but also how to live. Thus, for a holistic personality development, apart from academics there is a need to provide opportunities and facilities for sports, education in human values, yoga, meditation, NSS, and NCC, fine arts, etc. Leadership qualities, building communication skills, relationship management and developing team spirit are other areas on which our universities need to work and emphasize.

Thus, education is the most critical input in shaping human destinies. The natural potential of any person requires educational inputs to provide a framework for maximum development. The goal of education is to empower human beings for improving the quality of life of the society. While basic education provides a framework for skill development, it is higher education which empowers individuals and nations to compete and prosper in this world. University is about more than what is taught within the walls of a classroom. It is about getting involved and becoming a part of the campus life. Joining student organizations and volunteering to work in the community develops leadership skills. The personal development and growth that a student experiences will make him more organized, confident, and capable of handling the responsibilities of college and career. He will greatly enhance his ability to work in a more effective and efficient manner with a variety of people. Thus, people from all ages and backgrounds decide to enter higher education for a variety of reasons. For a country to grow meaningfully and in a sustainable way, the university systems and colleges have to become centers of excellence where the best minds apply themselves to the task of moulding India's coming generation. Before we discuss the basic philosophy and the aims and objectives of higher education, it becomes important to look into the development of a university institution through the ages both in India and abroad.

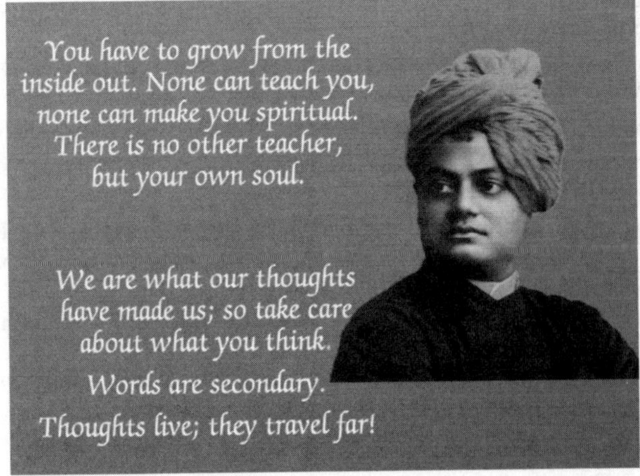

REFERENCES

Abbasi, A.N.M.S. (1987), "The Educational thoughts of Jawaharlal Nehru." In Buch, M.B. (Ed.) *Third Survey of Research in Education (1978-83)*, New Delhi: NCERT, p. 36.

A New Approach to Education. (1974), Pondicherry: Shri Aurobindo Society, pp. 29, 35, 39, 45, 52, 55, 65.

Barnett, R. (1992), The *Idea of Higher Education*. Buckingham: Open University Press.

Education of the Future. (1974), Pondicherry: Shri Aurobindo Society, pp. 4, 7, 29-30, 38, 40-41, 46, 51, 53, 55, 68, 70-72, 76, 79.

G. Terry Page and J.B. Thomas with A.R. Marshall, *International Dictionary of Education*. London: The English Language Book Society and Kogan Page, pp. 161, 354.

Government of India, Planning Commission (1996), p. 1.

Gandhi's Letter to Ranchhodlal Patwari, 10 June (1915), (*CW* 13, p. 105). In *Gandhi on Education*, New Delhi: N.C.T.E.

IGNOU, *Planning and Management of Higher Education*, MES 104, pp. 7-57.

Jaspers, K. (1960), *The Idea of University,* London: Peter Owen Limited, pp. 9-12.

K.B. Powar, "The Changing Role and Functions of Universities." *AIU Occasional Paper* 2000/2. New Delhi: Association of Indian Universities. pp 4-6.

Kulandaiswamy (1999), "Higher Education Leads towards Leadership", *University News.*

Kerr, I.T. (Ed.) (1976), In J.H. Newman, *The Idea of a University*, The Clarendon Press, Oxford.

Liam Atchinson (1997), *The Idea of a University: A Community Engaged in the Leisure of Scholarship*. © 1997 Mars Hill Review 9 Fall Issue 9: pp. 9-18.

Livingstone, H. (1974), *The University: An Organizational Analysis*, Blackie and Son, Glasgow.

Noam, E.M. (1995), "Electronics and the Dim Future of the University". *Science*, Vol. 270, 03 October, pp. 247-49.

Nehru, J.L. (1947), *Convocation Address*, Allahabad University, Allahabad.

Rabindranath Tagore, "My Educational Mission". In *The Modern Review*, June (1931), pp. 621-23.

Report of the Yashpal Committee on Higher Education: The Report on 'Renovation and Rejuvenation of Higher Education' (2008), Ministry of Education. Government of India, New Delhi.

Romain Rolland, *The Life of Vivekananda*, tr. E.K. Malcolm Smith. Kolkata: Advaita Ashrama.

Selections from the Complete Works of Swami Vivekananda. (2002), Publication Department Advaita Ashram, p. 538.

Soni, Rashmi. (2007), Intellectuals' Expectations from a University: An Exploratory Study. *Ph.D. Thesis*, Department of Education, University of Lucknow, Lucknow.

The Complete Works of Swami Vivekananda. Volume-III, Kolkata: Publication Department Advaita Ashrama, (2002), p. 302.

Tagore, Rabindranath (1941), In, *Vishwa Bharati Bulletin* (30) Paush, p. 2.

Universities in Great Britain, S.C.M. Press (1931), p. 9.

Varma, M., and Soni, R. (2005), "University Education as Dreamt by Gandhi", *Gandhi Marg: Journal of the Gandhi Peace Foundation*, New Delhi, Vol. 21, Oct- Dec 2005 & Jan- Mar 2006.

Websites

www.planningcommission.nic.in/reports/b-pubbody.htm

http://www.newmanreader.org/works/idea/

www.iotu.uchicago.edu/levine.html

Development of Universities Over the World

2

All advanced civilizations have needed higher education to train their ruling, priestly, military and other service elites, but only in medieval Europe did an institution recognizable as a university evolve: a school of higher learning combining teaching and scholarship and characterized by its corporate autonomy and academic freedom. The Confucian schools for the Mandarin bureaucracy of imperial China, the Hindu *gurukulas* and Buddhist *vihares* for the priests and monks of medieval India, the *madrasas* for the mullahs and Quranic judges of Islam, the Aztec and Inca temple schools for the priestly astronomers of pre-Columbian America, the Tokugawa *han* schools for Japanese samurai, all taught the high culture, received doctrine, literary and/or mathematical skills of their political or religious masters, with little room for questioning or analysis.

The same might be said for the monastic schools of early medieval Europe that kept alive Biblical studies and classical learning in the Dark Ages between the fall of Rome and the 12th century renaissance. Only in Europe from the 12th century onwards did an autonomous, permanent, corporate institution of higher learning emerge and survive, in varying forms, down to the present day. The university was the accidental product of a uniquely fragmented and decentralized civilization. Unintentionally, it evolved into an immensely flexible institution, able to adapt to almost any political situation and form of society. In this way, it was able to survive for eight centuries and migrate, eventually, to every country and continent in the world.

Designed originally for a cosmopolitan world in which scholars from every part of the Christian West could gather at key centers and communicate in Latin, it outlived that world and adjusted itself to a succession of divergent social and political systems. After helping to destroy the medieval world order at the Reformation, the universities were "nationalized" by the emerging nation-states in the religious wars between Catholics and Protestants; they served as instruments of propaganda warfare. During the 18th century Enlightenment, they declined to such an extent that the Scientific Revolution and the rise of new philosophies and social sciences bypassed them, and were in danger of disappearing altogether. Indeed, the French Revolution abolished them in France and the conquered territories, but resurrected them again in the form of the *grandes ecoles* and the Napoleonic University of France.

University of France

At the same time, the old universities were revitalized in Scotland and above all, in Germany, where a new model of professional organization combining teaching and research emerged and came to be emulated all over Europe and eventually, in countries overseas, including the United States and Japan. That form of university was especially suited to the needs of the new society produced by the Industrial Revolution, to which it belatedly but brilliantly adjusted.

Meanwhile, the expansion of Europe by conquest and colonization spread the university to other continents, from the 16th century in the Spanish Empire, from the 17th in the English and French colonies in North America, and later to other countries, including India, Australia and New Zealand, Africa and even to China, the Middle East and Japan. It became an instrument not only of modernization on the Western model but also, of the anticolonial reaction against Western domination of Asia and Africa in the shape of nationalist ideology and student unrest. Finally, in the worldwide expansion of higher education that followed World War II, it transformed itself once again, into the pivotal institution of a new kind of society. In this new post-industrial or professional society, agriculture and manufacturing became so efficient, partly with the help of the scientific research institutes, that most people came to work in service industries, increasing numbers of whom would require specialized high-level training.

This entailed the transition from elite to mass higher education, from a system catering to less than 5% of the student age group to one catering to more than 15% and even for as much as 30-50% in the most advanced countries. Not all of these were in universities but in increasing numbers of technical colleges, community colleges, short-cycle institutions, and the like, which had first arisen to serve the needs of industrial society and now came to train the second tier below the university level. In most countries, however, the university and its institutional offspring became so large and expensive, so dependent on the state for resources, and like the state itself, so bureaucraticized, that it was once more dominated by the superior authority. The cost of becoming the axial institution of modern post-industrial society is that the university has become, or is in danger of becoming, an integral organ of the state or the corporate economy and so of losing its autonomy and academic freedom.

The early history of higher education, therefore, is largely the history of the European university and its evolution into an institution or congeries of institutions, flexible enough to serve the needs of enormously different societies in every part of the world, culminating in its universal acceptance as the key institution of modern and developing societies everywhere. Its history can be told in five stages, viz. (i) the rise of the cosmopolitan European university and its role in the destruction of the medieval world order at the Reformation (12th century-1530s), (ii) the nationalization of the university by the emerging nation-states of the religious wars, and its decline during the 18th century Enlightenment (1530s-1789), (iii) the revival of the university after the French Revolution and its belated but increasing role in Industrialized Society (1789-1939), (iv) the migration of the university to the non-European world and its adaptation to the needs of developing societies and the anticolonial reaction (1939-1960) and (v) the transition from elite to mass higher education and the role of the university and its offshoots in post-industrial society (1960-present).

The University and the Medieval World Order

The first universities grew out of the cathedral and municipal schools of the reviving cities of the 12th century Europe (Hastings, 1895; Haskins, 1957; Cobban, 1975; Rudy, 1984; Stone, 1975). A demand arose for trained elites to serve the bureaucracies of church and state and the emerging professions of the clergy, law and medicine. These urban schools supplemented or replaced the monastic schools that had kept Biblical studies and ancient classical learning alive during the Dark Ages. Education had always been a lesser concern of the monasteries, whose main function was and remained the salvation of souls by prayer and meditation of the saints, but they needed to train their own novices and, sometimes, also trained neighbouring magnates' children. Where they were established in or near towns, they were only too willing to take advantage of the more specialized teaching of these new schools.

The new urban schools, called *studia*, came to serve the needs of a more secular, if still profoundly religious society, more settled if still warlike, for parish and diocesan clergy, lawyers and administrators, and medical practitioners. Most of them never became universities but taught the basic skills needed for the literate professions: grammar, rhetoric and dialectic. These three arts made up the *trivium*. The seven liberal arts were completed by the quadrivium—music, arithmetic; geometry and astronomy—making up all that an education man needed for the business of life. Such a man became a magister, a master qualified to teach others and to proceed to the higher faculties of theology, law or medicine. An arts *studium* that added one or more of the higher faculties and attracted students from far and wide could claim to be a *studium generale* and, in the course of time, petition the emperor or the pope to confirm its status by imperial charter and grant it the right of its masters to teach anywhere.

The first school to enjoy this status, at least in medicine, was at Salerno. Although given a monopoly of medical teaching by Frederick II, king of Naples, in 1231 and recognized as a *studium generale* by his successor Charles II of Anjou in 1280, it faded in the 13th century and its claim to be the first university is still disputed.

The first comprehensive universities in Europe were Paris and Bologna. In the 12th century renaissance of Greek philosophy, recovered through translations from the Arabic, the fame of the church schools of Paris—the schools of Norte Dame cathedral, St. Genevieve, and of the regular canons of St. Victor—attracted students from all over Northern Europe. Scholasticism became the key to understanding the visible world of men and things and the invisible worlds of Christian revelation and Platonic ideas. Its promise of esoteric knowledge and wisdom and its training in intellectual analysis and subtle argument excited generations of young scholars who flocked to Paris and other universities to learn the meaning of life and eternity.

Bologna University

Paris-Sorbonne University

By the 13th century, the schools of Paris had grown into a single *studium generale* with its privileges confirmed by the Pope (1194) and the French King (1200). The university began to take on corporate form or, rather, forms. Both masters and students organized themselves against the cathedral clergy, the citizens, and against each other. The word *universitas* meant no more than a society or guild, like the contemporary guilds of craftsmen or merchants in most medieval towns. The university originally signified not the studium but, in Paris and Northern Europe, the guild of masters and, in Bologna and the Italian universities, the guild of students. Those who passed the *trivium* became bachelors, equivalent to the craft bachelors or journeymen; and those fully qualified in all seven arts became masters, licensed to practice, that is, to teach the bachelors and apprentices. The term university, meaning the organization of masters and/or students, eventually became attached to the *studium* itself.

The college system also evolved in Paris. Originally, students lived in a lodging, hostel or hall rented by one of them or a resident master. The college tended to become permanent society of masters and students, in which the older members tutored the younger, at first to supplement the university lectures and later to replace them. The college system, in varying forms, came to be imitated at Oxford and Cambridge and at many other universities in Italy, Germany, Scotland and elsewhere, though it often took different forms in different places. In this and other ways, Paris became the model for most universities north of the Alps.

Bologna was the rival model. In the more advanced and sophisticated civilization of Italy, there was a demand for lawyers and administrators, and the university emerged from the municipal schools that taught the civil law of ancient Rome and the canon law of the papacy. Like Paris and the Northern universities, Bologna had its problems with the local townsfolk. Quarrels and riots led to migrations of scholars to Modena and Montpellier in the 1170s, to Vicenza in 1204, Arezzo in 1215 and Padua in 1222, thus establishing universities in those cities.

The brilliant success of Paris and Bologna models led to emulation, often by the classic process of migration. Oxford arose spontaneously about 1167 from one of the many arts studia in English towns, helped by the return of English students from France around 1167. Cambridge originated with a migration from Oxford after town and gown riots in 1209. In France, where Paris jealously guarded her supremacy in theology, her daughter universities, Orleans, Angers and Toulouse, all benefiting from the great dispersal of 1229, tended to concentrate on law. Many Italian cities competed for the honor and economic benefits of a university and wooed scholars to set up schools. Other Italian universities were recognized usually by the city authorities who petitioned the Pope for a bull, at Piacenza (1248), the City of Rome (1303), Perugia (1308), Ferrara (1391) and Catania (1444). Nearly all the Italian universities followed the Bologna model of student government, but reverted to professorial control in the later Middle Ages, when municipal salaries and magnificent buildings liberated the professors from student control.

The universities of the Iberian Peninsula were almost royal foundations, endowed by the various monarchs with church revenues and taxes from their own estates. The single university in Portugal was founded by the King in 1290 at Lisbon, but was continually shuttled between there and Coimbra before finally settling in the latter city in 1537. Spain was to become the parent of many institutions of higher education worldwide, as the Spanish conquerors exported the European university to other continents.

Until the 14th century, students from beyond the Rhine and the Alps went to France or Italy for higher education, a result of the slower development of city life in Northern and Central Europe. Arts studia *came* into existence to prepare them, but the first *studium generale* in the empire was established only in 1347, by Charles IV, King of Bohemia and emperor elect, in Prague. From 1419 Prague became in effect the first Protestant university in Europe, protected by the kings of Bohemia. Vienna, the first wholly German University, was founded by the Hapsburg Duke of Austria, Rudolf IV, in 1365 and soon took over the academic lead from Prague.

With the increasing dynastic nationalism of the later Middle Ages, other nations vied with each other to establish their own universities. The three medieval Scottish universities were founded at St. Andrews, Glasgow and Aberdeen by their bishops with royal backing in 1409, 1450 and 1494 respectively. They were much influenced by French and German examples and were, like them, to play a considerable part in the theological and philosophical disputes that led to the Reformation.

The Destruction of Medieval World Order

The four original universities in Europe that emerged in the 12th century, Salerno, Paris, Bologna, and Oxford, grew to 16 by 1300, 38 by 1400 and 72 by 1500. By that time, they were highly organized institutions with a rector or chancellor, a common seal and corporate personality that enabled them to own property and make contracts. They also had formal faculties—usually of arts, theology, law, medicine increasingly with endowed colleges—and enjoyed privileges guaranteed by the Pope and/or secular ruler that protected them from arbitrary interference by bishops and civic authorities and from sporadic violence by their urban neighbours. Though some of them were very small, like St. Andrews or Naples, others—like Paris, Bologna or Vienna—were very large, with several thousand students. The universities thus became almost a separate "intellectual estate", a third force between church and state. They were themselves divided in several ways, between reformers and conservatives, realists and nominalists, Aristotelian schoolmen and the new humanists who challenged scholastic logic-chopping and introduced the "new learning"—the rebirth of the ancient Greek and Latin literary classics—of the 14th century Renaissance.

The university's experience in the Reformation of the Church was ambivalent. On the one side, it helped to defeat the papacy and render the Church apart. On the other, it helped to bring about the resurgence of the Roman Church in the Counter Reformation. On both sides, it became an instrument of the embattled states in the religious wars of the 16th and 17th centuries, and many new colleges and universities were founded for that purpose, before they declined into a complacent somnolence in the ensuing reaction against "enthusiasm" in the 18th century Enlightenment (MacCulloch, 2003; Baldwin and Goldwaithe, 1972).

Renaissance carved stone corbel, 14th century or earlier possibly English or continental

The power of intellectual thought has no better material example than the dissolution of the monasteries in Protestant countries. The Reformation was about many theological disputes, yet the Reformation was a Pyrrhic victory for the universities. The only thing that saved the universities from complete subjection was the persisting pluralism of Europe, now divided monastic states that strove to attract academics to their side. The universities in England, for example, came within an ace of the fate of the monasteries. The Oxford and Cambridge colleges were quasi-monastic institutions and were often obliged by their foundations to say prayers for the souls of the founder and his kin and successors. In 1535, the teaching of canon law was banned, thus abolishing the largest graduate faculty.

With civil law already concentrated in the Inns of Court in London, the two universities, apart from a handful of unpractical physicians, were relegated to teaching arts and theology to the Anglican clergy. Sons of the gentry and the wealthier middle classes began to go in large numbers to Oxford and Cambridge, more for the general training in manners and political awareness than for intellectual improvement, for they often did not stay long enough to take the degree. Thus, in England, as elsewhere, the universities adapted themselves to a new social function, the general education of the ruling elite.

Both Catholic and Protestant rulers rushed to find new educational institutions to reinforce their hold on their subjects' minds. The spearhead of the Catholic counterattack was the Society of Jesus, which infiltrated or took over many of the older universities and founded many new ones. From their three great centers—Cologne, where they began to lecture in 1542; the Gregorian University, founded at Rome by Loyola himself in 1553; and Ingolstadt, near Munich, taken over by them in 1556—they spread throughout Europe. They established or took over institutions as far a field as Evora, Portugal, Bohemia in 1556, the great university of Vienna in 1622, Silesia in 1659 and Lvov, Poland in 1661.

As long as the religious wars lasted and required the ideological support of the universities, they thrived, and student numbers surged to new heights down to the mid-17th century. From then onwards a period of decline set in, as students and their elders wearied of the religious disputes of the last century began to repudiate "enthusiasm". By the 1680s, Oxford was "very dead for want of students", less than at any time before the Civil War. In Germany, student number in the 1780s at about seven thousand was smaller than a century and a half earlier.

One reason was the sheer exhaustion with religious controversy, but the principal cause was the rise of a new skeptical outlook associated with the "Enlightenment", a critical, rationalistic view of the world that eschewed the emotional fanaticism, as they saw it, of the old doctrinal wars. This undermined the universities as the homes of outmoded theoretical knowledge, still based largely on Aristotle and the medieval schoolmen and increasingly out of touch with observed reality. Why go to a university, it was argued, to learn old doctrine of little use outside a career in the Church? (Outram, 1995; Porter, 2001; Israel, 2002). The universities could not escape the new developments altogether and a few pioneers of modern science operated there, though often under difficulty. In the Netherlands, Leyden and other universities pioneered new and more practical systems of teaching medicine and the natural sciences and sent scientific missionaries out to Edinburgh, Vienna and Gottingen. For the most part the Scientific Revolution passed the universities by and managed to conquer them only after their reform in the 19th century.

In Germany, civil servants and politicians seriously discussed whether universities did more harm than good and ought to be abolished. Even the students lacked the energy to protest: perhaps because there was so little to protest against, there were fewer student riots in that century than before or after. In France, the revolutionaries did abolish the universities, in the territories they conquered. Paradoxically, however, the French Revolution, which temporarily abolished the universities, paved the way for their revival, not only in France but also in the rest of Europe.

The University and Industrial Society

The Industrial Revolution, which started in 18th century Britain and spread from there to Europe, America and the rest of the world, began outside the universities and for a long time was ignored by them. In the first half of the 19th century, most universities were still seminaries for the clergy and a few lawyers and administrators of the nation-state. The medieval curricula in the arts, theology, law and medicine were still largely intact, if somewhat updated, and Aristotle and Plato were still more important than Newton and Kant. So much was this the case that the applied science and technology needed for the new manufacturing, mining, and transport industries had to be taught in new institutions: mechanics' institutes in Britain, *technische hochschulen* in Germany and *grandes ecoles* in France, where Napoleon's new University of France (1806) embraced the whole education system down to the *lycees* (secondary schools) but still did not modernize the syllabus. Only gradually did the old universities catch up with the new natural and social sciences, and only then when they had been shamed into it by new institutions, including a new wave of universities.

Industrial society, nevertheless, eventually recreated the university in its own image. It invented the modern research university, the technical college and the research institute. New natural sciences like chemistry, biology and geology, new applied sciences like engineering, mineralogy, electricity, and practical medicine and new versions of the humanities like archive-based history, modern languages and vernacular literature, came into the curricula of new universities and spread to the older ones. In the later 19th century, student numbers expanded all over Europe from Britain and France to Germany and Russia and dramatically in the United States and for the first time women students began to appear in more than token numbers. Higher education at its widest was still very elitist, but in the 20th century the change was large enough to bring in some students from the lower layers of society.

The Emergence of the Research University

The modern university combining teaching and research began almost by accident in two poor and at that time marginal countries, Scotland and Germany. In 18th century Scotland, the new professors revolutionized old disciplines and pioneered new ones, like Colin Maclaurin, Newton's pupil, in mathematics, David Hume and Dugald Stewart in philosophy, William Robertson in history, Adam Smith in political economy, and John Miller in sociology and so on.

The Scottish model had a profound influence on the new English Universities of the 19th century. University College was founded in London in 1826 by Henry Brougham, Thomas Campbell and other Edinburgh graduates, with a slate of single-discipline professors in medicine, jurisprudence, political economy, chemistry, physics, modern languages, logic and philosophy, with others planned in engineering, mineralogy, design and education. The University of London acted as midwife and nurse to many of these provincial universities, as it was also to do to many colonial universities, especially in Africa, India, the West Indies and Malaya. From 1858 it offered external degrees to individual and college students anywhere in Britain or the Empire, and enabled colleges to earn their university status by awarding its degrees for a generation or more before becoming independent. Its admission of women to the external degree in 1878 was a landmark in women's education, not only enabling women's colleges to follow the same path but setting the precedent for other universities to admit them. Other new universities—in Ireland, Wales, India, South Africa, New Zealand and elsewhere—were founded on the same federal principle with affiliated colleges. London thus became the mentor or the pattern for a very large number of universities throughout the Empire and Commonwealth.

Founders Building Royal Holloway University of London

The older universities at Oxford and Cambridge dragged their feet but were eventually shamed by external critics, internal reformers, and royal commissions in the 1850s and

1870s into modernizing themselves. With the building of the Clarendon and Cavendish Laboratories in 1870 and 1872 Oxford and Cambridge began to play a leading role in science and technology.

The German and French Models

Most German universities in the 18th century were as moribund as elsewhere, and were lucky to escape abolition like the French. King Frederick William III of Prussia appointed Wilhelm von Humbodt, brother of the famous scientist-explorer Alexander von Humboldt, to reform the Prussian education system and found the University of Berlin (1810). Humboldt saw the university as the moral soul of society and the source of the nation's culture and survival. To ensure the highest form of knowledge (*wissenschaft*), absolute freedom of teaching and learning (*lehrfreiheit* and *lernfreiheit*) was imperative. Thus, began one of the paradoxes of the modern university that it increasingly came to depend on the state both for material support and for defense of its freedom from its most dangerous threat, the state. The paradox was intensified by the fact that academic freedom was most self-consciously proclaimed in Germany, the most authoritarian state west of Russia.

The Humboldt University of Berlin

The individual professors with their separate research institutes and unpaid assistants produced a surge of research with far-reaching consequences. Professors like Liebig in chemistry, Thaer in agricultural economics, Wundt in experimental psychology, even Ranke in history, had an effect on German development that was the envy of other countries. The new model attracted students in large numbers, far more than in any other country in Europe, though less than in United States. The French model after the Revolution was a two-tier system, with an upper tier of *grandes ecoles*—like the *ecole des mines*, the *ecole Polytechnique*, the *ecole des langues orientates vivantes*, and other specialized schools of elite studies—to which high-status research institutes were later added, over a lower tier of the Parisian and regional faculties of the Napoleonic University of France. All over Northern and Eastern Europe, from Scandinavia to Greece (Athens University, 1837) and Turkey (the Istanbul House of Science, 1863), the German specialized professor and the single-discipline department were imitated, and universities became geared, to varying extents, to the combination of teaching and research.

In Russia, the tsarist autocracy always had an ambivalent attitude toward higher education, as it did toward modernization, which for them meant Westernization, in general. Education and research were necessary for Russia to catch up with the wealth and military power of Western rivals, but students and intellectuals were a disruptive force that might become dangerous to the regime. At the opening of the 19th century Russia had only one university, Moscow, founded by the Empress Elizabeth in 1755.

If the universities followed the German model, and produced many eminent scholars and scientists, the technical institutes followed the French model, at a less prestigious level. But tsarist higher education was a tiny elite system, with about 127,000 students perched on top of a huge population of 174 million, two-thirds of whom were illiterate. This combination led not to modernization but to revolution. The German model was most admired and emulated in the United States and Japan. Meanwhile, the modern university, the technical college, and the research institute had, belatedly but successfully, been created by and helped to create that industrial society, which until Europe nearly destroyed itself in two world wars, gave the West almost complete mastery over the rest of the world.

Higher Education for the Excluded

One of the most important features of industrial society was its opening up of higher education to groups of the population previously excluded. More directly, the Industrial and French Revolutions combined to accelerate the trends toward democracy and equality, as working-class and feminist movements claimed rights denied to them in earlier societies. The widening of access was only a small beginning, but it laid the foundations for the post-World War II expansion of higher education. There was better hope for the disadvantaged student in non-university and part-time education, particularly in vocational education, which expanded in most countries in the early 20th century, though very erratically and foreshadowed the massive expansion of non-university education after World War II.

In the second half of the century, beginning in Britain and the United States, normal schools, teachers' colleges, and academic women's colleges were founded and the universities for the first time began to admit women, though often under restrictive conditions as to studying alongside men and taking full degrees. In England, Bedford College for women was established in 1849 by feminists and later incorporated in London University. Four women's colleges were founded at Oxford between 1878 and 1893, but women were not formally admitted to the university until 1920. London was the first university to admit women, via its external degrees in 1878, and was soon followed by most provincial, Welsh, and Scottish universities, often against the wishes of many professors and most male undergraduates.

In the United States, women were confined to seminaries, mostly founded between 1820 and 1850, until the last quarter of the century, when the leading women's colleges like Vassar and Mount Holyoke evolved from them. The extension of higher education to sectors of the population other than the male governing and professional elites was an expanding feature of industrial society, driven by the need for talent and the demands of the excluded. It was still, however, very limited until after World War II when, in a different, post-industrial society, the demand for much larger numbers of highly educated personnel would raise it to a higher level (Kaelble, 1985).

The University in the Wider World

The university first spread to the non-European world on the back of conquerors and colonists, and only later by the force of its own double-edged attraction. Its initial function was to educate the priests and ministers of the colonists and their governing and merchant elites. When it was later adapted to the education of the subject peoples, it imposed on them European intellectual and cultural values that they welcomed for the wealth and employment opportunities they promised but resented for the threat to native culture and values they imposed. Everywhere the university and its preparatory schools and satellites became the instruments of nationalism and anti-colonialism, and heralded the demise of four hundred years of Western hegemony.

Latin America

Spain, the first European power to achieve world supremacy, began to export education to its colonies from the beginning. Soon after the conquest of the Americas, the Spaniards founded universities in Santo Domingo on the island of Hispaniola in 1538 and Mexico City in 1551 along with Jesuit and Dominician schools in virtually all their colonies. There were soon said to be more institutions of higher education in Spanish America than in Spain itself. At least another 16 universities were founded there as well as numerous other colleges and seminaries, before Latin America achieved independence in the early 19th century. The universities were modeled on the charter and statutes of Salamanca, which supplied many of them with professors and administrators, and were open equally to Indians, Creoles and Spaniards.

The last century of Spanish rule, with cities larger and more splendid than any in contemporary North America, was the golden age of Latin America and higher education, with emphasis on native Indian languages as well as arts, philosophy, theology and medicine. The Latin American universities after independence mainly served the European elites, landlords and the priesthood; the emerging professional schools in agriculture, forestry, veterinary medicine, engineering and so on were mainly for a second level of technicians and administrators who rarely aspired to high rank. From 1918, these universities became famous for student unrest, with demands for participation that anticipated the 1960s student movement elsewhere; in 1950 they were described as untended gardens of obsolete learning, and only later blossomed into their current liveliness.

Latin America

The French and Dutch Empires

Apart from the Jesuit College at Laval (1635) in Quebec, the French founded no universities in their colonies until one for French pied-noirs in Algiers in 1879, which was considered an integral part of France, therefore merited a regional campus of the Napoleonic University. A new policy was adopted from 1945, when the other colonies became part of Metropolitan France and institutes of higher education were founded in Tunisia, Morocco and Senegal, those in Dakar and Tunis becoming universities in 1957 and 1960, just before and just after independence (Musselin, 2003; Manning, 1986; Behr, 1988).

In the Dutch East Indies, no university was founded until independence in 1947, when the University of Indonesia in Batavia (Jakarta), projected in 1942 but delayed by the Japanese invasion, was formed by the amalgamation of various colleges, including the Engineering College at Bandoeng (1920), the Law, Medical and Literary Colleges at Batavia (1924, 1927 and 1940), and the Agricultural College at Buitenzorg in 1940 (Hoong, 1973; Murray, 1973). On the Protestant side, the north German principalities, the Swiss cantons, the Dutch provincial estates, and the monarchs of Scotland and England also founded new educational institutions to spread the gospels of Luther, Zwingli, Calvin and the Arminian Anglicans. Meanwhile, as the religious wars swayed back and forth, many universities found themselves in the frontier zone between the armies and changed their political and religious allegiance, some more than once.

All nine colonial colleges founded before the American Revolution began as religious seminaries, instruments of the community and its faith. In time, they evolved from seminaries into liberal arts colleges, educating young gentlemen of the planter and business classes as well as of the cloth, and set the pattern for that general education that has been the mark of the American undergraduate experience down to the present. The University of New Brunswick was founded as the Provincial Academy of the Arts and Sciences at Fredericton in 1785, the first state institution in Canada and received a royal charter as King's College in 1828. When Canada achieved Dominion status and virtual internal independence in 1867 there were 18 degree-awarding institutions (including the French ones), most of them religious foundations. By 1939, there were 38 universities with 35, 903 students, about a quarter of them women.

The United States

American education had an eye for the practical as well as the intellectual and moral, but the great leap forward resulted from the third development, the import of the German model of the research university, beginning with John Hopkins in 1876 and soon to be imitated by Harvard, Yale, Columbia, Northwestern, Michigan and other universities, state and private, all the way across to Stanford and Berkeley on the West Coast. Yet the American research university bore little resemblance to the German model. Its highly funded research professors with their large teams and departments were able to bring to bear much larger resources than elsewhere on scientific and technological problems, with spectacular results. The United States in the 20th century became the Mecca for scholars from the whole world over, especially for European refugees from Hitler's Germany and Stalin's Russia.

The overwhelming features of American higher education have been its diversity and its restless expansion. Not only could any person find any study but any individual, group, church, city, state or private firm could found a college and open its doors to anyone willing to pay the tuition fees. Every state and large city had its state-funded university, often with several campuses and private universities sprang up to suit every kind of student. Today there are over 3,500 institutions of higher education, with more than twelve million students, over 70% of the age group (Veblen, 1954; Ashby, 1971; Clark, 1983).

In the White settler colonies of Britain, the Europeans wanted their own higher education, as they did in North America. In Australia, the government of each colony set up its own university. New South Wales founded Sydney University in 1850; Victoria, Melbourne University in 1853; South Australia, Adelaide University in 1874, Tasmania, its university at Hobart in 1890, Queensland, Brisbane University in 1909 and Western Australia, its own at Perth in 1911. In 1873, the Federal University of the Cape of Good Hope, patterned on the University of London, was set up, to which most of the South African colleges became affiliated. The only black college within the Union was the African Native College at Fort Hare, founded by the Free Church of Scotland in 1916.

India and Southeast Asia

The ancient civilizations of India and South Asia, on the other hand, had a long history of advanced education going back to Buddhist monasteries of the 7th century B.C. to the 3rd century A.D. Hindu Nalanda, and to the 11th century Islamic *madrasas*, although by the time of the British Raj such colleges were in low water. Both kinds of colony developed a love-hate relation with their imperialist rulers, however. Both wanted the advantages of education, at different levels, the more literate to compete for positions, however lowly, in the conqueror's system of administration and business, the illiterate to grasp at whatever means of gaining a living they could find in a poverty stricken environment. Schools and colleges provided the most promising way to arm themselves ideologically and acquire the necessary intellectual and moral means to gain independence (Ashby, 1964, 1966; Wandira, 1978).

India under the British possessed at least three traditions of advanced scholarship, in the Hindu *gurukulas,* the Buddhist *vihares,* and the Quranic *madrasas* of her three great religions. In the 18th century, the British encouraged native culture and Warren Hastings founded a new Islamic Madrasa at Calcutta in 1781 and John Duncan a Hindu College at Benaras in 1792. In the early 19th century, however, the influential James Mill and the English Utilitarians dismissed Indian culture as moribund and doubted the utility of teaching mere Hindu or mere Mohammedan literature and after a generation-long dispute between the Westerners and the Orientalists, persuaded the Indian government to found colleges of Western learning. The British Raj developed a policy, based on Lord Macaulay's famous minute of 1835, of educating the Indians in English language, literature and science with a view to state employment and a distant prospect, expressed as early as 1865, of self-government.

After much debate between the home and Indian governments, the Raj set up in 1857, after the Mutiny and the transfer of rule from the East India Company to Westminster, three federal examining universities on the London pattern in Calcutta, Bombay and Madras, supported by affiliated colleges.

Others, including the Muslim University at Aligarh (1875) and Lahore (1882), followed. There were 19 universities in all, plus scores of affiliated colleges by independence in 1947.

The Indian universities became immensely popular, and had 60,000 students by 1921 and twice that number by 1936. They served two major purposes, viz of educating Indians, especially Brahmins and Muslims, for the professions and minor posts in the Indian Civil Service, and that of preparing the way for independence. This preparation came most forcefully in ways not anticipated by the British rulers. The unintended effect was to provide recruits for the Indian Congress Party and the Muslim League and to fuel the nationalist movements that agitated for independence from before World War I until after World War II.

By independence in 1947, there were nearly 200,000 students in the Indian University system. In 1987, there were 3.6 million students, nearly a third of them women, about 8% of the age group. At independence Pakistan had three federal universities, Punjab (1882), Dacca (1921), and Sind (1947) with 106 affiliated colleges and perhaps 100,000 students, mostly men (Ashby, 1966; Singh and Altbach, 1973; Singh and Sharma, 1988). Outside British India itself, Rangoon College (1920, affiliated to the University of Calcutta), became the University of Rangoon after the separation of Burma from India in 1937, with over 4000 students, a quarter of them women, at independence in 1948. Ceylon University College (1921), affiliated to the University of Calcutta, amalgamated with the Ceylon Medical College (1870) to form the University of Ceylon in 1942. The University of Hong Kong was founded by the colonial government in 1911 and refounded in 1946 after its destruction by the Japanese. A separate Chinese University was founded in 1963. Thailand, the only independent country in Southeast Asia, did not escape Western influence, and its universities were based on the English model.

British Tropical Africa and the West Indies

Until after World War I, British governments took little interest in higher education in the tropics, believing that what largely non-literate societies needed first was elementary and vocational education. The first and until after World War I, only college in British West Africa was Fourah Bay College near Freetown in Sierra Leone, the British colony for slaves recaptured from the banned slave trade. Many attempts were made during the 19th century to raise it to a university status. It finally succeeded in 1876 with its affiliation for examination purposes to the University of Durham, but it averaged only between four and 14 degree students a year from then until 1926.

University of Durham

With the independence of Ghana in 1957 and most other African colonies in the 1960s, their university colleges threw off the tutelage of London and Durham universities and became full universities. In the West Indies, the only institution of higher education before World War II was the Imperial College of Tropical Agriculture in Trinidad (1921), which had only 51 students in 1948. As a result of a British educational commission in 1938, it became a constituent of the University of the West Indies, founded in 1949 to offer University of London sponsored external degrees to students from the 14 islands, eventually with three campuses in Jamaica, Trinidad and the Bahamas.

China, Iran and Japan

The Chinese education system is based on legalist and Confucian ideals. The teaching of Confucius has shaped the overall Chinese mindset for the past 2500 years. But other outside forces have played a large role in the nation's educational development. The First Opium War of 1840, for example, opened China to the rest of the world. As a result, Chinese intellectuals discovered the numerous Western advances in science and technology. This new information greatly impacted the higher education system and curriculum. Soviet influence in the early 1950s brought all higher education under government leadership. Research was separated from teaching. The government also introduced a central plan for a nationally unified instruction system, i.e. texts, syllabi, etc. The impact of this shift can still be seen today. Chinese higher education continues its struggle with excessive departmentalization, segmentation, and overspecialization in particular.

From 1967 to 1976, China's Cultural Revolution took another toll on higher education, which was devastated more than any other sector of the country. The enrollment of postsecondary students illustrates the impacts. The number dropped from 674,400 to 47,800. This has had a major impact on education in the 21st century. The decline in educational quality was profound. In 1977, Deng Xiaoping made the decision of resuming the National Higher Education Entrance Examination (Gao Kao), having profound impact on Chinese higher education in history. From the 1980s on, Chinese higher education has undergone a series of reforms that have slowly brought improvement.

Higher education in China is continuously growing, changing and developing. There are over 2,000 universities and colleges, with more than six million enrollments in total. China has set up a degree system, including Bachelor's, Master's and Doctoral degrees that are open to foreign students. The country offers non-degree programs as well. According to the Ministry of Education of the People's Republic of China, the government authority on all matters pertaining to education and language, higher education in China has played a significant part in economic growth, scientific progress and social development in the country "by bringing up large scale of advanced talents and experts for the construction of socialist modernization."

New trends in Chinese higher education are attracting the attention of educators around the world. Since China began to develop a Western-oriented university model at the end of nineteenth century, Chinese higher education has continued to evolve. Since the late 1980s, tremendous economic development in China has stimulated reforms in higher education that have resulted in remarkable improvements. In 2005, there were about 4,000 Chinese institutions. Student enrollment increased to 15 million, with rapid growth that is expected to peak in 2008. However, the higher education system does not meet the needs of 85 per cent of the college-aged population.

Peking University is the first formally established modern national university of China. It was founded as Imperial Capital University in 1898 as a replacement of the ancient *Guozijian*. The first modern institution, Peiyang University, was founded October 2, 1895, in Tianjin. The university changed its name to Tianjin University in 1951 and became one of the leading universities in China. Jiaotong University, the next, was founded in Shanghai in 1896. In the 1950s, a large portion of this university was moved to Xi'an, an ancient capital city in northwest China, and became Xi'an Jiaotong University; the part of the university remaining in Shanghai was renamed Shanghai Jiaotong University. Tianjin University celebrated its 100th anniversary in 1995, followed by Xi'an Jiaotong and Shanghai Jiaotong Universities in 1996. Other leading universities such as Zhejiang University (1897), Peking University (1898), and Nanjing University (1902) also recently celebrated their hundredth anniversaries, one after another.

In the Middle East, where most countries in the early 20th century were only nominally free, Iran, divided into British and Russian "spheres of influence", established Western-style universities in Tehran in 1934 and Tabriz in 1947, with about 5000 students in 1948 and 50,000 in 1970. Iraq, a British mandated territory, did not have a unified university but founded modern faculties of law, commerce and economics, agriculture, music and fine arts in the 1930s, with about 3,000 students in 1948 and 35,000 in 11 institutions by 1967. Turkey, which had a Quranic university in Istanbul since its conquest of the Byzantine Empire in 1453 and a naval engineering school since 1773, which developed other engineering faculties during the 19th century, built the "House of Science" in Istanbul in 1863 and acquired the same year Robert College, an American institution with Western staff, and an American College for Girls in 1890. Only after the overthrow of the sultan and the establishment of Ataturk's republic in 1923 did modern higher education take off in earnest, with the use of the Roman alphabet in 1928 and equality for women.

Egypt broke away from the Turkish Empire under Mehemet Ali Pasaha in 1830 and began to Westernize education but, apart from the Al-Azhar *madrasa* in the great mosque of Cairo, no modern university was founded before the American University in 1919. In Syria and Palestine, there was little higher education under the Turks, and the first universities came after World War I under the British and French Mandates, the Syrian University at Damascus in 1923 and the Hebrew University in Jerusalem, first projected by the Zionist movement in the 1880s in 1925.

The most spectacular example of Westernization in higher education, as in much else, was of course Japan. The revolutionary samurai who restored the Emperor Meiji in 1868 eagerly imported Western science, technology and education; in Prime Minister Ito's words it was "to maintain the nation's strength and to guarantee the welfare of the people." "A rich country and a strong army" was the watchword and the Han schools for samurai bureaucrats were replaced by imperial universities, at Tokyo (1886), Kyoto (1897), Sapporo on Hokkaido (1903) and Nagoya (1939). They were followed by many other colleges and institutes, more of them private than public. Initially on French lines with attached but separate research institutes, they soon ostensibly followed the German model of the combined teaching and Research University. The German model, like everything Western, was quickly modified to fit Japanese culture and society. With 30% of the age group going to college in 1985, Japan was one of the first countries to reach mass higher education, as befits the most successfully developed nation outside the West.

In higher education, as in technology, management and industrial relations, Japan set the pattern for post-industrial society. By the end of World War II, most advanced and some developing nations had adopted or were in the process of adopting, if in a highly modified form, the Western type of higher education that had done so much to reinforce, and in later cases to midwife, industrial society, with its promise of wealth and power but its heavy costs in drudgery and maldistribution of rewards. The world, unknowingly perhaps, was poised for another great leap forward, into a post-industrial phase in which the university and its satellites would become the key to further the development of human society (Blewitt, 1965; Cummings, 1979; Nagai, 1971).

The University and Post-industrial Society

The period since World War II has seen the greatest expansion of higher education since the 12th century. Three quarters of all universities, even in Europe, have been founded in the 20th century, 75% of them since 1945. Everywhere old universities have expanded in size, new institutions have come into existence and student numbers have increased to embrace ever-larger proportions of the relevant age group. In the leading countries, which already educated most of the children of their elite, the percentage of the student age group rose dramatically from under 10% in 1960 to a half or more by 2000. Most Third World countries were too poor and dependent on agriculture and craft industries to afford large expansions of higher education, but even they showed some increase.

Only the richest and most advanced countries have reached the post-industrial stage, but the pattern of development is clear. Even poor countries, like Malaysia, Indonesia and the

Philippines, have begun to move from the agricultural stage to the industrial, with the help of outsourced industries, not only of textiles and clothing but of sophisticated ones like cars, television sets and computers, for the West and Japan. In some cases, this has led to graduate employment in IT industries and the like, which require skilled managers and engineers, so that higher education is required on a growing scale. India with its tradition of speaking English has even begun to supply call centers for British railways and computer suppliers, processing of credit cards transactions, and the running of medical tests for health centers in the West. None of this could occur without advanced education for selective minorities of graduates.

This unprecedented expansion is due to the onset of what has been called the Third Revolution in human history, the transition to a society based on professional expert services. Usually called the post-industrial society, a negative definition that only tells what it is not, it entails the majority of the occupied in the most developed countries working not in growing good or manufacturing consumer and capital goods, but in services and especially in the ever more specialized services based on advanced training and education (Perkin, 1966).

Often called the "information society", emphasizing the significance of electronic communications and digital technology, or the "knowledge society" involving the application of many varieties of knowledge, notably in biology, medicine, arts and science, leisure and culture, strictly depends on the professional who serve it, and therefore, should be called the professional society. The professions include not only the traditional ones of clergy, law and medicine and the new sciences and technologies created by industrialism, but also the bureaucrats who run central and local government and the executives who have largely replaced the owner-managers of traditional industry. All these are now educated and qualified in the universities and business schools attached to them. This has made the university the axial institution of post-industrial society (Bell, 1973). It is for this reason that academics have become the key profession, the profession that educates the other professions (Perkin, 1969).

Universities normally adjust to meet the demands of the society, sometimes with a time lag. Before the modern universities came into existence few of them were interested in economic growth. Medieval universities were more concerned with theology and Aristotelian philosophy than with economic development, while early modern ones took little part in the Scientific or Industrial Revolutions. They came in the 19th century to pioneer training for new professions including science, engineering and technology, company law and accountancy, but it was only in the 20th century that they came to educate almost every profession required by the new society, including the social sciences and business management. Even then, across the Developing World especially, higher education still meant preserving the old traditions of thought and culture.

In the developed countries, this unprecedented expansion has achieved what T.R. McConnell and his colleagues have called the transition from aristocratic to meritocratic society. This means, first of all, a shift from higher education for the top 5% or less of the age group (mainly for the children of the rich and influential), to a system educating at the post-secondary level from a third to a half of the relevant age group. In the last three decades, the most advanced countries have already achieved mass higher education and some have gone beyond it. That is probably as far as one can go in the direction of universal higher education, since all societies need skilled and unskilled workers with little use for or interest in higher as distinct from further education. For the latter, more relevant perhaps is vocational education, as in Germany, where skilled apprenticeship is the norm for the non-student teenagers, now being copied elsewhere, as in the United Kingdom, France and other European countries.

The Globalization of Higher Education

Universities have always operated in an international context, as the European ones in the Middle Ages exchanged teachers, students and ideas through the *lingua franca* of Latin and the early modern ones eventually came to cooperate in the recovery of ancient learning and the scientific discoveries of the Enlightenment. The universities of post-industrial society, however, have raised this interchange to a higher plane to match the needs of a more global society. New ideas and discoveries are spread at the speed of light via the Internet, students are exchanged or are educated in other countries than their own, especially those from developing countries seeking degrees in the West. Academics in practically all disciplines collaborate through international journals, conferences and visiting professorships. Indeed, the very foundation and expansion of universities in the developing world have been carried out by colonizers from the imperial West or by imitation of Western models.

Higher Education and Social Mobility

Universities, while as educating elites, have always provided ladders for poor boys to climb to success in church, state and business. In post-industrial society, the need for expertise and the emphasis on meritocracy have had profound effects on social mobility for children of the working class and also on the expanded access to higher education for women of all classes. For women this began in the advanced countries soon after World War II. The enrollment patterns reflect the character of demand for graduates in the more advanced societies. Increased access by the children of all classes has been one of the main aims of the expansion, and this has certainly increased the numbers of workers' children on the campuses. Paradoxically, expansion seems in most countries to have benefited the wealthy and middle classes even more, through their knowledge and manipulation of the system and possession of material and social capital. In Western Europe, working class students began to make modest inroads into the student body after World War II. Higher education everywhere was becoming the high road for social climbing, replacing the self-made social climbers of the Victorian Age. Thus, higher education became an instrument of social engineering, as the new professional society drew educated specialists, in unequal proportions of course, from all levels of the population.

Distance Learning and the Internet

An unforeseen avenue of educational social mobility came in the mid-20th century with the founding of distance learning through such institutions as the British Open University founded in the 1960s, Deakin University in Australia, and similar institutions accessible to the adult populations in California, Singapore, Hong Kong, unitary in Malaysia and so on. An even freer development came with online degree education through the Internet in the late 20th century, which culminated in the UNESCO-affiliated International Council for Open and Distance Learning based in Norway representing 145 countries. These paths to a degree and certificates sold through the Internet might suggest that earthbound universities might become obsolete, but there seems to be no substitute for face-to-face learning, and least of all for the universities' role in research (Bell and Tight, 1993; Tiffen and Rajasingham, 2003; Taylor et al., 1985).

Deakin University in Australia

The Drawbacks of Post-Industrial Society

Post-industrial or professional society is the most productive society in the history of humankind, giving not only the elite but most of its members longer life, better health, greater comfort, more consumer goods and services, more leisure and holidays, more enjoyment of the arts and sciences, more access to education and social climbing, than any previous society. To that extent it owes its success mainly to higher education, which produces the research and professional experts as well as the trained experts on which most new industries and technology are based for service. But it is not all gain. There are three drawbacks as far as the universities are concerned.

Firstly, higher education has become far more expensive. The advanced countries generally spend between 5% and 8% of GNP on public education, of which they spend about a fifth to third on tertiary education (World Bank, 2003; Glenny, 1979). This has to be paid for by someone and taxpayers and governments are less and less willing to increase their share of the cost. Hence, the debate in almost every country on raising contributions from the private sector, either from business, alumni donations or from student fees in the shape of parental support or deferred student loans.

The second drawback is that universities have themselves become large-scale bureaucracies and subject to the threat of centralized, bureaucratic state control. This has had profound consequences for the status of the faculty and for academic autonomy and freedom. Firstly, increased state interference, audit, inspection and threatened control of the curriculum and research have undermined the autonomy and independence, which the medieval European universities had fought so hard to achieve. The ivory tower, which had produced so much independent thought to challenge the power of both state and church, has been eroded, and higher education is in danger of becoming an adjunct of the overbearing state. The very freedom and independence for which the university had been invented is subjected to the will of a single authority, the State.

A consequence of the increased dependence on the State was to extend the power of the administrators over the academics. European professors, in contrast to their American counterparts, long had a dual role, of academic work on the one hand and managing the university on the other. This may have led to inefficiency through the committee system, but it ensured academic control. The increasing size of the university made the system burdensome, so that full time administrators took over the bulk of the management. At the same time, the academic profession, grown to far greater numbers and therefore less prestigious, began to lose status and comparative income. Whereas professors had once been on par with doctors, lawyers, top civil servants and similar professions, they now found themselves slipping down the hierarchy and losing ground on the income ladder.

The third drawback of increased numbers and bureaucracy, provoking outrage in the West in the 1960s but subsiding in more recent decades, was student unrest. This was by no means new. It had accompanied the early days of the universities from the 12th century, and welled up from time to time throughout their history as at the Reformation, the English Civil War of the 17th century, the various revolutions in the 19th century Europe, Russia and South America and the demonstrations against globalization and world capitalism today. However, student generations are short and student rebels few; and the unrest in the West subsided as fast as it had risen.

Despite the drawbacks, the university and its offshoots are essential to post-industrial society. If it did not exist, it would have to be invented under another name. It is clear that in its origin the university owed its autonomy and creativity to its dual responsibility to State and church, which gave it the flexibility and productivity to think new and sometimes dangerous thoughts. No institution so flexible or so productive of new knowledge and adaptable experts has yet been discovered. Yet this flexibility and productivity still depend on the academic freedom to teach and to pursue knowledge wherever it can be found. Without the ability to protect themselves from the threat of the powerful forces, the university may well suffer the fate of those institutions in the non-

European world that never enjoyed the autonomy and freedom that the medieval division between church and State unintentionally bequeathed to academia.

TOP FIVE UNIVERSITIES IN ASIA 2011

Ranking	University
1	The Hong Kong University of Science and Technology
2	University of Hong Kong
3	National University of Singapore (NUS)
4	The University of Tokyo
5	The Chinese University of Hong Kong

Universities Ranking Report July 2010

The CSIC Cybermetrics Lab has just released the July 2010 edition of the Ranking Web of World Universities, viz. Webometrics. This new edition greatly expands coverage to Asia and reached the 20,000 higher education institutions analyzed, of which it provides the classification of the 12,000 first. The catalog has been revised and updating, making it the largest and most complete directory of universities exceeding the one offered by the UNESCO.

Top 500 Universities by Region

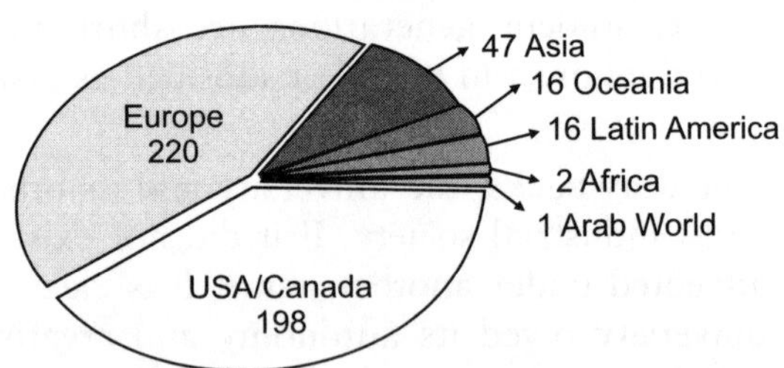

Changes of positions are scarce, because the American universities are still leading the results (Harvard, MIT, Stanford and Berkeley), with an excellent performance of Canadian institutions, which exceed in positions of privilege in the UK. In Europe, in addition to those English (Cambridge and Oxford but also the Scottish Edinburgh) highlights the Swiss (ETH Zurich) and Nordic (Helsinki, Oslo). Appear lagging German, French or Italian, due in large part because research in these countries takes place in independent institutions (Max Planck, CNRS, and CNR). In this new edition, Spain maintained their positions with a university among the 150 first (Complutense of Madrid). The polytechnics are also placed in good positions, but highlights the good job made by the University of the Basque Country (third in Spain, 202 of the world). The multi-domain problem seems Catalan universities, but explains that the University of Barcelona (214) does not reach a higher position. The University of Navarra (466) remains the first private Spanish Ranking. UNED (342) improves positions and remains the leader among distance universities.

In Latin America highlights the UNAM (70 in the world) from Mexico, being especially remarkable the large number of Brazilian universities, led by Sao Paulo, among the best in the region. The Universities of Chile and Buenos Aires are among those in Brazil and Mexico. Universities in Japan, Hong Kong and Singapore lead Asian ranking, after appearing Taiwanese and Korean. Chinese universities had not reached the levels of these countries and the Indian subcontinents are far behind. The research centers ranking complements the former, with a directory of over 7000 entries which provides the classification of early 4000. Institutes of Health in the USA and NASA are at the head of the ranking, followed closely by the CNRS. The Spanish CSIC is ranked 19 in the world, with seven of their centers from the first thousand.

REFERENCES

Perkin Harold (2006). History of Universities. In James J.F. Forest and Phillip G. Altbach (eds.), *International Handbook of Higher Education,* Netherlands: Springer, pp. 159-205.

http://www.webometrics.info/methodology.html

http://en.wikipedia.org/wiki/University

http://www.topuniversities.com/university-rankings/world-university-rankings/2011/subject-rankings/arts-humanities/history/

I personally acknowledge and pay regards to all the authors whose work I have quoted in this chapter from the book on *International Handbook of Higher Education* by Altbach and Forest.

Higher Education in India: History, Growth and Development

3

In the modern dynamic world, characterized by rapid transformations in all sectors of society, the role of universities has come under scrutiny. There is a feeling that the work and performance of universities, the world over, are not in keeping with the requirements of the societies they serve. This seems to be especially true for India where there is a growing demand for a reappraisal of their functions. Any such reappraisal should, however, take into consideration historical aspects, conventional roles and future requirements.

India's ancient seats of learning at Nalanda, Vikramshila, Vallabhi and Takshashila were essentially centers of religion and philosophy, though Takshashila also engaged in professional education (Jha, 1991). They had their own unique traditions and values. Ancient Indian civilization is one of the most important civilizations of the world. The system of education in ancient India served as an effective instrument for the transfer of oral and written tradition from one generation to another. The most striking feature of the ancient Indian education system was its predominantly religious character, though there is evidence of princes receiving training in the techniques of warfare and statecraft.

The Vedic period marked the beginning of Indian culture, literature and science. It was realized that the intellectual equipment and efficiency were the corner stone of human progress. Importance of education was emphasized by pointing out that Gods befriend only those who are wise and learned. It laid down that every person should undergo a period of training and discipline called *Brahmacharya* during the childhood and adolescence, when he or she should be initiated into sacred literature and trained in a profession.

Nalanda University

Vikramshila University

Takshila University

Gurukul System

Education continued to be regarded as the most vital factor for the well-being of the society in the Upanishad/Sutra period. Education was regarded as a process of illumination in the Dharamshastra period. It was believed that education transforms and illuminates a person's nature by promoting a progressive and harmonious development of the physical, mental, intellectual and spiritual powers and faculties. The rise of corporate institutions for higher studies is the most noteworthy development of the Puranic period. It had a profound influence on educational practice and method.

Students became a member of an educational colony with hundreds of teachers and students.

The Medieval centuries (12th-18th century) in the history of India signified a major phase of social and cultural synthesis, resulting from the interaction between widely diverse lifestyles of the new settlers from Central and Western Asia, on the one hand, and of the early inhabitants of the sub-continent, on the other. The early Indian education system and many of its centers continued, but not with their erstwhile grandeur, in the middle ages. There were important south Indian centers in the Chola, Pandaya and Hoysala kingdoms and later in the Vijayanagara empire and the Nyaka Kingdoms of its successors; in northern India, Varanasi, Prayag, Hardwar, Nadia, Ujjain and Mithila were noted for their pathshalas and tols of the early Indian pattern, where Brahmin teachers and scholars devoted their entire lives to the study of Vedas, Shastras and the Puranas.

Vijayanagara Empire in the post-Mughal India

Madrasa as a center of higher learning in northern India emerged with the transfer of the seat of political authority of Ghazanivids from Ghazni to Lahore, even though its history in India could be traced back to the first Arab contacts with the subcontinent. Later when Delhi became the capital of the Turkish rule, the city became one of the greatest centers of

Islamic higher learning in the East with almost the entire body of science and culture of the Islamic world getting imported into India by the middle of the 13th century.

These *madrasas* were intended to provide secular studies, but also took care of the religious and moral training of the students. Early in the 16th century the *madarasa* syllabus comprised over seven subjects, viz.: grammar, literature, logic, jurisprudence, commentaries on Quran and mysticism. Three of these, namely grammar, literature and logic had little bearing on theology, even though these three taken as instrumental disciplines did help in articulating the theological disputations and debates. In both Sanskrit and Arabic higher learning, much secular and scientific learning in law, medicine, mathematics, astronomy, etc. was cultivated besides literature, philosophy and theology with the help of books and discussion but chiefly through memorization.

Education under the Colonial Rule

The origin of the present system of education can be traced to the beginning of the nineteenth century when a controversy had been raging over the issue whether oriental learning and science should be spread through the medium of Sanskrit,

Arabic or Persian or Western sciences and literature be spread through English as the medium of instruction. A *madrasa* in 1780 at Calcutta and a Sanskrit College in 1791 at Benaras were established for pleasing the Muslims and Hindus. Charles Grant, an officer of the Company, in his famous essay "Observation" drew the attention of the British people towards the deplorable condition of education in India. As a result in the Charter of 1813, the British Parliament made the Company responsible for education of the Indian people. There was some progress in education during the period 1813-33. In 1814, the Board of Directors clarified the educational policy.

The period 1835-53 had been very important for Indian education as it saw many upheavals and ultimately was brought on a definite track. Before 1813, the Company's educational policy was influenced by Orientalism as the Company wanted to maintain the old educational system. The Orientalists contended that the Indians did not require the knowledge of European language, literature and culture so much as the English in India required understanding of the Indian culture and civilization.

By the beginning of the nineteenth century, England had become a great industrial country. They considered their language, literature, culture and civilization as superior to all others. The supporters of the Occidental point of view were young English men and in number they surpassed the Orientalist English men. These young men looked down at Indian languages, literature and culture and believed in introducing the study of English language and literature and European culture.

Lord Macaulay played a leading role in 1834 when he became the member of the Governor-General's Council and was appointed the President of the Committee of Public Instruction. He tried to ward off the Occidental and Oriental controversy, which ended finally during Auckland's period. Macaulay advocated the Occidental approach and laid down the educational policy accordingly. Lord Bentick also approved of the Macaulay's policy and issued a declaration based on his views. The indigenous schools got a setback, although they were allowed to continue with nominal financial assistance. Macaulay's policy produced clerks on the one hand, but also produced patriots on the other.

Lord Bentick

The idea of establishing universities in India, on the model of London University (i.e. a university of the affiliating type), was first given in Sir Charles Wood's Despatch of 1854, which has been described as the 'Magna Carta of English Education in India'. It described the aim of Indian education as the diffusion of Arts, Science philosophy and literature of Europe, and the study of Indian languages. These recommendations were enlarged to also include Law, Medicine and Engineering and were followed by the establishment, in 1857, of universities at Calcutta, Bombay and Madras. During the next 25 years, there was an increase in the number of colleges from 27 to 75. This led to the demand for more universities. The Allahabad University was established in 1887. By 1923 the number of universities had reached twelve. In order to facilitate coordination in the activities of these universities, the Inter-University Board (converted to the Association of Indian

Universities in 1973) was established in 1925. There was a steady growth in the subsequent years and 1943 a need was felt for a comprehensive plan of educational development. The Sargent Report of 1944 was the first attempt to formulate a national system of education in India. It pointed out the failure in making university education relevant to the community needs and suggested means for improvement (Mohanty, 1993). By the time India became independent, in 1947, it had 18 universities and total student strength of a little less than two lakhs.

Higher Education in the Post-independence Period

National movement was concerned not only with freedom from the British rule, but also with national culture and even, more significantly, education in Science and Technology and intellectual creativity. This goal was achieved by founding new institutions. Tagore created the Viswa-Bharati emphasizing Indian cultural roots, creativity and philosophical synthesis of the best that was in Western thought and Oriental philosophy. At Benaras, a whole new university was founded where Pt. Malaviya and his associates emphasized technological education. Seeing that Muslims had been left behind in Western education and hence government employment, the Muslim-Anglo Oriental College of Aligarh was founded, which later grew into Aligarh Muslim University. Here emphasis was on mastery of English, attributes, gracious living and sports.

Viswa-Bharti University

Tagore

Banaras Hindu University

Aligarh Muslim University

The University Education Commission (Radhkrishnan Commission) in 1948 was a major landmark in stating the goals and objectives of higher education in India after independence. It stressed amongst other things that Indian education must be rooted in its cultural heritage. It gave guidelines for the structuring of higher education and recommended the setting up of the University Grants Commission, which was formed in 1953 and given autonomous, statutory status by an Act of Parliament in 1956.

The state of higher education was re-examined by the Education Commission of 1964-66 (the Kothari Commission) which in its report (Government of India, 1966) emphasized the need for a built-in-flexibility in the system of education and for the necessity for education to be science based and in coherence with Indian culture and values. It visualized education as an instrument for the nation's progress, security and welfare. It advocated far reaching reforms. To quote:

> Indian education needs a drastic reconstruction almost a revolution. We need to...introduce work experience as an integral element of general education to improve quality of teachers at all levels...to strengthen centers of advanced studies and strive to attain in some of our universities at least, higher international standards; to lay special emphasis on the combination of teaching and research; and to pay particular attention to education and research in agriculture and allied sciences.

The Kothari Commission report emphasized that there had to be a radical improvement in the quality and standard of higher education and research; expansion of higher education to meet manpower requirements of the nation and the rising social ambitions and expectations of the people and improvement of university organization and administration.

Undoubtedly, great educationists, thinkers and philosophers laid down these recommendations keeping in mind the then state-of-art of higher education, but with great predicament it is felt that no specific *modus operandi* was suggested to implement the ideas. They did talk about science based education based on Indian culture and values but how and what courses will actually lead to such education, was not specified. Research, the most important aspect and factor to face the present globalization and privatization scenario, was not given much emphasis. Combination of teaching and research was opined but from then till now it is very rare that we see teaching that is based on researches.

Based upon Kothari Commission report, the National Policy of Education, 1968 was adopted. Twenty years later, in 1985, the Government of India document Challenge of Education recognized that "the general condition of universities and colleges is a matter of great concern to the nation". The National Policy of Education, 1986 accepted that the general formulations in the 1968 Policy did not get translated into a detailed strategy of implementation. The National Policy of Education, 1986 aims at not only developing manpower for serving the economy but also developing crucial values. The policy envisages education for equality. In the area of higher education emphasis is on consolidation and expansion of facilities. The strategies are outlined in the Ramamurti Committee Report of 1990 (Towards an Enlightened and Humane Society) and the Programme of Action, 1992. The question still lingers and holds importance even after twenty-thirty years of these policies as to how can Indian universities achieve manpower development and what steps should be followed for developing cultural values.

The Prime Minister's Council on Trade and Industry appointed a Committee headed by Mr. Mukesh Ambani and Mr. Kumarmangalam Birla to suggest reforms in the Educational sector. The Committee, which submitted its report in the year 2001, highlighted the important role of the State in the development of Education. Ambani and Birla in their report "A Policy Framework for Reforms in Education" emphasized that education is a very profitable market over which they must have full control and for their industrial requirements education must shape adaptable, competitive workers who can readily acquire new skills and innovations. Hence, they wanted a fundamental change in the mindset of seeing education only as a component of social development.

By not being market-oriented, the Indian education system fails to realize the potential of the information technology requirements. Consequently, private institutions enjoying brand equity and large market capitalization have come up forming a large non-formal education system of creating quality software professionals. However, none of these has developed into a world class institution, in the absence of needed investment, not available on account of the lack of opportunity to make profit.

The National Knowledge Commission (NKC) was constituted on 13 June 2005 and its recommendations on higher education were submitted to the Prime Minister on 29 November 2006. The Commission focussed on certain key areas such as education, science and technology, agriculture, industry, e-governance, etc. Easy access to knowledge, creation and preservation of knowledge systems, dissemination of knowledge and better knowledge services have been the core concerns of the commission. It focussed on creating a world class environment for creation of knowledge, promoting applications of knowledge for sustained and inclusive growth and using knowledge applications in efficient delivery of public places. The NKC gave recommendations regarding reforms in existing public universities, undergraduate colleges, regulatory structure, financing, quality, creation of national universities as centers of academic excellence and access to marginalized and excluded groups.

Dr. Manmohan Singh, in his speech at the launch of the NKC in 2005, emphasized some important issues. He opined that it is now commonplace to say that the 21st century will be the "Knowledge Century". It is not military power or economic power that will in fact determine a nation's place in the world now in the making, but its "brainpower". Brainpower should of course be reflected in a country's economic competitiveness as well as military prowess. More importantly it should be reflected in, what Amartya Sen has called, "human capabilities". Human capability is a function of the well-being of people and the investment we make in human capital formation. The ability of a nation to make best use of its brainpower will shape its place in the world in the present century. If capability created by knowledge is the foundation upon which our future is to be built then the need of the hour is to evaluate whether we are adequately equipped and prepared for the future. The paradox about India is that the answer to that question cannot be unambiguous. In many ways, we have the potential to make the best use of the opportunities that lie ahead of us. However, in many other ways we also have an enormous task ahead of us in being able to realize this vast latent potential of our country.

The enormity of this task is all the more due to the demographic transition underway now in the country. In the next few decades, India will probably have the world's largest set of young people. Even as other countries begin to age, India will remain a country of young people. And if we can find productive opportunities for our working population that of course would give us a big opportunity to leapfrog in the race for social and economic development and our growth rates should go up. These youth can be an asset only if we invest in their capabilities. A knowledge-driven generation will be an asset. Denied this investment, it will become a social and economic liability. Hence, we must invest in building the knowledge base of our coming generations. The task ahead is at many levels—from primary schools to higher education and research institutions of national excellence. At all levels, there is a need to improve both access and excellence. There are, of course, fiscal and administrative challenges to be tackled and there are intellectual and leadership issues to be addressed.

At the bottom of "knowledge pyramid" the challenge is one of improving access to the primary education. At the top of the "pyramid" there is need to make our institutions of higher education and research world class. There is a genuine funds constraint in the public sector that is being neutralized only in part by the private sector. Together, the public and private sectors are not able to cope with the demand for higher and professional education. However, there is an additional problem of quality at the top of the pyramid. The universities and centers of excellence are falling behind the best in the world both in terms of human capital and in terms of physical infrastructure.

With such a vast pool of qualified, English-speaking scientific and technological manpower, India must have the ambition to become a large base of research and development activity. We should be able to attract global investment into R&D activity at home. Finally, the Knowledge Commission should bring forward bold proposals aimed at improving excellence in research and teaching, especially in the frontier areas of mathematics, science, technology and management. India cannot afford to lag behind the rest of the world. The time has come for us to create a second wave of institution building and of excellence in the field of education, research and capability building in India so that we are better prepared for the 21st century.

A panel headed by Prof. Yashpal was set up in February 2008 with the mandate of studying the functioning of different agencies in higher education and suggest measures to restructure the system of higher education. The report on "Renovation and Rejuvenation of Higher Education", prepared after much consultation with all the stakeholders, including students and teachers was submitted to the Ministry of Human Resource Development (MHRD) on June 24, 2009. The report is a roadmap for future of education in India. Its recommendations are definitely pivotal for reforms. The committee suggested setting up of a National Commission for Higher Education and Research, which will be an apex body in education. The committee made several suggestions, including scrapping of regulatory bodies like the UGC and AICTE, granting full autonomy to universities and instituting a national commission to supervise them. It is however doubtful that a mammoth organization such as the proposed national commission would be free of the ills of the present apex bodies like UGC/AICTE, etc.; at least no safeguards have been suggested.

It is evident that over the years a lot of thought has been given to identify the problems faced by higher education in India and to formulating policies and programmes for their mitigation. However, we have woefully failed in implementing the reforms. Commenting on this situation, Valiathan (1993) regrets that "knowing what to do and not caring to do it has cast a shadow on (our) national endeavours". Altbach (1993) also concludes on a negative note that "the complexity of the social context in which higher education exists (in India) very likely makes systematic reforms impossible."

Final Remarks

Higher Education in India is in a state of doldrums. Bloated in size and resistant to change it is in danger of becoming irrelevant. The system has not been able to free itself from its colonial roots and identify itself with local needs. The outmoded affiliation model, with an unwieldy and unproductive examination system, still operates. Practically, all universities and institutions face a financial crisis. The maladies identified nearly three decades ago by the Kothari Commission still exist and the suggested reforms have been implemented only half-heartedly. This in spite of the Commission's warning that "tinkering with the existing situation and moving forward with faltering steps, and lack of faith, can make things worse than before" has apparently not received the attention it warrants.

During the last four decades of development planning, higher education has witnessed significant changes. A retrospect of developments in higher education indicates that, in spite of other various inadequacies and limitations; institutions of higher learning in India have helped in the accumulation of a pool of scientific and technical manpower which is the third largest and the oldest in the world. Given a wide range of accomplishments it is somewhat surprising that there is much to be done before the objectives of equity, quality and relevance are achieved.

The number of institutions and enrollment in higher education continue their rapid growth, but the quality of this education remains uncertain. A small number of state-subsidized institutions attract a thin top layer of talent from each year's cohort. High selectivity of admission to these elite institutions provides a screen valued by potential employers. Domestic and foreign demand for the services of these few thousand students has created an inflated reputation of the overall quality of India's higher education. The number of such graduates remains small relative to the population and the demands of India's economy for educated manpower. Reliable estimates of value-added by higher education, beyond the screening value of admission to elite institutions, are needed to assess colleges and universities, and to guide educational policy.

There is tremendous churning taking place in higher education the world over. It is changing radically, by becoming organically flexible in terms of diversity of programmes, in its structure, curricula and delivery systems. In addition, it is adapting itself to the use of information and communication technologies (ICT). Nations are struggling to cope with the diametrically opposite demands of quality education and a phenomenal increase in the number of students wanting to go in for higher education. Both the quality and quantity of education requires better academic and physical infrastructure and greater financial resources. Both basic education, which lays the foundation for a healthy, skilled and agile intellectual human force and lifelong education which enables countries to continually assess, adapt and apply new knowledge are equally important in a knowledge-linked society. The convergence of communication and computer technologies has opened new avenues for the spread of education as well as improving the quality of education. It is also capable of providing cost-effective solutions for the ever-expanding demand for higher education. Indeed, the ICT revolution greatly facilitates the acquisition and absorption of knowledge, and offers a country like India unprecedented opportunities to enhance its educational systems.

Graduate education continues in an alarming state of disarray with respect to both quality and quantity. Pressed by budgetary constraints, the government appears to have decided on profit-oriented privatization of higher education as the solution. Political and business classes, with significant overlap between the two, see higher education as a source of lucrative private returns on investment. There is little theoretical or empirical evidence that supports the prospects of success of a for-profit model in building quality higher education. Some recent proposals hold promise of radical reform and renovation, including regulatory restructuring. It remains unclear whether the government has the wisdom, determination, financing, and power to push reforms past the resistance from entrenched faculty and from the political and business classes.

A liberal university of the 21st century has to respond to the changing needs of the society, which are now technology driven and are becoming highly information and knowledge intensive, bringing in fundamental changes in the way human beings live, learn, interact, work and conduct their everyday activities. However, it is useful to note that learning is a personalized process not dependent on technology, whereas educating is a social process dependent on interaction between learners and teachers, which may make use of available tools and technologies. As a result, education has to keep pace with the worldwide changes taking place rapidly in all major sectors of the society, like social, cultural, economic and political, driven by the on-going ICT revolution.

Growth and Development: An Overview of India's Higher Education

India's emergence as one of the fastest growing economies on the globe, with the possibility of a double digit growth rate, poses a critical challenge of its preparedness to capitalize on opportunities on the horizon for its massive and growing work-force. More important is that the country is looking towards creating new ways to harvest this promise of growth through appropriate educational and training infrastructure. The revolution in ICT has been the mainstay of globalization of markets and knowledge systems. Availability of Internet-based services and communications has allowed distances and barriers to be reached in real time and that too at lower costs than ever imaginable.

Internet technology (IT) has found two broad applications in higher education or university system. First is its use in creating seamless administrative systems and interfaces, like online admission forms, status tracking, availability of results, course schedule, etc. In some cases, depending on how tech savvy faculty members are, online submission of assignments is also being done. The second application, which is significant in the Indian context, has been in changing the very manner in which education is delivered as a process and also as learning experience. It has taken higher education away from the confines of classrooms, libraries and individual lecture sessions.

Availability of online courses has allowed students and teachers from different parts of the world to converge. Online universities do not require physical infrastructure and thus have facilitated greater accessibility to education as a student need not commute or live on campus. Flexibility offered by online courses has brought in a new range of students, in terms of social and professional backgrounds. Acquiring specialized degrees is today seen as a sure means of creating possibilities of better jobs, as mid-life career changes become more frequent. Online education holds tremendous potential for India's massive population. The concept of e-education, especially at higher levels, is just beginning to be viewed seriously.

Growth Over the Years

The growth of higher education in India in the past 60 to 65 years has been a phenomenal story. The country's professional institutions can boast of powering the global IT industry and becoming a mainstay of health sector in several developed countries particularly in the United Kingdom. The growth can be ascertained from the fact that starting with only 263,000 students in all disciplines in 750 colleges affiliated to 30 universities in 1950, the numbers have grown to 11 million students in 17,000 degree colleges affiliated to 230 universities and non affiliated university level institutions in 2005. India's higher education system is the largest system of higher education in Commonwealth countries and second largest in the world with 25 central universities, 231 state universities, five institutions established through state legislation, 100 deemed universities, 31 institutes of national importance as on 31 December 2007. In 2008, the total number of university level institutions including 11 private universities was 431, number of colleges—20,677, teachers was 5.05 lakhs and the number of students enrolled was 116.12 lakh.

Indian has the third largest higher education system in the world now, next only to China and the United States of America. In mid-2011, it had 546 university level institutions, over 31,000 colleges, about 14.5 million students and a little less than 0.7 million teachers. The number of universities is expected to rise by 800+ in the next ten years, and the number of colleges by another 30,000.

At the beginning of the academic year 2009-10, the total number of students enrolled, in the formal system, in the universities and colleges has been reported at 136.42 lakhs—16.69 lakhs (12.24%) in university departments and 119.73 lakhs (87.76%) in affiliated colleges. The enrolment of women students at the beginning of the academic year 2009-10 was 56.49 lakhs constituting 41.40% of the total enrolment. Of the total women enrolment, 14.72% women have been enrolled in professional courses. The women enrolment as a percentage of total enrolment in States is the highest in Goa (59%) and the lowest in Bihar (30%). In terms of absolute numbers of women enrolment, Uttar Pradesh tops the list of States with 8.00 lakhs, followed by Maharashtra (7.8 lakhs). The number of doctoral degrees (Ph.D. only) awarded by various universities (during 2007-08) was 13,237. Out of which, the faculties of Sciences had the highest number with 4574 degrees, followed by the faculties of Arts with 4405 degrees. These two faculties together accounted for 67% of the total number of doctoral degrees awarded. The regular faculty strength in universities was 0.90 lakhs (15%) and 4.98 lakhs (85%) in colleges, totaling 5.89 lakhs in the beginning of the reporting year.

In spite of an impressive quantitative expansion, India lags behind the developed nations and also some of the developing nations in regard to access to higher education. The young Indians between age group of 17-26 years are large in number. These age groups of students are expected to be enrolled in higher education. It is a matter of great concern that approximately 93% have no access to higher education and only 6-7% of the said age group is enrolled for higher education. It covers hardly 12% of relevant age group. In countries like Canada, USA, Australia, the students' enrollment of the same corresponding age group is between 80-88%.

According to NASSCOM, India had a total of 650,000 IT professionals in 2002 and by February 2005, they rose to 813,500. According to Brain Bench Inc., India ranked behind the US in the number of certified software professionals with 145,517 against 194,211. India produces 400,000 engineers a year compared to 60,000 by US. In addition to this there are about 10 million students in over 6500 in vocational institutions. The enrollment is growing at the rate of 5.1% per year. This also presents a glaring contrast to massive illiteracy that still persists in our country. Over the years, rigid policies and red tape have compromised the quality of higher education, and in some cases marketability, as they have failed to keep pace with emerging knowledge systems and technology.

General Development Grants for Universities and Colleges

These are sanctioned to universities for their expansion activities and for developing new programmes. As the universities develop their maintenance grants but size of development grants does not increase proportionately. There are two kinds of grants for universities, institutions deemed to be universities and colleges, they are:

- Development (Plan) Grants
- Maintenance (Non-Plan) Grants

Central universities and colleges affiliated to them and institutions deemed to be university receive both the plan and non-plan grants. However, the state universities and their affiliated colleges receive only plan grants. The objective of providing plan assistance is not only to improve the infrastructure and basic facilities in the universities so as to achieve at least the threshold level but also to develop excellence in those who are already ahead. These are not intended to supplement the requirements under maintenance grant.

The UGC provides non-plan assistance to universities to meet the recurring expenditure on salaries of non-teaching and teaching staff and for maintenance of laboratories, libraries, buildings, as also for obligatory payments such as taxes, telephone bills, electricity and other purposes. Development assistance is utilized for consolidation of existing infrastructure and for modernizing teaching, research and administration and to meet the changing demands of the society.

The University Grants Commission continued to provide support to universities and colleges for their development during the XI Plan. While assistance to central and state universities is provided under the plan head, assistance to central universities, certain deemed universities and colleges affiliated to Delhi and Banaras Hindu University is being provided in the non-plan head too. The General Development Grant Assistance programme is intended for the overall development of the universities covering aspects like enhancing access, ensuring equity, imparting relevant education, improving equity with access, making management more effective and enhancing transparency in management for students, augmenting research facilities and any other plans of the universities. Infrastructure improvements, salary of staff, books and journals, campus development, innovative research activities, students' amenities, ICT requirements, etc. can be taken up by the assisted institution under this programme.

General Development Grants to Colleges

Development of colleges is an important area from the point of view of maintenance of standards and equalization of educational opportunities for disadvantaged and differently abled section of society, because colleges are responsible in a major way for undergraduate education and to a great extent account for postgraduate education. With a view to removing disparities and regional imbalances, special grants are also being provided to the colleges catering to the needs of Scheduled Castes and Scheduled Tribes, women students and for intensive development of colleges situated in backward/rural/border areas.

UGC gives plan and non-plan grants to central universities and plan grants to state universities but these grants do not go to affiliated colleges of the universities, in spite, they go for university campus only. For affiliated colleges UGC gives separate grant. Therefore, for affiliated colleges to state universities, UGC provides maintenance grants.

There are, at the time of report, 25,951 colleges of which, 7,362 are recognized under 2(f) and 5,997 colleges recognized under Section 2(f) and declared fit to receive grants under Section 12(B) of the UGC Act, 1956. All the eligible colleges have been financially supported for the development of undergraduate and postgraduate programmes. The main objectives of Development Assistance for Programme are to:

- Strengthen basic infrastructure and meet their basic needs like books and journals, scientific equipment, staff, campus development, teaching aids, etc. required for proper functioning.
- Provide special assistance to colleges catering to the needs of marginalized groups.
- Develop colleges situated in the backward/rural/hilly areas with a view to remove or reduce disparities and regional imbalances.
- Support financially the uncovered state colleges, etc. During 2009-10 (upto 31.12.2009), UGC has supported colleges in states to the extent of ₹ 449.39 crores including ₹ 67.00 crores for colleges located in North East Region. Assistance of ₹ 5.50 crores has also been provided to the affiliated colleges of University of Delhi. Maintenance grant to the tune of ₹ 675.86croresto Delhi University colleges, ₹ 8.12 crores to constituent colleges of Banaras Hindu University and ₹ 26.69 crores to University College of Medical Sciences has been released in the said period.

Quality and Excellence: Autonomous Colleges

The scheme of autonomous colleges was formulated by the UGC in the Fourth Five-Year Plan (1969-73). These colleges themselves prescribe their curriculum and conduct the evaluation of their students through a system of continuous evaluation. An autonomous college has freedom to determine and prescribe its own course; prescribe rules for admission in consonance with the reservation policy of the State Government; evolve methods of assessment of student work, the conduct of examination, and notification of results; use of modern tools of education technology to achieve higher standard and greater creativity.

The Commission provides financial assistance under this scheme to autonomous colleges to meet their additional and special needs. The normal financial assistance for undergraduate colleges having single faculty has been provided to the extent of rupees four lakh per annum and for multi faculty colleges rupees six lakh per annum. For both undergraduate and postgraduate level colleges, the assistance is rupees five lakh per annum for single faculty colleges and rupees eight lakh per annum for multi-faculty colleges. This is available or those colleges, which are offering not fewer than six programmes of which two may be at postgraduate level. The financial support to these colleges is divided into two parts: 50% of the grant is allowed to be used for items as indicated in the guidelines. For remaining 50% grant, the college will submit a proposal to the commission for approval, indicating their priorities and innovations proposed and specific requirements. Autonomous status covers only undergraduate and postgraduate programmes in colleges. The parent university will confer the status of autonomy upon a college, which is permanently affiliated, with the concurrence of the State Government and the UGC. The autonomy status will be granted initially for a period of five years. The university will review the functioning of autonomy in the college periodically with the help of a committee constituted for the purpose. The UGC regional offices are providing grants to these colleges.

To improve the quality of undergraduate education by delinking colleges of quality from the affiliating structure and to promote the concept of autonomy in affiliated colleges, the UGC has been regularly supporting potential colleges by providing grants. The target for the XIth Plan is to ensure that 10 per cent of eligible colleges achieve autonomous status by the end of the plan. Autonomous colleges have the freedom to: determine and prescribe own courses of study and syllabi and restructure and redesign the courses to suit local needs, prescribe rules for admission in consonance with the reservation policy, evolve methods of assessment of students performance, the conduct of examinations and notification of results and to use modern tools and technology to achieve higher standards and better quality. The autonomy granted is institutional and covers all academic courses in such institutions at present or at a later stage. All colleges including engineering colleges under Section 2(f)—aided, unaided, partially aided and self-financing, which are declared fit to receive grants under Section 12B—are eligible to apply for autonomous status. The pattern of assistance will be to the extent of ₹ 9.00 lakhs for the under graduate colleges with single faculty, ₹ 15.00 lakhs for under-graduate colleges with more than one faculty, ₹ 10.00 lakhs for colleges offering both undergraduate and postgraduate courses with single faculty and ₹ 20.00 lakhs for colleges with multi-faculty. The autonomous college is managed by its governing body, academic council, board of studies and finance committee. Upto 31.12.2009, 330 Union Territories have been given autonomous status. During 2009-10 (upto 31.12.2009), grants to the extent of ₹ 9.84 crores have been provided to these autonomous colleges.

Andhra Pradesh, Maharashtra and Rajasthan have appealed to the AICTE to stop granting permission for new engineering colleges in the respective states. In a request to the technical education regulator, they have requested that no more requests for engineering colleges must be sanctioned. The reason behind the "strange" request is the falling number of students opting for engineering courses. It may be mentioned here that these three states had seen mushrooming growth of private engineering colleges in the last decade. But now the situation has changed. The demand for the engineering has seen a slump and therefore, the State Governments have asked for the halt.

Notably, seats in IITs are also going vacant due to non-availability of students in courses. Besides, students are also leaving the institute after taking admission. Apart from these three states, Odisha, Tamil Nadu, Karnataka are also facing a crunch of students in their engineering colleges. However, they have not requested for any such ban. On the other hand, the AICTE (All India Council for Technical Education) has expressed amusement at the appeal since they, till now, were always faced with requests to hurry up the process of approval.

AICTE chairman S.S. Mantha said that this is not an extraordinary situation as about 15 to 20 per cent seats in engineering institutions remain vacant every year. The council can't refuse license to new colleges, just because of the State Governments' red flag, without supporting their claim with substantial logic, he affirmed. "Only these three states said they do not want new institutions. But they have not given details of the number of students clearing Class XII exams or the number of general and other professional institutions operating in these states. Unless we get those data, we cannot take a final decision on their demand. We have asked the states to furnish the additional data by December 31," the AICTE chief said.

He said that any decision on this matter will be taken only after the states come up with substantial data to establish their claims. However, the body has decided to let the engineering institutions conduct part-time courses in the evening hours from 2012-13 for working professionals, since there is already demand for such courses in metros and some other big cities.

Universities with Potential for Excellence

To achieve excellence in teaching and research, UGC has been assisting identified universities for granting the status of

"University with Potential for Excellence". During IXth Plan, five universities, namely Jawaharlal Nehru University (JNU), Hyderabad, Madras, Pune and Jadavpur Universities were given the status of universities with potential for excellence. During Xth Plan, four more universities, namely North Eastern Hill University (NEHU), Madurai Kamraj, Mumbai and Calcutta Universities have been accorded the status of university with potential for excellence. During XIth Plan, six more universities are to be identified for according such status. During 2009-10 (upto 31.12.2009), an amount of ₹ 10.00 crores has been provided to these Universities.

University Administrative block

Jawaharlal Nehru University

Colleges with Potential for Excellence

To achieve excellence mainly in teaching and inculcate the research culture, UGC has initiated the scheme of "Colleges with Potential for Excellence" (CPE). The scheme intends to identify potential colleges across the country and to support them financially to improve their academic/physical infrastructure, adopt innovation in teaching, modern methods and learning/evaluation, and to enhance the quality of the learning and teaching process by introducing a flexible credit based modern academic system. The colleges which are 10 years old or more and accredited by National Accreditation and Assessment Council (NAAC) are eligible for the status of CPE. Preference will be given to autonomous colleges. During 2009-10, as many as 149 colleges have been identified under the scheme. Till date, 246 colleges have been accorded CPE status. An amount of ₹ 2.21 crores has been provided to these colleges upto 31.12.2009 during the financial year 2009-10.

Financial and infrastructural stagnation are placing massive pressure on the higher education system with explosion in enrollment due growing population. High demand from primary and secondary education has led to the deterioration in the financial support provided by the government. So in order to compete in the globalized economy, with other developed countries having a coverage of about 30-40% of the relevant age group, India has the enormous task of creating huge infrastructure, excellence and quality in higher education, which requires financial resources not affordable to the Government of India. So, it becomes necessary to evolve some alternative way of enhancing quality and excellence, which calls for innovations in the higher education system.

Open University System

The sheer geographical expanse and a large population have made India look at open university for a long time now as a viable means of reaching out hundreds and thousands of people outside the mainstream university system. Indira Gandhi National Open University (IGNOU) has been a pioneer in the field and has over 11,87,100 students on its rolls. Currently, there are more than seven open universities in India offering over 500 courses. Modern communication technology can be harnessed to effectively provide education through this medium. A distance education council has been set up and a common pool of programmes is available for sharing.

> A National Mission for Education through ICT had been proposed by Human Resource Minister Arjun Singh. Under this plan all institutions of higher learning would be networked through broadband connectivity. A provision of INR 502 crore had been made for the Mission and substantial portion of this money would be used to provide high speed interconnectivity between 84 Central Educational and Research Institutions and for developing the e-course content.

Open universities can be highly cost effective as the cost of teaching through distance education comes down to a third compared to the traditional system. They also maintain a close relationship with the industry and are especially helpful to those who cannot afford a regular university degree.

Distance education is provided in academic, technical and professional subjects. Over thousands of students enroll for admissions to the distance-learning courses in various Indian states. These courses can be categorized under several disciplines, namely Arts, Science Commerce, etc. Students can opt for undergraduate and postgraduate degree as well as diploma courses. List of UG degree courses offered by distance learning institutes in India include B.A (English, History, Sociology, Psychology, Political Science, Hindi, Sanskrit), B.Com, B.Sc (Physics, Chemistry, Biology, Zoology, Economics and Geography), B.Lib. (Bachelor of Library Science), B.Ed. and BBA. Masters degree courses are also available through the distance-learning mode. A good number of students in India also pursue their MBA through correspondence. Some universities also offer Ph.D. programmes in selected disciplines.

The Indian states, where distance learning is offered include Delhi, Rajasthan, Madhya Pradesh, Maharashtra, Bihar, Gujarat, West Bengal, Uttar Pradesh, and others. Generally, open universities in the states offer distance-learning courses. Apart from open universities, there are many leading state universities like University of Delhi, University of Mumbai, Punjab University and Osmania University, which have a separate unit for distance learning. Indira Gandhi National Open University (IGNOU), a premier institute of distance learning in India, set up in 1985, offers Bachelor's, Master's as well as doctoral degree courses in a number of disciplines such as Arts, Education, Commerce, Science, Business Management and Library & Information Science among others. Students can also pursue Advanced Diploma, Diploma, PG Diploma and Certificate courses at various institutes offering distance learning in Indian states.

Distance Education Council (DEC) has been established as a statutory authority under the IGNOU Act, which provides development funds to open universities and distance education institutions from the funds placed at its disposal by the Central Government. It is an organization based in New Delhi, which maintains the standards, encourages and organizes the activities of Open and Distance Learning in India (ODL). The council encourages the State Governments and conventional universities to set up open universities and distance education centers. It also arranges for funds to run these universities. The assessment and accreditation of these universities is also conducted by the DEC. Facilitating and promoting distance education is the ultimate goal of the DEC.

Open Universities in India

There are many open universities in India at present; some of these have educational centers in different states of India. The universities include:

1. Indira Gandhi National Open University
2. Dr. B.R. Ambedkar Open University
3. Karnataka State Open University
4. Nalanda Open University
5. Netaji Subhash Open University
6. Kota Open University
7. Madhya Pradesh Bhoj Open University
8. Tamil Nadu Open University
9. Yashwant Rao Chavan Open University

10. Dr. Babasaheb Ambedkar Open University
11. Pt. Sunderlal Sharma Open University
12. Purshottam Das Tandon Open University.

Growing Role of Private Institutions

Since the late 1990s the higher education market is growing by 7% a year. With the growing demand for higher education and the need for aligning of content with the newer skill demands, the stage is set for private educational systems to come of age and assume much greater role than ever.

In 2000-01, of the 13,072 higher education institutions, 42% were privately owned and run catering to 37% of students enrolled into higher education. It will not be too ambitious to say that the growth in higher education sector itself is being propelled through private and unaided colleges or self-financing institutions. Many universities have now granted recognition or affiliation to unaided colleges and are also initiating self-financing courses in government and aided colleges. According to one estimate, close to 50% of the higher education in India is imparted through private institutions, mostly unaided. Privatization of education has also brought in a sea change in the way education is viewed. From being seen as service delivery, it has now become a quality product. Universities are actively pursuing students, especially foreign institutions, using a wide variety of strategies to market their courses. The student is now the customer or client. With globalization, universities are spreading their reach beyond geographical and political borders.

The British, Australian and American universities are setting up campuses in other countries, realizing that they can examine many more students than they can teach. Hence, many of them are collaborating with other institutions or franchisees to teach their courses under their brand name without getting involved in the direct business of imparting the education.

India has universities of every hue and caliber. By bringing in foreign universities, will it enhance the quality of higher education and contribute to economic well-being of the country are seminal questions. The Union Cabinet has approved the

Foreign Educational Institution (Regulation of Entry and Operation) Bill, 2010 which is being tabled before the Parliament. The exact details/provisions are not known. Arguments generally given in favour of foreign universities are that the best universities of the West will start quality programmes in higher education in the emerging areas in India. We already have different types of universities and university level institutions; Central universities, State universities, private universities, deemed universities and a number of institutions which are collaborating with Western universities and giving a degree of foreign universities. In addition, we also have institutions of eminence like NITs, IITs, IIMs, IIScRs, IISc and so on which are providing opportunities for excellent education and research. To the existing scenario, the government would like to add foreign universities. In what way will the addition of foreign universities enhance the quality of higher education and in what way it will contribute to economic well-being of the country are seminal questions.

As it is, there is a craze for foreign degree and some institutions cash on it: an institution that collaborates with a foreign institution normally charges heavily in the range of ₹ 10 to 12 lakh a year for a degree like MBA. This collaboration means a few teachers from abroad give one or two courses to an Indian institution and the institution is not bound by any regulations of higher education in the country. If by an Act of Parliament, an Indian institution in collaboration with a foreign university is permitted to give foreign degree it could encourage the prevalent practice. If, independently, a foreign university of repute establishes a campus in India, certainly it would attract people who can afford, denying the opportunity to the less fortunate people. Another important factor cannot be ignored; learning in a foreign country in their university has a definite advantage in terms of ambience, cultural environment and provides an international mix to the student as students from different countries will be studying in the same institution. Whereas, when a foreign university sets up a campus in India, it will be more of a subsidiary and naturally of a lower standing. In what way will it be different from our best institutions is not clear.

If special curriculum was to be evolved and research programmes developed keeping the Indian context in the picture, in addition to creating knowledge for its own sake, then they add significance. Most likely this would not happen. It is unlikely that many eminent academicians of the West will come to India to teach and do research but, many good ones already working in the Indian institutions would be attracted to these institutions because of prestige and higher salary. This will end up in making our good institutions mediocre. It may not be out of place to mention that the universities in this country in the early era suffered because the country started new institutions meant for excellence rather than raising the existing institutions to excellence. The result was even the best universities lost their good academicians to the new institutions and became second rate. This may happen again if foreign universities do establish their campuses here. It is not clear whether foreign universities will be judged by the same yardstick or an international yardstick will be evolved to evaluate both the Indian and foreign institutions. Quite often the employment market by itself does not determine quality.

Quality is essentially determined by the knowledge that the higher education and research institutions impart both in terms of knowledge per se and also the training provided to its students. Creation of knowledge takes place mainly in higher education institutions. This knowledge later gets converted to commodity or technology for the marketplace. From that point of view, creation of knowledge may not become a prime factor for the foreign universities. They are more likely to treat this as a financial endeavour. This can be seen in our industries and commercial activities that are now responsible for growth in GDP real knowledge contribution on a global scale comes essentially from foreign countries and a few of our eminent institutions, and our GDP growth is more due to our service industries using knowledge growth of the developed countries and not due to original contribution. Given this background, it is possible that we learn more about how to do better in the arena of higher education if the foreign universities' Bill is put to public debate and taken up at a later stage with relevant modifications. That way the country would be benefited rather than be harmed.

Scientific Research in Universities and Research Organizations

Universities in India have been traditional sources of research. With the advent of government R&D organizations, increase in the number of universities, poor funding and the escalating cost of infrastructure needed for research, research at universities had declined. The decline was certainly slowed down by government-sponsored research projects. There are only a few Indian universities, known for good standards in teaching and research. In a number of universities, there is very little research and even the classroom teaching is not regular. In such universities most part of the budget is spent on staff salaries and little is left for library, laboratory and other functions.

In last six decades or so there has been tremendous expansion of the knowledge base but most universities have not even made efforts to keep with it. The situation is highlighted by the fact that India is fast losing its competitive edge in research to other countries, which till recently were far behind; specifically India's share of world's scientific and technological research is steadily declining. To find a suitable place and to be able to compete in India and abroad, the Center and States in particular have to ensure a high rate of growth in the quality and quantity of the intellectual output from the universities.

However, in recent years there has been a serious decline in the quality of research carried out in the universities. Further it is a matter of serious concern that research in India is mainly carried out by the universities, national research laboratories and research organizations, unlike in the developed countries where much of the research is conducted in industrial establishments. In postgraduate colleges, practically no research work is done. In all the advanced countries, universities and university level institutes constitute strong centers of research. However, in India, the share of higher education in scientific research is pitiably low. Advanced countries are known to spend around 30% of their total research and development expenditure in the university sector. In India, the figure was calculated as 6%. Often, inadequate financial resources lead to the poor infrastructure and physical facilities that adversely affect the scientific research as well as development of new technology.

To realize the vision of India as an innovation hot spot, first we need to realize long-term academia-industry collaborative relationships with open access to and resources free of intellectual property (IP) entanglements and secondly, to put in place better integration of the corporate world with higher educational and research institutions to create a pipeline for skills that will support growth industries. Thirdly, we need to encourage multidisciplinary collaboration among business, government, academia and R&D laboratories, thereby creating an environment that supports technological development, which is aligned with and driven by industry needs.

Section II of the book deals in greater detail about scientific research in universities and research organizations.

Deemed Universities—Need for a National Debate

Yet another worrisome trend in higher education and research is the emerging government policy of according deemed university status to national labs and research institutes, so that these institutes can award their own Ph.D. degrees, without having to affiliate themselves to a university or fulfilling any other role of being a university. National laboratories include those under the Union Government's Council of Scientific and Industrial Research (CSIR), Indian Council of Medical Research (ICMR), Department of Atomic Energy (DAE), Defence Research and Development Organisation (DRDO), Department of Space (DOS), etc. Some DAE institutions have already obtained deemed university status, and the UGC has already recommended the case of CSIR for the commission's approval. It is not clear whether all the national laboratories are under consideration for this status, but it is most likely that all of them would eventually like to seek such a status.

The national laboratories were specifically established with the aim of making more direct contributions to the technological needs of the country in chosen areas such as medicine, agriculture, petroleum, metallurgy, energy, defence, space, etc. It was expected that these national (or regional) laboratories would employ selected scientific manpower generated from the colleges/universities and nurture their talents towards specific applied goals. But this did not happen, as the national labs became more sophisticated versions of university departments drawing better monetary and infrastructural support and publishing research papers, for which they need research students, who cannot be retained and tapped unless they are promised research degrees. The present demand for seeking deemed university status could therefore be an exercise to legitimize the current situation of the national labs, and redefine their original goals.

However, the country needs to decide whether it wants to develop glorified technicians and sycophants or make versatile scientists and conscious citizens. Barring a few exceptions, the monolithic hierarchy of national labs does not provide enough opportunity to young researchers to relate their research to broader social and national values. The more open intellectual environment of universities, which include natural and social sciences, is essential for interdisciplinary learning, personality development, national values and better citizenship. Thus, the issue of deemed universities calls for an open national debate, as it has major implications for our higher education and research in science and technology.

With the basic issues of equity and access to higher education still unresolved, the country is ill prepared to generate knowledge creators or knowledge workers of high quality to tap the opportunities of the emerging knowledge economy. There was a time when the country debated passionately about external brain drain of students going abroad and not returning, and internal brain drain of students taking up careers in areas quite different from their academic backgrounds, and what a waste of national resource this was. This situation has only worsened, with unemployment and underemployment in the era of liberalization and globalization, but we don't seem to even talk about it anymore.

Reforms may mean different things to different people, but for those students and teachers who are at the receiving end of their governments, reforms have come to mean withdrawal of government funding, no matter what happens. For those who believed that reforms in higher education would reduce bureaucratic controls, attract better talent, provide more operational freedom, improve transparency, increase accountability, remove corruption, encourage self-financing, reward productivity and punish laxity, to say that they are disappointed at the state of affairs in our country is an understatement.

Forward March for India

India, with a critical mass of skilled English-speaking knowledge workers, a functioning democracy and a massive domestic market, has many of the key ingredients for seizing the opportunity for making a transition to a knowledge economy. "India has a dynamic private sector, institutions of a free market economy, a well-developed financial sector, and a broad and diversified science and technology infrastructure. In addition, the development of the ICT sector in recent years has been remarkable. India is becoming a global provider of software services. Building on these strengths, India can harness the benefits of the knowledge revolution to improve its economic performance and boost the welfare of its people," reads a World Bank report titled "India and the Knowledge Economy: Leveraging Strength and Opportunities" (April 2005).

The time is very opportune for India to make its transition to the knowledge economy—an economy that creates, disseminates, and uses knowledge to enhance its growth and development. In India, great potential exists for increasing productivity by shifting labor from low productivity and subsistence activities in agriculture, informal industry, and informal service activities to more productive modern sectors, as well as new knowledge-based activities. In doing so, it can reduce poverty and touch every member of society.

India is uniquely positioned to reap the benefits of its economic gains by forging policies and strategies for effective use of knowledge to increase the overall productivity of the economy and benefit its own population. Some of the main issues, which the World Bank cites for strengthening India's education system include:

1. Efficient use of public resources in the education system, and making it more responsive to market needs, as well as ensuring expanded access to education.
2. Enhancing the quality of primary and secondary education.
3. Ensuring consistency between the skills taught in primary and secondary education and the needs of the knowledge economy.
4. Reforming the curriculum of tertiary education institutions to include skills and competencies for the knowledge economy.
5. Improving the operating environment for higher education and coordinating a system with multiple players.
6. Embracing the contribution of the private sector in education.
7. Establishing partnerships with foreign universities.
8. Increasing university-industry partnerships to ensure consistency between research and the needs of the economy.
9. Using ICTs to meet the double goals of expanding access to and improving the quality of education.
10. Developing a framework for lifelong learning, including programs intended to meet the learning needs of all, both within and outside the school system.

11. Making effective use of distance learning technologies to expand access to and the quality of formal education and lifelong training.

Higher Education Highlights in XIth Five-Year Plan

- Eight new IITs, four in Andhra Pradesh, Bihar, Rajasthan and Himachal Pradesh.
- Seven new IIMs, the first one at Shillong to start functioning from 2008-09 academic sessions.
- Three new Indian Institutes of Science Education & Research, one already functional at Mohali, work underway in Bhopal and Thiruvananthapuram.
- 16 Central universities in J&K, Punjab, Haryana, HP, Uttarakhand, Rajasthan, MP, Chhattisgarh, Bihar, Jharkhand, Orissa, Tamil Nadu, Kerala, Karnataka, Gujarat and Goa.
- 20 Indian Institutes of Information Technology in the Public-Private Partnership mode.
- Assistance to states for setting up 370 colleges in districts where access and participation rates are lower than the national average.
- Assistance to states for establishing a new polytechnic in those districts that do not have one. About 700 polytechnics to be created through PPP/Private mode.
- Establishment of an Indira Gandhi National Tribal University with countrywide jurisdiction to promote study and research into tribal history, economy, society, culture, etc. and to look into tribal issues, as well as to promote education of Scheduled Tribes.
- Proposal to launch a National Education Mission through ICT which will provide broadband connectivity to all the institutions of higher learning and make available high quality e-Content for dissemination through the connectivity to be provided under this Mission.

Concerns Arising Out of Growth Pattern

The expansion of higher education system in India has been chaotic and unplanned. The drive to make higher education socially inclusive has led to a sudden and dramatic increase in numbers of institutions without a proportionate increase in material and intellectual resources. As a result, academic standards have been jeopardized. There are many basic problems facing higher education in India today. These include inadequate infrastructure and facilities, large vacancies in faculty positions and poor faculty, outmoded teaching methods, declining research standards, unmotivated students, overcrowded classrooms and widespread geographic, income, gender, and ethnic imbalances. Education in basic sciences and subjects that are not market friendly has suffered. Research in higher education institutions is at its lowest ebb. There is an inadequate and diminishing financial support for higher education from the government and from society. Many colleges established in rural areas are non-viable, are under enrolled and have extremely poor infrastructure and facilities with just a few teachers. Apart from concerns relating to deteriorating standards, there is reported exploitation of students by many private providers. Moreover, the quality of education being provided by self-financing institutions is a major cause of concern. Ensuring equitable access to quality higher education for students coming from poor families is a major challenge. Students from poor background are put to further disadvantage since they are not academically prepared to crack highly competitive entrance examinations that have bias towards urban elite and rich students having access to private tuitions and coaching.

A series of judicial interventions over the last two decades and knee-jerk reaction of the government to the judicial pronouncements—both at the centre and state level, and the regulatory bodies without proper understanding of the emerging market structure of higher education in India has further added confusion to the higher education in the country. With changing circumstances, three near certainties about higher education: (i) it is supplied on national basis to the local students; (ii) it is government regulated and (iii) competition and profit are unknown concepts in higher education, have received a serious blow. With growing student mobility and the increasing demand in the global labour market for the highly skilled, higher education has now gone international. With the entry of a large number of private and foreign providers, there is intense competition in the higher education sector. The students and academics now have the choice to opt for the best deal. In the new global realties of competition and increased mobility of students and workforce, there is a need coherent and national strategic vision and policy framework for higher education in the country is called for, which would encourage all higher education institutions—public and private—to be more innovative and responsive. Public funded higher education has to be strengthened. At the same time, barriers to entry and operation of private institutions need to be removed.

There is a lot at stake in the present days because of the challenges being ushered in by the changing times and situation. All these challenges and problems could be resolved for a positive development in the near and distant future so that a stable higher education scenario can bring in the laurels to the country. These are the ground realities which need to be addressed on an urgent basis for setting the course of higher education on the right path.

REFERENCES

Agarwal, Pawan (2006). "Higher Education in India: The Need for Change", Working Paper No. 180 Indian Council for Research on International Economic Relations.

Altekar, A.S. (1957), *Education in Ancient India* (5th Edition), Varanasi: Nand Kishore and Bros.

Ambani, Mukesh and Kumarmangalam Birla (2000), *Report on a Policy Framework for Reforms in Education*, New Delhi: Government of India, Ministry of Education.

Basu, Aparna (1974), *The Growth of Education and Political Development in India, 1898-1920*, New Delhi: Oxford University Press.

Chaube, S.P. and Chaube, A (1999), *Education in Ancient and Medieval India*, New Delhi: Vikas Publishing House.

Government of India, *Report of the University Education Commission (1948-49)*, 1949, New Delhi: Ministry of Education.

Government of India, *Report of the Education Commission (1964-68): Education and National Development*, 1966, New Delhi: Ministry of Education.

Government of India, *National Knowledge Commission: Compilation of Recommendations on Education*, 2006, 07 and 08, New Delhi: Ministry of Education.

Government of India (2008), *Report of the Yashpal Committee on Higher Education: The Report on 'Renovation and Rejuvenation of Higher Education'*, New Delhi: Ministry of Education.

Jha, D.M. (1991), "Higher Education in Ancient India". In Raza, M. (Ed.), *Higher Education in India: Retrospect and Prospect*, New Delhi: Association of Indian Universities, pp. 1-5.

Raza, M. (Ed.) (1991), *Higher Education in India: Retrospect and Prospect*, New Delhi: Association of Indian Universities.

Nurullah, Syed and Naik, J.P. (1951), *History of Education in India during the British Period*, Bombay: Macmillan.

Naik, J.P. and Nurullah, Syed (1974), *A Students' History of Education in India: 1800-1976*, New Delhi: Macmillan.

N. Raghuram, *Combat Law*, Volume 5, Issue 1 (published 15 March 2006 in India Together).

Powar, K.B. (Ed.) (2000), "The Changing Role and Functions of Universities". In K.B. Powar (Ed.), *Higher Education for Human Development*, New Delhi: Association of Indian Universities.

Powar, K.B. (2012), *Expanding Domains in Indian Higher Education*, New Delhi: Association of Indian Universities.

Raghuram, N. (2005), Deemed university status to national laboratories: Need for a national debate, *Current Science*, Vol. 89, No. 1.

Rao, Jagdiswara (2003). A Status Report on Higher Education in India or the Deterioration of Standards in Indian Universities. www.Indiapolicyinstitute.org/debate/Notes/jagadiswara.html

Tilak, J.B.G. (2002). Privatization of Higher Education in India.

UGC Annual Report (2005-06), New Delhi: University Grants Commission and Selected Educational Statistics, New Delhi: Ministry of Human Resources Development.

University Grants Commission "Guidelines for general development assistance to Central, deemed and state universities during XIth Plan".

Websites

http://www.deccanherald.com/content/59156/do-we-need-foreign-universities.html

http://planningcommission.nic.in/aboutus/committee/wrkgrp12/hrd/wg_hiedu.pdf

http://deepaksharmaeducation.blogspot.in/2011/07/higher-education-in-india-issues.html

http://info.worldbank.org/etools/docs/library/145261/India_KE_Overview.pdf
http://www.thehindu.com/news/national/article2598268.ece
www.bc.edu/bcorg/avp/soe/cihe/newsletter/News29/text007.htm

Aims and Philosophy of Higher Education

4

The Higher Education system in India has constantly striven to build universities as places of culture and of learning open to all with corresponding reinforcement of lifelong learning. Participation and contribution in major debates concerning the direction and future of society is seen as a major task and a moral obligation of the university system.

The modern university has survived as an institution for over nine hundred years which is longer than many a nation-state. This has been possible because it has adapted itself to the changing needs and demands of its clientele. The fact that in the past the numbers were restricted, the academic community was relatively homogenous, and that the rate of change was slow, have perhaps all helped. The situation today is different. Academic institutions are growing in numbers and the multiversity has become a reality. The students cover the entire spectrum of the society. The life will be further influenced not only by the 'knowledge society' but also by the 'stakeholder society' and the 'market society'. The universities, while creating and disseminating knowledge, will have to cater to the interests and expectations of its various stakeholders (students, parents, faculty, government, society-at-large, etc.), and to the market demands.

University is a public institution meant to serve the public cause. A university can obviously not fulfill its role if it is not aware of the expectations of the society. Different stakeholders expect differently from the university. The society's expectations from higher education have however not always remained the same, but have kept changing with changing social concerns, economic situations and political conditions. In earlier times, when, by today's standards, universities were comparatively small, closed communities of scholars, there was little doubt about the university's objectives, viz. the discovery and dissemination of knowledge. Members of the faculty and the students found little difficulty in communicating with each other. However, the enormously increased demand for higher education, the explosion of knowledge and the social misgivings about the use to which the knowledge is being put, have not only made the university's objectives controversial but made meaningful communication between the faculty and students difficult, and in many universities, apparently impossible.

> **Fundamental to the rise of a vibrant democratic culture is the recognition that education must be treated as a public good–as a crucial site where students gain a public voice and come to grips with their own power as individual and social agents. Public and higher education cannot be viewed merely as sites for commercial investment or for affirming a notion of the private good based exclusively on the fulfillment of individual needs. Reducing higher education to the handmaiden of corporate culture works against the critical social imperative of educating citizens who can sustain and develop inclusive democratic public spheres.**

Higher education occupies a special position in the educational system of any nation because it is at the apex of the entire educational structure and thus influences all levels of education. The functions of universities can generally be discussed in two related aspects, viz. what they do for the society and what they do for the individual. Since the middle ages, universities have been valued and respected as centers for intellectual life. They have provided a place for scholars to work for the advancement of arts, letters and sciences. Noam (1995) rightly asserted that higher education is the place to which knowledge-seeking people make a pilgrimage and for which they take time off other activities to widen their intellectual horizons.

Aims of Higher Education: Changes Over the Years

Education today is the outcome of a long socio-cultural process of evolution. Enlightenment was the chief aim of ancient Indian education. Basic character of education is that it informs a person and enlightens him about things he does not know. In the primitive society, education was not a separate entity rather an experience that was transmitted from the older generation to the younger one. With time the aim of education got changed and it shifted to accommodate the real experiences of life. Later on education became a privileged act. The rulers provided education to a few due to the fear that others might get liberated by exposure to education.

Historically, the aim and objectives of higher education in India have been the development and perfection of the individual. Ancient Indian higher education aimed at spiritual perfection, i.e. attainment of salvation or emancipation. Thus, the aim was self-realization and salvation. Secondly, the aim was the pursuit and transmission of knowledge having many facets. The Vedic Indian scholars classified knowledge in two classes, viz. *paravidya*—knowledge that transcended human experience (spiritual knowledge), and *aparavidya*—knowledge that is based on human experience. Higher education was expected to cover both these types of knowledge and to transmit the same to the next generation.

Thirdly, education was expected to conserve and preserve knowledge and culture of the society, which was responsible for its progress. Education also took on a more active role, viz. that of enriching social heritage by adding on to it and by creating new knowledge, ideas, technologies and different forms of art and craft and by creating among students the urge to think independently. With changing times and growing industrialization, higher education functioned as an objective critic of the social order, i.e. its value and belief systems, its customs and traditions. These aims of higher education in ancient India undoubtedly got fulfilled by developing values, culture and consciousness in students. It brought about spiritual and intellectual perfection in true sense of the term.

Prime objective of the first three modern Indian universities were just to conduct examinations. In post-1857 era, the higher education in India was expected to expand and encourage knowledge and education, and to build the character of students. During the period of 1913-21, teaching was added to examination in the aims of universities.

Universities have been established as major institutions for providing higher education and research opportunities to the youth for shaping the future, and recognized as the most important indicator of a country's future. The UNESCO World Conference on Higher Education (Paris, 1998) has also observed that university education has become crucial in preparing a healthy, skilled and agile intellectual human force, empowered with the ability of lifelong learning that enables countries to continuously assess, adapt and apply new knowledge. Thus, Noam, 1995 rightly stressed that universities, for a variety of social, national and institutional reasons are not going to disappear; they are still here and continue to be a source of national and professional pride; they are still the gatekeepers of credible knowledge. They are the places where excellence is nurtured.

Philosophy of Higher Education in the Commissions and Policies

After independence India set about the task of reorienting the educational system to adjust to the needs and aspirations of a free nation committed to democracy, secularism and socialism. Intensive and widespread discussions among the various beneficiaries and stakeholders were conducted on the aims and objectives of higher education. These views found expression in important national documents like reports of commissions and committees and statements of national policies. These commissions from time to time till today have stressed different aspects of education in general and the aims and objectives of higher education in particular.

The formulation of the essential purpose of university education in independent India can be traced back to the statement of Jawaharlal Nehru, the first Prime Minister of India, who addressing the graduates of Allahabad University in 1947 said:

> A University stands for humanism, for tolerance, for reason, for the adventure of ideas and for the search of truth. It stands for the onward march of human race toward higher objectives. Universities are places of ideals and idealism. If the Universities discharge their duties adequately, then, it is well with the nation and the people.

These great words highlight the basic truth that universities have a crucial part to play in the life, welfare and strength of a nation. The universities can, however, fill this role only if they owe uncompromising loyalty to certain fundamental values of life. They are essentially a community of teachers and students where, in some way, all learn from one another or, at any rate, strive to do so. Their principal objective is to deepen man's understanding of the universe and of himself—in body, mind and spirit, to disseminate this understanding throughout society and to apply it in the service of mankind. They are the dwelling places of ideas and idealism, and expect high standards of conduct and integrity from all their members. Theirs is the pursuit of truth and excellence in all its diversity—a pursuit which needs, above all, courage and fearlessness. *Great universities and timid people go ill together.*

Our universities today, however, are far removed from this ideal, and the courses and programmes they offer remain, to a large extent, traditional and unimaginative. There is no excitement among students about learning, no thrust towards innovation and enterprise which should be of prime value to a rapidly changing society as ours. There is very little relationship of these programmes with employment opportunities. Everywhere the link with environment and society is weak. This lends a largely peripheral or irrelevant character to higher education and is perhaps responsible for the pursuit of a degree rather than of education. There is no doubt about the fact that the students have to be empowered for lifelong learning and for a meaningful role in society.

A crucial step by the Ministry of Education in higher education was to appoint in 1947 a Commission on University Education, headed by Dr. S. Radhakrishnan. The Commission stated in its report:

> Democracy depends for its very life on a high standard of general, vocational and professional education. Dissemination of learning, incessant search for new knowledge, unceasing effort to plumb the meaning of life, provision for professional education to satisfy the occupational needs of our society are the vital tasks of higher education.

The Commission set out the aims of university education basically as dissemination of learning and provision for professional education to satisfy the occupational needs of our country. Higher education policies and programmes should be related to the social purposes, which we profess to serve; there should be a sufficient unity of purpose in the diversity to produce a community of values and ideas among educated men and women. Institutional forms may vary as time and circumstances require, but there should be a steadfast loyalty to the abiding elements of respect for human personality, freedom of belief and expression for all citizens, a deep obligation to promote human well-being and faith in reason and humanity.

Dr. Radhakrishnan recognized that "if India is to confront the confusion of our times, she must turn for guidance not to those who are lost to the exigencies of the passing hour but to her men of letters and men of science.... These intellectual pioneers of civilization are to be found and trained in the universities, which are the sanctuaries of the inner life of the nation."

He emphasized that mere vocational and technical education, important though they are, does not necessarily serve the spirit, as there might be a number of scientists without conscience and technicians without appropriate attitude who would find a void—a moral vacuum, within themselves. It is important to preserve the values of democracy, justice, liberty, equality and fraternity. Universities must stand for these ideals, which can never be lost so long as men seek wisdom and follow righteousness. Thus, the University Education Commission did not place much emphasis on vocational and professional training which is the need of the society today.

The university Education Commission laid down the following specific aims of university education:

- The universities have to provide leadership in politics, administration, education, industry and commerce.
- University should be organized as a center of civilization to train intellectual pioneers of civilization.
- The aim of university education should be to produce intellectual adventurers.
- Universities should produce such wise persons who may make an incessant search for new knowledge and unceasing effort to plug the mission of life.
- The contents of education must accept the best of what modern advancement has to offer but without neglecting the cultural heritage from the past.
- One of the main functions of universities is to bring about the spiritual development of the students.
- Universities should preserve the culture and civilization of the country. To be civilized, we should sympathize with the poor, respect women, love, peace and independence and hate tyranny and injustice. University education should infuse these ideals into the youth.
- University education should discover the innate qualities of a person and develop them through training.

- Attention should be paid not only to the mental but also to the physical development of students in universities.
- Universities should give the most important place to the mother tongue in general education.

Thus, the Commission emphasized that in the modern times the university should promote a rational outlook and nurture scientific temper in the youth. It should wipe out dogmatism, fundamentalism and prejudices from the minds of the youth. On the other hand, it should develop right kind of temperament and ability to judge between right and wrong and good and evil. The predicament is that the ideals set by the Commission years back have not been met to a large extent.

The Mudaliar Commission was appointed in 1952 with Dr. Lakshman Swami Mudaliar as the Chairman of the Commission. It was basically appointed to guide the country's Secondary Education but it laid down the aims and objectives of education, certainly applicable for higher education. It emphasized on development of democratic citizenship, development of personality, education for leadership, improvement of vocational capability and efficiency and inculcation of world citizenship.

Kothari Commission (1964-66) has also reiterated in its report: "While the fundamental values to which the Universities owe their allegiances are largely unrelated to time and circumstances, their functions change from time to time. Their tasks are no longer confined to the two traditional functions of teaching and advancement of knowledge. They are assuming new functions and the older ones are increasing in range, depth and complexity."

The expectation of The Education Commission from higher education was to deepen man's understanding of the universe and of himself, in body mind and spirit, and to disseminate this understanding throughout society. The Education Commission stated: "The destiny of India is now being shaped in her classrooms. This, we believe, is no more a rhetoric. In a world based on science and technology, it is education that determines the level of prosperity, welfare and security of the people."

The report thus emphasized that the universities are the dwelling places of ideas and idealism, and expected high standards of conduct and integrity from all the members. They must be continuously engaged in the pursuit of truth and excellence in all its diversity, a pursuit that needs above all, courage and fearlessness.

The Indian universities should strive to assist the schools in their attempts at qualitative self-improvement. Universities should conduct experimental schools, run advanced courses for teachers in various school subjects, assume greater responsibility for the training of teachers at all levels, and develop new curricula, textbooks and teaching materials. Most important responsibility is to lower the dominant place given to examinations, to improve the standard in every aspect and by a symbiotic development of teaching and research, to create at least a few centers comparable to those of their type in any other part of the world.

The Commission set out the functions of the universities in the modern world:

1. to seek and cultivate new knowledge to engage vigorously and fearlessly in the pursuit of truth and to interpret old knowledge and beliefs in the light of new needs and discoveries;
2. to provide right kind of leadership in all walks of life by helping the individuals develop their potential;
3. to provide society with competent men and women trained in all professions who, as individuals, are endowed with a sense of social justice;
4. to reduce social and cultural differences through diffusion of education to foster in the teachers and students, and through them in the society generally, the attitudes and values needed for developing the 'good life' in individuals and society, and lastly

5. to bring the universities closer to the community through extension of knowledge and its applications for problem solving.

The purpose of higher education in India has been fully explored by eminent academicians and statesmen from time to time. In the words of Swami Vivekananda, "We want that education by which character is formed, strength of mind is increased, the intellect is expanded and by which one can stand on one's own feet. Education is the manifestation of the perfection already in man."

National Education Policies and Programmes

Two decades later, the Government of India undertook a comprehensive review of the nation's education policy. The policy statement, which emerged following this review, reaffirmed: "Education is a unique investment in the present and the future. This cardinal principle is the key to the National Policy on Education." The educational policy and progress were reviewed in the light of the goal of national development and priorities set from time to time. In the National Policy of Education, 1986 (updated in 1992), special efforts were made to assign specific responsibilities for organizing, implementing and financing the higher education as well. It was also stated that though education is in the concurrent list of the constitution, the State Governments should play a very major role in the development of education. India also recognizes that the new global scenario poses unprecedented challenges for the higher education system.

It laid down that in our national perception education is essentially for all. This is fundamental to our all-round development, material as well as spiritual; education promotes culture. It refines sensitivities and perceptions that contribute to national cohesion, scientific temper and independence of mind and spirit, thus furthering the goals of socialism, secularism and democracy enshrined in our Constitution; education develops manpower for different levels of economy. It is also a forum in which research and development flourish; this is the ultimate guarantee of national self-reliance and once again it emphasized that education is a unique investment in the present and the future.

Higher education provides people with an opportunity to reflect on the critical social, economic, cultural, moral and spiritual issues facing humanity. It contributes to national development through dissemination of specialized knowledge and skills. It is therefore a crucial factor for survival. Being at the apex of the educational pyramid, it has a key role in producing teachers for the education system. In the age of knowledge explosion, higher education has to be dynamic as never before, constantly exploring unexplored areas. Also, large number of universities and colleges in the country need an all-round improvement; the emphasis in the immediate future should be on their consolidation as well as expansion.

The University Grants Commission (UGC) has appropriately recognized the challenges and has stated that a whole range of skills will be demanded from the graduates and postgraduates of humanities, social sciences, natural sciences and commerce, as well as from the various professional disciplines such as agriculture, law, management, medicine or engineering.

Responding to these emerging needs the UGC emphasized that, "The University has a crucial role to play in promoting social change. It must make an impact on the community if it is to retain its legitimacy and gain public support." It seeks to do so by a new emphasis on community-based programmes and work on social issues. Emphasis has to be laid on curricular change and interdisciplinary courses should gradually replace discipline-oriented learning. Also field learning experiences for students in graduate and postgraduate programmes; more career-oriented courses and response to local needs for human resource in specific work-related opportunities need to be stressed. The need of the hour is that the university be seen not only as a seat of learning and new knowledge through its research and extension functions but also as a focal point for the dissemination of information to the community through continuing education, extension education and through field outreach activities.

The universities will have to prove equal to the faith reposed in them by the UGC as the third dimension of education, i.e. to play its due role in directly impacting on the community for social development and change. However, as universities abandon their catnap and start gearing up to meet the new challenges by re-organizing their curriculum and programme at all levels, the bureaucratic mind-set impedes their onward march forgetting that education is not a discipline imposed from above on an apathetic if consenting nature. In most states of the country and at central level, higher education is fragmented and placed under the control of various government departments such as education, health, agriculture, commerce, industries and the like. Sometimes even a bifurcation between science and technology and general education takes place. The coordinating machinery is either non-existent or ineffective. This state of affairs mars planning as well as effective implementation. Above all it leads to a failure to integrate higher education in national planning, resulting in unemployment of graduates and postgraduates, wasteful duplication of efforts and lack of adequate mobilization of scarce resources.

A report of the International Commission on Education for the Twenty-First Century (Delors Report), entitled "Learning: The Treasure Within" (UNESCO, 1996) visualized four functions for the universities, viz. to prepare students for research and training, to provide training courses oriented to the needs of society, to be open to all to foster lifelong learning in its broadest sense and to strive for international cooperation. Just two years after, the Indian National Commission for Cooperation with UNESCO presented a paper entitled "Higher Education in India: Vision and Action", in 1998. It reflected the following views on aims of higher education:

- Education aims at liberation from bondage and ignorance, backwardness and gravitational pulls of the lower human nature;

- Education, being an evolutionary force should aim at developing a new type of humanity, highly humane, cultured and integrated;
- Education should be developed as a harmonizing force, which tries to relate the individual, environment and cosmos in a total harmony by the purification and cultivation of various domains of outer space and inner space;
- Education should be so designed as to become a powerful carrier of the best of the heritage and it should, therefore, aim at transmitting to the new generations the lessons of the accumulated experiences of the past for further progress in the present and the future.

The concept of education and hence educational institutions has undergone a great change in recent years. Education is no more limited to the building up of knowledge, skills and character of the students and hence educational institutions cannot be mere ivory towers with total academic freedom to do what they like with their programmes. Education now has to have social concerns, for the employment of the youth and for the value system to be inculcated in keeping with the ideals enshrined in our constitution. Research and creative activities of the students and institutions are to be channelized for tackling specific problems of regional and national development. This new concept has great potentialities for making education an investment as visualized by the National Policy on Education rather than merely a social service. It should be able to attract far more funds for its programmes and pay back to society handsome dividends through not only human resources development, but also through participation and intervention in the whole process of socio-economic and cultural development. Through its linage with research institutions, industry, agriculture, a variety of services and the government, the university should be in a position to offer enriched academic programmes without in any way adversely affecting its autonomy.

The Birla-Ambani Report: Aims of Higher Education

The Prime Minister's Council on Trade and Industry appointed a committee in 2000 headed by Mr. Mukesh Ambani and Mr. Kumarmangalam Birla to suggest reforms in the educational sector. The committee submitted its report in the year 2001. It highlighted the important role of the State in the development of education. Education is universally recognized as an important investment in building human capital, which is a driver for technological innovation and economic growth. Education is becoming even more vital in the new world of information, where knowledge is rapidly replacing raw materials and labour as the most critical input for survival and success. India has to see education not just as a component of social development, but as a means of securing her future in an information society, resplendent with knowledge, research, creativity and innovation.

The challenge in education in India is to bridge the large divide between the education have not's and the haves, while simultaneously, radically upgrading education content, delivery and processes. Given the magnitude of the challenge and the complexities involved, this will call for a national mission unprecedented in the history of mankind. The vision for education in India should be "to create a competitive, yet co-operative, knowledge based society".

Ambani and Birla in their report "A Policy Framework for Reforms in Education" emphasized that education is a very profitable market over which they must have full control and for their industrial requirements, education must shape adaptable, competitive workers who can readily acquire new skills and innovations. Hence, they wanted a fundamental change in the mindset of seeing education as a component of social development. By not being market-oriented, the Indian education system fails to realize the potential of the information technology. Consequently, private institutions enjoying brand equity and large market capitalization have come up forming a large non-formal education system of creating quality software professionals.

Funding the huge expenditure demand should be by both an increase in quantum of public spending and increase in efficiency of public spending on education. Government has to reallocate public spending to education from other publicly funded activities such as defense and inefficient public sector enterprises. Private financing should be encouraged either to fund private institutions or to supplement the income of publicly funded institutions. There are basically three mutually reinforcing methods that could overcome some of the problems in financing education. The first method is to recover the public cost of higher education and reallocate government spending on education towards the level with the highest social returns, i.e. in primary education. The second method is to develop a credit market for education, together with selective scholarships, especially in higher education. The third method is to decentralize the management of public education and encourage the expansion of private and community-supported schools.

The report emphasized the establishment of world-class higher education facilities at every district headquarters. The creation of state-of-the-art professional research-based education institutions in all disciplines should be encouraged. Thus, both Birla and Ambani desired India to create an environment that does not produce industrial workers and labourers but fosters *knowledge workers*. Since education has a major role to play in shaping knowledge workers, Birla and Ambani want to first capture higher education and make huge profits, and then use the 'knowledge workers' in their unorganized sector to make further profits.

The National Knowledge Commission (NKC): Aims of Higher Education

In the words of the Prime Minister, Dr. Manmohan Singh, "The time has come to create a second wave of institution building and of excellence in the field of education, research and capability building so that we are better prepared for the 21st century." The universities perform a critical role in economy and society. They create, assimilate and disseminate knowledge. Therefore, they must be flexible, innovative and creative. They have to be accountable to the society. The number of universities and colleges has to be increased several times to meet the demands so that all deserving students have access to higher education, irrespective of their socio-economic background.

With this broad task in mind, the National Knowledge Commission (NKC) was constituted on 13 June 2005 with a time frame of three years, from 2 October 2005 to 2 October 2008. The NKC recommendations on higher education were submitted to the Prime Minister on 29 November 2006. The NKC's "Report to the Nation 2006" states "destiny of India is in the hands of 550 million people below the age of 25 who will benefit the most from the new knowledge initiatives. The proportion of our population, in the age group 18-24, that enters the world of higher education is around 7 per cent, which is only one-half the average for Asia." The NKC therefore recommends creation of "1500 universities nationwide that would enable India to attain a gross enrolment ratio of at least 15 per cent by 2015." Of these, 50 new national universities may be established to provide education of the highest standard. As an example for the rest of the nation, these would train students in a variety of disciplines. These institutions would have provisions for frequent curricula revision, an appropriate system of appointments and incentives to maximize productivity of faculty, a great deal of autonomy in management coupled with accountability and freedom to set student fee levels as well as to tap other sources of generating funds. The NKC has given recommendations regarding reforms in existing public universities, undergraduate colleges, regulatory structure, financing, quality, creation of national universities as centers of academic excellence and access to marginalized and excluded groups.

The emerging knowledge society and associated opportunities present a set of new imperatives and new challenges for our economy, polity and society. The concerns about the higher education need a systematic overhaul, so that we can educate much larger numbers without diluting academic standards. Indeed this is essential because the transformation of economy and society in the 21st century would depend, in significant part, on the spread and the quality of education among our people, particularly in the sphere of higher education. And it is only an inclusive society that can provide the foundations for a knowledge society.

The Yashpal Committee: Aims of Higher Education

With a strong idea of creating 'world-class universities', a committee headed by Prof. Yashpal was set up in February 2008. The mandate was to study the functioning of different agencies in higher education and to suggest various measures to restructure the system of higher education. The report on "Renovation and Rejuvenation of Higher Education" was submitted to the Ministry of Human Resource Development (MHRD) on June 24, 2009 providing a roadmap for future of education in India. University was visualized not only to impart knowledge to young people but also to give them opportunities to create their own knowledge. Active and constant engagement with the young minds and hearts of the society also implies that the universities are to serve the society as a whole, and in order to achieve this, considerable investment in continuing education is essential. University education should no longer be considered as a good in itself, but also as the stepping-stone into a higher orbit of the job market, where the student achieves a concrete monetary return, and consequently in this perception, of today a university is expected to be in tune with the emerging needs of the society and market demands.

The Yashpal Committee regarded university as the trustee of the humanist traditions of the world and an institution beyond all geographical, cultural and political boundaries. University should aim to develop a scholarly and a scientific outlook. Also, the university should at the same time aspire to encompass the world of work in all its forms constituting the human sphere where knowledge and skills are born and where knowledge takes shape in response to social and personal needs. The committee emphasized that since a university is based on the fundamental principle of transcendence and meeting of minds from diverse backgrounds, higher education should be a means to overcome caste and class hierarchy, patriarchy and other cultural prejudices and also a source of new knowledge and skills, a space for creativity and innovations. Higher education, therefore, was and continues to be considered a national responsibility and the state has to make necessary provisions to realize its potentials.

The committee further suggested setting up of a National Commission for Higher Education and Research, which will be an apex body in education. The committee made several recommendations, including scrapping of regulatory bodies like the UGC and AICTE, granting full autonomy to universities and instituting a national commission to supervise them.

There is a general appreciation of the fact that higher education provides the competencies that are required in different spheres of human activity, ranging from administration to agriculture, business, industry, health and communication, and extending to the arts and culture. The World Bank document. "Higher Education: The Lessons of Experience" (World Bank, 1994) allocates a low priority to higher education in its scheme of funding, yet admits:

> Higher education is of paramount importance for economic and social development. Institutions for higher education have the main responsibility for equipping individuals

with the advanced knowledge and skills required for positions of responsibility in government, business and the professions.

Today, education is being subjected to the competitive laws of the market. Governments are expected to encourage universities to develop an entrepreneurial, if not commercial, approach. There is a mad rush to internationalize education, not because of its social, cultural and diplomatic benefits, but in order to generate additional income. Those in authority in India must accept the fact that higher education is essential for national development and that in the first decade of the new millennium it should receive the highest priority.

Objectives of Higher Education in the Changing World

Government, universities, colleges and polytechnics alike now recognize the need to expand higher education. More technology is needed to perform the jobs previously attended to by people and more technology requires larger number of educated labour force to use it. Higher education institutions must adapt by providing what the learner wants and should select students in, not out. That is to say, they should find ways to include new groups of students rather than constantly operate a student-selection process to filter and exclude. This means that institutions must do market research and change what they provide accordingly. It may well mean that—

Higher Education must:

1. provide many more short courses and part-time courses.
2. develop short modules that can be accumulated to gain academic awards.
3. remove the stigma of failure by encouraging dropping in and dropping out.
4. take courses to factories and other outside centers rather than always expecting students to come to the college.
5. assess prior experiential learning to select students.
6. develop activities and learning methods suitable for mature students and others with experience to relate.
7. devise more consultancy courses for professional groups.

In short, what is needed is more 'continuing education' and higher education needs to be seen as part of it, rather than something separate that happens to be organized by a department in the same institution. Thus, it can be said that higher education is needed:

1. To develop attitudes and emotional adjustment

The education of the emotions must become a major aim of higher education. Higher education is no longer a supplement to basic education. It must attend to the basics itself. Four aims given by the Robbins Committee in 1963 are—

- Instruction in occupational skills (develop the nation's economy)
- To promote the general powers of the mind (develop the intellect of the individual)
- The advancement of learning (develop knowledge) and
- The transmission of a common culture and common standards of citizenship (develop society).

2. To provide a base of adaptable occupational skills

Courses have to be designed, validated and often accredited by the professionals before a college can advertise for applicants. At this stage students' choice of career is more influenced by what they think they would enjoy doing—that is expected job satisfaction—than by expectations of high financial rewards. Graduates have to be trained for specific jobs, which require specific mental skills based on a combination of sub-skills with much wider application. Understanding, application and exercising critical judgement are important educational aims of higher education too. Much of higher education consists of learning, testing and applying generalizations.

3. To promote the general powers of the mind

Universities and now other institutions of higher education are the major institutions in our society for the acquisition, preservation, assembly, classification, interrelation, testing, interpretation and dissemination of knowledge, particularly new knowledge. They therefore have a major role in the advancement of our society. It is not the quantity of knowledge or what the knowledge is about, that gives knowledge its quality, rather it is the way that knowledge is learnt, related, justified and applied, that is important. It is the method that matters. It is a matter of attitudes and abilities in thinking. What one thinks about is less important than the quality of thought.

4. To advance learning

Higher education employs people whose job is not only to keep up to date on the latest knowledge in specialist areas, but also to rub shoulders with people who are up to date in other areas of knowledge so that cross-fertilization can take place. Higher education is most important in carrying out fundamental research.

5. To develop culture and standards of citizenship

It is concerned with the ability to see things in different ways and to exercise balanced judgement in the light of varied perceptions. It is concerned with the ability to see different sides of a question, to understand different points of view, to appreciate the value of diverse objects and activities and to understand nations other than our own. This involves having many different concepts, which can be used to interpret any situation.

6. Aims from other perspectives

Higher education is an agent of change. Diversity is desirable in higher education. It produces a creative tension because each perspective emphasizes some values more than others. Single mindedness is detrimental to higher education. The university should promote an imaginative blend of various disciplines to prepare students for challenging careers such as modern business, engineering, etc.

Kneller (1969) voiced that the primary purpose of the university is to provide an environment in which the faculty and students can discover, examine critically, preserve and transmit the knowledge, wisdom and values that will help to ensure the survival of the present and future generations with improvement in the quality of life.

The universities in India are going through a crisis today. Lack of discipline, unrest in campuses and the influence of party politics are the main causes that have contributed to this crisis. The number of teachers devoted and dedicated to the profession is fast disappearing. Instead of being examples of centers of excellence in teaching and research, the universities are fast becoming centers of mediocrity, partisan, politics and conflicts. It will be a Herculean task to reform and revitalize the universities and re-establish their credibility. In this great task, reorganizing the present system of governance that exists in most of our universities should be the first priority.

Aims of Higher Education: Views of Some Great Philosophers

Although an idea of a university a visualized by great philosophers and educationists have been mentioned in the first chapter, yet a need was felt to discuss their views in detail regarding the specific aims and functions of higher education.

Gurudev Rabindranath Tagore

A national system of education in India should try to discover the characteristic truths of its civilization. Those truths are not commercialism, imperialism or nationalism, but rather universalism. The aim was all-round development of the individual personality through harmonious interaction and union of the spirit with the environment. Visva Bharati, Gurudev Rabindranath Tagore's conception of a world university, was founded at the end of the First World War with a determination to go beyond aggressive nationalism and to build friendship with all nations. He emphasized co-operation between East and West, in the field of humanistic studies and culture. From children's education and rural development, he increasingly shifted his attention to university education and developing the surrounding villages as one of the university's functions during this third phase. He dreamt of an alternative form of education.

In every nation, education is intimately associated with the life of the people. For most of us, modern education is relevant only to turning out clerks, lawyers, doctors, magistrates and policemen.... This education has not reached the farmer, the oil grinder, nor the potter. No other educated society has been struck with such disaster.... If ever a truly Indian university is established, it must from the very beginning implement India's own knowledge of economics, agriculture, health, medicine and of all other everyday science from the surrounding villages. Then alone can the school or university become the centre of the country's way of living. This school must practice agriculture, dairying and weaving using the best modern methods. Tagore was convinced that no form of education offered in India, be it at school or at university level, would be complete without knowledge of patterns of rural living and without an effort by the universities to rejuvenate rural life. He considered this to be an important aspect of Visva Bharati's total activity.

The main task of universities is to produce knowledge; its dissemination is its secondary function. We must invite those intellectuals and scholars to our universities who are engaged in research, invention or creative activity. It was important to borrow knowledge and experience from abroad, but not to use them as the foundation for Indian education. Even so, if there was one European quality which Indian university students must acquire it was "the desire to know, to find out about the laws of nature and to use them for the betterment of the conditions of human beings".

Science and its applications in the form of technology have led to the power and prosperity of Western countries. Unless India acquired knowledge of science and technology through its universities and schools, poverty and powerlessness would continue. To transform life and make it richer, healthier and more educated, it was imperative to resort to technology and science. But Tagore wanted science to be taught along with India's own philosophical and spiritual knowledge at Indian universities. However, science without the constraint of self-knowledge, without appreciating that the quest for knowledge is the most important aim of human existence, leads to an endless desire for material goods and well-being, and the meaningless pursuit of the instruments of war and power, which are often the origin of conflict between nations and end, ultimately, in the suppression of the weaker by the stronger. That is why both spiritual and scientific knowledge are considered by Tagore as equally important.

In an address on the functions of the university, Tagore argued that a university is an attempt by a nation to aggregate knowledge at one place, to develop it and to disseminate it to the younger generation. Long before universities in the West had been established, there existed in India universities such as Nalanda and Vikramshila, where various branches of knowledge had been pursued by scholars for centuries during the Buddhist period of India's history. Students came to these universities from far and near in Asia to learn about the subjects taught, and to live with the teachers who were respected for their exemplary way of life. When universities came to be founded in Europe, the hold of religion was loosened. New methods of acquiring knowledge led to rapid growth in the fields of social, physical and life sciences.

Modern universities collect existing knowledge in various fields from within a country or abroad, preserve and develop it and make it available to the younger generations. But contemporary Indian universities had not been concerned about collecting and preserving the national heritage, and enriching it by fusing it with knowledge coming from abroad. Neither had they been concerned about improving life in the villages. "Universities here are like a lighted railway compartment in a train passing through the countryside which is enveloped in darkness." In Tagore's view, the higher aim of education was the same as that of a person's life, that is, to achieve fulfillment and completeness. There was a lesser aim that of providing the individual with a satisfactory means of livelihood, without which a person would not be able to satisfy his/her basic requirements and thus fail to achieve either of these two aims.

He wanted Indian universities to integrate themselves with society and make an effort to educate people living in the countryside. He did not want education to remain confined to the cities and to particular classes of society. Tagore wanted his students to acquire a scientific temper; in other words, he wanted teachers to stimulate constructive doubt, the love of mental adventure, the courage and longing to conquer the world by enterprise and boldness in thought and in action. These were the virtues, cultivation of which had made the West forge ahead.

Aurobindo Ghosh

The first principle of true teaching is that nothing can be taught.

—Sri Aurobindo

Education is meant to bring out the best in Man, to develop his potentialities to the maximum, to integrate him with himself, his surroundings, his society, his country and humanity to make him the "complete man", the "integrated man". In Sri Aurobindo's words:

> That alone will be a true and living education which helps to bring out to full advantage, makes ready for the full purpose and scope of human life all that is in the individual man, and which at the same time helps him to enter into his right relation with the life, mind and soul of the people to which he belongs and with that great total life, mind and soul of humanity of which he himself is a unit and his people or nation a living, a separate yet inseparable member.

If this is the meaning of education, then what passes in its name today in our educational institutions, is obviously very far from the mark. The purpose of education cannot be, even at its best, to merely create a literate individual, or a highly informed person crammed with information and facts, or to prepare an individual to find a job, or to create a good worker, a skilled technician and scientist, or an efficient doctor or lawyer, or a capable industrialist or politician, even to create a good and law abiding citizen. These may be needed but they are not sufficient in themselves. Nor do they create the whole man or a great nation.

They do not take into account the even more important aspects of the individual—his character, his personality, and his values. We all want our youths to be truthful, courageous, generous and benevolent. The question is of bringing out the best in man. India has always seen in him not merely a body, an emotional and aesthetic being, a rational and thinking mind, but much more fundamentally a soul, evolving gradually into a higher consciousness, towards truth, light, freedom, harmony and immortality. It is this concept which has made India a nation apart and our education too must reflect this attitude. It must lay stress on the emergence of the spirit, not rejecting but embracing and perfecting matter and life.

To learn for the sake of knowledge, to study in order to know the secrets of Nature and life, to educate oneself in order to grow in consciousness, to discipline oneself in order to become master of oneself, to overcome one's weaknesses, incapacities and ignorance, to prepare oneself to advance in life towards a goal that is nobler and vaster, more generous and more true, has been the aim of higher education for Aurobindo.

Sri Aurobindo was aware of the significance of variations in the concept of man, his life and destiny, of the nation and of humanity and the life of human race, which get reflected in the respective philosophies of education, and developed his scheme of integral education rooted in "the developing soul of India, to her future need, to the greatness of her coming self-creation, to her eternal spirit". In devising a true and living education, three things according to Sri Aurobindo—the man, the individual in his commonness and his uniqueness, the nation or people and universal humanity—should be taken into account.

The education of the intellect, says Aurobindo, divorced from the perfection of the moral and emotional nature, is injurious to human progress. The best kind of moral training for a man, that Sri Aurobindo conceives of is, "to habituate himself to the right emotions, the noblest associations, the best mental, emotional and physical habits and the following out in right action of the fundamental impulses of his essential nature". No religious teaching, according to Aurobindo, is of any value unless it is lived, and the use of various kinds of sadhana (spiritual self-training and exercise), is the only effective preparation for religious living. Aurobindo also speaks of mental and psychic education, but his real interest was in a still higher stage, which according to him is spiritual or supra-mental education. This does not imply the extinction of the individual but his enrichment through contact with the Absolute.

The educational doctrine of Sri Aurobindo is closely linked with his futuristic vision of human destiny. He visualized a system of education which would help expression of unrealized potentialities, in line with his concept of life. This called for a creative vision and an extraordinary adventure. For him human destiny is an ascent towards the super mind, towards realization of the Godhead and his philosophy of education provides a forceful and resilient framework to attain this goal.

Swami Vivekananda

Amongst the contemporary Indian philosophers of education, Swami Vivekananda is one of those who revolted against the imposition of British system of education in India. He criticized the pattern of education introduced by the British in India. He pointed out that the then current system of education only brings about an external change without any reflective inner force. According to Swami Vivekananda, there are several aims for education. They are self-development, fulfillment of *Swadharma,* freedom of growth and character formation.

In contrast to the contemporary system of education, Vivekananda advocated education for self-development.

Education, according to most of the Western educationalists, aims at man's adjustment with the environment. According to the Indian philosophical tradition, true knowledge does not come from outside, it is discovered with the individual, in the self which is the source of all knowledge. According to Vivekananda, the function of education is the uncovering of the knowledge hidden in our mind.

Vivekananda supported the idea of *Swadharma* in education. Everyone has to grow like himself. No one has to copy others. External pressure only creates destructive reactions leading to stubbornness and disorderliness. In an atmosphere of freedom, love and sympathy alone, the child will develop courage and self-reliance. Each child should be given opportunities to develop according to his own inner nature. The teacher should not exert any type of pressure on the child. The child should be helped in solving his problems himself. The teachers should have an attitude of service and worship. Education ultimately aims at realization.

To him education plays a vital role in curing the evils in society, and it is critical in shaping the future of humanity. The goal of education—general or ultimate—is essentially laid down by society and therefore varies from society to society. Even as every society tries to keep pace with the contemporary world, societies with a stable and older tradition cherish some higher goals of everlasting value. Education, he said, must provide "life-building, man-making, character-making assimilation of ideas" (*CW*, Vol. III, p. 302). The ideal of this type of education would be to produce an integrated person—one who has learned how to improve his intellect, purify his emotions, and stand firm on moral virtues and unselfishness.

Training the mind should be a student's highest priority, and not simply the accumulation, the memorizing and the repeating of facts. In the long run, stuffing one's mind with information, technical skills and useless trivia only creates more problems if one's mind is not nourished and strengthened and made healthy. Yet training of the mind in all its aspects is conspicuously absent in today's education. Learning to concentrate the mind was the focus in the Swami's scheme. He said: "To me the very essence of education is concentration of mind, not the collecting of facts" (*CW*, Vol. VI, p. 38).

Talking about the importance of science, Swamiji believed that science is systematic pursuit of knowledge at empirical level. The scientific method gives a very good training to the mind. It was by applying the scientific method that Western countries made tremendous advancement in technology and acquired great wealth and power. Swami Vivekananda was one of the first among religious teachers to understand the importance of science and technology. In the first place, Swamiji saw that poor countries like India would be able to overcome poverty and backwardness only by mastering technology. Secondly, Swamiji saw that science is not contradictory to the eternal spiritual principles, which is the foundation of Indian culture. Both science and eternal religion are concerned with truth. Science seeks truth in the physical world, whereas religion seeks truth in the spiritual realm. Thus, religion and science are complementary.

Mahatma Gandhi

Mahatma Gandhi, in his article titled "National Education" published in *Young India* on 1 September, 1921, has written that it might be true regarding other countries but in India where 80% of the population is occupied with agriculture and 10% of it with industries, it is an offence to make education merely literary. It is apparent from these lines that according to Mahatma Gandhi, education is not only to gain literary knowledge. Each and every student should have a definite aim before he enters the field of higher education; otherwise it is meaningless to pursue higher education.

True education is all-round development of the faculties, best attained through action. It bases itself on the fact that knowledge and understanding develop in relation to problems set right by action. Information thrust on the mind only burdens the memory and causes intellectual indigestion, casting learning into oblivion. Education must be concrete and interconnected, not abstract or given in isolated sections. Concrete education allows the learner to manipulate problems or sets of problems and study their relationships, character and artistic sense. It allows the mind, heart, hand and eyes to work simultaneously in a correlated manner, resulting in a harmonious and well-balanced personality.

Tertiary Education should either lead to the responsibilities of adult family life or some form of professional training in the university. Each individual must develop "a scientific attitude of mind". It means a clean intellectual curiosity to know the "how" and "why" of things; the patience detachment to test all phenomena, all ideas and all traditions by the standards of truth; the courage and power to think for oneself; the intellectual and moral authority to abide by all the facts.

Having become a graduate with technical knowledge any young boy or girl would be capable of seeking self-employment in a country with a population as large as in India and it will be comparably easy for him/her to get a government or non-government job. He or she can also pursue his or her studies further while doing his/her job. In this way, being self-dependant, a young boy/girl can continue his/her studies further to fulfill his/her aim and object. This is what Gandhi wanted. One who is self-employed will not have to run about after graduation for post-graduation or any other higher degree. Apart from this, he will not be required to waste precious time and money. It will naturally bring down the unnecessary crowding in colleges and universities. Besides, education will be purposeful and will be able to guide in the right direction. In short, these are Mahatma Gandhi's views on higher education and keeping them in mind, the system of education in India will have to be reformed. These views of Mahatma Gandhi can be our guide and can contribute to the management of our educational system.

Mahatma Gandhi had talked about self-sufficiency of colleges and universities. It meant that these institutions instead of depending on government aid should be self-financed. India is an agricultural country. Most of the industries are based on agriculture. Gandhi wanted that more and more self-financed agriculture-colleges should be opened and they should be attached to related industries which would turn out graduates according to their requirement. Not only this, they should bear the expenses of their education and the training-staff. Gandhi wanted the same system to be adopted for graduates of engineering and medical colleges. Engineering graduates should be attached to the related industry and medical graduates to hospitals. Law, commerce and arts colleges can be managed by voluntary organizations and donations can be procured according to their requirement. Mahatma Gandhi was never in favour of government aid. He, however, wanted the universities' control over the colleges and that of the government over the universities.

He stressed that the educational system must be one in which the highest development of mind and soul is possible and which instills courage and self-reliance in the individual, while at the same time, helping them cultivate the highest intellectual scientific, moral, and ethical accomplishments. Gandhiji aimed at developing a society, "a socially conscious 'man' dedicated to truth and non-violence." His educational scheme was nationalist in setting, idealist in nature and pragmatic on one hand while social in purpose and spiritual in intent on the other hand.

He had very specific ideas about research, higher education and the accumulation of knowledge. In Gandhi's scheme, higher education performed the essential function of providing training and properly motivating human power for national needs and there was an urgent need for the purposive expansion of such education. He declared, "...under my scheme, there will be more and better libraries, more and better research institutes. Under it we should have an army of chemists, engineers, and other experts who will be the real servants of the nation and answer the varied and growing requirements of the people who are becoming increasingly conscious of their rights and wants."

J. Krishnamurthy

Though there is a higher and wider significance to life, of what value is our education if we never discover it? We may be highly educated, but if we are without deep integration of thought and feeling, our lives are incomplete, contradictory and torn with many fears; and as long as education does not cultivate an integrated outlook on life, it has very little significance.

In our present civilization, we have divided life into so many departments that education has very little meaning, except in learning a particular technique or profession. Instead of awakening the integrated intelligence of the individual, education is encouraging him to conform to a pattern and so is hindering his comprehension of himself as a total process. To attempt to solve the many problems of existence at their respective levels, separated as they are into various categories, indicates an utter lack of comprehension. The individual is made up of different entities, but to emphasize the differences and to encourage the development of a definite type leads to many complexities and contradictions.

Education should bring about the integration of these separate entities—for without integration, life becomes a series of conflicts and sorrows. Of what value is it to be trained as lawyers if we perpetuate litigation? Of what value is knowledge if we continue in our confusion? What significance has technical and industrial capacity if we use it to destroy one another? What is the point of our existence if it leads to violence and utter misery? Though we may have money or are capable of earning it, though we have our pleasures and our organized religions, we are in endless conflict.

Education is not merely a matter of training the mind. Training makes for efficiency, but it does not bring about completeness. A mind that has merely been trained is the continuation of the past, and such a mind can never discover the new. That is why, to find out what is right education, we will have to inquire into the whole significance of living. To most of us, the meaning of life as a whole is not of primary importance, and our education emphasizes secondary values, merely making us proficient in some branch of knowledge. Though knowledge and efficiency are necessary, to lay chief emphasis on them only leads to conflict and confusion.

Our present education is geared to industrialization and war, its principal aim being to develop efficiency; and we are caught in this machine of ruthless competition and mutual destruction. If education leads to war, if it teaches us to destroy or be destroyed, has it not utterly failed? Education is not merely acquiring knowledge, gathering and correlating facts; it is to see the significance of life as a whole. But the whole cannot be approached through the part—which is what governments, organized religions and authoritarian parties are attempting to do.

The function of education is to create human beings who are integrated and therefore intelligent. We may take degrees and be mechanically efficient without being intelligent. Intelligence is not mere information; it is not derived from books, nor does it consist of clever self-defensive responses and aggressive assertions. One who has not studied may be more intelligent than the learned. We have made examinations and degrees the criterion of intelligence and have developed cunning minds that avoid vital human issues. Intelligence is the capacity to perceive the essential and to awaken this capacity, in oneself and in others, is education.

Education should help us to discover lasting values so that we do not merely cling to formulas or repeat slogans; it should help us to break down our national and social barriers, instead of emphasizing them, for they breed antagonism between man and man. Unfortunately, the present system of education is making us subservient, mechanical and deeply thoughtless;

though it awakens us intellectually, inwardly it leaves us incomplete, stultified and uncreative. Without an integrated understanding of life, our individual and collective problems will only deepen and extend. The purpose of education is not to produce mere scholars, technicians and job hunters, but integrated men and women who are free of fear; for only between such human beings can there be enduring peace.

J. Krishnamurti

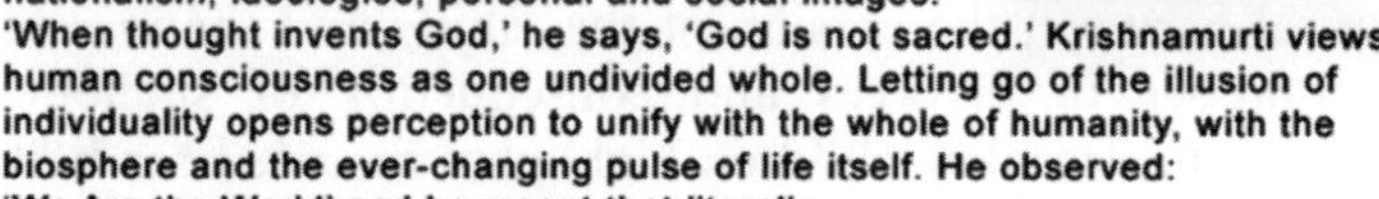

A true revolutionary J. Krishnamurti is one of the most influential teachers of the 20th century. He challenges the conditioning that traps the mind in habitual patterns, patterns that inventively breed personal and global conflict, organized religions, nationalism, ideologies, personal and social images. 'When thought invents God,' he says, 'God is not sacred.' Krishnamurti views human consciousness as one undivided whole. Letting go of the illusion of individuality opens perception to unify with the whole of humanity, with the biosphere and the ever-changing pulse of life itself. He observed: 'We Are the World' and he meant that literally.

Education should not encourage the individual to conform to society or to be negatively harmonious with it, but help him to discover the true values which come with unbiased investigation and self-awareness. When there is no self knowledge, self-expression becomes self-assertion, with all its aggressive and ambitious conflicts. Education should awaken the capacity to be self-aware and not merely indulge in gratifying self-expression.

Throughout the world, engineers are frantically designing machines which do not need men to operate them. In a life run almost entirely by machines, what is to become of human beings? We shall have more and more leisure without knowing wisely how to employ it, and we shall seek escape through knowledge, through enfeebling amusements, or through ideals. Right education comes with the transformation of ourselves. We must re-educate ourselves not to kill one another for any cause, however righteous, for any ideology, however promising it may appear to be for the future happiness of the world. We must learn to be compassionate, to be content with little, and to seek the Supreme, for only then can there be the true salvation of mankind.

The recent debate about professional—vocational education versus liberal—humanistic education has added a new dimension to the discourse on educational curricula. While allowing technology to permeate our lives and classroom environment, we must emphasize that technology must ever remain a means; it can never become an end from the point of view of education. In other words, the role of technology must be facilitative and usually near—peripheral. The task of humane development of the learners, of fostering their inquisitiveness and of encouraging them to undertake humanistic pursuits would ever remain primary and the more cherished. The forces of change unleashed by electronics-led communication revolution, the invasion through satellite channels on our cultural heritage, the erosion of the family and the increase in the number of divorces and consequently of single-parent families and latchkey children highlights the need for building up a strong component of value based education. Value education needs to be participatory rather than sermon-based and it should support and strengthen the holistic development of the learners' personality.

The growing alienation of our youth from our cultural heritage, secularism derived from our multi-culturism and spiritualism necessitate that curricula in education should enable them to discover the best in our culture and also in other cultures. Curricula in education should provide and promote critical insight into our cultural heritage and also help develop the ability to separate the deadwood from the vital. It can hardly be denied that much of the present-day education, in terms of structure and content, is a reflection of the colonial legacy and the Westernized mindset. In our zeal to preserve the British system, we have de-emphasized even the worthwhile in our indigenous system. Indian experiments and the achievements rooted in our native soil should now be given their legitimate place in educational curricula. Tagore, Sri Aurobindo, Mahatma Gandhi, Jiddoo Krishnamurthy, Vivekananda, to name a few, have contributed a great deal through their thought and experiments to reconstruction of our society through education. The Indian achievements in the discipline of education, theoretical as well as practical, should be included in courses of study at the undergraduate and the postgraduate level.

One of the twentieth century's most original metaphysicians and a major figure in mathematical logic, Alfred North Whitehead was also an important social and educational philosopher. While Whitehead's metaphysical and logical writings merit his inclusion in any pantheon of twentieth-century philosophers, his work in social and educational philosophy is marked by singular qualities of imagination, profound analysis, and personal commitment. His thought resembles much in the philosophy of John Dewey (1859–1952). In the philosophy of higher education, where Dewey wrote very little, Whitehead is probably the most important figure since John Henry Cardinal Newman (1801-90).

Alfred North Whitehead

"Education is the acquisition of the art of the utilization of knowledge." This simple sentence from Whitehead's introductory essay in his *Aims of Education* (1929, p. 4), epitomizes one of his central themes: Education cannot be dissected from practice. For Whitehead, education is a temporal, growth-oriented process, in which both student and subject matter move progressively. The concept of rhythm suggests an aesthetic dimension to the process, one analogous to music. Growth then is a part of physical and mental development, with a strong element of style understood as a central driving motif. There are three fundamental stages in this process, which Whitehead called the stage of romance, the stage of precision, and the stage of generalization.

Romance is the first moment in the educational experience. All rich educational experiences begin with an immediate emotional involvement on the part of the learner. The primary acquisition of knowledge involves freshness, enthusiasm, and enjoyment of learning. The natural ferment of the living mind leads it to fix on those objects that strike it pre-reflectively as important for the fulfilling of some felt need on the part of the learner. All early learning experiences are of this kind and a curriculum ought to include appeals to the spirit of inquiry with which all children are natively endowed. The stage of precision concerns "exactness of formulation" (Whitehead, 1929, p. 18), rather than the immediacy and breadth of relations involved in the romantic phase. Precision is discipline in the various languages and grammars of discrete subject matters, particularly science and technical subjects, including logic and spoken languages. It is the scholastic phase with which most students and teachers are familiar in organized schools and curricula. In isolation from the romantic impetus of education, precision can be barren, cold, and unfulfilling, and useless in the personal development of children.

Generalization, the last rhythmic element of the learning process, is the incorporation of romance and precision into some general context of serviceable ideas and classifications. It is the moment of educational completeness and fruition, in which general ideas or, one may say, a philosophical outlook, both integrate the feelings and thoughts of the earlier moments of growth, and prepare the way for fresh experiences of excitement and romance, signaling a new beginning to the educational process.

It is important to realize that these three rhythmic moments of the educational process characterize all stages of development, although each is typically associated with one period of growth. So, romance, precision, and generalization characterize the rich educational experience of a young child, the adolescent, and the adult, although the romantic period is more closely associated with infancy and young childhood, the stage of precision with adolescence, and generalization with young and mature adulthood. Education is not uniquely oriented to some future moment, but holds the present in an attitude of almost religious awe. It is "holy ground" (Whitehead, 1929, p. 3), and each moment in a person's education ought to include all three rhythmical elements. Similarly, the subjects contained in a comprehensive curriculum need to comprise all three stages, at whatever point they are introduced to the student. Thus, the young child can be introduced to language acquisition by a deft combination of appeal to the child's emotional involvement, its need for exactitude in detail, and the philosophical consideration of broad generalizations.

> The university imparts information, but it imparts it imaginatively.... This atmosphere of excitement, arising from imaginative consideration, transforms knowledge. A fact is no longer a bare fact: it is invested with all its possibilities. It is no longer a burden on the memory: it is energizing as the poet of our dreams, and as the architect of our purposes. Imagination is not to be divorced from the facts: it is a way of illuminating the facts. It works by eliciting the general principles which apply to the facts, as they exist, and then by an intellectual survey of alternative possibilities which are consistent with those principles.... (Whitehead, 1929)

> The development of students' intellectual and imaginative powers; their understanding and judgment; their problem-solving skills; their ability to communicate; their ability to see relationships within what they have learned and to perceive their field of study in a broader perspective. HE must aim to stimulate an enquiring, analytical and creative approach, encouraging independent judgment and critical self-awareness (in the context of disciplinary knowledge). (UK Council for Academic Awards)

Scenario Today

India has seen a consistently high rate of economic growth in the recent years. It has now become a major player in the global knowledge economy. Skill-based activities have made significant contribution to this growth. Such activities depend on the large pool of qualified manpower that is fed by its large higher education system. It is now widely accepted that higher education has been critical to India's emergence in the global knowledge economy. Yet, it is believed that a crisis is plaguing the Indian higher education system. While the National Knowledge Commission (NKC) calls it a 'quiet crisis', the Human Resource Minister calls higher education 'a sick child'. Industries routinely point towards huge skill shortages and are of the opinion that growth momentum may not be sustained unless the problem of skill shortages is addressed, especially the communication skills.

There appear to be endless problems with the Indian higher education system. The higher education system produces graduates that are unemployable, though there are mounting skill shortages in a number of sectors. The standards of academic research are low and declining. An unwieldy affiliating system, inflexible academic structure, uneven capacity across subjects, eroding autonomy of academic institutions, low level of public funding, archaic and dysfunctional regulatory environment are some of its many problems. Finally, it is widely held that it suffers from several systemic deficiencies and is driven by populism, and in the absence of reliable data, there is little informed public debate.

More than 35 years ago, Nobel laureate Amartya Sen, while analyzing the crisis in Indian education, rather than attributing the crisis in Indian education to administrative neglect or to thoughtless action, pointed out that the "grave failures in policy-making in the field of education require the analysis of the characteristics of the economic and social forces operating in India, and response of public policy to these forces" (Amartya Sen, "The Crisis in Indian Education", Lal Bahadur Shastri Memorial Lectures, 10-11 March 1970). He emphasized that "due to the government's tendency to formulate educational policies based on public pressure, often wrong policies are pursued." Unfortunately, it is believed that policy-making suffers from similar failure even today. Rather than pragmatism, it is populism, ideology and vested interests that drive policy. It seeks to achieve arbitrarily set goals that are often elusive and, more than that, pursued half-heartedly.

During the last four decades, mankind has moved from the modern era to the post-modern era. The typical post-modern individual is very much unlike his counterpart of the modern era. While the modern man had faith in rationality, progress and in long-term planning, the post-modern man finds himself unhinged from his roots; unlike the modern man who lived more for the future than in the present, the post-modern man has chosen to live in and for the present rather than for the future. The post-modern man is committed to the pursuit of the images and symbols of his desire; for this he is ready to disregard the established structures of society but he lacks the strong faith that would enable him to function as the agent of normative social change. Haunted by his alienation from his traditional social milieu and fearful of what lies hidden in the womb of future, the post-modern man has chosen to pursue instant gratification of his desires. Unlike modernity which was looked upon as worthy of pursuit, post-modernity has emerged as a challenge to cope with. This has led to decline of idealism and erosion of altruism as values in life; advances in technology during the last two decades have inexplicably been accompanied by streaks of blind faith and superstition in some quarters.

Our formal education system has been essentially a reactive rather than a proactive one. Instead of visualizing the future and providing for it, Indian education has been content to be a follower of changes in various sectors in India as well as elsewhere. Newer technologies like Internet, telematics, world wide web, e-mail and now e-commerce are impacting education. Private initiative in higher education is readily willing to embrace what the formal system has so far been skeptical about. Our education system has yet to assimilate and use research, especially that conducted in the West in various fields like learning disabilities, giftedness, as well as multiple intelligences, to name a few. The corporate sector is far ahead of the formal education system. On the one hand, research conducted in the education sector has increased in terms of sheer quantity; on the other hand, it is mostly not in tune with the acknowledged priority areas. Besides, the fund available for research has shrunk. The corporate sector has lately become more liberal in funding research; it uses research findings for organizational restructuring, updating its available technologies and boosting productivity. Research in formal education is not ploughed back into the system to accelerate its development or to make it more functional. The formal education sector can learn some lessons from the corporate sector for optimizing its functioning through need-based research geared to its development.

The challenges and problems of harnessing India's pluralism for national developmental await our attention. 'Unity in diversity' is yet to become a living faith in our society. Our rich social collage should not only strengthen 'Unity in diversity' but also allow a thousand flowers to bloom through socio-emotional unity underlying our social psyche. Revisiting and re-discovering the age-old genius of our society in accepting and assimilating diverse cultures and sub-cultures and thereby developing a composite culture can truly be our asset today provided Indian education chooses to serve it and to draw its sustenance from it. The challenges emanating from updating and restructuring of school education, greater popularity of open learning systems, the pressures, endogenous as well as exogenous, to achieve and excel international standards have obvious implications for updating educational curricula especially those of teacher education. Indian education can no longer afford to remain a sleeping titan. 'Update or perish' is the need of the time.

Recent Developments in Indian Higher Education

Higher education has received a lot of attention in India over the past few years. There are four reasons for this recent focus. First, country's weak higher education system is being blamed for skill shortages in several sectors of economy. Second, reservation quotas in higher education institutions, particularly the more reputed ones that provide access to high status and best-paid jobs became a highly discordant issue, central to the policy of inclusive growth and distributive justice, and hence politically very important. Third, in the backdrop of the first two developments, it began to be argued that the country would not be able to sustain its growth momentum and maintain competitiveness unless problems with higher education are fixed. Last, demand for higher education continues to outpace the supply due to growing population of young people, gains in school education, the growing middle class and their rising aspirations.

It is widely believed that technological advances and a shift in demographic provide India with a window of opportunity to productively engage its huge pool of human resources, and become a leader in both the rapidly expanding sectors of services and highly skilled manufacturing. This would, however, require revamping the higher education sector. Hence, many steps have been taken to augment supply, improve quality and fix many of the problems faced by higher education. The National Knowledge Commission (NKC) that was set up to examine the higher education sector (amongst other things) made several useful and important recommendations. The Government of India has increased funding significantly during the Eleventh Five-Year Plan. Many new institutions have been planned and some of them are already operational. There are many good ideas in the plan document. All these efforts, however, appear to be somewhat disconnected. Some even appear to be at cross-purposes with each other. Several suggestions appear to be merely impressionistic views of individuals, rather than being supported by data and research. Overall, these efforts do not give a sense of an integrated reform agenda for Indian higher education. And in absence of credible data and good analysis, the media continues to perpetuate and exacerbate certain fallacies and inconsistencies.

With ambiguity in defining its purpose and vagueness about its quality, debate on higher education is usually full of rhetoric. As pointed out by Kapur and Crowley, "for the higher education sector whose main purpose is to train people with strong analytical skills, it is ironical that its own self-analysis is replete with homilies and platitudes, rather than strong evidence" (Kapur and Crowley, 2008). Institutions of higher education today are an integral organ of the state and economy. They are embedded in the history and culture of a nation and are shaped by its contemporary realities, ideologies and vested interests. India's large size, long history and diverse culture and the complicated nature of Indian polity and policy process make Indian higher education a very complex enterprise.

Of late, the private sector is entering into the business of higher education. Soon it will capture that part of the market which is remunerative. Yet, it is doubtful that the private sector in higher education will deliver goods needed for the prosperity of the nation. At that, the left-over part of the market, unattended by the private sector, will have no ability or willingness to pay. This latter one will be quite sizeable. It will be impractical to launch at self-financing of higher education in the public sector. Thus, unless we are ready to restructure the system of higher education, we will have only two alternatives: first not to press upon the institutions of higher education to earn their own sustenance, and the second to constrain them to do so and wait for their doomsday. If one plans to erect a new structure on the debris of the present one, it is an entirely different matter.

Additionally, one must think on a singularly different role of higher education. A function of higher education relates to keeping the students, the adolescent and youth forces, engaged in some pursuit for several years. Age mallows us on account of many reasons—wisdom, attachment, tapering rate of creative energy, emotional stability, realization of factual situation, disillusionment and so on. Thus, higher education suppresses the tendency to revolt against the contradictions in the social system. It works as a great sedative. If economic constraints eject the adolescents and youths without providing them with an alternative, it would perhaps backfire violently. This possibility should concern us.

At present, research in most of the institutions of higher learning is disorganized, unstructured, mostly repetitive and irrelevant. It is needed that universities should promote directed research. The industrial houses or the government, semi-government and autonomous institutions should back up most of the research activities. To this end, teachers should be encouraged to approach these institutions. The university should chalk out a well thought out program to reward the teachers who perform and penalize the teachers who do not perform. One must remember that pressure accelerates the pace of development. Pressure from above, pressure from sides and pressure from below must be generated.

Leakages that do not allow building pressure fail the most potent explosive. The university should go in for promotional advertisement and approach business and industrial houses, government, etc. and make them aware of its research capabilities and how it can help them with research. If the business and industrial houses sponsor research, it will fetch enormous financial resources to develop and strengthen research activities in the university. Furthermore, the research students will develop connection with their potential employers and will have no employment problem after completion of their research. The university may take necessary steps to patenting the knowledge or the product developed through research. The researcher and the university may have joint intellectual property right of patents. Education programs in the institutions of higher learning should not be limited to offering degrees and diplomas to the youngsters. Utility-based training programs useful to the personnel in industrial and business house, in government organizations, etc. may be a significant source of revenue to the institutions of higher learning.

To do all these things, the university authorities must be earnest, effortful, watchful, thoughtful and sensitive. They must shun perfunctory democratization. To earn money one has to be industrious and that means adieu to the policy of laissez faire. One must reflect everyday on prudence, innovation, cane-candy principle, fixing of responsibility, exploitation of comparative advantages, reliance on interdependency and cooperation, removal of conflicts, indifferences and bottlenecks and subversive tendencies, clear, self-consistent and explicit goal setting, rational choice of paths to the goals, inculcation of positive attitudes, minimization of wastages, utilization of untapped potentials and so on. In several institutions of learning, there are telling instances of idle capacities—non-teaching centers, non-performing units, sleeping research cells—that only add to the burden on the public exchequer. Those institutions, nevertheless, have thousand and one reasons not to utilize those idle capacities for a productive purpose, but behind all that there is a poor will to economize, a poor will to develop, a paralyzing indifference.

What is needed is to evaluate the economic worth of an activity before it gets financial support from the university. Lastly, there cannot be any 'mantra' to earn money and go in for self-financing. Each institution of higher learning has to reflect on its own prospects and constraints and firmly stride on its path to progress. Nature has a provision for everyone but one must make efforts. It cannot be believed that an organization that enshrines a vast army of the intelligentsia, commands a treasure of knowledge, possesses the skill to understand the nature of things and change them to serve the interest of the society, would stagnate for want of resources from the government. It is true that history is replete with the instances when universities of great fame in the past disintegrated, crumbled down and vanished for want of the government support. But the power of man lies in changing the history, redirecting its run and stopping it to repeat itself.

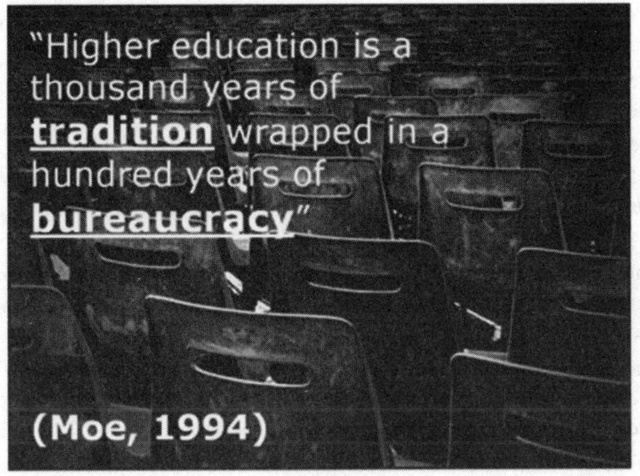

REFERENCES

Altekar, A.S. (1957), *Education in Ancient India* (5th edition), Varanasi: Nand Kishore and Bros.

Ambani, Mukesh and Kumarmangalam Birla (2000), *Report on a Policy Framework for Reforms in Education,* New Delhi: Government of India, Ministry of Education.

Aurobindo, S. (1971). *Social and Political Thought.* Pondicherry, Sri Aurobindo Ashram.

——. (1972*a*). *On Himself.* Pondicherry, Sri Auronbindo Ashram (Centenary Edition, Vol. 26).

——. (1972*b*). *The Synthesis of Yoga.* Pondicherry, Sri Aurobindo Ashram (Centenary Edition, Vol. 21).

——. (1990) reprint. *On Education.* Pondicherry, Aurobindo Ashram.

Butterfield, Herbert (1965). *The Universities and Education Today,* The Lindsay Memorial Lectures at the University College of North Staffordshire, London: Routledge & Kegan Paul Ltd. pp. 1-30.

Brumaugh, Robert S. (1982). *Whitehead, Process Philosophy, and Education.* Albany: State University of New York Press.

Chaudhury, H. (1972). "The Philosophy and Yoga of Sri Aurobindo". *Philosophy: East and West,* Vol. 22, pp. 5-14.

Das, M. (1977). *Sri Aurobindo.* New Delhi, Sahitya Akademi.

——. (1999). *Sri Aurobindo on Education.* New Delhi, National Council for Teacher Education.

Datta, B. (1993). *Swami Vivekananda, Patriot-Prophet—A Study.* Calcutta: Nababharat Publ.

Dunkel, Harold B. (1965). *Whitehead on Education.* Columbus: Ohio State University Press.

Gokak, V.K. (1973). *Sri Aurobindo : Seer and Poet.* New Delhi, Abhinav Publications.

Gambhirananda, Swami (1996). *Yuganayak Vivekananda* (Vivekananda, the leader of this era). 3 Vols. Calcutta: Udbodhan Karyalaya.

George, K.K. and Raman, R. (2003). "Changes in Indian Higher Education—An Insider's View". Support material for the book entitled *Transformation in Higher Education—Global Pressures and Local Realities in South Africa.* See at www.chet.org.za/papers/India.doc

Government of India, *National Knowledge Commission: Compilation of Recommendations on Education,* 2006, 07 and 08, New Delhi: Ministry of Education.

Government of India (2008), *Report of the Yashpal Committee on Higher Education: The Report on 'Renovation and Rejuvenation of Higher Education',* New Delhi: Ministry of Education.

Government of India, Ministry of Human Resource Development, Department of Education, *National Policy on Education (1986),* New Delhi.

Heehs, P. (1989). *Sri Aurobindo : A Brief Biography.* Delhi, Oxford University Press.

——. (1998). *The Essential Writings of Sri Aurobindo.* Delhi, Oxford University Press.

Hetherington, Hector Sir (1953), *The Social Function of the University.* The Essex Hall Lecture, London: The Lindsey Press, pp. 8-29.

Jawaharlal Nehru: Speeches (1949-1953), Delhi: Publication Division, Ministry of Information & Broadcasting Govt. of India, 1954, pp. 360, 365, 395-96, 428, 433.

Joshi, K. (1975). Education for Personality Development. (National Institute of Education Lecture Series delivered at National Council of Educational Research and Training, New Delhi, 22 and 24 February 1975.)

——. (1998*a*). Sri Aurobindo. (Lecture delivered at Indian Institute of Technology, New Delhi, 21 November 1998.)

——. (1998*b*). Philosophy and Yoga of Sri Aurobindo. (Lecture delivered at Rajendra Bhawan, Deen Dayal Upadhayaya Marg, New Delhi, 23 November 1998.)

——. (1998*c*). An Experiment in Eduction for Tomorrow (Lecture delivered at Indian Institute of Technology, New Delhi, 22 November 1998.)

——. (1972). "The Experiential Basis of Sri Aurobindo's Integral Yoga". *Philosophy: East and West,* Vol. 22, pp. 15-23.

Johnson, Allison H. (1958). *Whitehead's Philosophy of Civilization.* Boston: Beacon.

Kneller, George F. (1971). *Foundations of Education.* New York: John Wiley & Sons, Inc. p. 568.

Kumar, D. (1988), "Challenges of Rural Development and the Responsibilities of Universities". In *What can We Do for Our Countries? The Contribution of Universities to National Development,* ACU, London, pp. 457-65.

Levi, Albert W. (1937). "The Problem of Higher Education: Whitehead and Hutchins." *Harvard Educational Review* 7:451-465.

Lewis, W.A. (1959). *The Theory of Economic Growth*. Allen & Unwin, London.

Lord, Butler (1970), *Survival Depends on Higher Education*, Azad Memorial Lectures, New Delhi: Vikas Publications. Indian Council for Cultural Relations, pp. 9-42.

MHRD and NIC (2000). UNESCO Conference on Higher Education in India—Country Paper. Govt. of India (atshikshanic.nic.in/cd50years/).

Mishra, S.K. and Panda, N.M. (2000). "Unit Cost of Higher Education: A Case Study of North Eastern Hill University". *Journal of Educational Planning and Administration*, XIV (3).

Ministry of Education, Government of India (1949). *Report of the University Education Commission (1948-49)*, New Delhi: Chapter I.

Ministry of Education, Government of India (1953). *Report of the Secondary Education Commission (1952-53)*, New Delhi.

Ministry of Education, Government of India (1966). *Report of the Education Commission (1964-66)*, New Delhi: Chapters: XI, XII and XIII.

Myrdal, Gunnar (1972). *Asian Drama* (abridged by Seth S. King; originally published in 1968, three volumes). New York: Vintage Books.

North Eastern Council (2000). Basic Statistics of North Eastern Region 2000. Ministry of Home Affairs, Govt. of India, Shillong.

Noam, E.M. (1995). "Electronics and the Dim Future of the University". *Science*, Vol. 270, pp. 247-49.

Patil, V.T. (2002). *Studies in Higher Education.*/edited. Virat Publications, Pondicherry.

Powar, K.B. (1997). Higher Education in India Since Independence: Retrospect and Future Options, AIU *Occasional Paper* 97/1, AIU, New Delhi.

Powar, K.B. The Changing Role and Functions of Universities. *AIU Occasional Paper* 2000/2. New Delhi: Association of Indian Universities, pp. 4-6.

Powar, K.B. (Ed.) (2000). *Higher Education for Human Development* (Papers presented at the International Conference on Higher Education for Human Development, held at New Delhi on Feb 22-24, 2000), AIU: New Delhi.

Raina, M.K. (1979). "Education of the Left and the Right". *International Review of Education* (Hamburgh), Vol. 25, pp. 7-20.

——. (1997). 'Most dear to all the muses' : Mapping Tagorean networks of enterprise—A study in creative complexity. *Creativity Research Journal* (New Jersey, USA), Vol. 10, pp. 153-73.

Rolland, R. (1992). *The Life of Vivekananda and the Universal Gospel*, trans. from French by E.F. Malcolm-Smith. Calcutta: Advaita Ashrama.

Satprem (1984). *Sri Aurobindo or the Adventure of Consciousness*. New York, Institute for Evolutionary Research.

Sen, I. (1952). *Integral Education*. Pondicherry, Aurobindo International University Centre.

Sorokin, P.A. (1960). "The Integral Yoga of Sri Aurobindo". In Chaudhari, H. Spiegelberg, F., eds. *The Integral Philosophy of Sri Aurobindo*. London, Allen and Unwin.

Soni, Rashmi (2007). *Intellectuals' Expectations from a University: An Exploratory Study, Ph.D. Thesis, Department of Education, University of Lucknow, Lucknow.*

Tewari, D. (1998). Auroville: An Experiment in Eduction. (Lecture delivered at Indian Institute of Technology, New Delhi, 22 November 1998.)

The Report of the Robbins Committee on Higher Education (1963). Memorandum by the Chief Secretary to the Treasury and Paymaster General. In *Report of the National Committee of Inquiry into Higher Education,* Chapter 5.

UNESCO (1996). '*Learning: The Treasure Within*', Report of the International Commission on Education for the Twentyfirst Century (Delors Report), UNESCO, Paris.

UNESCO (1998). *Higher Education in the Twenty-first Century: Vision and Action*, UNESCO, Paris.

Vrekhem, G.V. (1999). *Beyond Man.* Delhi, Oxford University Press. Quotations bearing the reference *CW* in the text is taken from: *The Complete Works of Swami Vivekananda*. Volumes I–IX. Calcutta: Advaita Ashrama, 1989. (Mayavati Memorial Edition.)

Varma, M. and Soni, Rashmi (2005). *Transcripts of Open Conversations with Intellectuals Belonging to Different Fields—India and Abroad,* 06 and 07.

Varma, M., M.S. Sodha and R. Soni (2007). "Teachers' Expectations from Their University: A study in context of Lucknow University", NCERT: *Journal of Indian Education*, XXXIII, pp. 70-84.

Varma, M. and Soni, Rashmi (2005). "Higher Education beyond Academics", *University News*, New Delhi: AIU, Vol. 43 (44), pp. 8-14.

Whitehead, A.N. (1951). *The Aims of Education*, USA: The McMillan Company, pp 95-103.

World Bank (1994). *Higher Education: The Lessons of Experience*, The World Bank: Washington, D.C.

Structure and Organization of Higher Education in India

5

Higher education in India is primarily a public-funded activity. However, its structure and organization are complex and varied. There are different agencies and departments involved in its operation. The agencies are mainly the Ministries at the Federal and State levels, autonomous organizations set up by the Ministries and the private organizations or trusts. The Indian higher education system is both vast and complex. This complexity arises from the great variety in the university level institutions and from the multiplicity in nomenclature.

Structure of Higher Education

In the Indian system, higher education includes the education imparted after the 10+2 stage—ten years of primary and secondary education followed by two years of higher secondary education. The first degree, the Bachelor's degrees, is obtained after three years study in the case of liberal arts, and four years in the case of most professional degrees (four and half in case of medicine and five/six years in case of law). The Master's program is usually of two years duration. It could be course work based without thesis or rarely research alone. Admission to postgraduate programmes in engineering and technology is made on the basis of Graduate Aptitude Test in Engineering or Combined Medical Test, respectively.

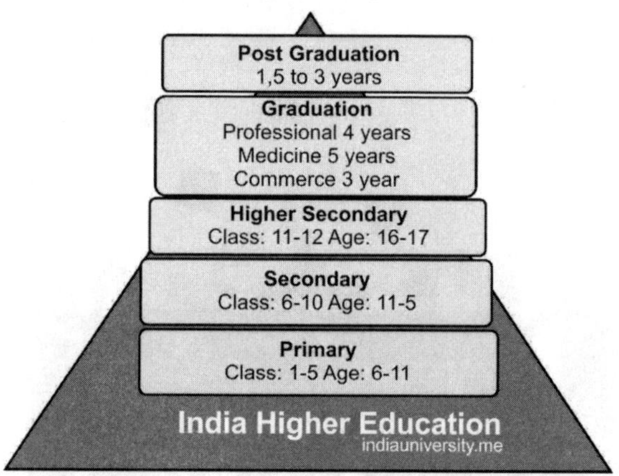

The research degrees (M.Phil. and Ph.D.) take variable time depending upon the individual student. Ph.D. maybe awarded two years after the M.Phil. or three years after the Master's degree, which generally takes longer. There are also postgraduate diploma programmes open to graduates, and certain professional programmes like those in education and law require a first degree as a pre-condition for admission in most places.

The postgraduate degree programs involve two years of study after first degree. These include M.Tech, MD, MS and MDS programs, which take two years after B.Tech and MBBS/ BDS respectively. M.Phil. program is of one and half year duration. It is a preparatory program for doctoral level studies. Ph.D. program is research study for two years and can take several years while D.Sc. and D.Litt. are awarded by some universities after Ph.D. in three years or seven years after Master's degree.

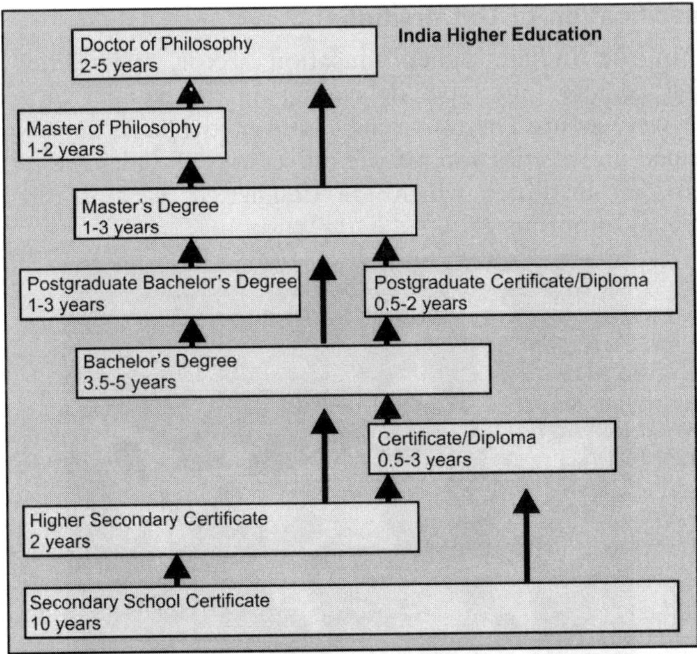

In addition to the degree programs, a number of diploma and certificate programs are also available in universities. Their range is wide and they cover anything from poetics to computers. Some of them are undergraduate diploma programs and others are postgraduate programs. The duration varies from one to three years.

Universities, deemed universities and institutions of national importance are largely autonomous institutions empowered by law to design, develop and offer programs which they consider relevant and appropriate for the national needs. Colleges and other institutes, in turn, are expected to be regulated by the universities with which they are affiliated or associated. Given the wide reach and variety of institutions and programs of higher education, a number of professional, regulatory bodies and councils have been established to ensure proper development of higher education in the country in a coordinated manner.

Classification of Universities

In the Indian higher education sector, universities are classified into four types depending on the manner in which they were set up. These are central universities, state universities, deemed universities and private universities. Besides these four, there are institutes which are designated as "institutes of national importance".

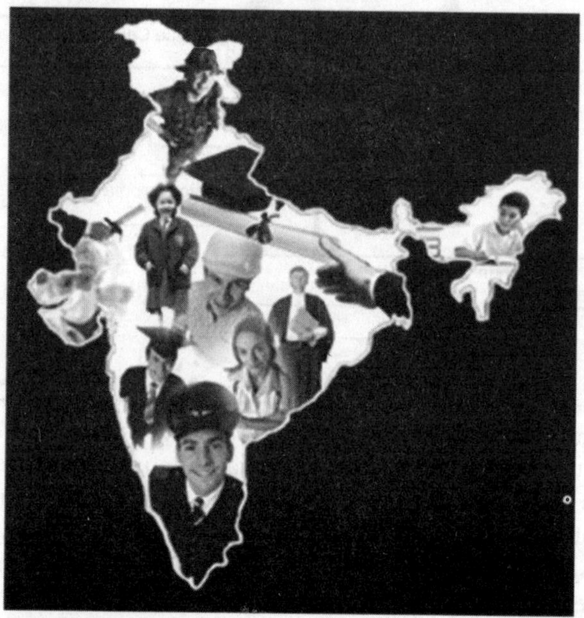

The universities in India are of various kinds: with a single faculty or many faculties; teaching, unitary or affiliating, or teaching-cum-affiliating; single-campus or multi-campus; agricultural universities; medical universities; technological universities; language universities (Hindi, Sanskrit, Tamil, Telugu, and Urdu); and women's universities. Besides these there are specialized institutions in medicine, science, engineering and technology, management and social sciences.

In the case of unitary universities (e.g. BHU), the teaching and research is conducted in a single campus and there is a provision for both undergraduate and postgraduate teachings, as well as for research. Affiliating universities are those that have central campus on which there are departments or schools that impart postgraduate instruction and conduct research in a variety of disciplines. They prescribe the courses of study for the affiliated colleges and conduct examinations and award degrees. The colleges mostly engage in undergraduate teaching, though some of them may be permitted to conduct post-graduate classes in selected subjects. Most Indian universities are of the affiliating types with the larger ones like Kolkata, Mumbai, Osmania and Bangalore having more than 300 affiliated colleges.

The institutions of higher learning can be classified into the following categories:

1. Universities which are established by an Act of Parliament or State Legislature and are of unitary or affiliating type;
2. Institutions of national importance—such as the Indian Institutes of Technology—that are established under Acts of Parliament and are empowered to award degrees.
3. Institutions deemed to be universities, which are given university status under a provision in the UGC Act. Some of these institutions offer advance level courses in a particular field of specialization, while many of them award general degrees.
4. Institutions, which award only diplomas and are neither established by legislation nor declared as deemed to be universities. The Indian Institutes of Management are in this category.

Thus, the university level institutions in the Indian higher education system are basically of three types—the conventional universities, usually referred to simply as universities; the deemed-to-be universities, or deemed universities; and the institutions of national importance. An idea of different types of universities in India can be obtained from the following table:

Present System of Universities in India—Important Features

University Type	*Established By*	*Important Features*
Conventional	Central/State Governments	(i) Unitary: Teaching (UG/PG) and research on campus (main/sub); Many faculties; (ii) Affiliating: Teaching (PG) and research on campus (main/sub); Many faculties; Affiliated colleges(UG mostly) and some Autonomous colleges(UG/PG) in its jurisdiction; *Nearly 50% of Universities in India belong to this category.*
Professional	State Governments	Specialized instruction(UG/PG) and research on campus(main/sub); Single faculty; Professional areas like engineering, medicine, law covered; Both unitary and affiliating types functioning now; Many States have established Universities in this category.
Agricultural	State Governments	Agricultural studies (UG/PG), including forestry, horticulture, veterinary science, research and extension; Many faculties; Mostly unitary; Most States have established these Universities.
Deemed	Central Government	University level institutions engaged in PG teaching and research, with close interactions between both functions, for mutual benefit;
	Private/Joint Sector (UGC Approved)	*Very few institutions in this category, IISc being an example.* University status to institutions of long standing (or even de novo) and high academic reputation; UG/PG teaching and research; Single/ Multiple faculties; *Many institutions already, numbers increasing.*
Open	Central/ State Governments	Open and flexible education offered through the distance mode using correspondence courses/modern educational technology like interactive TV; Wide variety of programmes-UG/PG/Research; *Many Universities functioning; their number steadily increasing.*
Other	Central Government	(i) Unitary; Teaching/Research in close contact between students/teachers - classroom lectures, tutorials, seminars etc;
	Private/ Joint Sector	*Very few Universities of this type; JNU an example.* (ii) Elitist: Institutions offering professional (UG/PG) teaching /research on the campus, to talented and carefully selected students; *IITs/NITs/IIMs/ Law Institutes fall in this category.* (iii) Private (under State Act); Teaching (UG/PG)/Research; Unitary/Affiliating; Single/ Many faculties; With/Without UGC approval; *Already in few States, numbers increasing.* (iv) Virtual: Institutions using multimedia providing intra/ internet, based *any-time, any-where, any-discipline learning in professional subjects; Already in some States, expanding.* (v) Foreign: Universities singly or jointly with local partners, offering UG/PG Teaching/ Research programmes in the country; *Rapidly upcoming type.*

Models of Universities

A number of models have been recognized in the European and North American scene. Indian universities vary considerably in terms of traditions, objectives, organizational structures, disciplines—taught and source of funding (Powar, 2002). Models that are represented in India include:

1. *The Humboldtian research university model* in which there is emphasis on postgraduate teaching and research, and on close interaction between the two functions for their mutual enrichment. Typical examples are the Berlin University in Germany and amongst others, Stanford and John Hopkins in the United States. In India university-level institutions that approach this model include the Indian Institute of Science, Bangalore and the Central University, Hyderabad.
2. *The British residential university model or the Oxbridge model* that stresses close formal and informal contact between teachers and students, through classroom lectures, tutorials, seminars and other forms of personal contacts. The British examples are Oxford and Cambridge Universities. In India, these ideals are being sought to be met in the single campus universities like Jawaharlal Nehru University, New Delhi and the Banaras Hindu University, Varanasi.
3. *The French grandes ecoles model* imparting elitist professional education, mainly in science and technology, to the most talented, and intellectually select, students. The Indian counterparts are the Indian Institutes of Technology, and the Indian Institutes of Management.
4. *The Chicago liberal education model,* launched by Hutchins at the University of Chicago, which has a strong liberal arts orientation that places emphasis on the development of independent and critical thinking. A few Indian institutions like Viswa Bharati University replicate this model.
5. *The affiliating university model*, based on the University of London of the nineteenth century, wherein there is a

central campus for postgraduate studies and research with a number of affiliated colleges spread over the university area. In spite of an overt central control the standard of education imparted by the colleges varies considerably. There are about 120 universities in India that are based on this model.

6. *The agriculture university model,* developed on the lines of the land grant colleges of the United States, that concentrate on agricultural studies, including forestry, horticulture and veterinary sciences. The utilitarian approach is exemplified by a strong emphasis on extension services. There are presently 35 agricultural universities in India based on this model.
7. *The professional university model*, that provides for higher education in one of the professional areas like engineering, and medicine and health services. This is a new trend that seeks to separate education in the professional subjects from the mainstream of higher education. Examples are the universities for science and technology, for law, and for medicine and health services, established in some states of India. These may also be set up to regulate a number of colleges offering professional degrees.
8. *The 'deemed university' model,* by which institutions noted for their noteworthy contributions in specialized subjects or disciplines are granted the status of universities. As of today there are 32 such institutions in India. Examples are the Deccan College Postgraduate and Research Institute, Pune, the Birla Institute of Technology and Science, and the Manipal Academy of Higher Education, Manipal.
9. *The open university model,* that provides education through the distance mode, to those denied access otherwise; it promotes the concept of lifelong education for all. U.K. Open University, Milton Keynes and the Indira Gandhi National Open University, New Delhi, are some typical examples.

In what follows the above models on which different types of universities exist in India have been discussed.

What is a Central University?

Central universities are set up by an Act of Parliament. At present, there are 40 central universities of which, 38 are being given maintenance and development grants by University Grants Commission (UGC). The UGC is the agency that provides funding for maintenance and development of these universities. President of India is a visitor at all central universities. Indira Gandhi National Open University (IGNOU) and the Central Agricultural University, Imphal are not being funded by UGC directly; these are assisted by the Ministry of Human Resource Development and the Ministry of Agriculture, respectively. The University of Delhi, Allahabad University, Jawaharlal Nehru University (JNU), Aligarh Muslim University (AMU) are among the central universities. During 2009-10 (upto 31.12.2009), an amount of ₹ 1764.37 crore under Non-Plan assistance and grants of ₹ 712.62 crore including ₹ 206.18 crore for central universities in North East Region, under Plan assistance have been made available to the central universities.

Improving the quality and access to higher education and research in India has become all the more important keeping in view the growing need of qualified human resource in various sectors of the economy. Therefore, it can only be hoped that there would be more central universities in India in the immediate future. The Central Government has also been empowered by a special Act of the Constitution to maintain a particular standard conducive to the educational health of the country. The Central Government lays special emphasis on research and development carried out in technical as well as other institutions. Recently, new central universities have been established or are in the process of being established.

What is a State University?

Universities set up or recognized by an act of the State Legislature are known as state universities. Three of the country's oldest institutions of higher learning, University of Calcutta, University of Madras, and University of Mumbai are state universities. State Governments are responsible for establishment of state universities and provide Plan grants for their development and non-Plan grants for their maintenance. The UGC makes budgetary plan allocation for 113 state universities. As per Section 12B of the UGC Act, state universities established after June 17, 1972 will not be eligible to receive any grant from the Central Government, UGC, or any organization receiving funds from the Government of India, unless the UGC makes an exception.

At present, there are 296 state universities of which, the UGC has provided budgetary support to 130 state universities, excluding medical and agricultural universities which are funded by the Ministries of Health and Agriculture, respectively. Special grants are being provided to other state universities with Departments of Engineering and Technology. Such grants facilitate the creation, augmentation and upgradation of infrastructural facilities that are not normally available from the State Government or other sources of funds. During 2009-10 (up to 31.12.2009), Plan grants amounting to ₹ 279.46 crore has been provided to state universities for their general development as well as for specific programmes.

The University of Madras

University of Mumbai

What is an Open University?

The open universities in India are regulated by the Distance Education Council of India (DEC). It is an organization based in New Delhi, which maintains the standards, encourages and organizes the activities of open and distance learning in India (ODL). The council encourages the State Governments and conventional universities to set up open universities and distance education centers. It also arrange for funds to run these universities. The assessment and accreditation of these universities is also processed by the DEC. There are 14 open universities in

India at present. These have educational centers in various states of India. Facilitating and promoting distance education is the ultimate goal of the DEC. Some famous open universities are Indira Gandhi National Open University, Dr. B.R. Ambedkar Open University, Karnataka State Open University, Nalanda Open University and Kota Open University.

What is a Deemed University?

Institutions of higher learning, which are not universities, recognized for the high caliber of education are granted the status of a university. Such institutions are known as deemed to be university, or deemed university. Institutions deemed to be universities enjoy the academic status and privileges of universities. The status of a deemed university is accorded by the UGC. Section 3 of the UGC Act, provides for the conferring of this status of autonomy granted to high performing institutes. Deemed university status enables not just full autonomy in setting course work and syllabus of those institutes and research centers but also allows it to set its own guidelines for the admissions, fees and instructions for the students. As in other universities students are conferred degrees on completion of their programme. Thus, the deemed universities in India get the opportunities to develop their own unique course structure to prepare the students to enter diverse fields after the completion of their study. Those deemed universities, which, continue to perform well eventually, get the status of a full-fledged university.

At present, there are 130 institutions which are deemed to be universities, of which, 10 institutions are being allocated both maintenance and development grants and 23 institutions are being allocated only development grants. During 2009-10 (upto 31.12.2009), non-Plan grant amounting to ₹ 120.01 crore and Plan assistance of ₹ 30.01 crore (including ₹ 1.82 crore for institutions located in North East Region) has been provided to institutions deemed universities. The formal declaration of the status of a deemed university is made on the recommendation of University Grants Commission (UGC) of India.

National Institutes of Technology (formerly known as Regional Engineering Colleges), Manipal Academy of Higher

Education, Symbiosis International Education Centre, Pune comprising Symbiosis Institute of Computer Studies and Research, Symbiosis Institute of Business Management, Symbiosis Society's Law College, Narsee Monjee Institute of Management Studies, Indian Institute of Information Technology and Management, Indian Institute of Science, Bangalore are some of the deemed universities.

Deemed universities obtain many concessions from the University Grants Commission and the government. Such institutions can now use the term "university" in their title and initiate teaching programs at both the undergraduate and the postgraduate levels in disciplines of their choice. This brings them at par with public universities.

What is an Agricultural University?

As agriculture plays a very important role in the Indian economy, setting up of adequate number of agricultural universities was considered very important in India. While the Royal Commission, set up in 1926, emphasized the importance of a strong research base for agricultural development in India, the second National Education Commission (1964-66) headed by the then University Grants Commission Chairman Dr. D.S. Kothari recommended the establishment of at least one agricultural university in each of the Indian state. The importance of agricultural universities has increased tremendously in the recent years as the growth of the agricultural sector has seen a sharp decline for over a decade now. It has not been able to keep pace with the other sectors of the Indian economy although nearly 60% of the workforce is engaged with agriculture in India.

The contribution of agriculture to the Gross Domestic Product (GDP) of the country's economy has been below 25% in the recent years. At such a juncture, people involved with agricultural universities and other research organizations will have to come up with some innovative ideas to deal with the challenges that the sector is currently facing. There are at present 45 agricultural universities in India. Out of these, five are deemed universities and two are Central Agricultural

Universities. All these universities are members of the Indian Agricultural Universities Association (IAUA). It was established primarily to promote agricultural research and education in the country. IAUA holds annual convention and also brings out a journal in order to exchange and promote ideas.

What is a Private University?

A private university is an institution of higher learning established through a State or Central Act by a sponsoring body, such as a society registered under the Societies Registration Act, 1860, or any other corresponding law for the time being in force in a state or a public trust or a company registered under Section 25 of the Companies Act, 1956. Setting up of private universities through State Acts is a recent phenomenon. For an institution to be given the status of a private university, the State Legislature conferring the status has to pass an act by which the institution will receive the status of a university. Private universities have to be recognized by the UGC so that the degrees awarded by them have to be of any value. The Birla Institute of Technology and Science at Pilani in Rajasthan, which is funded and run by the Birla Group Trust, became an officially recognized university in 1964.

For private universities, a suitable regulatory mechanism is essential by way of laying down the conditions specifically for the establishment and operation of such universities for safeguarding the interests of the student community with adequate emphasis on the quality of education and to avoid commercialization of higher education, etc.

Over the past 20 years, the higher education capacity in the country has increased largely through private institutions. Currently, 43 per cent of institutions and 30 per cent of enrollments are in the private sector. Until recently, these private institutions consisted mostly of colleges. These private colleges are subject to government control through the public universities with which they are affiliated. They lack the autonomy to offer new programs, innovate curricula and evaluation, or change policies in matters of admissions and fees. Many people believe that the affiliating structure is a bane on

Indian higher education. However, the affiliating system did ensure rapid expansion, while maintaining the sanctity of admissions and fees. Wherever academic supervision was effective, it also ensured that minimum standards were maintained.

By the mid-1990s, promoters of private colleges saw the regulatory control of the affiliating university and State Governments as cumbersome, impending the full utilization of the colleges' market potential. Thus, they wanted university status to wriggle out of control of State Governments and the affiliating universities. This resulted in the proliferation of private universities and private deemed universities. In 1995, the Private Universities (Establishment and Regulation) Bill was introduced in the Parliament. While a central legislation for private universities is still pending for want of a consensus, several State Governments have established private universities through state legislation. The UGC list of private universities from 10 February 2012 lists 106 private universities.

Private Deemed Universities

The Human Resource Development Ministry under, Mr. Kapil Sibal, in a virtual rebuff to his predecessor, Mr. Arjun Singh's policy of conferring "deemed university" status to 126 institutions, submitted in the Supreme Court that only 36 institutions were fully qualified to be upgraded. A big step was taken after clearance from the Prime Minister Manmohan Singh and UPA Chairperson Sonia Gandhi and is also an indictment of the manner in which the "deemed" status was doled out during the tenure of the last HRD Minister, Arjun Singh. Although the list includes many that were given deemed status during Murli Manohar Joshi's time, the list of those red-penciled indicates how during Arjun Singh's tenure, the "deemed" status was virtually up for grabs.

The HRD Ministry emphasized that the affected students would be taken care of. The Ministry's task force has recomended that institutions not found fit for deemed university status "revert to status quo ante as an affiliated college of the State university of jurisdiction so that students would be able to complete their ongoing courses and obtain degree from the affiliating university." Similarly, medical and dental colleges not found suitable can affiliate to state university or state medical university.

In case, the institution is unable to obtain affiliation, efforts would be made to facilitate the migration/re-enrolment of the affected students in other institutions. Doctoral students will have to re-register in affiliating universities and those in distance education should either go to IGNOU or state open universities. While these safeguards have been recommended, the students are nonetheless likely to go through a phase of uncertainty as they move from one university to another.

In an affidavit filed in the Supreme Court in the *Viplav Sharma* v. *Union of India* case, the HRD Ministry said the review committee found only 38 institutes fit to have the deemed university status. Another 44 were found "deficient" in some aspects which need to be rectified over the next three years. With Supreme Court likely to approve HRD's action, it is unlikely that government will have to face any litigation.

These 44 deemed universities have 1,19,363 students at the undergraduate and postgraduate levels. In addition, there are 2,124 students pursuing research at MPhil and PhD levels and another estimated 74,808 students pursuing distance education programmes. As many as 41 of the 44 deemed universities have several constituent institutions under them, which would further swell the number of affected students.

Tamil Nadu has the distinction of having 16 of the 44 derecognized deemed universities, 15 of them private and one government-sponsored. Among those found undeserving of deemed status in Tamil Nadu is Bharath Institute of Higher Education & Research—with six constituent institutions—run by S. Jagatharakshakan, MoS Information and Broadcasting. Karnataka has six derecognized deemed universities; Uttar Pradesh four; Haryana, Uttarakhand, Rajasthan and Maharashtra three each; Gujarat, Orissa, Andhra Pradesh, Delhi, Bihar, one each. The three government-run institutions to be de-recognized are Nava Nalanda Mahavira in Bihar, Rajiv Gandhi National Institute of Youth Development, Tamil Nadu, and National Museum Institute of the History of Art, Conservation and Museology, New Delhi.

Autonomous Colleges

The total number of universities in India is 563. There are universities of some kind in each and every of the 28 states of India as well as three of the union territories, Chandigarh, Delhi and Puducherry. The state with the most universities is Tamil Nadu with 55 universities. It is also the state with the most deemed universities, numbering 29. Andhra Pradesh has the most state universities (32), Rajasthan the most private universities (24), while Delhi has six central universities, the largest number of all the States and Union Territories.

Apart from the above universities, other institutions are granted the permission to autonomously award degrees. However, they do not affiliate colleges and are not officially called “universities” but “autonomous organizations” or “autonomous institutes”. They fall under the administrative control of the Department of Higher Education. These organizations include the Indian Institutes of Technology, the National Institutes of Technology, the Indian Institutes of Science Education and Research, the Indian Institutes of Management (though these award diplomas, not degrees) and other autonomous institutes.

The affiliating system of colleges was originally designed when their number in a university was small. The university could then effectively oversee the working of the colleges, act as an examining body and award degrees on their behalf. The system has now become unwieldy and it is becoming increasingly difficult for a university to attend to the varied needs of individual colleges. The colleges do not have the freedom to modernize their curricula or make them locally relevant. The regulations of the university and its common system, governing all colleges alike, irrespective of their characteristic strengths, weaknesses and locations, have affected the academic development of individual colleges.

In 1964-66, the Education Commission pointed out that the exercise of academic freedom by teachers is a crucial requirement for development of the intellectual climate of our country. Unless such a climate prevails, it is difficult to achieve excellence in the higher education system. With students, teachers and management being co-partners in raising the quality of higher education, it is imperative that they share major responsibility. Hence, the Education Commission recommended college autonomy, which in essence is the instrument for promoting academic excellence.

The concept of autonomous colleges was crystallized with a view to providing academic freedom for the colleges, especially in designing their curricula, evolving new methods of teaching, research and learning, framing own rules for admission, prescribing own courses of study and conduct of examination. The intention was to provide greater opportunities to the teachers to play a crucial role in the promotion and development of an intellectual climate, which is conducive to the pursuit of scholarship and excellence.

The UGC constitutes review committees in order to assess the quality of the university programmes. Instruction for almost 80% of the enrolment in first-degree programmes is imparted in colleges. Since the universities concerned prescribe the courses, set the standards and conduct the examinations, the large body of college teachers are left with very little option in deciding what to teach and how. The UGC has, therefore, evolved a scheme to confer autonomous status on selected colleges, which would enable them to prescribe the courses, determine the content and decide the teaching-learning processes. The colleges would continue to remain affiliated to the universities whose major functions would be to approve the courses, hold the examinations and award the degrees. The experiment has led to the review and renewal of the curricular content of the programmes offered by the autonomous colleges and imparting the programmes, some measure of relevance.

Acts of most of the older universities do not provide for the grant of autonomy to their colleges. Some universities have a provision to restrict the scope of implementing the autonomy within the framework of the conditions laid down by the University, e.g. the U.P. State Universities Act, 1973 states that the extent to which the courses may be varied and the manner of holding the examination conducted by such (Autonomous) College shall be determined in each case by the University; such a college shall be declared in the manner prescribed, as an Autonomous College. Perusal of the Acts of several Universities revealed the complete absence of provision for granting autonomy to its departments.

Talking of the present scenario, the overall situation is not very encouraging as there are only 328 autonomous colleges in 17 states of the country. There is a wide difference in number of autonomous colleges in different states. Such as Tamil Nadu leads the tally with 120 such colleges poorly followed by Andhra Pradesh (49), Karnataka (46), Bihar, Uttrakhand, Nagaland (01). It is interesting to note that Nagaland which is supposed to be an educationally backward state enjoys the distinction of having the only autonomous college in the entire north-eastern region. Alphonse sourced this information from the UGC list of autonomous colleges in October 2009.

The same kind of wide differences appear also in one more aspect. Another source points out that Tamil Nadu and Andhra Pradesh have 11 and 7 universities, respectively empowered to confer autonomous degree status to colleges whereas the rest of the 15 states have just about six and less number of universities with such a power. So the result is also reflective of the same. Tamil Nadu leads the list with 119 autonomous colleges out of a total of 280 colleges in the state with 11 universities allowed to confer such a status.

On the other hand, the original UGC plan for converting at least 10% of the total colleges of the country into autonomous ones remains a pipe dream till date as there seems to be hardly any taker for the scheme. This is because the number 328 is slightly more than one per cent of the total of around 26,000 undergraduate colleges in the country. The lacunae seems to be that either the scheme itself is flawed or not being implemented properly.

A lack of understanding of the concept of autonomy at various levels, including universities, state and regulatory bodies, remains the biggest hurdle in efforts to promote autonomy among colleges. According to PES Chairman Gajanan Ekbote, "Concerns among college employees about a change in their service conditions in case their institution goes autonomous, are misplaced. The State Government's circular of February 14, 2005, issued at the behest of the Governor, is quite clear that there will be no reduction in the salary grants to autonomous institutions."

Pandit Vidyasagar, director of the University of Pune's Board of College and University Development, called for a change in the mindset at all levels to understand and encourage autonomy. He said apprehensions about college managements losing control over the institution or teachers losing their jobs were misplaced, considering the good experience of those colleges which preferred autonomy.

"Flexibility in approach is the biggest advantage of autonomy," he said and added, "the institutions ought to be disciplined and totally non-complacent in responding to the changes in order to survive as an autonomous establishment." Sharing his experience as head of an autonomous college, IndSearch director Ashok Joshi said, "There aren't many problems as far as internal operations of an autonomous institution are concerned, but there are problems with external relationships vis-à-vis universities, state and regulatory bodies that continue to treat autonomous colleges as affiliated colleges and try to impose their will."

"There is no clarity and no proper modus operandi in the universities for implementation of the autonomy scheme. Few people understand the concept," said Joshi. This makes an independent call for autonomy essential, he added.

TECHNICAL EDUCATION

Technical education plays a vital role in human resource development of the country by creating skilled manpower, enhancing industrial productivity and improving the quality of life. Technical education covers courses and programmes in engineering, technology, management, architecture, town planning, pharmacy and applied arts and crafts, hotel management and catering technology. The development of science and technology has greatly influenced the modern age; the effects are perceptible all around. During the past five decades, there has been a phenomenal expansion of technical educational facilities in the country. The technical education system in the country covers engineering, technology, management, architecture, pharmacy, etc. The Ministry of Human Resource Development caters to programmes at undergraduate, graduate, postgraduate and research levels.

The credit of first starting degree classes in mechanical and electrical engineering and in metallurgy belongs to the Banaras Hindu University, thanks to the foresight of its great founder, Pt. Madan Mohan Malaviya (1917). About fifteen years later, in 1931-32, Bengal Engineering College at Sibpur started mechanical engineering courses; electrical engineering courses in 1935-36, and courses in metallurgy in 1939-40. Courses in these subjects were also introduced at Puna about the same time. Quite a number of engineering colleges have been started since August 15, 1947. It is due to the realization that India has to become a great industrial country, and would require a far larger number of engineers than could be supplied by the older institutions. In some cases, existing lower type institutions have been raised to the status of degree-giving colleges.

The technical education system at the central level comprises the following:

A. Indian Institutes of Technology (IITs)

The Indian Institutes of Technology (IITs) are a group of autonomous engineering and technology-oriented institutes of higher education. The IITs are governed by the Institutes of Technology Act, 1961 which has declared them as "institutions of national importance", and lays down their powers, duties, framework for governance, etc. They were created to train scientists and engineers, with the aim of developing a skilled workforce to support the economic and social development of India. IITs are listed as societies under the Indian Societies Registration Act.

The 1961 Act lists seven institutes, which are, in order of establishment, IIT Kharagpur in Kharagpur (1950; as IIT

1951), IIT Bombay in Mumbai (1958), IIT Madras in Chennai (1959), IIT Kanpur in Kanpur (1959), IIT Delhi in New Delhi (1961; as IIT 1963), IIT Guwahati in Guwahati (1994) and IIT Roorkee in Roorkee (1847; as IIT 2001).

Indian Institute of Technology (IIT) Delhi

Main Building, Indian Institute of Technology, Roorkee

In addition to the seven IITs, the Institutes of Technology (Amendment) Act, 2010 seeks to add nine new institutes to the list. Of these, eight are new institutes, in order of establishment, IIT Ropar in Rupnagar (2008), IIT Bhubaneswar in Bhubaneswar (2008), IIT Gandhinagar in Gandhinagar (2008), IIT Hyderabad in Hyderabad (2008), IIT Patna in Patna (2008), IIT Rajasthan in Rajasthan (2008), IIT Mandi in Mandi (2009) and IIT Indore in Indore (2009). These IITs are registered as societies and are in various stages of consolidation and development. The ninth is Institute of Technology, Banaras Hindu University (IT-BHU), which is currently a faculty under the administration of Banaras Hindu University, Varanasi, which is to be named "Indian Institute of Technology (Banaras Hindu University), Varanasi", which is to be abbreviated as IIT-BHU. The Bill was approved by the Indian Cabinet in February 25, 2011, and the Lok Sabha passed the Bill on March 24, 2011. It is still to be adopted by the Rajya Sabha.

Indian Institute of Technology (IIT-Kanpur)

Each IIT is an autonomous university, linked to the others through a common IIT Council, which oversees their administration. They have a common admission process for undergraduate admissions, using the very selective Indian Institute of Technology Joint Entrance Examination (IIT-JEE), which in 2011 had an acceptance rate of less than 1 in 50 (485,000 candidates and only 9,618 seats). Undergraduate students receive a B.Tech. degree in Engineering. The graduate level program that awards M.Tech. degree in engineering is administered by the older IITs (Kharagpur, Bombay, Madras, Kanpur, Delhi, Guwahati, Roorkee) and the Indian Institute of Science, Bangalore. M.Tech. admissions are done on the basis of the Graduate Aptitude Test in Engineering (GATE). In addition to B.Tech and M.Tech programs IITs also award other graduate degrees such as M.S. in engineering, M.Sc in Math, Physics and Chemistry, MBA and more. Admission to these is through Common Admission Test (CAT), Joint Admission Test to M.Sc. (JAM) and Common Entrance Examination for Design (CEED). About 15,500 undergraduate and 12,000 graduate students study in the IITs, in addition to research scholars.

The IITs offer a number of postgraduate programs including Master of Technology (M.Tech.), Master of Business Administration (MBA) (only for engineers and postgraduates in science), and Master of Science (M.Sc.). Some IITs offer specialized graduate programmes such as the Postgraduate Diploma in Information Technology (PGDIT), Master in Medical Science and Technology (MMST), Master of City Planning (MCP), Master of Arts (MA), Postgraduate Diploma in Intellectual Property Law (PGDIPL), Master of Design (M.Des.), and the Postgraduate Diploma in Maritime Operation and Management (PGDMOM).

The IITs also offer the Doctor of Philosophy degree (Ph.D.) as part of their doctoral education programme. In it, the candidates are given a topic of academic interest by the professor or have to work on a consultancy project given by the industries. The duration of the program is usually unspecified and depends on the specific discipline. Ph.D. candidates have to submit a dissertation as well as provide an oral defence for their thesis. Teaching Assistantships (TA) and Research Assistantships (RA) are often provided. Some of the IITs offer an M.S. (by research) program; the M.Tech. and M.S. is similar to the US universities' non-thesis (course based) and thesis (research based) masters programs, respectively. The IITs, along with NITs and IISc, account for nearly 80% of all Ph.Ds. in engineering.

The IITs also offer an unconventional B.Tech. and M.Tech. integrated educational program called "Dual Degree". It integrates undergraduate and postgraduate studies in selected areas of specialisation. It is completed in five years as against six years in conventional B.Tech. (four years) followed by an M.Tech. (two years). Integrated Master of Science programs are also offered at few IITs which integrates the undergraduate and postgraduate studies in science streams in a single degree program against the conventional university system. This programme was started to allow IITians to complete postgraduate studies from IIT rather than having to go to another institute. All IITs (except IIT Guwahati) have schools of management offering degrees in management or business administration.

IIT alumni have achieved success in a variety of professions. Most of the IITs were created in early 1950s and 1960s as the Institutes of National Importance through special acts of Indian Parliament. The success of the IITs led to the creation of the Indian Institutes of Information Technology (IIIT) in the late 1990s and in the 2000s.

IITs In India

Name	*Short Name*	*Established*	*City/Town*	*State/UT*
Current IITs:				
IIT Kharagpur	IITKGP	1951	Kharagpur	West Bengal
IIT Bombay	IITB	1958	Mumbai	Maharashtra
IIT Madras	IITM	1959	Chennai	Tamil Nadu
IIT Kanpur	IITK	1959	Kanpur	Uttar Pradesh
IIT Delhi	IITD	1961 (1963‡)	New Delhi	New Delhi
IIT Guwahati	IITG	1994	Guwahati	Assam
IIT Roorkee	IITR	1847 (2001‡)	Roorkee	Uttrakhand
New IITs:				
IIT Ropar	IITRPR	2008	Rupnagar	Punjab
IIT Bhubaneswar	IITBBS	2008	Bhubaneswar	Orissa
IIT Hyderabad	IITH	2008	Hyderabad	Andhra Pradesh
IIT Gandhinagar	IITGN	2008	Gandhinagar	Gujarat
IIT Patna	IITP	2008	Patna	Bihar
IIT Rajasthan	IITJ	2008	Jodhpur	Rajasthan
IIT Mandi	IIT Mandi	2009	Mandi	Himachal Pradesh
IIT Indore	IITI	2009	Indore	Madhya Pradesh
IIT (BHU) Varanasi	IITBHU	1916 (2012‡)	Varanasi	Uttar Pradesh

‡ - Year converted/planned to convert to IIT

B. Indian Institutes of Management (IIMs)

The Indian Institutes of Management (IIMs) are a group of autonomous management institutes of higher education in India. The establishment of IIMs was envisioned and initiated by the first Prime Minister of India Jawaharlal Nehru. They were set up with the objective of providing management education and to assist the industry through research and consulting services. The IIMs offer postgraduate diploma programmes, fellowship programmes in management and other short-term courses.

The IIM Council oversees the administration of these autonomous institutes. The IIM Council consists of Directors of all IIMs, bureaucrats of Ministry of Human Resource Development and is headed by the Union Minister of Human Resource Development.

Indian Institutes of Management

Indian Institute of Management Calcutta	IIM-C	1961	Kolkata	West Bengal
Indian Institute of Management Ahmedabad	IIM-A	1961	Ahmedabad	Gujarat
Indian Institute of Management Bangalore	IIMB	1973	Bengaluru	Karnataka
Indian Institute of Management Lucknow	IIML	1984	Lucknow	Uttar Pradesh
Indian Institute of Management Kozhikode	IIMK	1996	Kozhikode	Kerala
Indian Institute of Management Indore	IIMI	1996	Indore	Madhya Pradesh
Indian Institute of Management Shillong	IIMS	2007	Shillong	Meghalaya
Indian Institute of Management Rohtak	IIM-R	2010	Rohtak	Haryana
Indian Institute of Management Ranchi	IIM-R	2010	Ranchi	Jharkhand
Indian Institute of Management Raipur	IIM-Rp	2010	Raipur	Chhattisgarh
Indian Institute of Management Tiruchirappalli	IIMT	2011	Trichy	Tamil Nadu
Indian Institute of Management Udaipur	IIMU	2011	Udaipur	Rajasthan
Indian Institute of Management Kashipur	IIM-Kpv	2011	Kashipur	Uttarakhand

Indian Institute of Management, Bangalore

The growth of management education in India has been phenomenal, with new management schools opening almost every month in some part of the country. However, students find it difficult to choose the right school, except when it comes to the premier institutes. Within the university system, the faculty of management studies of the University of Delhi was the first to launch a full-time MBA programme in 1967, which was followed by several other universities in India. A good number of universities also started offering part-time and correspondence courses in management. The Indira Gandhi National Open University today offers a wide range of courses in management.

Indian Institute of Management, Calcutta

While in the early 1990s there was only a handful of management schools in the country, a Supreme Court judgment in 1993 led to a surge in the number of management schools. In Kerala, only a few institutions such as the School of Management Studies, Cochin University of Science and Technology (CUSAT); Department of Commerce and Management Studies, Calicut University, and the Institute of Management in Kerala, University of Kerala, were offering MBA programmes in the early 1990s. However, there are many new institutions now offering MBA degree programmes.

One cannot compare the performance of a university department with that of a private school as there will be big differences in factors such as faculty strength and infrastructure.

University departments tend to have better quality faculty but poorer infrastructure compared with many new private schools. Universities have realized the need to involve industry professionals in framing the curriculum. Currently, interaction with industry is restricted to industry personnel handling special classes at management institutions.

It is important that to foster a mutually beneficial climate with industry, universities provide for adequate number of industry personnel on the Board of studies in management and commerce, faculty of management and commerce and also in the governing bodies, revise the curriculum as per the requirements of industry and have continuous interaction with leaders in industry for the same, have close interaction with industry by setting up Chair centers, have more interaction with the Confederation of Indian Industry (CII), the Federation of Indian Chambers of Commerce and Industry (FICCI) and other chambers of commerce and conduct industry-relevant projects and training programmes.

To conclude, in 2011-12, as per the statistics put out by the All India Council of Technical Education, the number of applicants for (establishing) management institutions was only 400. In another five years, only those that can sustain their faculty, impart training to them, have a close link with industry, offer niche specializations and choose students with a focus on cross-subsidizing fees will be able to survive.

C. Indian Institute of Sciences (IISc)

The IISc, Bangalore is one of the premier institutes in the country that carry out research work in science and engineering and allied fields. The Institute was established in the year 1909. In 2011, IISc was the only Indian institute ranked by the Academic Ranking of World Universities, at 301—400 overall. It was also ranked 49 in Chemistry and 76—100 in Engineering/ Technology and Computer Science. In the QS World University Rankings, it was ranked 142 in Natural Sciences, 96 in Engineering and IT and 188 in Life Sciences, with no overall ranking.

IISc, Bangalore

D. National Institutes of Technology (NITs)

The National Institutes of Technology (NITs) are a group of higher education engineering institutes in India. Comprising thirty autonomous institutes, they are located in one each major state/territory of India. On their inception decades ago, all NITs were referred as Regional Engineering Colleges (RECs) and were governed by their respective State Governments. A parliamentary legislation in 2002 brought them under the direct purview of India's Federal Government. In 2007, through legislation, the Indian Government declared these schools as Institutes of National Importance at par with the Indian Institutes of Technology.

NITs were founded to promote regional diversity and multi-cultural understanding in India. Therefore, in the NIT school system, half of the student population in each batch is drawn from the respective state of the NIT and the other half is drawn from the rest of India on a common merit list. This is different than the Indian Institutes of Technology or IITs—another prominent engineering school system in India. An IIT need not accept specified number of students from any region of India as the IIT admission criteria is based only on the performance of a student in an entrance examination.

NITs offer degree courses at bachelors, masters, and doctorate levels in various branches of engineering and technology. Various nationwide college surveys rate most of the NITs over other colleges in India, except for the IITs and a few other institutions. NITs function autonomously, similarly to IITs, sharing only entrance tests. The autonomy enables the NITs to set up their own curriculum, thereby making it easier to adapt to changing industry requirements.

With the Indian technology industry's continuing growth, the government decided to upgrade twenty National Institutes of Technology to full-fledged technical universities. Parliament passed enabling legislation, the National Institutes of Technology Act in 2007 and took effect on 15 August of that year. The target is to fulfill the need for quality manpower in the field of engineering, science, and technology and to provide consistent governance, fee structure, and rules across the NITs in both Houses of Parliament. The law designates each NIT an Institute of National Importance (INI).

VOCATIONAL/PROFESSIONAL EDUCATION

Vocational education or vocational education and training (VET) is an education that prepares trainees for jobs that are based on manual or practical activities, traditionally non-academic, and closely related to a specific trade, occupation, or vocation. It is sometimes referred to as technical education as the trainee directly develops expertise in a particular group of techniques. An important stream of higher education is the professional/vocational one. For this a network of public and private polytechnics and vocational institutions, controlled and supervised by the councils specializing in each discipline, exist. There are nearly 10 million students in about 6,500 institutions. Integration of the university and vocational education has been attempted in India as was done in Australia. In a recent innovation, vocational curriculum has been introduced at the bachelor's degree level by permitting one of the three subjects to be a vocational one. A number of subjects have been introduced including agriculture related activities. Nearly 1,500 colleges have been provided the facilities for vocational education.

Vocational education may be classified as teaching procedural knowledge. This can be contrasted with declarative knowledge, as used in education in a usually broader scientific field, which includes theory and abstract conceptual knowledge, characteristic of tertiary education. Vocational education can be at the secondary or post-secondary level and can interact with the apprenticeship system. Increasingly, vocational education can be recognized in terms of recognition of prior learning and partial academic credit towards tertiary education (e.g. at a university); however, it is rarely considered in its own form to fall under the traditional definition of higher education.

Up until the end of the twentieth century, vocational education focused on specific trades such as, for example, those of automobile mechanic or welder, and it was therefore associated with the activities of lower social classes. As a consequence, it carries some social stigma. Vocational education is related to the age-old apprenticeship system of learning. However, as the labor market becomes more specialized and economies demand higher levels of skill, governments and businesses are increasingly investing in the future of vocational education through publicly funded training organizations and subsidized apprenticeship or traineeship initiatives for businesses. At the post-secondary level, vocational education is typically provided by an institute of technology, or by a local community college.

Vocational education has diversified over the 20th century and now exists in industries such as retail, tourism, information technology, funeral services and cosmetics, as well as in the traditional crafts and cottage industries. Vocational training in India is provided on a full time as well as part time basis. Full time programs are generally offered through I.T.I.s (industrial training institutes). Part time programs are offered through state technical education boards or universities who also offer full-time courses. Vocational training has been successful in India only in industrial training institutes and that too in engineering trades. There are many private institutes in India which offer courses in vocational training and finishing, but most of them have not been recognized by the government.

India is a pioneer in vocational training in Film and Television, and Information Technology.

Statutory Professional Councils

Professional councils are responsible for recognition of courses, promotion of professional institutions and providing grants to undergraduate programmes and various awards. The Statutory Professional Councils are:

1. All India Council for Technical Education (AICTE)
2. Distance Education Council (DEC)
3. Indian Council for Agricultural Research (ICAR)
4. Bar Council of India (BCI)
5. National Council for Teacher Education (NCTE)
6. Rehabilitation Council of India (RCI)
7. Medical Council of India (MCI)
8. Pharmacy Council of India (PCI)
9. Indian Nursing Council (INC)
10. Dental Council of India (DCI)
11. Central Council of Homeopathy (CCH)
12. Central Council of Indian Medicine (CCIM)

ORGANIZATION OF HIGHER EDUCATION IN INDIA

Higher education in India has evolved in distinct and divergent streams with each stream monitored by an apex body, indirectly controlled by the Ministry of Human Resource Development. The 433 universities/institutions are mostly funded by the State Governments. However, there are 40 important universities called Central Universities, which are maintained by the Union Government and because of relatively large funding, they have an edge over the others. The engineering education and business schools are monitored and accredited by the All India Council for Technical Education (AICTE) while medical education is monitored and accredited by the Medical Council of India (MCI). Likewise, agriculture education and research is monitored by the Indian Council for Agriculture Research. Apart from these, National Council for Teacher Education

(NCTE) controls all the teacher training institutions in the country. The country has some world-class engineering, management and medical education institutions which are directly funded by the Ministry of Human Resource Development of the Union Government. Admission to all professional education colleges is done through all-India common admission tests of which the IIT-JEE, AIEEE, CAT and CPMT are the most popular ones. Most of the institutions reserve a small percentage of seats for foreign students.

The position of higher education in the Indian polity is regulated by Entry 66 of the 7th Schedule in the Union List of the Constitution of India as well as the placement of the subject of education in the concurrent list insofar as it relates to higher education. This makes it clear that the Union Government and States exercise joint responsibilities. As a result, while the role and responsibilities of the States in regard to education remains unaltered, the Union Government accepts a larger responsibility to reinforce the national and integrated character of education, to maintain quality and standards, to study and monitor the educational requirements of the country as a whole in regard to manpower for development, to attend to the needs of research and advanced study, to look after international aspects of education, culture and human resource development, and in general, to promote excellence at the tertiary level of the educational pyramid throughout the country.

Universities, irrespective of whether they are sponsored by the Central or State Government or by any other agency, should be treated as national institutions working harmoniously to provide trained and educated manpower, which the country needs and to push the frontiers of knowledge. This objective made it imperative to set up a national body to coordinate and harmonize the work of universities and to maintain standards on a national scale. The University Grants Commission (UGC) was therefore established by an Act of Parliament for promotion and coordination of higher education with a view to determining and maintaining the standards of teaching, examination and research. This coordination and cooperation between the Union and the States is brought about in the field of education through the Central Advisory Board of Education (CABE), which needs regular strengthening.

Ministries and Agencies in Higher Education

Department of Higher Education is the department under Ministry of Human Resource Development that oversees higher education in India. However, higher education in India is not the exclusive responsibility of the Department of Education. There are many other ministries and agencies directly involved in higher education. The first is the Ministry of Human Resource Development. It is the major agency concerned with higher education. It operates normally through the UGC. The All India Council for Technical Education (AICTE) is responsible for coordination of technical and management institutions. The other statutory bodies are Medical Council of India (MCI), Central Council of Indian Medicine, the Homeopathy Central Council, the Indian Council of Medical Research (ICMR), Indian Nursing Council, the Dental Council and the Pharmacy Council, which are in the jurisdiction of the Ministry of Health. The legal education is under the Ministry of Law. The Bar Council of India is concerned with the legal studies in India. The Indian Council of Agricultural Research (ICAR) comes under the Ministry of Agriculture. All the agricultural universities function under ICAR. There are also certain specialized agencies for the promotion of research. The Council of Scientific and Industrial Research (CSIR), and the Department of Science and Technology, are planning and coordinating body operating through a chain of national laboratories and institutions. The Indian Council of Social Science Research (ICSSR), Indian Council of Historical Research (ICHR) and Indian Space Research Organization (ISRO) are some specialized agencies for the promotion of research in India.

There are also bodies at the state level such as State Councils of Higher Education that were established recently. There is yet another type of coordinating agency called Association of Indian Universities (AIU), which was earlier known as Inter-University Board of India. All the universities and other equivalent institutions of higher education are members of the AIU. The AIU has no executive powers, but plays an important role as an agency of dissemination of information and as an advisor both to the government and/or UGC and universities. It also provides for equivalence of foreign degrees.

University Grants Commission

The University Grants Commission (UGC) of India is a statutory organization set up by Union Government in 1956, for the coordination, determination and maintenance of standards of university education. It provides recognition for universities in India, and provides funds for government-recognized universities and colleges. Its headquarters are in New Delhi, and it has six regional centers in Pune, Bhopal, Kolkata, Hyderabad, Guwahati and Bangalore. The head office of the UGC is located at Bahadur Shah Zafar Marg in New Delhi, with two additional bureaus operating from 35, Feroze Shah Road and the South Campus of University of Delhi as well.

University Grants Commission was recommended in 1945 and formed in 1946 to oversee the work of the three Central Universities of Aligarh, Banaras and Delhi. In 1947, the Committee was entrusted with the responsibility of dealing with all the then existing universities. After independence, the University Education Commission was set up in 1948 under the Chairmanship of Dr. S. Radhakrishna and it recommended that the UGC be reconstituted on the general model of the University Grants Commission of the United Kingdom. University Grants Commission (UGC) was formally inaugurated by late Abul Kalam Azad, the then Minister of Education, Natural Resources and Scientific Research on 28 December 1953. In 2009, the Union Minister of Education made public the Government of India's plans to close down UGC and the related body AICTE—due to corruption and inefficiency charges against the bodies—in favour of a higher regulatory body with more sweeping powers.

The primary responsibility of the Commission is to promote and coordinate university education in the country and to ensure that the standards are maintained in teaching, research and examinations. In performing these functions, the UGC allocates and disburses grants, placed at its disposal by the Central Government, to the universities, after an assessment of their needs. The Commission provides development and maintenance grants to universities established by the Central Government and also provides development grants to the other universities established by the State Governments and colleges.

The major initiatives taken by the UGC in improving the quality and standards of higher education are:

- Improvement in the quality and standards of teaching and research through programmes for setting up Centers of Advanced Study and Research, improvements in college teaching, strengthening research and infrastructure, etc.
- Periodic review and renewal of the curricular content of courses in various disciplines, and special schemes for introduction of emerging areas of education and training.
- Establishment of common facilities for research and networking of resources for information and documentation.
- Induction of electronic media in higher education.
- Provision of scholarships and fellowships to students.
- Launching of special programmes for greater participation of women, disadvantaged groups and the weaker sections in higher education.

All-India Council for Technical Education (AICTE)

The All-India Council for Technical Education (AICTE) is the statutory body and a national-level council for technical education, under Department of Higher Education, Ministry of Human Resource Development. Established in November 1945 first as an advisory body and given statutory status by an Act of Parliament in 1987, AICTE is responsible for proper planning and coordinated development of technical and management education system in India. As per its charter, the AICTE accredits postgraduate and graduate programs under specific categories at Indian institutions. It is responsible to evolve suitable performance appraisal system for technical institutions and universities imparting technical education, and incorporating norms and mechanisms for enforcing accountability; it lays down norms and standards for courses, curricula, physical and instructional facilities, staff pattern, staff qualifications, quality instruction, assessment and examinations. It approves grants for starting new technical institutions and for introduction of new course or programmes in consultation with the agencies concerned.

In the performance of its functions, the AICTE works in close coordination with the UGC as far as technical education programmes offered by the universities are concerned. The major programmes are related to review and renewal of the curriculum for education and training of engineers and technicians, modernization of the laboratories and workshops, removal of obsolescence, establishment of community polytechnics, technology forecasting, manpower planning, training of teachers, preparation of norms and standards for programmes of education, training in various disciplines at different levels, and extending the benefits of technical training to the backward and rural areas.

It is assisted by 10 Statutory Boards of Studies, namely UG Studies in Engineering and Technology, PG and Research in Engineering and Technology, Management Studies, Vocational Education, Technical Education, Pharmaceutical Education, Architecture, Hotel Management and Catering Technology, Information Technology, Town and Country Planning. The AICTE has its headquarters in Indira Gandhi Sports Complex, Indraprastha Estate, New Delhi, which has the offices of the chairman, vice-chairman and the member-secretary, plus it has regional offices at Kolkata, Chennai, Kanpur, Mumbai, Chandigarh, Guwahati, Bhopal and Bangalore, Hyderabad and Gurgaon.

In 2009, the Union Minister of Education formally communicated the intention of closing down AICTE and the University Grants Commission due to corruption and inefficiency charges against the bodies in favour of a larger regulatory body.

The National Board of Accreditation, which currently operates under the wing of AICTE, will be converted into an independent body.

The AICTE Act, stated verbatim reads:

> To provide for establishment of an All-India Council for Technical Education with a view to the proper planning and co-ordinated development of the technical education system throughout the country, the promotion of qualitative improvement of such education in relation to planned quantitative growth and the regulation and proper maintenance of norms and standards in the technical education system and for matters connected therewith.

In order to improve the present technical education system, the current objective is to modify the engineering curriculum. It should place greater emphasis on design-oriented teaching, teaching of design methodologies, problem-solving approach; greater exposure to industrial and manufacturing processes; exclusion of outmoded technologies and inclusion of the new appropriate and emerging technologies and greater input of management education and professional communication skills.

National Council for Teacher Education (NCTE)

The National Council for Teacher Education (NCTE) was set up in 1973 by a government tesolution as a national expert body to advise Central and State Governments on all matters pertaining to teacher education. The Council was made a statutory body by an Act of Parliament in 1993. The National Council for Teacher Education is designed to ensure planned and coordinated development of teacher education and determination and maintenance of its standards. For the performance of this function, the Council lays down norms for specified categories of courses and guidelines for granting recognition to teacher training programmes offered by various institutions including universities and colleges.

NCTE

As of 2007, the NCTE has its headquarters in New Delhi apart from regional representations in many other cities. Four officials 'Regional Committees' of NCTE operate from Jaipur, Bangalore, Bhubaneswar and Bhopal handling the Northern, Southern, Eastern and Western regions respectively. The councils are responsible for recognizing 'teacher training institutions'. It is reported that as on 1 January 2007, "7461 teacher training institutions offering 9045 courses have been recognized by NCTE with an approved intake of 7.72 lakh teacher trainees."

Indian Council of Agricultural Research (ICAR)

Indian Council of Agricultural Research (ICAR), New Delhi, is an autonomous organization under the Department of Agricultural Research and Education, Ministry of Agriculture, Government of India. Formerly known as Imperial Council of Agricultural Research, it was established on 16 July 1929 as a registered society under the Societies Registration Act, 1860 in pursuance of the report of the Royal Commission on Agriculture. The ICAR has its headquarters at New Delhi.

The Council is the apex body for coordinating, guiding and managing research and education in agriculture including horticulture, fisheries and animal sciences in the entire country. With over 90 ICAR institutes and 45 agricultural universities spread across the country, this is one of the largest national agricultural university systems in the world.

The ICAR has played a pioneering role in ushering Green Revolution and subsequent developments in agriculture in India through its research and technology development that has enabled the country to increase the production of food grains by four times, horticultural crops by six times, fish by nine times (marine five times and inland 17 times), milk six times and eggs 27 times since 1950-51, thus making a visible impact on the national food and nutritional security. It has played a major role in promoting excellence in higher education in agriculture. It is engaged in research at cutting edge areas of science and technology development and its scientists are internationally acknowledged in their fields.

The 'Committee to Advise on Renovation and Rejuvenation of Higher Education' (Yashpal Committee, 2009) has recommended setting up of a constitutional body, viz. the National Commission for Higher Education and Research, which would be a unified supreme body to regulate all branches of higher education including agricultural education. Presently, regulation of agricultural education is the mandate of ICAR, Veterinary Council of India (Veterinary sub-discipline) and Indian Council of Forestry Research and Education (Forestry sub-discipline). The UPA Government had included Yashpal Committee recommendations in its '100 day's agenda'.

National Accreditation and Assessment Council (NAAC)/ National Board of Accreditation (NBA)

In order to ensure a measure of accountability and to evaluate the performance of institutions on the basis of objective criteria, a system of accreditation of institutions of higher learning was an issue of discussion following the 1986 Policy statement. As far as universities are concerned, the UGC took the initiative and established a body called National Accreditation and Assessment Council (NAAC) as an autonomous council under the aegis of the UGC to carry out periodical assessment of universities and colleges in the country. The methodology developed by NAAC for assessment involves:

- a self-appraisal by each university/college on the basis of specified parameters and documenting its performance with reference to each of them;
- an assessment of the performance by an expert committee on the basis of probes identified in respect of each parameter;

- a peer review of the self-appraisal and expert's evaluation; and
- a judgement of the performance.

The NAAC has developed the instruments for carrying out the evaluation studies and several universities and colleges have offered themselves for this assessment. The AICTE Act of 1988 envisages the establishment of accreditation mechanisms for institutions offering technical education programmes. The AICTE has since established a National Board of Accreditation (NBA) to initiate the accreditation of technical institutions. As a first step, the NBA undertook a detailed exercise for benchmarking the performance of premier institutions so that a frame of reference for the evaluation of the performance of the institutions can be initiated. The AICTE has also set up a body similar to NAAC for accreditation of institutions under its jurisdiction.

Distance Education Council (DEC)

Distance Education Council (DEC) is an organization based in New Delhi, India responsible for the promotion and coordination of the open university and distance education system and for determination of its standards in India. The Council was constituted under the Indira Gandhi National Open University Act (1985). It is consistent with the duty of the university that takes all such steps as it may deem fit for the promotion of the Open University and distance education systems in the educational pattern of the country and for the coordination and determination of standards of teaching, evaluation and research in such systems; and in pursuance of the objectives of the university to encourage greater flexibility, diversity, accessibility, mobility and innovation in education at the university level by making full use of the latest scientific knowledge and new educational technology, and to further cooperation between the existing universities. It was considered necessary and expedient to establish a Distance Education Council as an authority of the university under Section 16 of the Act. IGNOU has received international attention and recognition and the Commonwealth of Learning has recently conferred the status of excellence in distance education on the IGNOU.

Bar Council of India (BCI)

The Bar Council of India is a statutory body that regulates and represents the Indian bar. It was created by Parliament under the Advocates Act, 1961. It prescribes standards of professional conduct and etiquette and exercises disciplinary jurisdiction. It sets standards for legal education and grants recognition to universities whose degree will serve as a qualification for students to enroll themselves as advocates upon graduation. Section 7 of the Advocates Act, 1961 lays down the Bar Council's regulatory and representative mandate.

The functions of the Bar Council are to lay down standards of professional conduct and etiquette for advocates, lay down procedure to be followed by disciplinary committees, safeguard the rights, privileges and interests of advocates, promote and support law reform, deal with and dispose of any matter which may be referred by a State Bar Council, promote legal education and lay down standards of legal education, determine universities whose degree in law shall be a qualification for enrolment as an advocate, conduct seminars on legal topics by eminent jurists and publish journals and papers of legal interest, organize and provide legal aid to the poor, recognize foreign qualifications in law obtained outside India for admission as an advocate, manage and invest funds of the Bar Council and provide for the election of its members who shall run the Bar Councils.

Medical Council of India (MCI)

The Medical Council of India (MCI) is the statutory body for maintenance of uniform and high standards of medical education in India. It was first established in 1934 under the Indian Medical Council Act of 1933. The Council was later reconstituted under the Indian Medical Council Act of 1956. The Council grants recognition of medical qualifications, gives accreditation to medical colleges, grants registration to medical practitioners, and monitors medical practice in India. The main functions of the Medical Council of India are recognition of medical qualifications granted by medical institutions of India, recognition of foreign medical qualifications in India, accreditation of medical colleges (medical schools), maintenance of uniform standards for undergraduate medical education, regulation of postgraduate medical education in medical colleges accredited by it. The National Board of Examinations is another statutory body for postgraduate medical education in India. Registration of doctors with recognized medical qualifications is usually made by State Medical Councils. A directory of all registered doctors, called the Indian Medical Register is maintained by MCI.

Rehabilitation Council of India (RCI)

The Rehabilitation Council of India (RCI) is the apex government body, set up under an Act of Parliament, to regulate training programmes and courses targeted at disabled, disadvantaged, and special education requirement communities. It is the only statutory council in India that is required to maintain the Central Rehabilitation Register which mainly document's details of all qualified professionals who operate and deliver training and educational programmes for the targeted communities. In the year 2000, the Rehabilitation Council of India (Amendment) Act, 2000, was introduced and notified consequently by the Government of India. The amendment brought definitions and discussions provided within the earlier Rehabilitation Council of India Act, 1992, under the ambit of a larger Act, namely Persons with Disabilities (Equal Opportunities, Protection of Rights and Full Participation) Act, 1995.

Pharmacy Council of India (PCI)

The pharmacy education and profession in India up to graduate level is regulated by the Pharmacy Council of India (PCI), a statutory body governed by the provisions of the Pharmacy Act, 1948 passed by the Indian Parliament. The Pharmacy Act, 1948 was enacted on 04.03.1948 with the following preamble: "An Act to regulate the profession of pharmacy; whereas it is expedient to make better provision for the regulation of the profession and practice of pharmacy and for that purpose to constitute Pharmacy Councils". The PCI was constituted on 09.08.1949 under Section 3 of the Pharmacy Act. The objectives of PCI are:

1. Regulation of the pharmacy education in the country for the purpose of registration as a pharmacist under the Pharmacy Act.
2. Regulation of profession and practice of pharmacy.
3. Prescribing the minimum standard of education required for qualifying as a pharmacist, i.e. framing of educational regulations prescribing the conditions to be fulfilled by the institutions seeking approval of the PCI for imparting education in pharmacy.
4. Ensuring uniform implementation of the educational standards throughout the country.
5. Approving the courses of study and examination for pharmacists, i.e. approval of the academic training institutions providing pharmacy courses.
6. Withdrawing approval if the courses of study does not continue to be in conformity with the educational standards prescribed by the PCI,
7. Approving qualifications granted outside the territories to which Pharmacy Act, 1948 extends, i.e. the approval of foreign qualification and
8. Maintaining Central Register of Pharmacists.

Dental Council of India (DCI)

The Dental Council of India was incorporated under the Dentists Act, 1948 to regulate dental education and the profession throughout India. It is financed by the Ministry of Health and Family Welfare and operates through the local State Dental Councils. The main objectives are to maintain uniform standards of dental education in India, to regulate the curriculum in the training of dentists, dental hygienists, dental mechanics, and to regulate the level of examinations and qualifications.

Indian Nursing Council (INC)

Indian Nursing Council, an autonomous body under the Government of India; Ministry of Health and Family Welfare was constituted by the Central Government under Section 3(1) of the Indian Nursing Council Act, 1947 of Parliament in order to establish a uniform standard of training for nurses, Midwives and health visitors.

Central Council of Homoeopathy (CCH)

It is a statutory apex body under the Ministry of Health and Family Welfare, Department of Indian Systems of Medicine and Homoeopathy. It was set up by Government of India in 1973, and is a part of the Professional Councils of University Grants Commission (UGC), formed to monitor higher education in India. CCH prescribes and recognizes all homoeopathic medicine education in India; any university or medical institutions desiring to grant a medical qualification in homoeopathy is required to apply to the Council. Above all it prescribes course curriculum, evolves standards of education and maintains central registers of homoeopathy physicians.

Any university or similar institution in India offering either a degree or a diploma in homoeopathy can do so only if it is approved by CCH, apart from being listed under the Schedules of the Central Council of Homoeopathy Act, 1973 (Act 59) above-mentioned Act. The CCH also defines specific course curriculum and notifies benchmarks that need to be maintained by homoeopathy teaching institutions, apart from maintaining a central registry of all homoeopathy physicians in India.

In 2007, the Union Health Ministry set up the "National Council for Clinical Establishments" to "determine minimum standards" for clinical establishments, a CCH representative is also a formal member of this National Council. In June 2008, a notice was issued to CCH by the Punjab and Haryana High Court when Sri Guru Nanak Dev Homeopathic College, Ludhiana, India, challenged the powers of the CCH in controlling the intake into the college's homoeopathic courses.

As a result of the order issued by the Ministry, the selection committee conducting counselling sessions had to stop the process midway on May 30. The petitioner stated that according to Amendment Regulations Notification, 2001, published in the Government of India Gazette on November 5, 2001, the universities concerned might allow the admission of external candidates to appear in postgraduate examinations for eight years from the commencement of the Homoeopathy (Post-graduate Degree Course) MD (Homoeopathy) (Amendment) Regulations, 2001, for three subjects. But subsequently the universities were directed not to conduct any counselling after 2007-08 session. Baba Farid University, however, wrote back to the Department of Ayurveda, Yoga and Naturopathy, Unani, Siddha and Homoeopathy (AYUSH) on May 23 that universities could give admissions for MD (Homoeopathy) course for external candidates till 2009.

Central Council of Indian Medicine (CCIM)

It is a statutory body under Department of Ayurveda, Yoga and Naturopathy, Unani, Siddha and Homoeopathy (AYUSH), Ministry of Health and Family Welfare, Government of India, set up in 1971 under the Indian Medicine Central Council Act, (Act 48) which was passed in 1970. It is one of the professional councils under University Grants Commission (UGC) to monitor higher education in Indian systems of medicine, including Ayurveda, Siddha and Unani.

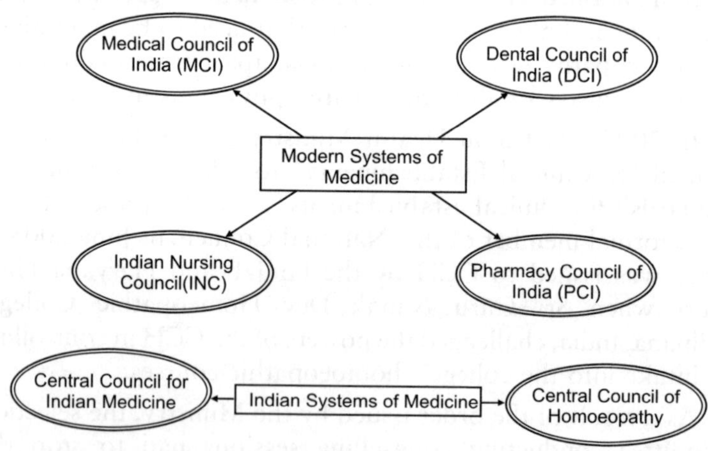

Existing Structure of Governance in Medical Education

CCIM's, office is located in New Delhi, India. CCIM was set up to suggest the benchmarks and practices to be followed in Indian medicinal systems. CCIM has also been involved in regulating the Ayurveda, Siddha and Unani Tibb education courses at the graduate and postgraduate streams. The Siddha course recognition system of CCIM was questioned through public interest litigation. The main objectives are to prescribe minimum standards of education in Indian Systems of Medicine, viz. Ayurved, Siddha, Unani Tibb, to advise Central Government in matters relating to recognition (inclusion/withdrawal) of medical qualification in/from Second Schedule to Indian Medicine Council Act, 1970, to maintain a Central Register on Indian Medicine and revise the register from time to time and to prescribe Standards of Professional Conduct, Etiquette and Code of Ethics to be observed by the practitioners.

AUTONOMOUS RESEARCH ORGANIZATIONS

Research is not an immutable part of the higher education enterprise. As Clark points out, "research as a central function of the university dates back only to the establishment of the University of Berlin in 1810, based on Wilhelm von Humboldt's model". The Humboldtian idea, with its reliance on Lehrfreiheit and Lernfreiheit—*the freedom of the professor to teach his or her specialty and the freedom of the student to choose what to study*—emphasized research. To upgrade the quality of higher education and research, certain autonomous research organizations have been established by the Central Government that play the parental role towards quality research. (http://www.education.nic.in/AutonomousSec.asp#top)

1. University Grants Commission (UGC)

(It has been discussed above in detail)

2. Indian Council of Social Science Research (ICSSR)

Indian Council of Social Science Research (ICSSR) was established in the year of 1969 by the Government of India to promote research in social sciences in the country. It supports a network of 27 ICSSR research institutes, including:

- Institute for Social and Economic Change (ISEC), Bangalore
- Institute of Public Enterprise, Hyderabad
- Institute of Studies in Industrial Development, New Delhi

- Govind Ballabh Pant Social Science Institute, Allahabad
- Centre for Studies in Social Sciences, Calcutta
- Centre for Policy Research (CPR), New Delhi
- Centre for Multi-Disciplinary Development Research
- Centre for Women's Development Studies (CWDS), Delhi
- Madras Institute of Development Studies

3. National Council of Educational Research and Training (NCERT)

NCERT is an autonomous organization under the Ministry of Education, which was set up in 1961 in order to promote, organize and foster research in all branches of education, to organize advanced level training and to act as a clearing house. It undertakes special studies, surveys and investigations.

4. Indian Council of Historical Research (ICHR)

ICHR, set up in 1972 with office in New Delhi, reviews the progress of historical research and encourages scientific writing of history. It operates research projects, finances research projects by individual scholars, awards fellowships and undertakes publication and translation. The main objectives of ICHR are:

- to bring historians together and provide a forum for exchange of views between them;
- to give a national direction to an objective and scientific writing of history and to have rational presentation and interpretation of history;
- to promote, accelerate and coordinate research in history with special emphasis on areas which have not received adequate attention so far;
- to promote and coordinated a balanced distribution of research effort over different areas;
- to elicit support and recognition for historical research from all concerned and ensure the necessary dissemination and use of results.

5. Indian Council of Philosophical Research (ICPR)

ICPR functioning from 1977 with office in New Delhi and Lucknow reviews the progress and sponsors or assists projects and programmes of research in philosophy and gives financial assistance to institutions and individuals to conduct research in philosophy and allied disciplines.

6. Indian Institute of Advanced Study (IIAS)

IIAS, Simla is a residential center for advanced research in humanities, social sciences and natural sciences. It was set up by the Ministry of Education, Government of India in 1964 and it started functioning from October 20, 1965. The Institute is administered by a society and a governing body, the members of which come from varied backgrounds. A statutory finance Committee advises the Governing body in financial matters. The Director of the Institute is assisted by a Secretary, a Deputy Secretary a Public Relations Officer and other supervisory staff.

7. National Council of Rural Institutes (NCRI)

NCRI was set up in 1995 as an autonomous organization fully funded by the Central Government to promote rural higher education on the lines of Mahatma Gandhi's revolutionary ideas on education and promote research as a tool of social and rural development.

8. Association of Indian Universities (AIU)

AIU is an apex voluntary educational organization of universities with the major objective of promoting and coordinating activities of higher educational institutions. Some of the major activities of AIU in the fields of higher education include disseminating information, carrying out research studies, publication and promotion of literature, cooperation among institutions in the area of cultural, sports and allied areas.

9. National Assessment and Accreditation Council (NAAC)

NAAC was established based on the recommendations of the National Policy on Education (1986) and the Programme of Action (1992), by the University Grants Commission as an autonomous body in the year 1994 with its headquarters at Bangalore. It has evolved a methodology of assessment that involves self-appraisal by each university/college and an assessment of performance by an expert.

Role of Regulatory Bodies with Reference to Quality

Higher education in India is coordinated by several agencies. While most of general higher education falls within the jurisdiction of the UGC, professional institutions are coordinated by different bodies. The AICTE is responsible for coordinating technical and management education institutions. The other statutory bodies are Medical Council of India (MCI), Central Council of Indian Medicine, the Homoeopathy Central Council, the Indian Council of Medical Research (ICMR), Indian Nursing Council, the Dental Council, the Pharmacy Council, the Bar Council of India, and the Indian Council of Agriculture Research (ICAR), etc. There are also a few such bodies at state level such as State Council of Higher Education that were established currently. There is yet another type of a coordinating agency, called AIU, which was earlier known as Inter-University Board of India. AIU has no executive powers, but plays an important role as an agency of dissemination of information and as an adviser both to the government and/or UGC and University.

There are significant differences in their mandate, powers and functions. The councils have rules and regulations of their own. There is large overlap of their functions with the functions of the UGC, other professional councils and even function of universities in some cases. In five cases, namely—Medical Council of India, Pharmacy Council of India, All India Council for Technical Education, Indian Nursing Council and the Bar Council of India, there are also State Councils; and there are overlaps in functions of the national councils and state councils. Today in this scenario there is very little of clearly defined policy for promoting and regulating institutions and especially the private initiatives. "Whatever policies exist, they are of ad-hoc nature prescribed by either the central regulatory bodies and/or by the various States and UT's. Often because of inconsistencies, ambiguities, and vagueness—especially in the light of different legal mandates of these agencies and the concurrent status of higher education—there have been a plethora of legal battles resulting in enormous expenditure to the governments and the institutions" (M. Anandakrishnan, *Policy Orientation for Private Initiatives in Higher Education: Issues and Options*, 2003).

In order to encourage full participation of private education providers, the regulatory bodies have to play the role of facilitators and not regulators. There should not be any inconsistency in the policy for the growth of different types of higher education institutions. There is a need to establish a system whereby there is a minimum procedural consistency among the regulatory bodies in establishing new higher educational institutions; since there are different types of institutions coming up in the same premises under the responsibilities of different agencies which create more confusion and delay. So harmonizing the processes of different agencies would require willingness on the part of the agencies themselves and amendments in their Acts and statutes.

The point that has to be kept in mind is that too much interference exerted by the regulatory bodies would result in discouraging their initiative and autonomy. There are multi-layered regulations, which have to be made more simple and supportive. It can also be thought that all that is required to ensure quality across the board is to have a national level overseeing body that is teethed with powers to grant permission to establish a university and to derecognize an already established university if it fails to maintain the prescribed standards. It is also essential that the functioning of such a central authority is transparent and its decision are nor arbitrary. To ensure such transparent governance authority should prescribe its parameters for granting permission to establish an institution/university. Similarly, it should also make it known to the participating agencies as to on what lines the performance of a university is assessed to declare it as eligible for its continuation or not.

Taking a cue from the experiences it is time that we had one central body to oversee the functioning of higher institutions/ universities—both in public and private management and evaluate them on prescribed quality parameters to ensure excellence in education. This anomaly needs to be corrected if the credibility of Indian Higher Education system is to be sustained in the coming years under severely changing competitive environment. It can only be possible if the different approaches in policies between the various regulatory bodies and agencies are harmonized. Review of the existing structure of regulatory system in India and the way it regulates various aspects of higher education show that the existing regulatory procedures are extremely burdensome and counter-productive. They often control supply limiting choice by erecting formidable entry barriers for new institutions to be set up through private enterprise.

Time consuming, non-transparent and complex procedures applied arbitrarily, create conducive environment for rent seeking and patronage. It makes higher education institutions less accountable. The system is strait-jacketed and inhibits innovation. Overall, the system works towards standardization in higher education and not for maintenance of standards. There is a widespread feeling that regulatory bodies in India have miserably failed to discharge their responsibility towards maintenance of standards. Summing up the situation, Mehta and Kapur (2004) conclude that the existing laws regulating higher education in India tend to promote adverse selection. It deters genuine investment in education, but encourages those who are adapting at manipulating the licence quota raj in the system.

In a recent survey of the degree of regulatory control of the major higher education systems in the world, *The Economist* has noted that whereas, most nations in the world (including China) are working towards loosening of statutory control over their higher education systems, India is moving in reverse direction and tightening government control in institutions of higher education. It is also clear from the mapping of the regulatory system in India that there is a diarchy in higher education in India. While UGC is expected to oversee it, the State Governments regulate it in practice. In addition, the higher education institutions are subjected to a multi-layered regulatory and control process involving a number of agencies and bodies. Despite all this, higher education in India has virtually remained an unbridled horse (Pinto, 1984).

In view of the above, it is no surprise that many of the better known institutions of higher education in India such as the Indian Institutes of Technology (IITs), the Indian Institutes of Management (IIMs), National Institute of Fashion Technology (NIFT), National Institute of Design (NID), Indian Institute of Science (IISc), Tata Institute of Social Sciences (TISS) and Birla Institute of Technology and Sciences (Pilani) are all outside the conventional university system in India. IIMs, NIFT and NID do not even have degree granting powers and offer only diplomas. Complex and dysfunctional regulatory arrangements for higher education in India have raised serious concerns about the credibility of the Indian higher education system. There is a need to safeguard its integrity and enhance its credibility. Loss of this credibility would have serious repercussions. Our competitive advantage as a nation with huge reserve of highly qualified and trained manpower may be lost. Many countries are shying away in signing mutual recognition agreements with us because of horror stories that they hear about deteriorating standards of higher education in India. This would become more difficult in the years to come, if we allow any further compromise on the standards of higher education in the country.

Being blamed for all its ills, it is often argued that total deregulation of higher education in India would serve the public interest best. This argument is based on the simple principle of economics that if the market regulates institutions more efficiently and effectively than the state, then task of regulation should be left to the market; facilitating oversupply would be the best way to subject market sensitive institutions to the regulations of the market. The manner in which clearing of demand and supply takes place in higher education suggests that leaving higher education to market forces may not be most viable option. Though academics would normally object to the concept of regulation especially as it relates to academic quality, however, it needs to be understood that due to its very nature, academic standards need to be determined and coordinated across universities requiring some kind of external scrutiny. This makes regulation important; though equally important is as to the nature of regulation, who is responsible to develop and who would implement these regulations.

The Union Cabinet has given its nod for the establishment of National Commission of Higher Education and Research (NCHER), an overarching body in higher education to oversee universities and technical institutes. It will subsume all existing regulatory bodies, including UGC, AICTE and Council of Distance Education. These agencies monitor various components of higher education in the country. The body will have 70 members, with representatives from every state and regulatory bodies. The proposal to establish NCHER was suggested by Prof Yash Pal Committee and it was based on the recommendations of National Knowledge Commission.

NCHER will cover all areas and disciplines, including general, technical and professional education, and according to sources, also some research components in the field of medicine. Earlier, the setting up of NCHER was disrupted when the HRD Ministry announced taking over the medical education under the Bill. The Health Ministry had opposed it and approached the cabinet for clearance of National Commission for Human Resources for Health (NCHRH) Bill.

Final Comments

It can be concluded after a detailed description of the structure and organization of Higher Education in India that undoubtedly the organization is a complex one. The type of universities normally included are—central universities, state universities and deemed universities. Some of them fall within the purview of the UGC, while the others are looked after by different agencies working under the respective ministries. The various ministries and their specialized agencies are involved with professional higher education in the country. However, there are certain specialized agencies like CSIR, ICMR, ICHR, ICSSR, ISRO, etc., which have the overall responsibility of planning and coordinating high quality research in their respective specialized areas.

Universities in India have been traditional sources of research. With the advent of government R&D organizations, increase in the number of universities, poor funding and the escalating cost of infrastructure needed for research, research at universities had declined. The decline was certainly slowed down by government-sponsored research projects. There are only a few Indian universities, known for good standards in teaching and research. In a number of universities, there is very little research and even the classroom teaching is not regular. In such universities, most part of the budget is spent on staff salaries and little is left for library, laboratory and other functions.

In last six decades or so there has been tremendous expansion of the knowledge base but most universities have not even made efforts to keep with it. The situation is highlighted by the fact that India is fast losing its competitive edge in research to other countries, which till recently were far behind; specifically India's share of world's scientific and technological research is steadily declining. To find a suitable place and to be able to compete in India and abroad, the center and states in particular have to ensure a high rate of growth in the quality and quantity of the intellectual output from the universities.

In 2004, India produced around 5,900 science, technology and engineering Ph.Ds., a figure that has now grown to some 8,900 a year. This is still a fraction of the number from China and the United States, and the country wants many more, to match the explosive growth of its economy and population. The government is making major investments in research and higher education—including a one-third increase in the higher education budget in 2011-12—and is trying to attract investment from foreign universities. The hope is that up to 20,000 Ph.Ds. will graduate each year by 2020, says Thirumalachari Ramasami, the Indian Government's head of science and technology.

Teaching and research are the twin foundations of a university because the creation of new knowledge should go hand in hand with the dissemination of that new knowledge for the betterment of society. Hence, in any university, teaching should be seen as an activity, which is integral to the life of an academic, and not as an inferior adjunct to research. It is best of all if teaching is combined with live research, with original work that is still in progress. The quality of teaching and research is the backbone of development of any nation. Research is one of the prominent indicators of the quality of university education. Production and dissemination of knowledge and excellence is directly related to research. Thus, being recognized as center of excellence and producer of knowledge research has to be one of the primary agendas of universities. There is a need for the universities to strike an appropriate balance between research and teaching as one strengthens the other and vice-versa.

Thus, if we focus our efforts around a clear enunciation of our goals arising from an understanding of our needs, endowments and competencies and all of us—government, academia, scientific community, business, civil society and citizens—work together to realize a merit-based accessible quality education system and excellence in research as a mission, India will definitely become an innovation super power by 2030.

REFERENCES

Altbach, Philip G. (2005a). "Higher Education in India". *The Hindu*, April 12, 2005.

Altbach, Philip G. (2006b). "The Private Higher Education Revolution: An Introduction". *University News.* January 2-8, 2006. Vol. 44, No. 01.

Anandakrishnan, M. (2004). Higher Education in Regional Development: Some Key Pointers. Indo-UK Collaboration on Higher Education —Policy Forum Workshop, 12-13 February 2004.

Anandakrishnan, M. (2006). "Privatization of Higher Education: Opportunities and Anomalies". *Privatization and commercialization of higher education* organized by NIEPA, May 2, 2006. New Delhi.

Béteille, André (2005). "Universities as Public Institutions". *Economic and Political Weekly*, July 30, 2005.

CABE Committee (2005a). *Report of the Central Advisory Board of Education*, Committee on Autonomy of Higher Education Institutions. Government of India. June 2005.

Delors, Jacques (1996). Learning the Treasure Within. *Report to UNESCO of the International Commission on Education for the Twenty-first Century.* UNSECO Publishing, Paris.

Gartia, Radhakanta and Dash Jagannath (2009). "Higher Education in India: A Reality Check". *University News*, 47 (02), January 12-18.

Government of India, Ministry of Human Resource Development, Department of Higher Education, Organizational Structure. www.education.nic.in/orgastru.asp

IGNOU, Planning and Management of Higher Education, MES 104, pp. 7-57.

Jha, D.M. (1991). "Higher Education in Ancient India." In Raza, M. (Ed.), *Higher Education in India: Retrospect and Prospect*, AIU, New Delhi, pp. 1-5.

Jayaram, N. (2002). "The Fall of the Guru: The Decline of the Academic Profession in India. In Philip G. Altbach (Ed.), *The Decline of the Guru: The Academic Profession in Developing and Middle Income Countries* (pp. 207-39), Centre for International Higher Education. Boston College.

Kapur, Devesh and Pratap Bhanu Mehta (2004). Indian Higher Education Reform: From Half-Baked Socialism to Half-Baked Capitalism. CID Working Paper No. 108. Harvard University. Center for International Development.

Mehta, Pratap Bhanu (2005). "Regulating Higher Education". *Indian Express*, New Delhi. July 14. MHRD (2006). Annual Report. Ministry of Human Resource Development, Department of Secondary and Higher Education. Government of India. New Delhi.

NASSCOM-Mckinsey Report 2005.

Nayyar, Deepak (2005), *Indian Express*. New Delhi. May 25, 2005.

Pinto, M. (1984). *Federalism and Higher Education: The India Experience.* Bombay, India: Orient Longman, 28.

Agarwal, Pawan (2006). Higher Education in India, the Need for a Change, ICRIER, Working Paper No. 179.

Planning Commission (1999). Approach Paper to the Tenth Five-Year Plan (2002-2007). Planning Commission. New Delhi.

Planning Commission (2006), *Towards Faster and Inclusive Growth: An Approach to the 11th Five-Year Plan,* Government of India, New Delhi.

Powar, K.B. (1990), "The AIU at Seventy Five". *University News*, 37(12):1-2, March 22, 1999.

Powar, K.B. (2002), *Indian Higher Education: A Conglomerate of Concepts, Facts and Practices*, Delhi: Concept Publishing Co.

Powar, K.B. The Changing Role and Functions of Universities. *AIU Occasional Paper* 2000/2. New Delhi: Association of Indian Universities.

Report of the Central Advisory Board of Education (CABE) Committee on Financing of Higher and Technical Education. Government of India. June 2005.

Singh, Amrik (1988), "Foundation and Role of UGC". In Amrik Singh and G.D. Sharma (eds), *Higher Education in India: The Social Context*, Delhi: Konark Publishers Pvt. Ltd., pp. 234-51.

Singh, Amrik and G.D. Sharma (eds) (1989). *Higher Education in India: The Institutional Context*, Delhi: Konark Publishers Pvt. Ltd.

Sector Overview, Government of India, Ministry of Human Resource Development, Department of Higher Education.

Stella, Antony (2002). *External Quality Assurance in Indian Higher Education: Case Study of the National Assessment and Accreditation Council* (NAAC). International Institute for Educational Planning. Paris.

The Economist (2005a). Survey of Higher Education 2005. September 10.

The Economist (2005b). Free Degrees to Fly: Special Report on Higher Education, February, 26, 2005.

The Economist (1997). A Survey of Higher Education. October 2, 1997.

UGC Annual Report 1996-97 and 2005-06 (New Delhi: University Grants Commission); and Selected Educational Statistics (New Delhi: Ministry of Human Resource Development).

UGC Annual Report (2004-05). University Grants Commission, New Delhi.

UGC, *Model Act Committee Report*, New Delhi, 1964. p. 8.

UGC (2005). Research Handbook: Towards Nurturing Research Culture in Higher Education Institutions in India. University Grants Commission. New Delhi.

University Act (RSBC 1996). Chapter 468, 2005, Queen's Printer, Victoria, British Columbia, Canada.

World Bank (2003). A policy note on the grant-in-aid system in Indian education. South Asia Human Development Sector. Report No. 3. November, 2003.

World Bank (2004). "Measuring Trade in Services Liberalization and its Impact on Economic Growth: An illustration", World Bank Group Working Paper, downloadable from http://econ.worldbank.org/files/2373_wps2655.pdf

World Bank (2005). Dahlman, Carl and Utz, Anuja. Indian and the Knowledge Economy: Leveraging Strengths and Opportunities. Washington DC.

Websites

www.iotu.uchicago.edu/levine.html

http://www.campusfrance.org/promotion/inde/doc/HIGHER_INDIA.doc

http://www.education.nic.in/uhe/uhe-inst-Councils.asp

http://www.education.nic.in/Higedu.asp

www.education.nic.in/ed50years/x/7H/Book7H.htm

Governance and Administration of Higher Education in India

6

In India, the higher education institutions exist in two significant categories—university and college. Universities are autonomous bodies whereas colleges are affiliated to universities. Universities, therefore, have the prime responsibility of developing the higher education system and maintaining the quality. The dimensions of our higher education system warrant a very serious consideration of the issues of management. There is a dire need to review the governance issues for all aspects of the higher education system prevalent in India. We should begin examining the manner in which the governance had been evolving since pre-independence period to the present. Models of institutional governance and administration with particular reference to autonomy and accountability are the most important issues of governance which need much pondering. Besides these, governance issues of higher education in the current scenario of establishment of institutions under Public Private Partnership (PPP) model, establishment of foreign institutions in India jointly with Indian counterparts or otherwise and issues concerning the role and responsibility of statutory bodies interacting with and regulating the university system vis-à-vis the State and Central Governments also need serious consideration.

Affiliating System of the University

India has lived with the affiliating system for several years. The system in place was primarily designed to help college enrollment to adopt the university education programmes to maintain the norms and standards at par with the university system itself without being a university! What a paradox? This worked well for the initial period of independent India. As it happens in all sectors of development, with massive expansion in the college sector many ills and scarcity of resources embraced the university academic system, particularly the expansion plan. Thus, the affiliating system soon started creating immense hurdles for good higher education. In fact, the sudden expansion of higher education enrollment in the university and college sectors mutually started hurting each other. The affiliating college sector started being treated as unwanted burden on the university and the college sector felt that the university wanted only to collect revenue, conduct examinations and award degrees. Educationists in India have argued against the affiliating system long enough. Autonomous college system has been promoted by UGC with appropriate financial support, but still no viable solution has emerged for the governance of the college system in general.

Of late, the participation of the private sector in the establishment of university level institutions is increasing substantially. The opening of the economy world over has resulted in the exposure of Indian higher education system and its pattern in global context. So, we should consider the cross-country collaboration in higher education. All these issues need sharp focus for design of appropriate strategies befitting to our needs and for consultations by the State/Central Governments and statutory bodies.

External and Internal Governance

Governance of institutions can be divided into two major groups:

1. External governance
2. Internal governance

External Governance

The agencies/authorities for external governance are the Central/State Governments, their organizations/bodies, and national/international accreditation authorities. This includes any policy directive concerning the national agenda/scenario through the statutory bodies like the UGC and other regulating bodies for governing the performance of the higher education institutions in terms of course, content/duration of courses of study, etc. and maintenance of uniformity of norms and standards. The apex authorities and organizations in this regard have been discussed in previous chapters.

The governance of the institutions in pursuing the subject areas of studies and the areas of research are by and large through broad policy directions as prescribed by the national bodies. Internal systems of institutions have significant scope of autonomy through their Academic Councils and the Governing Boards. For appointment to the position of the Vice Chancellor/ Director (Head of the Institution), the Central/State Government maintains its privilege in respect of government funded institution/university. The Central/State Government enforces the recommendations of the statutory bodies with respect to appointment/promotion of faculty/non-faculty in the context of the prescribed qualifications and experience and related service conditions and pay scales. Calendar of events, namely commencement of academic session, semester breaks, vacation periods, etc. is generally maintained uniformly in the country to facilitate mobility among students from one institution/university to another for postgraduate studies, and also facilitate them for joining national and international admission tests for further studies. It is true that some States are always unable to maintain the calendar resulting in great hardships to students. This is undesirable and hence the uniformity of the calendar of events is an important issue for discussion.

Internal Governance

The internal governance within an institution is governed by the structure, prescribed by the Acts/Statutes/regulations, etc. which provide for the apex authority of the university/ institute, namely, the Board of Governors called by many names like University Court, the Senate, and Governing Council, etc. These apex authorities are supported through various other bodies, namely Academic Council, Board of Studies, Research Board, Planning Board, Admission Committee, Faculty Selection Committee, and many others.

While we compare the internal governance mechanism of the universities and other institutions of higher education, we find that the model adopted by IITs and IIMs are functionally the best of the prevalent ones. The Board of IIT is chaired by a nominee of the Government of India from among the persons who are distinguished in their own fields of pursuit from science and technology, industry or administration and many other walks of life. In almost all other Central/State sector institutions (other than IITs), the structure of the apex bodies is unwieldy and needs a serious review for efficiency and efficacy of the performance. In the state universities, highest body is presided over by the Governor of the State as Chancellor whereas in case of central universities the Central Government appoints an eminent person to be the Chancellor. Private institutes/ universities are normally headed by the chairperson or president of the sponsoring trust with significant number of family members in the Governing Council.

Constitution of Universities

Management is universal in approach and effective governance and management is the key to success for any and every institution. Its application is essential in the efficient running of institutions and organizations. Every organization requires the making of decisions, the coordinating of activities, the handling of people and the evaluation of performance directed towards group objectives. Management facilitates this and here lies its importance. Universities are autonomous and self-governing institutions. Every university has two important decision-making bodies. The Executive Council (Board of Management or Syndicate) is the principal executive body dealing with all the functions of the first category, and the Academic Council (in some cases called the Senate) is the principal academic body, taking all academic decisions.

This duality in the decision-making processes a unique feature of university management. It is necessary for the health of the university that the two bodies function organically, with mutual respect and co-ordination, though in practice it is not unusual to see conflicts arising between the two. It is inherent in the nature of functions of the universities that there is always some tension between the academics and the administrators, sometimes also institutionalized in terms of the conflicts between the Executive and Academic Councils. Normally, while prescribing the composition and functions of these two bodies, the legislation also takes care to specify the matters on which, and the manner in which, either body consults the other. However, since execution of any decision requiring funds, people and facilities is in the domain of the Executive Council, this body is perceived to have an edge over the Academic Council in terms of power and authority. With this understanding of a significant complexity in the structure and pattern of governance of universities, it becomes important to understand the constitution of these bodies, the functions they perform and the power they exercise.

The Acts provide for "Authorities" which have defined powers, and "bodies" which are generally advisory in character. There has been a general uniformity in the constitution and composition of the authorities and bodies, despite some minor variations in the mode of election/nomination of certain section of members in these bodies.

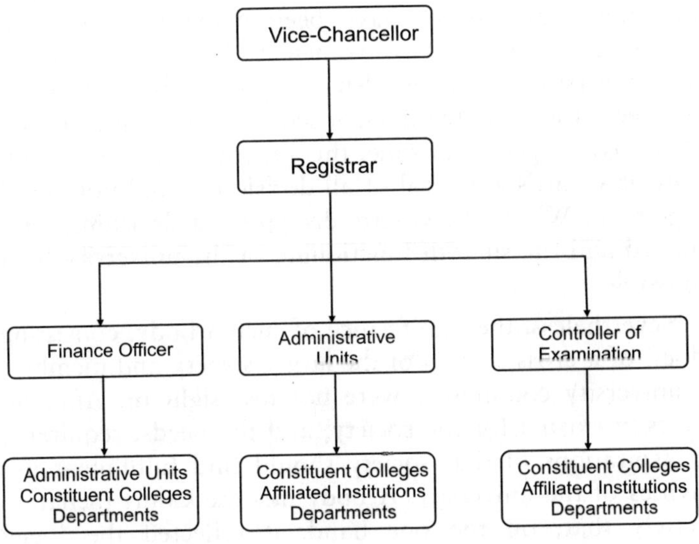

Senate/Court

The structure of governance described above is the pattern that has emerged in the last three decades or so in India. Prior to that, most universities in the country had a Court (for central universities) and Senate (for state universities). This body was the supreme authority of a university. It worked in the older days, but with the growing complexity in the functioning of universities, there has been a review and reformulation of the composition, functions and powers of this body. Traditionally, the Court/Senate consisted of a cross section of the academic community (teachers, administrations and students) and representatives of different sections of the general community outside the university (legislators, civil servants, representatives of business/industry, the learned professions, former students, and so on).

In a few universities such as Banaras Hindu University and Allahabad University, the Senate consists of mostly nominated members. In Kerala University and Bombay University, a wide cross-section of the society finds representation in the Senate. In Delhi University and Aligarh Muslim University, the Senate includes their former Vice-Chancellors also. In Karnataka State Universities, reservations have been made for one woman registered graduate and two women students. In the Courts of some universities, there is also a representation of students, employees other than teachers, Scheduled Castes and Scheduled Tribes. Over a period of time, this practice became difficult to follow as Court's approval of all decisions could not be taken for granted. Where the Courts disapproved decisions, friction followed and the smooth functioning of the university became impossible.

Nevertheless, the significance of such a body, consisting as it does, of a cross-section of the larger society and members of the university community were not lost sight of. After all, a university existed for the society, and the needs, requirements and aspirations of that society should find fulfillment in the activities of the university. A body like the Court (Senate) did precisely that; on the one hand, it reflected the society's expectations through the members representing the larger society, and on the other, it provided a window of opportunity to the university community to inform the general society about its policies, programmes and problems. This function of building bridges, of reviewing progammes and policies on the basis of informed views and making them responsive to social needs was considered a vital function for the management of the university.

In recognition of this role, the Court (Senate) in later legislations were designated as a "deliberative" body reviewing policies and progammes, making suggestions for improvements and development, and to express views on the overall performance of the university on the basis of its annual performance reports. With this major change in its powers and functions, the Court (Senate) continues to be a body provided in the Acts of most universities in the country. Their composition as indicated above also remains more or less unchanged. With this change in the functions and powers of the Court (Senate), it is no more saddled with the burden of having to over-rule decisions of the university. For that reason, some of the more recent legislations have altogether dispensed with the provision to constitute a Court (Senate) for universities established under them.

The Executive Council

The Executive Council (also called Syndicate or Board of Management) is the authority that takes all executive decisions and implements them. All administrative and financial powers are exercised by this body. It should be a compact body capable of functioning with unity of purpose. The body consists of administrators, educationists and people who have made a name in their professions like engineers, doctors and businessmen people; these persons give serious thought to higher education issues. Only the persons well versed with and interested in the university's affairs and activities should be made the members of Executive Council.

Generally, the Executive Council consists of the Vice Chancellor as its Chairman, a Pro-Vice Chancellor, two Deans, three or four representatives of teachers, two or three representatives (generally Heads) of colleges or institutions affiliated to the university, three or four nominees of the government, and two or three members of the Senate who are external members. There could be minor variations in this broad pattern of composition from university to university. The significant point is that it has the majority of its members from within the university, and an adequate representation of interests from outside. The internal and external representation is generally in the ratio of 3:2 with the total membership ranging between 15 and 20.

The Executive Council should be an instrument to run the university effectively and to see that the larger objectives and purposes for which the university is supported by public funds are fulfilled. The important functions of the Executive Council are making statutes and ordinances which govern the conduct of all the sub-systems of the university, control of the finances and properties, management of personnel (recruitment, promotion, conditions of service, welfare), supervision over the management of institutions/colleges affiliated to the university, redressal of grievances of teachers, staff and students. It should be noted however that the power of legislation (rule-making) in all academic matters can be exercised only after consulting the Academic Council. The syndicate should have a fixed calendar of meetings. The effective functioning of the syndicate/executive council largely decides the efficient functioning of the university.

The Academic Council

The Academic Council is the principal academic authority of the university. All decisions regarding programmes, courses, teaching methods, evaluation systems, academic standards, creation of new departments, etc. fall within the purview of the Academic Council. However, the scheme of university management envisages a sharing of powers and authority between the External Council and the Academic Council, with the former enjoying a slight edge over the latter. The Academic Council is essentially a body comprising of the academics of the university. It is chaired by the Vice Chancellor and consists of the Pro-Vice Chancellor(s), all Deans, all Heads of Departments, representatives of the Heads of affiliated institutions and colleges, and representatives of all categories of teachers both from the Department and the affiliated institutions, and in several cases also of representatives of students. Depending upon the size and nature of the university, the Academic Council can be a body of 50-250 members. Where the number of teachers is large, representation is provided normally through the method of election, and where the number of teachers is small, a system of nomination or rotation is followed.

The important functions of the Academic Council are laying down the academic policies of the university; supervision of the academic policies and giving directions on methods of instruction, evaluation of research and improvements in academic standards; inter-faculty coordination for joint projects, programmes, etc.; recommending statutes/ordinances concerning academic matters like establishment of departments, laboratories, research centers, committees for admission and examination, qualification of teachers, award of degrees, diplomas and other qualifications, conduct of examinations, institution of scholarships and fellowships, student fees, etc. Generally, the universities will also have a set of academic regulations that provide for procedures to be followed in various matters like admission, examination, declaration of results, etc. These regulations are also framed by the Academic Council. To the extent statutes/ordinances/regulations are internal legislations, they require the approval of the Executive Council. In general, all decisions of academic council need the approval of the executive council.

Faculties and Boards of Studies

Faculties and Boards of Studies are discipline based. They are not flexible enough and have very little scope of inducting experts from industries, national laboratories, public undertakings, etc. While newer university Acts have prescribed statutory and other committees to discharge academic and other roles of the universities, this is not so in many of the older universities. Most of the older universities for instance do not have provision for Planning Boards, College Development Council, Boards of Extension, and Curriculum Development Cell, etc. However, anybody can be invited to any meeting of these bodies by the chairman.

The authorities of the university system, i.e. the Senate, Syndicate and Academic Council, do not have mutually exclusive powers and functions. Most of the decisions taken by one authority are to be approved by or remitted to for information or ratification by other authorities. Though the Syndicate is the apex executive body managing the administration of the university, it has to seek the policy approval and budget-sanction from the Senate. The Academic Council is primarily concerned with the academic curricula, syllabi and regulations. However, it does not have the ultimate authority over them as most of these are provided under Ordinances, which have to be approved by the Syndicate and not disapproved by the Visitor/ Chancellor.

Finance Committee

The Finance Committee of a university is not an independent decision-making body. It can only make recommendations on financial matters to the Executive Council which alone can take decisions on them. Some Acts provide that certain matters which involve continuing financial commitments like creation of new positions and revision of pay scales should not be considered by the Executive Council unless the Finance Committee has considered them in the first place, and made its recommendations. All universities have Finance Committees which prepare the budget, set the ceilings of expenditure and manage the university fund. It decides on investment of funds which are not required for immediate expenditure, considers and recommends purchases of equipment and stores, construction of buildings, considers and makes recommendations on the annual accounts, and so on.

The Finance Committee is chaired by the Vice Chancellor. But its most important members are the nominees (mostly officers) of the government which provide the finances. There are, in addition, one or two members of the Executive Council and one or two external members on the Finance Committee. In actual practice, however, the nominees of the funding agencies play a dominant role in the proceedings of the Finance Committee.

Planning and Evaluation Board

The Planning Board presided over by the Vice Chancellor should be a compact body. It should consist of some seven to nine members. The Chancellor, on the advice of the Vice Chancellor, should nominate the members of the planning board and their membership should be strictly on merit and provision may be made for adequate administrative support to the board.

Planning being a very important function from a developmental point of view, every university should have a Planning and Evaluation Board. It should be the principal planning body of the university. The planning board should consist of managerial and educational experts. It should be responsible for formulating the short-term and long-term plans of the university and should also be responsible for monitoring the development of the university in terms of the objectives of the university. It should have the right to advise the syndicate and the academic council on any matter, academic or administrative, which it considers necessary for the fulfillment of the objectives of the university.

ADMINISTRATION OF HIGHER EDUCATION AT THE STATE LEVEL

The administrative structure varies among states. Usually, there are three different structures dealing with educational administration at the state level. They are the Secretariat, the Directorate and the Inspectorate.

The Secretariat and the Directorate are more important as far as higher education is concerned. The Secretariat is headed by the Education Secretary. Some states have only one Education secretary who is responsible for all levels of education. Some states, on the other hand, have two or more Secretaries looking after the different levels/sectors of education. In states where there is only one Education Secretary, there are other functionaries such as Special Secretary/Deputy Secretary, exclusively dealing with higher education.

At the union level, only general and technical education falls under the purview of the Secretary. The Secretaries of the respective ministries look after professional education. A few states have established Higher Education Commission chaired by the Education Minister. An eminent educationist serves as the Vice-Chairman. The Commission is responsible for improving the organization and promoting higher education in the state. It is also responsible for determining and maintaining the standards of teaching, examination and research in the universities of the state. The functions of the Commission are similar to that of the UGC at the national level.

Generally, all the states have directorates of higher education. There are, normally, two directorates dealing with higher education such as directorates of collegiate education and directorates of technical education. A director, who takes care of the administration at the collegiate and technical education level, heads each of these directorates.

ADMINISTRATIVE STRUCTURE AT THE UNIVERSITY LEVEL

Universities in India are autonomous institutions. They have their own administrative structures and management styles different from the state. The responsibility for the smooth functioning of any institution rests upon its authorities/staff. They are the pivotal links between the public and the institute's authorities. In the context of a university, the hierarchy maintained by these functionaries is all the more interesting to observe. The different functionaries and authorities within a university system have been discussed hereby.

The Visitor/Chancellor

The President of India/Governor of the respective states is usually the "Constitutional head" of the central/state universities respectively in their capacity as the Visitor/Chancellor. The Governor by virtue of his office is also the Chancellor of the state-financed universities in the state. His role as Chancellor ensures creating right environment and conditions for the universities so as to enable them to make greater contribution to the cause of higher education in the state. It is the Chancellor's responsibility to steadily and continuously enhance the statute and quality of the university education. Without meddling in the day-to-day administration, he as the Chancellor has to share his vision, experience and thoughts in furthering the interests of the higher education. He interprets the university Act, supervises the formulation of Statutes in accordance with the University Act and resolves the conflicts between different authorities of the university. The Chancellors in some universities (e.g. U.P. State Universities Act, 1973) have rather sweeping powers to suspend/remove the Vice Chancellors. To quote Section 12, sub-sections (12) and (13) of U.P. State University Act, 1973;

> If in the opinion of the Chancellor, the Vice Chancellor willfully omits or refuses to carry out the provisions of this Act, or abuses the powers vested in him or if it otherwise appears to the Chancellor that the continuance of the Vice Chancellor in office is detrimental to the interests of the university, the Chancellor, may, after making such inquiry as he deems proper, by order, remove the Vice Chancellor. The Chancellor shall have the power to suspend the Vice Chancellor during the pendency or contemplation of any Inquiry referred to above"(S. 15 of the Act).

As per the UGC report of the Committee on Model Act for Universities, the Chancellorship should be an Office of honour to which the Court may elect a person. The Chancellor may preside at convocations and other ceremonial functions. The Chancellor, by virtue of his position and eminence in public life, could be of assistance to the university in settling conflicts and smoothening generally the relationship between various authorities of the universities.

The Report of the Committee on Governance of Universities and colleges (1971), contemplated the appointment of a Chancellor, and recommended that the Chancellor should have the privilege of presiding over the convocations of the university, but he should not be given any administrative responsibility or authority. It was suggested that the Chancellor might be nominated by the Visitor on the recommendation of the Executive Council, for a period of three years.

Undoubtedly, the post of a Chancellor is an important post as understood above but the important issue for discussion is just not having a post for name sake but make it effective. Generally in any university Chancellor of that university is nowhere seen in the picture no matter what happens in the university. If there has to be a post of a Chancellor, he/she should be given responsibility and authority so that the person can intervene in university matters. Also he/she should be a regular visitor in the university campus.

The Pro-Chancellor

In many state universities, the concerned State Education Minister is the ex-officio Pro-Chancellor with a few honorary/ conventional role during convocations, etc. In some technical/ professional universities also such as Agricultural Universities and Health Universities, the concerned Minister happens to be the Pro-Chancellor. Among the central universities, the University of Delhi has the Chief Justice of the Supreme Court of India as it's Pro-Chancellor.

The office of Pro-Chancellor is a decorative post. Ordinarily, Pro-Chancellor is next to the Chancellor and a number of University Acts provide that in the absence of the Chancellor, the Pro-Chancellor may perform such functions as may be assigned to him by the Chancellor. It often leads to political interference in the university's autonomy. The guidelines issued by the University Grants Commission prohibit the designation of a minister-pro-chancellor and that there should be a no provision for a minister-pro-chancellor.

In the Central University of Delhi, the Chief Justice of India is ex-officio Pro-Chancellor of the university. Eight Universities of Agricultural Sciences have the Minister of Agriculture of the state concerned as the ex-officio Pro-Chancellor. In the two universities of Jammu and Kashmir, the Chief Minister of the state is ex-officio Pro-Chancellor. The Ministers of Education of the state is the Pro-Chancellor in the Universities of Cochin, Calicut, Kerala, Madras, Madurai and Kamaraj. Some other universities earlier had the office of Pro-Chancellor, but the same was abolished by amendments of their Acts. There are however still many universities which need urgent amendment in their Acts for the removal of such decorative posts just for name sake.

The Vice Chancellor

The Vice Chancellor is the principal academic and administrative officer of the university. He or she chairs the Council of the university, the General Board of the Faculties and the Finance Committee of the Council. Among the main tasks of the Vice Chancellor are to provide leadership, academic and administrative to the whole university; represent the university externally; secure a financial base sufficient to allow the delivery of the university's mission, aims and objectives; and carry out certain important ceremonial and civic duties.

Vice Chancellor is the custodian of the integrity of the university. He should be a person who can provide multiple fora for its constituents, to get together beyond their own respective subject and to think beyond their subject. Also, once a certain set of rules has been set up, it is the duty of the Vice Chancellor to ensure that those rules are followed. On the qualities of a Vice Chancellor, the words of Clerk Kerr (1976), a former President of the University of California are worth quoting:

> A University President should be firm and gentle, sensitive to others but insensitive to himself, have vision, affability, broad perspective and be a seeker of truth where the truth may not hurt too much. He should sound like a mouse at home but roar like a lion abroad.

As the academic and executive head of the university, the Vice Chancellor has to play the most significant role as the leader of the university system both in the executive and academic wings. He functions as a "bridge" between the executive and the academic wings of the university. According to the UGC Model Act Committee report, the Vice Chancellor is by far the most important functionary in a university, not only at the administrative side but also for securing the right atmosphere for the teachers and the students to do their work effectively and in the right spirit.

The Vice Chancellor enjoys wide ranging powers in the administration of the university. But he has to seek the approval of the Executive Council/Syndicate and other bodies wherever necessary. The term of office for the Vice Chancellor in the central university is normally five years, with no provision for seeking a second term; in most of the state universities the Vice Chancellor holds office for a term of three years, with a provision for a second term. Vice Chancellors are mostly chosen either from university professors or from Principals of colleges. There are instances where Supreme Court/High Court Judges as also IAS/IPS or other services officers were appointed as Vice Chancellors. But most of the universities have their Vice Chancellors drawn from the teaching profession.

The Radhakrishnan Commission favoured the idea of selecting the Vice Chancellor by the Chancellor, but on the positive recommendation of one name by the Executive Council empowering the Chancellor to ask for fresh name if he considers the name unsuitable. The Kothari Commission while agreeing with the idea of the Radhakrishnan Commission suggested that as the necessary conditions are created the choice of the Vice Chancellor should eventually be left to the university concerned.

Appointment of the Vice Chancellor is made in most of the universities out of a panel of at least three names by the Governor/Chancellor, if it is state university and by the Visitor in the case of the central universities. The panel of names is prepared by a committee constituted in accordance with the provision of the Act or the Statute of the university concerned. The UGC committee on "Governance of Universities and College" (UGC, 1971) has in its report, after considering several alternatives, recommended that the Vice Chancellor may be appointed by the Visitor (or Chancellor) from amongst a panel of names submitted by a committee specially constituted for the purpose.

It is important that there must be some guidelines for the appointment of a Vice Chancellor (Sodha, 2005). The Vice Chancellor should be an academic person—academically good in his own field, he should have held some administrative position and he must have a mental framework regarding higher education system in the country, which should be evidenced by his publications on higher education. There should be a committee with senior most professors as its members to contribute in the selection procedure. The appointment procedure can be comprised of some tests to prove that the candidate for the post is academically active. The short-listed candidates should be invited to make a presentation about their vision of the university for which they are being appointed. The presentation should be made publicly in the presence of teachers, students and other representatives from the community, which will help in maintaining transparency.

In the Gajendragadkar Committee report on the governance of the university, it has been stated that the Vice Chancellor should be the principal executive and academic officer of the university and should exercise general supervision and control over the affairs of the university and give effect to the decision of all its authorities. He shall be the ex-officio Chairman of the Court, Executive Council, Academic Council, Finance Committee and Selection Committees and shall, in the absence of the Chancellor, preside at any convocation of the university for conferring degrees. It shall be the duty of the Vice Chancellor to see that the provisions of the Act, Statutes and Ordinances and Regulations are fully observed and he should have the power necessary for the discharge of this duty. His position has to be detached from the State Government.

Even if the higher education sector will in the future offer the most important recruitment base, it should of course be possible to recruit Vice Chancellors from other sectors of the community. In view of the basic assumptions presented above, however, academic leadership and professional legitimacy is an important factor. This means that the qualifications currently required should be retained. For the institutions of higher education in the arts, the artistic background required of the Vice Chancellors is indispensable and here too the current qualification requirements should of course continue to apply.

Analysis also shows that the most frequent pattern in the countries studied is for Vice Chancellors to be appointed by the governing bodies of the higher education institutions. Indeed, international comparison reveals that the appointment of Vice Chancellors by governments is the exception. From an international perspective, issues such as transparency and secrecy are central to any discussion of the process of recruiting Vice Chancellors. Various tendencies can be discerned, from total secrecy to full transparency. The most frequent pattern would appear, however, to be secrecy to begin with, followed by transparency when a limited number of candidates have been singled out.

There is a general need to assure the quality of the appointment procedures. This is a task for a national agency. It can be achieved by means of a number of complementary measures. One would be for the agency to use the experience it has acquired in undertaking this survey for the government to produce a brochure on good practice in connection with the appointment of Vice Chancellors. Another would be for the agency to arrange an annual meeting of representatives of all the governing bodies that will soon be recruiting new Vice Chancellors so that they, together with representatives of the institutions which have recently made an appointment, can discuss routines and problems.

The Pro-Vice Chancellor

There is a provision for the appointment of a Pro-Vice Chancellor in many universities who shall be appointed by the

Visitor/Chancellor on the recommendation of the Vice Chancellor or the Executive Council. In some universities, there is a provision for Rector instead of Pro-Vice Chancellor. In many universities (Tamil Nadu Universities and Karnataka Universities), where there is no provision for Pro-Vice Chancellor, the Vice Chancellor is found overburdened with all routine matters leaving little time to devote sufficient attention to the academic planning and development of the universities. The Pro-Vice Chancellor should be an eminent educationist with adequate administrative experience.

Registrar

The Registrar has traditionally been the permanent administrative head of a university. The very aspect of permanency gives the Registrar enough experience, which is at the disposal of the Vice Chancellor who has a fixed tenure. The Registrar is the ex-officio secretary of the Court/Executive Council/Syndicate. He/she is the custodian of the records, the university seal and all the other properties of the university that the Executive Council entrusts to his/her care. He/she must sign all contracts and agreements made on behalf of the university. The Registrar is expected to maintain correspondence with other statutory bodies. He/she is not an administrator but a facilitator and of the status of a professor—someone who has administrative skills, and who is sensitive to the feelings of students and teachers. He/she convenes meetings of all the bodies as per the advice of the Vice Chancellor. He/she is also responsible for the preparation of the Annual Report on the activities of the universities and other sundry matters. The practice of having a cadre or no cadre Registrar, appointed by the government, is detrimental to the university because he owes allegiance to the government and the interest of the university is secondary to him.

Dean of Faculty/School

The Dean is the head of the school/faculty of studies. Mostly, the Vice Chancellor appoints the Dean for two years, by rotation on the basis of seniority from amongst the professors of a faculty. He/she is responsible for the conduct and standards of teaching and research in his/her faculty. He/she coordinates and generally supervises these functions through heads of the departments. His/her responsibility may include arrangement for the examinations of the university in accordance with such directions as may be given by the Academic Council in respect of the students of his/her faculty/school.

Head of the Department

The Head, otherwise known as the Chairman of a Department or Center is appointed by the Vice Chancellor, for a period specified in the statutes, on a rotation basis. He/she is appointed from among the professor or readers in the department. In some of the state universities, even a lecturer can become the Head of the department. The Head convenes and presides over the meetings of the department under the general supervision of the Dean. He/she organizes teaching and research in the department and is in-charge of maintaining discipline in the classroom, laboratories, etc. He/she assigns to the teachers of the department, such duties as may be necessary, for the proper functioning of the department. The major activities undertaken by the head are to plan, execute and monitor the working of his/her department in the fields of teaching, research, consultation and extension activities.

Other Functionaries

There are some other authorities responsible for both the administrative and academic matters. The most important in this category are the Controller of Examinations, Finance Officer, Deputy Registrars and also Assistant Registrars. The position of Controller of Examinations is of immense value as examination is an important and confidential matter connected with the university administration. Another important officer appointed on deputation from the government is the Finance Officer of the university. He/she is trained in accounts and advises the university authorities regarding all financial matters. He/she has the responsibility for preparing annual budget estimates and gives it a final shape; thus, he is the custodian of the university's finance.

A UGC Committee on Alternate Models of Management with Prof. A. Jnanam as chairman submitted in January 1990 a report titled "Towards New Educational Management", which made important recommendations on various aspects of university governance. Some of the recommendations regarding the Authorities, Bodies and Committees are that the university senate or court should be a deliberative and consultative body and not a decision-making authority. It should have representation from various sections of society; that the Syndicate/ Executive Council/Board of Management should be the principal executive body; and it should not normally over-rule the decisions of the academic council in academic matters; that the Academic Council should be the principal authority as far as academic affairs are concerned; that every academic discipline should have a Board of Studies and that every university should have a finance committee, Manning and Monitoring Board, Board of Research, Board of Evaluation/Examination/Board of Extension Work and Grievance Rehearsal Committee.

The National Knowledge Commission (NKC) report in 2006, perceived the need for establishing an Independent Regulatory Authority for Higher Education (IRAHE) to better govern the higher education system in India which it noted was "over-regulated but under-governed". The British university system, on the other hand, is governed through "the noble traditions" than "rules" and "regulations". However, the role of Higher Education Funding Council of England (HEFCE) stands out in the governance, of universities and other higher education institutions in England. The funding method of the council incorporates the essentials of good governance, i.e. transparency, predictability, accountability, fairness and efficiency. The funding formula based on students, subjects and research provides the essence of financial governance in England which India may emulate to improve the university education system. The Browne Report and White Paper on British higher education also suggest students' participation in the governance process and that the increased level of fee will play a bigger role in the days to come, this will make it easier to address the issue of governance.

In developing countries like India eradication of corruption appears to be most important element of improving governance. It is pervasive in the university system as well. Incorporating objectivity will also help in mitigating the prevailing corruption in the university system. The NKC pointed out the need for improving governance of higher education. It has emphasized control over regulation. It has opined to raise fee. The NKC notes that it is for the universities to decide the level of fees but as a norm fees should meet at least 20 per cent of total expenditure in universities. The commission also suggested that to safeguard the interest of poorer students, there should be fee waivers and scheme of scholarships to help them. At the same time the UGC should not penalize by reducing grants to those universities that are able to raise more resources through fees or other means.

In view of the resource crunch and continuously declining strength of regular teaching staff in universities in India, if the university system has to survive and be able to better compete in the modern world, governance reforms and financial restructuring is needed and then surely the British experience will be a good guide along with the national mandates.

The Recommendations of the Yashpal Committee

The committee in its final report, submitted to the Ministry of Human Resource Development (MHRD) on June 24, recommended that further recognition of deemed university status be abandoned and that all deserving deemed universities be either converted to full-fledged universities or scrapped and a GRE like test be evolved for university education. The committee also said that plethora of regulatory bodies like UGC, AICTE, NCTE and the like should be replaced by a seven-member Commission for Higher Education and Research (CHER) under an Act of Parliament. It has also recommended that the position of chairperson of the proposed commission be analogous to that of Election Commissioners. Thus, buffering the new regulator against political pressures, also said that the jurisdiction of other regulators, viz. Medical Council of India, Bar Council of India and others be confined to administrative matters, with universities taking up their academic responsibilities.

Finalized on June 22 and given to HRD Minister Kapil Sibal on June 24, the report said that IITs and IIMs should be encouraged to diversify and expand their scope to work as full-fledged universities. Expressing concern on the mushrooming of engineering and management colleges, that had "largely become business entities dispensing very poor quality education", Yashpal Committee lamented the growth of deemed universities and called for a complete ban on further grant of such status. Existing ones, the committee said, should be given three years to develop as a university and fulfill the prescribed accreditation norms. Raising doubts about the source of funding of private education providers, the committee said mostly it was either "unaccounted wealth from business and political enterprises or from capitation fees". It said the system of conferring academic designations as chancellors and Vice Chancellors to members of the promoter's family should be done away with. They should submit to a national accreditation system. However, the committee underlined the need for private investment in higher education. The committee also criticized the UPA Government's policy of setting up IIMs and IITs indiscriminately, saying that mere numerical expansion, without any understanding of symptoms of poor education, would not help.

The committee has, in its interim report, suggested "creation of an all-encompassing Commission for Higher Education, a central statutory body to replace the existing regulatory bodies" like the University Grants Commission, the Medical Council of India, All India Council for Technical Education, NCTE and many others The proposed autonomous statutory body will comprise six members and a chairman appointed by the President. State Higher Education Councils, along the lines of those existing in West Bengal, Kerala and Andhra Pradesh, will form the second tier of the system.

Taking a firm stand against the liberal granting of deemed university status by the UGC in recent years, the committee recommended that approval for deemed universities be stopped forthwith. Further, all existing ones must submit to new accreditation norms within three years failing which they ought to lose their deemed university status. The committee has stressed the need for more attention to undergraduate programmes and a multi-disciplinary approach to learning. The IITs and IIMs, "which are bright spots in the otherwise dismal higher education scenario" should, while keeping intact their unique features, expand their academic reach to include the humanities and arts, and function as full-fledged universities. The committee recommends that all research bodies connect with universities in their vicinity, and that all universities combine teaching and research.

Some Thoughts on Governance of Higher Education

The centre/state universities and deemed universities present two existing models of governance. While the system of governance in the deemed university is based on the wealth of experience in the universities, no reverse flow of learning by experience has occurred. The deemed universities have developed a flexible system of governance, which combines the essential elements of academic autonomy with functional efficiency, consistent with rapid response to the fast changing world and rapid advances in knowledge in research, teaching and consultancy efforts. It is obvious that the structure of governance of a deemed university cannot be applied as such to a normal university on account of the large difference in the available infrastructure, the number of students, the student/teacher ratio, the financial support per student, the seriousness and level of the students and the quality of the faculty, but a number of features in the governance of deemed universities can be incorporated in the governance of normal universities, to improve their performance.

The structure of governance in the universities in India, which has changed very little with time, is based on authority, centralization, conformity and discouragement of initiative and innovation; the emphasis is on strict adherence to rules, rather than high level of performance. Some aspects of governance, which need attention are the act, the statutory academic and executive bodies, decentralization of authority and responsibility, autonomy at all levels, the recruitment/service rules and rotation of heads/deans, etc. these should be examined in view of available experience. Changes in the governance must be made to improve the performance and make the introduction of modern management techniques/practices possible and desirable.

Many aspects of participatory management are already present in the university system. Teachers are represented on a number of committees, which take executive and academic decisions. Students also have a union, which in principle can interact with the faculty and the administration for evolution and implementation of academic and related programs. The employees do not in general have any role in management except fighting for the protection and welfare of the members.

The present system, despite its inherently representative structure is great, only for preserving status quo and discourages significant changes like new disciplines, new academic programmes and innovations in teaching, consultancy and extension. It is not uncommon in universities, to remain immune to new disciplines, needed by the changing world. Innovation and continued relevance can only be ensured, when authority and responsibility can be given to a department or group of teachers, who have a worthwhile venture in mind; the system must not only enable this to take place but also positively encourage it. Other aspects of participatory management, which may be applicable to the management of the university, are:

(i) evaluation of teaching programmes and teachers by students;

(ii) peer evaluation of teachers and candidates for teachers;

(iii) encouraging suggestions and complaints;

(iv) joint committees (teachers, students, employees) to consider/implement new programmes;

(v) quality circles; and

(vi) incentives, etc.

Principles of University Management

Mathai, Pareek and Venkateshwara Rao have outlined some general principles applicable to university management; these are:

University and People

(i) The goals should be challenging, fairly focused and shared by the members of the university community and society at large.

(ii) Enough trust should be put in the members, who should

be given autonomy, consistent with work towards accepted goals.

(iii) Committed key people should be identified and empowered, before undertaking significant tasks.

(iv) The matrix organization, where persons in a given discipline are put in a department and persons from different departments are chosen to form a team for an interdisciplinary task, may be most desirable.

(v) Healthy traditions and culture should bc nurtured.

(vi) Linkage with interacting systems should be built and strengthened.

(vii) Working and thinking together is essential for healthy development.

(viii) Delicate balance between individual autonomy and group effort towards a common goal should be maintained.

(ix) Self-renewal should be a continuous process.

(x) The leader should be fully committed, non-competitive, respectful of other's contribution, willing to provide autonomy, capable of establishing linkages to interacting system, ready to learn from experience and able to effectively dispossess the institution, which he has built.

Organizational Structure

(i) The university organization should be transparent and as flat as possible, in other words it should have minimum number of levels; this applied to academic as well as non-academic sides.

(ii) The structure should be like a matrix. The columns represent fairly autonomous departments, while rows represent centrally administered tasks like postgraduate programmes, research and sponsored research and consultancy, etc. organized by a Dean, etc.

(iii) Decision-making should be based on an interconnected system of committees, which involves a high cost of time but results in much wanted participation by the faculty and other sections of the university. Members of faculty should take part in committees concerned with administrative officers should participate in academic committees.

Emphasis on Academics

(i) Academic roles should be given much more importance than non-academic ones so that there is an urge to be excellent teacher/researcher rather than Head of Department or Dean.

(ii) Non-academic appointment like Dean, etc. should be term appointments only and not carry any financial incentive; some relaxation of teaching load may be given.

Norms and Culture

(i) Professional and peer relationship should be encouraged. Professional excellence must be the most important criterion for recognition.

(ii) Seniority alone should not be the criterion for administrative appointment; the rationale system should not be automatic.

(iii) Mature organizational behaviour, particularly, when a person assumes or gives up an administrative appointment must be cultivated.

Thus, there is need for more decentralization in the administrative set-up of the universities. Every university has to provide for systematic management training for all levels of functionaries in the university with a view to not only making them function effectively but also preparing them to shoulder higher responsibilities as they move up in the hierarchy. Good governance is essential to achieve rapid and inclusive development. In the context of the university, good governance has to achieve academic excellence, academic needs and welfare of students, quality faculty participation including their retention and to provide them with all necessary facilities and freedom. It is also important to ensure quality service to faculty and students through skilled and committed support services, and finally fulfill public expectations and provide full transparency. Good governance has many entry points as depicted in the following diagram:

Good Governance has many entry points...

REFERENCES

Government of India, *Report of the Education Commission (1964-66) Education and National Development,* 1966, GoI, New Delhi.

IGNOU, *Planning and Management of Higher Education*, MES 104, pp. 7-57.

Kerr, I.T. (Ed.) (1976). In J.H. Newman, *The Idea of a University*, the Clarendon Press, Oxford.

Mathai, R.J., Pareek U. and Rao, Venkateshwara T. (1994). "Designing Effective University System", in M.V. Mathur, R.K. Arora and M. Sogani (eds), *Indian University System: Revitalization and Reform,* 1994, Wiley Eastern Ltd., New Delhi, p. 92.

Pylee, M.V. (1994). "Governance of Universities", In M.V. Mathur, R.K. Arora and M. Sogani (eds), *Indian University System: Revitalization and Reform,* Wiley Eastern Ltd., New Delhi, p. 139.

Sengupta, Kamna, Reena Srivastava and M.S. Sodha (2003). "Governance of Universities: Some Aspects, Higher Education Policy and Practices", *University News*, 1, pp. 43-50.

Sodha, M., and K. Srivastava (1998). "Management of Change in Universities", *University News*, 36(31), pp. 4-11.

Soni, Rashmi (2007). Intellectuals' Expectations from a University: An Exploratory Study, Ph.D. Thesis, Department of Education, University of Lucknow, Lucknow.

UGC (1964). Model Act Committee Report, New Delhi, p. 8.

UGC (1971). *Report of the Committee on Governance of Universities*, New Delhi, pp. 66-69.

UGC (1971). *Report of the Committee on Governance of Universities and Colleges (Gajendragadkar Committee)*, UGC, New Delhi.

UGC (1990). *Towards New Educational Management*, New Delhi: UGC.

Varma, M. and Sodha, M.S. (2005). *Transcripts of Open Conversations with Teachers of University of Lucknow.*

Vaish, L.P. and R.N. Srivastava (1994). "University Administration". In M.V. Mathur, R.K. Arora and M. Sogani (eds.), *Indian University System: Revitalization and Reform,* Wiley Eastern Ltd., New Delhi, p. 169.

Higher Education Management 7

There has been considerable effort in improving schools and building new universities to increase the quality of the workforce, or human capital, in order to improve economic growth, military security, public health, cultural vitality and political judiciousness (Bowen, 1977; Schultz, 1981). Building of a nation depends on the development of intellectual capacity. Higher education has become, and is likely to remain, a central activity of developed and many developing countries. It is now the preferred approach to prepare a country's able young people for tomorrow's Darwinian social environment. From Mexico, Brazil and Poland to Malaysia, South Korea and China the number of universities and specialized institutes has multiplied and enrollments have swelled (Altbach, 2002).

Naturally, questions have arisen about how these universities should be managed, and by whom. How should they be governed? Which students should be admitted? Who should be the teachers, and toward what ends should the students be educated? And how can they be financed, or who should pay for all this expanding advanced education? The possible answers to these and other salient questions are complicated by the fact that higher learning is expanding at the time when major social upheavals are erupting in many areas of the world. The questions that are largely internal to universities are influenced by fundamental external changes in the societies in which the universities carry out their activities. These pressures have led to the giving away of traditional patterns in the way universities are run (Keller, 2004). The unhurried decision-making, the inward-looking and pre-occupied concerns, and the feeble and unremarkable administration by university executives have been forced to yield to stronger management, swifter and deeper changes, and the creation of new, more thoughtful strategies so that the colleges and universities can respond more adequately to threats and opportunities.

The Factors Affecting Change

Most universities are shaped appreciably by external factors and large shifts in their environment, though many professors consider themselves to be the principal architects of their academic lives. These external developments have become quite powerful and appear to be multiplying. A growing challenge for university faculty and administrators is the extent to which colleges and universities should yield or adapt to these new conditions.

An example can be quoted with reference to the rapid advance of digital technology, connecting the world through the Internet. Computers have become ubiquitous in much of the developed world and are increasingly available in developing nations. The information and data obtainable from software programs now competes with that in esteemed university libraries. How should universities incorporate the new technology and to what extent should they modify pedagogy and research, or increase collaboration with other academics, or deliver more courses online to new, enlarged audiences? Should nations follow India's lead in the field of software engineering? Or for that matter Great Britain's lead in distance education?

There have also been several shifts in the political atmosphere that affect higher education. These shifts differ greatly from country to country, but a few trends are apparent. One is the changing role of government in the patronage, financing and control of their universities. As V. Lynn Meek observes, "Higher education is characterized by a common trend whereby governments increasingly refrain from detailed steering of their respective higher education systems in favour of more global policies that determine the boundary conditions under which institutions may operate" (Amaral, Meek and Larsen, 2003). Governments now prefer to concentrate on such matters as results, efficiency of operations and service to national needs rather than giving specific directions. This trend allows higher education institutions more freedom to design their own practices, but it compels them to become more strategic, better managed, financially entrepreneurial and educationally productive and innovative. As higher education becomes more essential to each nation's future prospects, pressures are likely to continue so that colleges and universities become more inclusive and representative.

The Problems

Perhaps the most challenging problem for anyone connected with higher education management is the finance. The costs of higher education have been increasing faster than rise in the cost of living in most countries. For governments that have built new colleges or universities and enlarged their existing institutions, there is the need for much greater appropriations for higher education. More sophisticated scientific equipment, larger libraries corresponding to the exponential growth of knowledge, the growing expenses for digital technology, rising cost of employees, greater financial aid for needy students, larger salaries for the faculty, and increased staff for management and student services have all contributed to the escalating costs of the universities.

To add to the financial difficulties, some countries such as Finland refuse to charge tuition; other nations also believe that attendance at a university is a public good not a private benefit, and thus ought to be kept as inexpensive for students and their parents as possible. For instance, Oxford and Cambridge have astonishingly low fees even though many students come from leading families. In America, the State of California charges its public university students very little, even at its prestigious research universities with their noted and highly paid professors and expensive facilities. However, the World Bank has classified higher education as non-merit.

At the root of the financial problem is the desire of more and more nation-states to have the most highly educated and trained population possible to compete in world markets and the new knowledge-based economy. This is because knowledge is the key factor in the increasingly post-industrial world. This recognition has had profound consequences for higher education. It has moved colleges, research institutes and universities into a central position in society (Kerr, 1964; Keller, 2003). Governments worry more about the quality of these institutions, while students, keen to get enrolled in classes, see them as pathways to position, wealth and privilege. What used to be education for an elite minority has increasingly become higher education for the masses. The finest professors and scholarly researchers have gained new prominence, with some of the best professors—especially in the United States—now receiving six-figure salaries or being allowed to start up businesses based on their discoveries (Slaughter and Rhodes, 2004).

While this is certainly not the first time major social changes have impacted higher education; the multitude of demographic, technological, political, economic and religious developments at the present time demands a penetrating analysis of the challenges that academic managers, faculty and governments need to confront. Nearly every facet of higher education appears to be under scrutiny and even assault. This becomes evident from some of the basic questions surrounding higher education today. Some of the issues are as follows:

1. *Who is to be taught?* Should universities be reserved for the brightest and the best? Or should they reach out to and include mediocre students, young people from poor family households, and under-represented minorities? Clearly, the issue—for whom a country should design its higher education system—is undergoing interrogation and in some countries, it is leading to aggressive debates and decisions in the courts.
2. *What should the colleges and universities teach?* Should the universities teach what the faculty thinks is best or what the marketplace of students wants to learn? Should states, provinces and national governments—or others, like religious groups—have a powerful say in what young people need to know? How should global teaching

be? To what extent should science, engineering, and business education be available to all students?

3. *How should students be taught?* Should there be large lectures or smaller classes and seminars? What role should technology play in today's pedagogy? How extensively should modern technology—film, tapes, the Internet, CD-ROMs, television, videoconferencing and the like—be used?
4. *How long should students study at the level of higher education?* Should undergraduate study be for two, three or four years? Should online courses be available at any time? How long should training in the professions take? How many years of study should be required for a doctoral degree? Should brilliant students be allowed to progress faster?
5. *Who should teach?* Should professors be engaged largely full-time or mostly part-time, as in Latin America and China? Should they be mainly scholars and researchers with doctoral degrees or mainly skilful practitioners or former experienced workers or executives? Should universities bring in famous persons as speakers or invite learned or expert practitioners to teach for short periods as scholars-in-residence? Should graduate students teach the basic courses, freeing professors for research, consulting, or advanced instruction?
6. *Where should the teaching take place?* Is it best to locate universities in the major cities or in more pastoral, less diversion-rich settings? Should contemporary universities establish branches in other areas of their region or in other countries as an increasing number of American institutions have done? How much learning should take place in homes, offices or workplaces, either online or in off-campus deliveries?
7. *How much research?* Should most professors be expected to conduct research and engage in high level scholarly activity and publish? How much teaching should the best

research faculty do? Should universities collaborate with industry in research? If so, to what extent?

8. *Who should pay for higher learning?* Should university costs be borne largely by the national government, or by the nation's provinces, states or leading cities? Or should the costs be paid largely by the students and their parents (Johnson, 1986; St. John, 2003)? Should universities seek to raise money through quasi-commercial enterprises, patents, faculty enterprises, sports events and the like (Bok, 2003)? For the growing number of private universities in many countries, should governments help support them or their students? Should there be large scale for needed students? Should the rich pay for the poor?
9. *How should universities be governed?* Who should set policy for a country's universities? The Central Government, the regional or local political and business leaders or each university? Who within each university should be involved in helping to shape the policies, programs and practices of the institution? How can colleges and universities best adapt to the new conditions they face (Clark, 1998; Keller 1983)?
10. *To whom should universities be accountable?* The national or state government? All those who help support the university? Some licensing or accrediting body? A board of trustees or overseers? Who should assess the accounts? What contributes to quality for an institution?
11. *How much independence should universities have?* Should public universities be free to establish their own programs and hire their professors? Or should the state limit the offerings and help screen the appointment and retention of teachers for instance in Arab states (Mazawi, 2004)? How free should professors be to teach what they believe in is most important? Should universities be free to engage in politics? In religious discussions? In cultural and economic reform movements?

Approach

Clearly, there is a plethora of management challenges facing the higher education system in every nation. The combination of internal pressures and powerful external forces of change requires that each college and university create a satisfactory process for decision making and a strategy for survival, growth and increasing expenses. The new importance—and rising costs—of higher learning, training, and research for a country's economy, polity and culture has tugged numerous national governments into establishing fresh national policies for their universities. Also, as more corporate and commercial enterprises depend on research, special knowledge, and advanced training to be successful in the increasingly competitive global economy, the business sector of most nations has become more concerned with the management and content of their country's colleges, universities and research institutes.

Thus, higher education today is often engaged in a three-way tussle, with government, business and academic battling for changes that each believes is vital. In some countries such as the United States and several Latin American nations, the students and their parents are becoming more influential in what the universities teach, how they teach and how much they charge. In other countries, religious leaders are gathering an increasing arsenal of weapons to shape their nation's educational content in a more devout direction. To some extent, the struggle to dominate the operation of universities is an age-old one (Barker, 1930; Marsden, 1984; Rashdall, 1936). But the intensity of the discussions and maneouvers seems to have grown considerably.

National governments and their leaders have chosen to manage their universities in different ways. South Korea, for instance, sensing expanded competition from China, the United States, and Japan, has decided to press its universities to be more research oriented. In Austria, on the other hand, the universities have long been regarded as state agencies, with faculty having lifetime civil service appointments. And the management of the universities, except for teaching and research, has been in the hands of legislators and government bureaucrats, in a kind of dualism. But in recent years a radically new higher education policy has been enacted. The Australian Government has cut its universities loose to compete, plan their own strategies and contend for students, professors and dollars. Management has shifted from state control and mandates to individual university rectors, governing boards and faculty managers, who will exercise greatly enhanced powers.

Just as many colleges and universities have begun to set their own directions and decide on their own priorities, national governments from Brazil to Bulgaria have begun to re-examine their policies toward higher education. They are faced by many of the same factors, viz. the need for a better educated workforce, the desire for improved research and teaching, the growing demand from the young for higher education, the government's diminishing ability to pay for the necessities, and a recognition that in-house managers and their faculty are more likely to build useful houses of intellect than government ministers. For many countries, the changes in state policy have meant a significantly enlarged role for the university's leaders and an increased need for them to create an appropriate strategy to steer their academic vessels through more turbulent waters.

New Ingredients for a Strategy

Today, a growing number of academic institutions need to make hard choices. To do so, universities require "a steering mechanism" (Clark, 1998), e.g. a small group of academic executives and concerned faculty who can agree on a competitive strategy to pilot their institution. As the number of public and private institutions increases, the competition among them for students, faculty and financial support intensifies. As external conditions change, universities must decide how to adjust to them. Strategic decision making has become imperative.

If colleges and universities now need more focus, efficiency, and responsiveness to the rapidly changing environment, the question arises: Who should decide on the strategy? The opinion is that the efforts to make difficult choices and set bold, new directions by consensus among the entire faculty, key staff persons and the managers have been fruitless and time-squandering. However, there is almost equal disdain for corporate-like designs from the top by a strong-willed president, rector, chancellor or governing body. Such designs have proven to be too idiosyncratic and difficult to implement. So contemporary strategy mailing and execution seems to demand more determined but skilful academic leaders who can solicit faculty contributions and win an acceptable degree of concurrence. Universities, like hospitals and high technology firms, are entities in which the "workers" are highly talented, expert and professional colleagues. Managing a university is largely a matter of managing intellectual talent and expertise.

This recognition has caused more institutions to change the requirements for their presidents. The appointment of politically connected, locally popular, or intellectually notable persons is yielding to a wider search for diplomatic change agents who are financially wise. In addition to improved central leadership, numerous universities are deciding that they need to engage in strategic planning, an activity that began in the early 1980s in countries such as the United States and Great Britain (Keller, 1983). Colleges and universities face increased financial strictures and new and increased competitive threats from the expanding number of other higher education institutions, many of which were scraping to climb in enrollment, quality and prestige. Universities also need to respond to the increased diversity of students, to demands by working adults for continuing higher education, to the rapid advance of computers and other technologies. Universities are expected to respond as institutions, not as separate collections of academic departments or schools, or as individual scholars.

Strategic planning is a form of planning and priority action steps initiated to counteract threats and exploit opportunities. It is an entity to protect oneself or overcome those elements that are threatening. It is also a core or chain of strategic moves that allows a group or organization to seize new opportunities, to win a victory, gain market share, overcome discrimination, or achieve new stature. In recent years, many colleges and universities have either felt threatened or seen new opportunities for growth in the changes taking place in the higher education landscape. Or they were newly established and needed a strategy to decide how to structure themselves, who to serve, what to teach and how to finance their operations among the existing institutions.

The Experimental Steps

However, colleges and universities have for centuries been largely faculty-driven collegial associations pursuing their own scholarly interests, unused to thinking about how their entire organization can and should respond to major societal shifts and needs, or how it might shrewdly maneouver the organization to anew and more prominent position in the constellation of higher education. So, stronger management and competitive strategies did not graft easily. The older ideas about academic governance and management are also being refuted by an increasing number of successful college and university transformations (Clark, 1998; Graham and Diamond, 1997; Keller, 2004).

To introduce strategy formulation, colleges and universities had to devise new processes for joint governance and management so that both the old tradition of faculty direction setting and the introduction of stronger management could be combined. Some institutions have leaned heavily on maximum faculty input and wide participatory involvement, which numerous proponents of continued faculty autonomy advised (Bensimon and Neumann, 1993; Birnbaum, 1991; Duke, 2002).

Others installed stronger management teams to tug the professors into collective decision making about the university's future emphases, cheered on by advocates of stronger leadership and clearer purposes (Duderstadt, 2004; Fisher and Koch, 1996). Other scholars argued that the process of strategic design depends on the particular "culture" of the college or university, no two of which have similar histories and arrangements of decision making (Eckel and Kezar, 2003; Kuh and Whitt, 1988); thus, some universities have employed novel processes to select the future priorities that work best for their institutions.

The process for a university's strategic planning is complicated by the faculty's nostalgia and reluctance to accept the resulting effects of their advocacy for more higher learning. The substance of strategic planning and enactment is also undergoing renovation. The glacial shifts affecting society are prompting more universities to pay attention to conditions outside higher education such as demographics, technology, and international development and cultural and political values. A university's strategy formulation must increasingly consider other institutions in its ecosystem: local and national governments, important business firms, the media, its graduates and supporters, powerful interest groups, and its student markets.

Financial worries are getting worse, so attracting monetary support from corporations, foundations and affluent citizens has become a major consideration for colleges, universities and research institutes everywhere, compelling everyone to become mendicants. Lifetime positions are being reserved for only a minority of the finest professors. Given the pace of change, strategic decision making and implementation have become swifter; and given the growing number of discontinuities in modern times, the strategies should be more flexible and open to alteration (Keller, 1997). Such rapidly derived new strategies or modifications of an existing strategic set of actions call for better justifications and communication with all the persons affected or curious; and they should be abundant and honest.

Strategic thinking should concern itself with more than a university's own programs, campus facilities, and personnel. If it is not located in an area with such amenities, the university should plan to facilitate the development of such a network of facilities nearby that supports intellectual, cultural and personal growth alongside its classroom explorations.

Finally, universities may need to look beyond strategic actions, which are primarily directed at competition against perceived rivals, and imagine and create structural changes in the way they conduct their operations. Technological innovations are forcing structural changes in pedagogy. The spread of mass instead of elite higher education is bringing a more engaged and practical kind of higher learning and creating new vestibules to college for immigrants or the inadequately prepared short institutes instead of traditional semesters are being introduced for certain areas of learning or for new adult constituencies of learners.

An Insight

A deeper understanding is required for successfully meeting the new challenges and devising helpful strategies. A university's members can easily mistake attempts at appropriate adaptive change as an overthrow of tradition, a power grab by administrators, an expanding disrespect of faculty voice, a foolish attempt to predict the future, a dangerous increase in bureaucracy, a pandering to student demands, or an attempt to lessen the hard-won freedom of academic inquiry. Blame game needs to be replaced by a more profound analysis of the new centrality of knowledge and the universities that dispense knowledge and of the novel elements and glacial shifts of 21st century societies. Numerous universities and governments are struggling to discern the new currents and find better ways to deal with them, while clinging to what is essential for free and higher learning. The challenges are many and real. Definitely, the strategies need to be meaningful and insightful.

REFERENCES

American Association of University Professors (AAUP) (1995). *AAUP Policy Documents and Reports,* 8th edition. Washington, DC: American Association of University Professors Press.

Baldridge, J. Victor (1971). *Power and Conflict in the University: Research in the Sociology of Complex Organizations.* New York: J. Wiley.

Baldwin, Roger G., and Chronister, Jay L. (2001). *Teaching without Tenure: Policies and Practices for a New Era.* Baltimore: Johns Hopkins University Press.

Birnbaum, Robert (1988). *How Colleges Work: The Cybernetics of Academic Organization and Leadership.* San Francisco: Jossey-Bass.

Birnbaum, Robert (2000). *Management Fads in Higher Education: Where They Came From, What They Do, Why They Fail.* San Francisco: Jossey-Bass.

Bolman, Lee G. and Deal, Terrence E. (1997). *Reframing Organizations: Artistry, Choice, and Leadership,* 2nd edition. San Francisco: Jossey-Bass.

Berger, Joseph B. and Milem, Jeffrey (2000). "Organizational Behavior in Higher Education and Student Outcomes." In *Higher Education: Handbook of Theory and Research,* Vol. XV, ed. John C. Smart. New York: Agathon.

Bryson, John M. (1988). *Strategic Planning for Public and Nonprofit Organizations*. San Francisco: Jossey-Bass.

Council for Higher Education Accreditation (2002). *1998 Recognition Standards*. Retrieved in January 2002. http://www.chea.org

Etzioni, Amitai (1964). *Modern Organizations*. Englewood Cliffs, NJ: Prentice-Hall.

Fisher, James L., and Koch, James V. (1996). *Presidential Leadership*. Phoenix, AZ: ACE/Oryx Press.

Gieger, Roger (1986). *The Growth of American Research Universities, 1900–1940*. New York: Oxford University Press.

Hyman, Harold M. (1986). *American Singularity: The 1787 Northwest Ordinance, the 1862 Homestead and Morrill Acts, and the 1944 GI Bill of Rights*. Athens: University of Georgia Press.

Holmes, Jeffrey (1985). *20/20 Planning*. Ann Arbor: Society for College and University Planning.

Kerr, Clark (1963). *The Uses of the University*. Cambridge, MA: Harvard University Press.

Keller, George (1983). *Academic Strategy: The Management Revolution in American Higher Education*. Baltimore: Johns Hopkins University Press.

—— (1997). Examining What Works in Strategic Planning. In *Planning and Managing for a Changing Environment*, edited by M.W. Peterson, D.D. Dill, L.A. Mets, and Associates. San Francisco: Jossey-Bass.

—— (1999-2000). "The Emerging Third Stage in Higher Education Planning". *Planning for Higher Education* 28(2): 1-7.

—— (2006). "Higher Education Management: Challenges and Strategies". In James J.F. Forest and Phillip G. Altbach (eds.), *International Handbook of Higher Education*, Netherlands: Springer, pp. 229-42.

Mintzberg, Henry (1994). *The Rise and Fall of Strategic Planning*. New York: Free Press.

Millett, John (1984). *Conflict in Higher Education: State Government Coordination Versus Institutional Independence*. San Francisco: Jossey-Bass.

Penn, State (1997). *Academic Excellence: Planning for the Twenty-First Century*. University Park, PA: Office of the President.

——. (2002a). *CIC Institutions' Strategic Planning Practices*. University Park, PA: Center for Quality and Planning.

——. (2002b). *Strategic Indicators: Measuring and Improving University Performance*. University Park, PA: Center for Quality and Planning.

Pusser, Brian (2000). "The Contemporary Politics of Access Policy: California after Proposition 209." In *The States and Public Higher Education:*

Affordability, Access, and Accountability, ed. Donald E. Heller. Baltimore: Johns Hopkins University Press.

Rowley, Daniel James and Herbert Sherman (2001). *From Strategy to Change: Implementing the Plan in Higher Education.* San Francisco: Jossey-Bass.

Schmidtlein, Frank A. (1990). Why Linking Budgets to Plans Has Proven Difficult in Higher Education. *Planning for Higher Education* 18(2): 9-23.

Schmidtlein, Frank A. and Toby H. Milton (1990). (Editors) *Adapting Strategic Planning to Campus Realities.* New Directions for Institutional Research No. 67. San Francisco: Jossey-Bass.

Slaughter, Sheila and Leslie, Larry L. (1997). *Academic Capitalism.* Baltimore: Johns Hopkins University Press.

Veysey, Laurence (1965). *The Emergence of the American University.* Chicago: University of Chicago Press.

Woo, Carolyn (1998). Strategic Planning Workshop. Presentation at the CIC Academic Leadership Program, University of Illinois-Chicago.

Governance and Administration of Higher Education Around the World

8

Governance and Administration: Meaning and Concept

Governance in higher education refers to the means by which higher educational (also tertiary or post-secondary) institutions are formally organized and managed, though often there is a distinction between definitions of management and governance. It refers to the structure and processes by which decisions are made at institutions of higher education. This includes the role of certain groups within the institution as well as the specific decision-making style being practiced. Simply, university governance is the way in which universities are operated.

Administration refers to the structure and processes by which the institution is led and managed. The leadership group (e.g. vice-rectors, associate deans, deputy provost) forms the management or executive team to whom all administrative units have to report. The team's responsibility usually includes functional areas like marketing, finance or infrastructure. The administrators are employed by the college or university for a very specific job (e.g. marketing manager or enrollment officer) for which they receive a yearly budget, personnel and support. They report to the university leaders and are accountable for the rcsults.

Administration: The Role of Leadership and Management

The administration of academic organizations is a complex process given their distinctive nature. Colleges and universities have ambiguous goals, are "people-processing' institutions, engage in problematic technologies, involve professionals to provide core services and are vulnerable to a changing environment. Consequently, they cannot be defined as standard bureaucracies.

Quality has been evolved as the guiding concept for university administration, especially in Europe. Countries like Sweden, the Netherlands and Denmark have built their policies around the concept of quality and self-evaluation. The U.K. has linked resource allocation to performance indicators. U.S. colleges and universities have been autonomous and market oriented for decades, and hence have a longer tradition of "total quality management" (Dill, 1993; Rhoades and Sporn, 2002). The meaning of quality assurance and assessment, particularly as they relate to strategic management of institutions in the U.S. are quite different from their counterparts in Europe. Context matters in terms of long standing political and professional structures, such as the strength of campus administrations and weak State Governments in the U.S. versus the power of national ministries, civil servant status and corporatism in Europe. In Europe, quality assurance has been linked to resource allocation to an extent that it has not been in the U.S. Yet strategic management at the institutional level has been undertaken in the U.S. in ways that have not been tried in Europe.

With increased autonomy, institutions of higher education have been accountable for their performance by setting specific goals through contracts. As a consequence, the funding is connected to specific output indicators. Academic institutions can autonomously manage their enterprise and are accountable for the results. The role of administration and leadership vis-à-vis the faculty has seen some major shifts as well. In Europe, the delegation of authority to the institutional level has meant the need to increase the capacity to manage and lead the university. In the U.S. this trend has been in place for many decades, and the capacity of administration shows in its size. In general, leaders and administrators gained more authority in speaking and deciding for the institutions. Conflicts with the faculty have been a natural consequence.

Administration and governance of higher education have become complex processes. On the one hand, institutional autonomy provides the necessary flexibility to design and manage the enterprise in an environment of constraints and opportunities. On the other hand, the funding of higher eduction has become increasingly more competitive. Public institutions can no longer count on the state to pay the bill. Private institutions need to constantly refine and renew their mission. Colleges and universities in general need to apply strategic management, management by objectives, and quality management to create a sustainable future for the institution. Administrators and institutional leaders are at the heart of the operational functioning of the institution. Through board control they are accountable for the success or failure of any one academic year. Faculty need to concentrate their activities on the core academic "product"—research and teaching—and have to be involved and engaged in institutional management through efficient and effective governance structures. Departing from the past, this would mean leaner teams or structures and delegates representing the interests of specific groups. Only through a balance and a viable working relationship are colleges and universities able to succeed.

Modern Governance Structures: Three Models

There are three models of modern governance structures and trends, viz. the shared governance, corporate/entrepreneurial approaches, and flexible/learning architectures.

Shared governance refers to the political aspect of academic organization. It stresses the importance of negotiations as well as the role and power of different stakeholders. Decision-making under this shared approach prescribes participation of all relevant groups with their different goals and values. Conflicts are an integral part of this system and limit the formal authority of institutional leaders. Political groups and their interests impede a rational and objective decision-making process.

Corporate models of governance emphasize the entrepreneurial character of colleges and universities. Like Clark pointed out in his seminal work, the entrepreneurial university looks different from the traditional 'Humboldt University'. Basically, only a few layers of governance exist within higher education organizations. The role of the state is purely supervisory. Policy and strategy are delegated to the institutions. A board of supervisors serves as a buffer between the institution and state. The real power lies at the executive board level, with the rector or president as the leader. The senate has purely advisory functions, especially for academic issues. All academic leaders like deans or department heads are represented in the executive committee. With this new structure, governance has become faster and more efficient. At the same time, it has become more contested.

Another approach is that of a *flexible governance structure* which enhances learning and adaptation (Dill, 1999). Over the years, more flexibility was necessary to compete in (and adapt to) an increasingly dynamic environment and market. As a result, ad-hoc project structures emerged, serving as governing or working groups and work on important decisions for the institution. Applying the learning framework (Senge, 1990) to higher education, learning is defined as systematic problem solving, learning from own experience, learning from others, experimentation with new approaches, transferring knowledge and measuring learning. Governance would take a different form. A joint committee overseeing teaching and learning experiments, external advisory committees to comment on curricula, university-wise evaluation committees or a committee of associate deans of teaching are among the examples which describe the new architecture (Dill, 1999). The participation of different stakeholders is important, but should focus on outcomes rather than on political consensus (Kezar and Eckel, 2002).

Thus, governance structures are changing and should support fast reaction times of colleges and universities. Nevertheless, ample opportunity needs to be guaranteed for involvement and engagement of all important groups of the university. The challenge seems to be to find ways to reunite shared governance models with the recent need for flexible actions. Colleges and universities are increasingly developing answers to this question in order to stay successful for many years to come.

Governance: Its Current Form and Future Trends Toward a Market Model

The roles and responsibilities for governing institutions of higher education have been changing substantially over the last decade. Especially at European universities, senior faculty and the state ministers have played a very important role in decision-making. Over the years, with a shift towards marketization and deregulation, the institutional or middle level (i.e. deans, rectors, presidents) has gained increased power. A new distribution of power and responsibility has been established between the state, the board, the senate and the institutional leadership. Governing bodies remain a key element in institutional governance. Partnerships between different groups represented in these bodies can improve institutional efficiency and effectiveness. At the same time, "over-governing" can discourage innovation and enhance academic opportunism and quick decision-making. The art of finding the right balance is a crucial factor of successful university management.

The role of the state has changed with the 1990s and new policy agendas in Europe. Financial constraints triggered the shift from a state control to a state supervision model, targeted towards navigation from a distance. Ex-ante control has been replaced by ex-post control and the rise of the evaluative state (Dill, 1998). Contracts between universities and the state define funding and output. Basic funds are allocated based on performance indicators for core services in teaching and research. Additional financial resources are project and competition based.

Boards have been created to oversee institutional activities. In many countries, they serve as representatives of the general public and the owners of public universities. Many different models exist for the composition and authority of boards in Europe. Although the U.S. board model emphasizes the importance of lay membership, the European model is often a mixture of lay and academic membership. Their power can reach from purely advisory to the state bureaucracy to a supervisory function similar to the corporate world. In Europe, boards are becoming increasingly important. In the U.S. their role has been contested given the very political nature of their appointment or election (Gumport and Pusser, 1999).

In general, boards have evolved into an important management component of modern universities in Europe. In the past they have been supporting fund-raising. Nowadays, their functions include the resolution of university problems, financial forecasting and advising in strategic choices. For the institution, boards can provide technical and professional advice, take a long-term perspective, act as the referee for internal arguments, audit and oversee university activities, scan the environment, and appoint institutional leaders. The nomination process of board members is clearly important. The entrepreneurs have a right to select board members and share this with senate or institutional representatives.

Another very important governing body is the senate or academic board. Senates are certainly internally focused and make institution-wide decisions, mostly in academic and programmatic matters. The composition of academic boards or senates resembles a democratic or representative body. Only very few ex-officio members are allowed. Basically, a senate should represent the overall faculty and its departments. A recent development have led to the increasing power of the management team—or, like it is often called, the executive committee—which consists of the head of the institution (e.g. rector, president, vice chancellor) and deputy leaders. This body incorporates the key academic and administrative officers. It is essential to bring together these persons who are directly responsible for the core activity of the college or university. It has been referred to by Clark as "strengthened steering core", entrusting the "steering of the weekly business of the university to those bodies best qualified to deal with it and tackling some of the most difficult and sensitive issues itself" (Shattock, 2003). A management team can consist of the leadership team, the deans and some of the most important senior administrators. It can also be the hub for a governing body structure in close touch with other bodies within the institution. It must act speedily and decisively on behalf of the university and should coordinate business, settle contested issues and monitor implementation of decisions. Participation in this executive committee should be active, dynamic, resilient and enjoyable. It should be a stimulating experience for everybody.

Given the very complex nature of academic governance, it is important to stress the need for keeping the governing powers in balance. The relationship between the senate, the board and the leadership/executive committee is extremely important. Very often this balance is achieved by very accurately defining the different areas of responsibility. For example, the senate is responsible for all academic matters, like study programs and academic evaluation. Boards are mostly charged with overseeing academic activities, appointing institutional leadership and fund raising. Executive bodies are meant to manage the institution and see after resource allocation, personal issues, student service and the like.

In this context, it is most important to maintain a climate of collaboration. Different governance structures need to actively work together. A climate of protest or destruction has adverse effects on all parts of the institution. Even though many areas of academic governance have changed, one key issue remains: the need to find a productive and trusting relationship between the administration and the faculty in order to move the institution forward. Otherwise, quick successes will turn into failures and destroy the willingness of members of the academic community to become involved.

The dominant ideals of the organization and governance of universities have changed over the last few decades. The organizational and decision-making structures within universities are based on two broad sets of ideas about university governance. According to the first, we may consider the university as a *republic of scholars* whereas the second regards the university as a *stakeholder organization*. In the former, institutional autonomy and academic freedom are seen as two sides of the same coin, which means that leadership and decision making are based on collegial decisions made by independent scholars. In the latter, institutional autonomy is considered a basis for strategic decision making by leaders who are assumed to see it as their primary task to meet the interests of major stakeholders and where the voice of academics within the institutions is but one among several stakeholders. Academic freedom is therefore circumscribed by the interests of other stakeholders, and decision making is taking place within hierarchical structures designed to provide leaders the authority to make and enforce strategic decisions within the organization. Whereas power is vested in the professoriate both regarding major decisions and the management of daily affairs according to the first ideal, it needs to be vested in stakeholders when major decisions are to be made and in leaders and strong managerial structures in connection with day-to-day management.

International Trends

The last decades have undoubtedly been characterized by a move from the "republic of scholars" ideal towards the "stakeholder university" ideal, and has been observed and commented upon by a number of observers (Keller, 1983; Teichler, 1988; Neave and Van Vught, 1991, 1994; Becher and Kogan, 1992; Dill and Sporn, 1995; Etzkowitz and Leydesdorff, 1997; Slaughter and Leslie, 1997; Bleiklie, 1998, 2005; Clark, 1998; Neave, 1998; Gornitzka et al., 2005; Olsen, 2005). However, two questions need to be addressed in this connection. First, it is relatively easy to demonstrate that the notion of a move is valid if one looks at ideologies, beliefs and values as they are expressed by policymakers, higher education leaders and other interested parties. Changing beliefs and ideals do not necessarily lead to new practices. In order to understand the extent of change beyond the initial ideological shift, one must observe actual structures and behaviour at various levels within higher education institutions (Kogan et al., 2006). Second, in a period where notions of globalization are in vogue, the move is often seen as a globalizing process that leads to the transformation of traditional universities governed like republics of scholars into "stakeholder universities" across the globe. This development in turn means that universities in different locations and countries are converging towards a common type of organizational structure. Again, there are reasons to ask whether these assumptions are true despite evidence to the contrary from various nation-states (Teichler, 1988; Neave and Van Vught, 1991; Musselin, 1999; Hood et al., 2004).

Within different national regimes, different components of the internal structures may be balanced in different ways, communication between teaching and research may vary as may the sub-division of universities in departments, schools and curricula. The main structural changes that have been noted are as follows:

- A far stronger role for central authorities in the determination of university objectives and modes of working: This is true of universities that used to be under detailed central controls and those that used to enjoy large degrees of autonomy such as the Anglophone universities (Neave, 1998; Musselin, 1999, 2004; Kogan et al., 2006). Therefore, introduction of macro steering mechanisms, through national funding systems, evaluation and accreditation regimes or legislation, may all be tightly linked to and may profoundly affect governance at the institutional level.
- The creation of powerful managerial infrastructures that now parallel and to some extent replace the academic structures of deans, heads of departments and professors: In the latter case, the implication is that government by professionals or academics that used to be based on collegial decision-making bodies have become integrated into the administrative line of the organization and thus become part of top-down decision-making structures. This reverses the basis of legitimacy and the movement of decision-making premises. Whereas decision making used to be based on collegiate bodies that at each level of the organization were composed of representatives from the organizational level below, decisions are now often trusted with leaders who are appointed by and are supposed to implement the policies of leaders on the organizational level above their own so that department chairs are appointed by deans and deans by rectors.

These structures are supported by the creation of directorates concerned with the economic development, marketing, quality assurance and international connections of the university.

- In many countries, the power of academically dominated senates has been paralleled or replaced by councils, boards or trustees who incorporate representation from the world of business, public services and politics. These and their chairpersons in particular reinforce the corporate nature of the reformed university. The power of the academic had already been substantially modified from the 1960s onwards by the admission of junior academics and students to senates and other decision-making bodies.
- A movement of power so that institutional leaders—rectors, presidents or vice-chancellors—who used to act as *primi inter pares* (the first among equals or first among peers, is Latin phrase describing the most senior person of a group sharing the same rank or office) are now nearer the position of chief executives running a corporate institution. This means less detailed interference from central authorities through laws and regulations in day-to-day operations and budgetary decisions and more focus on goal management by objectives and result.

These movements add up to a situation in which the working conditions of the institutions are becoming standardized at the political level, institutional leadership is being strengthened, new managerial structures are being established and collegial structures are being weakened and replaced by stakeholder boards and a stronger bureaucratic line organization with a firmer top-down grip on internal organizational processes.

A powerful force lending support to the growth of managerialism has been the assertion of penetrative quality assurance procedures that replace the hitherto "trustful" relationships between academics and their institutions as the belief in "transparency" has replaced trust in expert and professional knowledge. Both research and teaching and learning are assessed by a variety of measures including various forms of external review, benchmarking, and performance indicators that shift judgements from the academic profession towards that of external bodies and institutional management. The use of peer reviews and in some cases significant participation by academics (e.g. in connection with the Research Assessment Exercise in the UK) in developing performance indicators, however, means that managerialism does not necessarily exclude participation by the academic profession.

These changes all add up to regimes appropriate to a stakeholder university. Independently of, but perhaps interacting with the different national higher education regimes, there are several current drivers for change in different university systems such as introduction of new degrees, changing funding criteria, direct regulation or competition.

From the organizational perspective outlined here, it may seem somewhat paradoxical that the call for change has been justified in terms of an organizational ideal that emphasizes efficiency as a general organizational quality and the organization as an instrument rather than having some set of institutional values. This fact should not, however, be exaggerated without a closer scrutiny of empirical evidence. Initially, it is important to be aware of the fact that organizational ideals come in packages where more than one set of values are bundled together. Secondly, one cannot necessarily deduce actual practices in specific instances from general trends or ideals in policy documents or organizational plans.

As already indicated, the organizational ideals that we find in academia based on principles such as *professional self-regulation* under which academics independently run their research and teaching operations, *representative democracy* that grants participatory rights to staff and students in institutional decision-making processes, *bureaucratic steering* by which the state regulates publicly funded educational institutions and *corporate management* as a means to render higher education institutions efficient and accountable are not mutually exclusive, but the degree to which they are emphasized and dominate varies over time and across institutions and educational systems. Whereas in the 1960s and 1970s it shifted from professorial self-regulation towards some form of representative model although still dominated by academics, the emphasis since the late 1980s has (at least ostensibly) shifted towards a business model, while the representative model has been under attack as a prime example of "weak" leadership. In addition, bureaucratic steering has always been an aspect of the way in which public and private universities have been managed.

Universities, Public Policy and Organizational Change

The rising influence of the business enterprise model as an organizational ideal has constituted an increasing institutional contextual pressure for change over the last decades in many countries. There is little doubt that the expectations that face universities and their performance are changing. A number of processes have been identified as drivers behind the changing ideals that institutional leaders are supposed to sustain (Bleiklie and Byrkjeflot, 2002). The rise of mass education during the 1980s and 1990s made higher education and its costs more visible and contributed to a more intense focus on how higher education institutions are organized and managed. New ideas about university management and funding have altered the political rhetoric and discourse about higher education issues (Neave, 1998, 2002).

The idea that universities ought to be organized and managed as business enterprises and become "entrepreneurial" universities (Clark, 1998) has deeply influenced the normative debate about organization and leadership in higher education. Thus, enthusiasts who envisage new alliances and forms of cooperation between economic enterprise, public authority and knowledge institutions as necessary and with desirable consequences for academic institutions and knowledge production have had a strong influence on the public debate on these issues (Gibbons et al., 1994; Etzkowitz and Leydesdorff, 1997). Skeptics of these trends have, on the other hand, suggested that stronger external influence over academic institutions, symbolized by the rise of "academic capitalism" (Slaughter and Leslie, 1997) and the "ruin" of the university as a cultural institution (Readings, 1996), leads to the breakdown of internal value systems that sustain academic freedom and independent, critical scholarship. Enthusiasts and skeptics alike, however, tend to share the assumption that a radical change has taken place and focus on how new ideals and policies based on those ideals change the operating conditions for universities. The implications of such changing expectations are, however, contested issues. At least two empirical questions may be raised in this connection.

The first question focuses on the nature of organizational change. In the higher education literature, Becher and Kogan (1992, 176) have adapted two classical assumptions about organizational change to higher education. The assumption of *radical change* implies that change means that new ideals and goals simply replace established ones. The alternative is the assumption of *organic growth* or sedimentation. In this case, change is viewed as processes where new ideals come in addition to and are "layered on top" of established ones. Much of the literature on change in higher education focuses on how traditional ideals are replaced by new ones, under the assumption that new ideals almost instantly lead to the introduction of new organizational structures and changed behaviour by organization members so as to represent the ideals adequately. If this is true, then universities have undergone a process of radical change. Alternatively, one may assume that new ideals are layered on top of existing ones in a process of sedimentation. Institutions are therefore faced with a number of expectations, based partly on traditional and partly on more recently adopted ideals. The structural and behavioural implications are therefore much more ambiguous and thus leave room for different interpretations and struggles as part of the implementation process.

The answer to the first question has implications for the second question. If organizational ideals develop in a goal replacement process, one may hypothesize that organizational forms develop through structural redesign processes. This kind of process gives the impression of well-integrated organizations in which activities and changes in one part of the organization have clear consequences for what goes on in the rest of the organization. This is the prevailing notion about organization in much of the management literature and among administration practitioners (Olsen, 2005). If organizational ideals develop in a sedimentation process, then this might also be true for how organizational forms are affected by such ideals—that is through a process of gradual change in which new structures are added to existing ones. This second process gives the impression of a more complex, loosely coupled organization in which activities and changes in one part of the organization have no or only diffuse implications for activities in the rest of the organization. Traditionally, organization theorists have conceptualized universities as complex (Damrosch, 1995), multifunctional (Parsons and Platt, 1973; Kerr, 1995) and loosely coupled organizations (Weick, 1976). Indeed, the very ideas of loose coupling and corresponding processes were developed by students of decision making in universities (Cohen et al., 1972). The new trends that face universities may be regarded as attempts at changing the organizational characteristics that used to be regarded as essential to universities. The two perspectives sketched above produce highly divergent expectations as to the likely outcome of such attempts.

Reforms are often presented as radical changes introduced as the outcome of thorough and well-planned structural redesign, and based on the assumption that human behaviour easily lends itself to steering by changes in formal structures. Actual reform processes, however, tend to depart from this ideal. More often than not the gradual and organic processes of change, means that reforms, for better or worse, tend to accomplish less than originally announced. Yet, in order to make choices among political alternatives, one sometimes needs models that clearly represent the principles on which the alternatives are based.

Although academic institutions develop gradually and the introduction of new social values adds to their complexity rather than changing them radically, this does not mean that change cannot take place abruptly and be radical. But it does mean that the circumstances under which rapid change takes place are relatively unusual and specific. Both external pressure and internal dynamics are important in accounting for the conditions for rapid organizational change (Greenwood and Hinings, 1996).

Starting with the process of transformation from elite to mass higher education, the story runs more or less as follows: from the 1960s onwards, and with the until now last wave of expansion during the 1990s, the transformation was an international process that affected educational systems and societies, at least in Europe, North America and Austral-Asia, in a uniform way with respect to a number of general characteristics (Ramírez, 2003). Increased participation rates made higher education and research important to much larger population groups than before and this, in turn, made it less exclusive and less associated with elevated social status. The number of university faculty grew and, with their loss of exclusiveness, they experienced a loss of social status and power within their institutions.

From the 1980s, globalization and neo-liberalism have put increasingly strong pressures on universities to behave like businesses. It is argued that this will make them more efficient in providing education and research services in large quantities, more competitive on the international marketplace and better able to secure outside funding, and so to reduce their dependence on public support. In order to enable universities to meet these challenges, university reformers have set out to integrate universities, tightening the links between the different parts of the university organization in order to make them more efficient, manageable and accountable.

Correct as this argument may be, it is important to keep in mind that universities, no less than previously, are pursuing multiple goals, serving various constituencies and interest groups. They are embedded in different and powerful national settings (Krücken et al., 2007). The replacement of goals or addition of new goals such as efficiency, manageability, accountability and profitability, does not necessarily have any direct implications for leadership and organizational behaviour. Teichler (1988) has demonstrated how the exact implications of the transition to mass higher education systems have varied across countries depending on what institutional and organizational patterns that were developed in order to deal with higher education expansion. Comparative evidence from countries such as Australia, France, Germany, Japan, the Netherlands, Norway, Sweden, United Kingdom and the United States suggests that the solutions have been contested and shaped by established institutional structures (Musselin, 1999; Hood et al., 2004; Kogan et al., 2006). The evidence demonstrates how reforms, apparently justified in terms of common ideals such as autonomy, accountability, efficiency and quality, were not only introduced in institutional settings that were quite different but also followed different paths.

National Variation

One common characteristic that applies to European countries is that higher education, because of its sharply increasing size and budgetary significance, has become more politically salient over the last decades. Accordingly, Central Government authorities, whatever their leaning, have become more concerned about the cost of higher education and more interested in affecting its product in terms of students and research than before. This means that although governments might steer in a more decentralized manner than before, they are interested in steering a wider array of affairs. In this latter sense, power has become centralized although discretion and responsibilities have become decentralized to individual institutions.

The comparative evidence indicates that the general ideological pressure in individual countries is mediated through specific national policies based on experiences and issues that constitute powerful political, legal and financial operating conditions. These national influences have moulded and given shape to the general trends that affect systems internationally. This means that although the values that justify the policies are quite similar, the countries that are affected by them started out from different positions characterized by considerable variation as to the extent of institutional autonomy, and have since moved in quite different directions. For example, English universities did enjoy considerable autonomy until about 1980 and have since then experienced stronger government control and less autonomy; Swedish universities experienced a move towards more autonomy, whereas Norway until recently found itself in a middle position characterized by a less drastic and more mixed combination of reform measures (Kogan et al., 2006).

Considering organizational change, one might say that formerly, the ideal university governance arrangement claimed authority in its capacity to represent the professoriate as members of an egalitarian and autonomous disciplinary community. Now, governance arrangements claim authority on a basis that is radically different from representing the collective of faculty members. Today's managers claim authority by formulating strategies that the organization's stakeholders request, and by giving directions to their academic staff that shall induce them to contribute to the pursuit of the strategic goals of their institution. The tension between these ideals is alive and well within today's universities and they may be illustrated by the following formulation by Kogan and Hanney (2000, 195): "One of the genuine challenges for any head of institution is to ensure there is a balance between managerial accountability and giving a say to the academic community". Although national trajectories vary regarding the development of institutional autonomy, current developments seem to challenge the link between academic autonomy at the institutional level and individual autonomy of academics within the institutions.

The situation in the US seems to be somewhat different from the European one. The pattern of higher education organization and management structures appears to be more stable. The system expanded earlier and is of a size and diversity that make it unusually capable of absorbing growth and change while retaining its basic structural features.

As pointed out before, institutional governance arrangements are often shaped to a considerable extent by national governance structures through legislation, funding systems and systems for evaluation, accreditation and control. Therefore, if we consider the forms of public sector control that are applied and how they may combine in different ways to form specific governance regimes, it may be easier to form a more complete picture of governance arrangements and their development at the institutional level. A study comparing changes in government regulation of higher education in eight countries—Australia, France, Germany, Japan, the Netherlands, Norway, United Kingdom and the United States—during the late 1980s and 1990s found a number of differences that are relevant in this context (Hood et al., 2004).

The study focused on the use of four types of government regulation of research and higher education as one of three public sectors. The four types of regulation—"oversight", "mutuality", "competition" and "contrived randomness"—were developed in order to be able to analyze formal and informal forms of government control comparatively across nations, across different public sectors and their development over time. "Oversight" corresponds roughly to a classic form of government control through laws, regulations and other forms of control from above. "Mutuality" means control by formal or informal group processes and may have many shapes and forms, but in academic life the typical form is the collegiate body that we find in traditional university governing bodies dominated by professors, hiring committees, peer review bodies, research funding councils and so on. "Competition" may be any form of institutionalized rivalry such as in competition for research funds or academic positions. Finally, "contrived randomness" is understood as any way in which control of individuals may be exercised to make their lives unpredictable, for example, by random inspections or audits, selection of office holder by lot or other random selection processes.

The following pattern was revealed. The US stood out from the other countries by being less exposed to direct regulation or "oversight". The UK stood out as the only country where random control ("contrived randomness") plays a certain role. Autonomous collegial decision making ('mutuality') still plays an essential role in all university systems, but enjoys a stronger position in continental Europe than in the Anglo-American countries and Japan. Conversely, competition plays a stronger role in systems with many and influential private institutions

(Japan, the US) and countries that have pursued more radical New Public Management Policies (Australia).

The business enterprise ideal has influenced governance of the university systems analyzed above, and of the institutions within them, only to a limited extent. The research has demonstrated that being affected by common external forces pushing all systems in the same direction does not necessarily mean that they are becoming more similar to one another. National distinctive features still exert a heavy influence on the formulation of current reform policies, and previous findings of this sort continue to be supported by more recent projects (Paradeise, 2007). The findings reported above indicate that national peculiarities have survived and that some of the oft-cited differences between regions such as the Anglo-Saxon world and continental Europe still persist.

Furthermore, we may draw two conclusions about current organizational characteristics for universities in Europe and North America. Universities still enjoy considerable institutional autonomy. However, the connection between institutional and individual autonomy has been seriously weakened, if not severed, in many countries (Bleiklie, 2005; Kogan et al., 2006). If one wishes to sustain some measure of individual academic freedom as an essential part of university teaching and research, then the question arises "What are the values on which such autonomy might be based?"

University Governance and Emerging Knowledge Regimes

Modern universities and higher education systems are influenced by a number of developments that have created a thrust towards an extended concept of knowledge comprising both its theoretical and practical aspects, and with a stronger emphasis on utility and social demand (Bleiklie and Byrkjeflot, 2002). Emerging knowledge regimes may be separated into at least two main groups. On the one hand, there is *an academic capitalist regime*, driven by university-industry alliances, economic interests and a commercial logic. In spite of its huge influence on the discourse about higher education and as a symbol of current changes in higher education institutions, the notion of "academic capitalism" (Slaughter and Leslie, 1997) or "entrepreneurial universities" (Clark, 1998), industry funding is an important source for relatively few top research universities, particularly in the US (Powell and Owen-Smith, 1998; Turk-Bicacki and Brint, 2005). In fact, the dominant pattern is that most higher education institutions are publicly funded and owned by national or regional governments. This might be taken as an argument to the effect that stability prevails in the face of all rhetoric about fundamental change. Managers, informed by the stakeholder university ideal, however, may support the spread of "capitalism" and be supported by a combination of public austerity policies and stronger influence by external stakeholders through funding arrangements and university board positions.

Although universities are still predominantly public in most countries, the way in which public authorities run them has changed fundamentally, and this has been heavily influenced by notions of "academic capitalism" and "entrepreneurial universities". It manifests itself in the notion of universities as business enterprises and the introduction of quasi-market mechanisms in order to promote competition and cost effectiveness. Furthermore, in many countries public universities have introduced student fees and they are playing an increasingly important part in funding higher education. Such *public managerialist regimes* are driven by university-state alliances, political-administrative interests and a semi-competitive logic based on incentive policies where public support depends partly on teaching and/or research performance. They come, however, in different versions that may be understood against the backdrop of the previous public regimes from which they have developed. Comparative studies of national systems have demonstrated how public regimes that dominated the European systems until the 1980s or 1990s were different in important respects. Although all in principle were public, different actor constellations, alliances and interests characterized the regimes (Musselin 1999; Kogan et al., 2006).

In countries like England, Norway and Sweden (Kogan et al., 2006), France and Germany (Musselin, 1999), one finds different institutional environments that distribute actors differently from country to country. Although English reforms in the 1980s and 1990s were radical, important features at systems level as well as the institutional level were preserved. The former may be illustrated by the continuous important role played by co-opted academic elites in designing systemwide regulation such as the Research Assessment Exercises, and the status and role of the Vice Chancellors at the institutional level. In Sweden, reform processes from the mid-1980s were characterized by early politicization and corporatist features with a strong role of the unions in higher education policies. Swedish reforms tended to be relatively radical but susceptible to change as the political balance has shifted back and forth between the political left and right. These features are quite different from the reform pattern of neighbouring Norway.

Traditionally, reform policies have been a matter handled within a rather close relationship between the institutions and the Ministry of Education. Policies have developed gradually in a consensual way that sustains established relationships and regime features. The radical institutional governance reforms introduced with the quality reform of 2003 have affected the organizational landscape profoundly, but at the same time institutions have been given the opportunity to adopt the reforms to the extent and at the speed they prefer. Similarly, in France, Musselin (1999) demonstrated how French reforms for a very long time have been moulded by the "disciplinary logic" that has characterized the French higher education system since the Napoleonic University reforms as opposed to logic by "organization" that characterizes German reforms.

Thus, within the same main regime type, university systems may vary considerably with regard to important characteristics on key dimensions such as the role and strength of academic elites (cf. England), corporatist features (cf. Sweden), state structures (cf. Norway), academic institutions (cf. Germany) and academic disciplines (cf. France). The five countries mentioned were characterized by the prominent position of one of these characteristics, which in turn shaped national policy processes as well as organization and leadership structures at the institutional level.

National systems, furthermore, appear to include both capitalist and managerialist regime features (Teixeira et al., 2004). Thus, public funding plays an important role for American research funding, and many US states own and contribute substantially to funding comprehensive state systems. On the other hand, many public systems incorporate capitalist elements, which may be illustrated by the way in which foreign students' tuition payments contribute in important ways to the funding of English and Australian universities.

Conclusion

The discussion throws light on the idea that when new knowledge regimes arise, their impact may be partial and may vary depending on the conditions with which they are faced. The emerging capitalist and managerialist regimes may be viewed as different responses to a number of general trends such as higher education expansion, the rise of "knowledge society" and a different understanding of the purpose of higher education and research. What we have called an academic capitalist regime has in many ways become a global yardstick, despised by some, espoused by others. It has until now had a stronger impact on ideology and discourse than on the way in which universities are operated and funded. It may therefore express standardized norms with a global ideological impact that are far from being always backed up by organizational arrangements and practical realities (Frank and Meyer, 2007; Meyer and Schofer, 2007). This is even clearer if we move from the systemic level to individual institutions where we are likely to find considerable variation across institutions within national systems (Musselin, 2004; Kogan et al., 2006).

The practical impact of a commercial logic on Western university systems is still limited and in the field of research, it concerns mainly a relatively small number of major research universities. In many public systems in Europe, a semi-competitive logic between institutions has been introduced in which they are supposed to compete for students and research funding. This semi-competitive logic may provide an important rationale for organizational reforms whereby corporate structures are introduced. The way in which this might develop, however, depends on the extent to which corporate enterprise ideals are counter-balanced by existing institutionalized systemic features shaped by academic elites, corporative structures, state structures, academic institutions and disciplines (Bleiklie, 2007). It is an open question as to what implications these processes will have for institutional arrangements sustaining academic individual as well as institutional autonomy as fundamental characteristics of academic research and teaching. It is still early to determine how and to what extent the competitive or semi-competitive drive based on ideas of production efficiency will affect academic institutions internationally. Until recently, the extent to which it had gained a foothold varied considerably, weakened by still apparently quite resilient alternative values.

To summarize, the organizational and structural trends for administration and governance in higher education show a clear—but also contested—direction. As institutions move towards more market-oriented, entrepreneurial models, governance will-be concentrated more in the hands of the top leadership. Administration will move towards professional management. The balance between the authority of the faculty and the power of administration is at stake. Only if both groups are accountable, based on well-accepted and objective measure, can this be achieved. Governance and administration need to address these issues for institutions of higher education to stay competitive. With constrained resources, the future of higher education will only become more competitive. Colleges and universities need to be flexible and strong enough to meet these challenges. Shared governance and professional administration could be possible success factors.

REFERENCES

Altbach, G.P. (2005). "Patterns in Higher Education Development." In P.G. Altbach, R.O. Berdahl, and P.J. Gumport, (Eds.), *American Higher Education in the Twenty-First Century: Social, Political, and Economic Challenges* (2nd ed.). Baltimore: The Johns Hopkins University Press.

Association of Governing Boards of Universities and Colleges (2001). "AGB Statement on Institutional Governance" and "Governing in the Public Trust: External Influences on Colleges and Universities." The Fundamentals Board Basics. Washington, D.C.: Author.

Australian Vice Chancellors' Committee: The Council of Australia's University Presidents (2003). "Chancellors and AVCC statement on university governance."

American Association of University Professors (1966). "Statement on Government of Colleges and Universities." Retrieved September 26, 2002, http://www.aaup.org/AAUP/issuesed/governance/default.htm

American Federation of Teachers (2002). "Shared Governance in Colleges and Universities", Retrieved September 27, 2006 [3] http://www.aft.org/higher_ed/news/2002/shared_governance.htm

Brubacher, J.S. (1982). *On the Philosophy of Higher Education.* San Francisco: Jossey-Bass Publishers.

Becher, T. and Kogan, M. (1992). *Process and Structure in Higher Education*, Milton Keynes: Open University Press.

Berger, S. and Dore, R. (eds.) (1996). *National Diversity and Global Capitalism*, Ithaca and London: Cornell University Press.

Bleiklie, I. (1998). "Justifying the Evaluative State. New Public Management Ideals in Higher Education", *European Journal of Education*, 33(3): 299-316.

—— (2004). "Norway: Holding Back Competition?", in C. Hood, O. James, B.G. Peters and C. Scott (eds.) *Controlling Modern Government*, London: Edward Elgar, pp. 114-18.

—— (2005). "Academic Leadership and Emerging Knowledge Regimes", in I. Bleiklie and M. Henkel (eds.) *Governing Knowledge: A Study of Continuity and Change in Higher Education*, Dordrecht: Springer.

Clark, B.R. (1998). *Creating Entrepreneurial Universities: Organizational Pathways to Transformation*, Oxford, New York, Tokyo: IAU Press/Pergamon.

Coaldrake, P., Stedman, L. and Little, P. (2003). "Issues in Australian University Governance." Brisbane: QUT.

Dearlove, J. (1997). "The Academic Labour Process: From Collegiality and Professionalism to Managerialism and Proletarianisation?" *Higher Education Review*, Vol. 30, No. 1: 56-75.

Damrosch, D. (1995). *We Scholars. Changing the Culture of the Universities*, Cambridge and London: Harvard University Press.

Dill, D. and Sporn, B. (1995). *Emerging Patterns of Social Demand and University Reform: Through a Glass Darkly*, Oxford: IAU Press/Pergamon.

Etzkowitz, H. and Leydesdorff, L. (eds.) (1997). *Universities and the Global Knowledge Economy: A Triple Helix of University-Industry-Government Relations*, London: Cassell.

Frank, D.J. and Meyer, J.W. (2007). "Worldwide Expansion and Change in the University", in G.A. Krücken, A. Kosmützky and M. Torka (eds.) *Towards a Multiversity? Universities between Global Trends and National Traditions*, Bielefeld: Transcript Verlag.

Gornitzka, Å., Kogan, M. and Amaral, A. (eds.) (2005). *Reform and Change in Higher Education. Analyzing Policy Implementation*, Dordrecht: Springer.

Greenwood, R. and Hinings, C.R. (1996). "Understanding Radical Organizational Change: Bringing Together the Old and the New Institutionalism', *Academy of Management Review*, 21(4): 1022-54.

Hall, M. and Symes, A. (2005). "South African Higher Education in the First Decade of Democracy: from Cooperative Governance to Conditional Autonomy." *Studies in Higher Education*, Vol. 30, Issue 2, pp. 199-212.

Huisman, J. and Toonen, T. (2004). "The Netherlands: A Mixed Pattern of Control", in C. Hood, O. James, B.G. Peters and C. Scott (eds.) *Controlling Modern Government*, London: Edward Elgar, pp. 108-13.

Kaplan, G. (2001). "Preliminary Results from the 2001 Survey on Higher Education Governance." Sponsored by the American Association of University Professors and the American Conference of Academic Deans.

Kezar, A., and Eckel, P.D. (2004). "Meeting Today's Governance Challenges." *The Journal of Higher Education*: Vol. 75, No. 4: 371-98.

Keller, G. (1983). *Academic Strategy*, Baltimore and London: The Johns Hopkins University Press.

Kerr, C. (1995). *The Uses of the University*, Cambridge: Harvard University Press.

Kogan, M. and Hanney, S. (2000). *Reforming Higher Education*, London and Philadelphia: Jessica Kingsley Publishers.

Kogan, M., Bauer, M., Bleiklie, I. and Henkel, M. (eds.) (2006). *Transforming Higher Education: A Comparative Study*, 2nd edn, Dordrecht: Springer.

Krücken, G.A., Kosmützky, A. and Torka, M. (eds.) (2007). *Towards a Multiversity? Universities between Global Trends and National Traditions*, Bielefeld: Transcript Verlag.

Levine, A. (2001). "Higher Education as a Mature Industry", in P. Altbach, P.J. Gumport and B. Johnstone (eds.) *In Defense of American Higher Education*, Baltimore: Johns Hopkins University Press.

Lapworth, S. (2004). "Arresting Decline in Shared Governance: Towards a Flexible Model for Academic Participation." *Higher Education Quarterly*, Vol. 58, No. 4: 299-314.

Leadership and Governance in Higher Education. Handbook for Decision-makers and Administrators. (2011). Raabe Academic Publishers. http://www.lg-handbook.info

Middlehurst, R. (2004). "Changing Internal Governance: A Discussion of Leadership Roles and Management Structures in UK Universities." *Higher Education Quarterly*, Vol. 58, No. 4: 258-79.

McMaster, M. (2007). "Partnerships between Administrative and Academic Managers: How Deans and Faculty Managers Work Together. Association of Tertiary Education Management, Retrieved May 10, 2007, http://www.atem.org.au/downloads/doc/018_mcmaster.doc

Moore, R., Jr. (1992-2004). "In Shared Governance, What Role for the AAUP?" *Conversations on Jesuit Higher Education*, 28:26.

Meyer, J.W. and Ramírez, F. (2000). "The World Institutionalization of Education", in Schriver, J. (ed.) *Discourse Formation in Comparative Education*, New York: Peter Lang Publishers, pp. 111-32.

Meyer, J.W. and Schofer, E. (2007). "The University in Europe and the World: Twentieth Century Expansion", in G.A. Krücken, A. Kosmützky and M. Torka (eds.) *Towards a Multiversity? Universities between Global Trends and National Traditions*, Bielefeld: Transcript Verlag.

National Education Association (1987). "NEA Policy Statements: Faculty Governance in Higher Education." Retrieved September 26, 2006, http://www2.nea.org/he/policy6.html

—— (1989). "NEA Policy Statements: Statement on Community College Governance." Retrieved September 26, 2006, http://www2.nea.org/he/policy-cc.html

Neave, G. (1998). "The Evaluative State Reconsidered', *European Journal of Education,* 33(3): 265-84.

Neave, G. (2002). "The Stakeholder Perspective Historically Explored", in J. Enders and O. Fulton (eds.) *Higher Education in a Globalizing World. International Trends and Mutual Observations*, Dordrecht: Kluwer.

Neave, G. and Van Vught, F.A. (eds.) (1991). *Prometheus Bound: The Changing Relationship between Government and Higher Education in Europe*, Oxford: Pergamon.

—— (1994). *"Government and Higher Education Relationships across Three Continents: Winds of Change*, Oxford: Pergamon.

Parsons, T. and Platt, G. (1973). *The American University*, Cambridge, MA: Harvard University Press.

Powell, W.W. and Owen-Smith, J. (1998). "Universities and the Market for Intellectual Property in the Life Sciences", *Journal of Policy Analysis and Management,* 17(2): 253-77.

Ramírez, F. (2003). "World Society and the Socially Embedded University", unpublished paper, School of Education, Stanford University.

Readings, B. (1996). *The University in Ruins*, Cambridge, MA and London: Harvard University Press.

Sporn, B. (2003). "Convergence of Divergence in International Higher Education Policy: Lessons from Europe." *Publications from the Forum for the Future of Higher Education*, Retrieved February 2007, http://www.educause.edu/content.asp?page_id=666&ID=FFPFP0305&bhcp=1

Scott, C. (2004a). "Australia: Linking Oversight to Mutuality and Competition", in C. Hood, O. James, B.G. Peters and C Scott (eds.) *Controlling Modern Government*, London: Edward Elgar, pp. 119-23.

—— (2004b). "The UK: Hyper-regulation and Regulatory Reform", in C. Hood, O. James, B.G. Peters and C. Scott (eds.) *Controlling Modern Government*, London: Edward Elgar, pp. 124-29.

Scott, C. and Hood, C. (2004). "Overview", in C. Hood, O. James, B.G. Peters and C. Scott (eds.) *Controlling Modern Government*, London: Edward Elgar, pp. 75-85.

Teichler, U. (1988). *Changing Patterns of the Higher Education System: The Experience of Three Decades*, London: Jessica Kingsley.

Teixeira, P., Jongbloed, B., Dill, D. and Amaral, A. (eds.) (2004). *Markets in Higher Education. Rhetoric or Reality?* Dordrecht: Kluwer.

Turk-Bicacki, L. and Brint, S. (2005). "University-industry collaboration. Patterns of growth for low and middle-level performers", *Higher Education*, **49**(1-2): 61-89.

Weber, M. (1978). *Economy and Society*, Berkeley, Los Angeles, London: University of California Press.

Weick, K.E. (1976). "Educational Organizations as Loosely Coupled Systems", *Administrative Science Quarterly*, 21: 1-19.

Structure and Organization of Higher Education Abroad

9

HIGHER EDUCATION IN UNITED STATES OF AMERICA

U.S. higher education borrows its structure from both the British undergraduate college and German Research University, but its character is profoundly influenced by three major philosophical beliefs that shape American public life. Inspired by the Jeffersonian ideals of limited government and freedom of expression, states, religious communities and individuals established and maintained a range of higher education institutions and continue to protect these institutions from the level of government control seen in most other countries. The second set of influences is capitalism and belief in the rationality of markets. American colleges and universities compete for students, faculty and funding with the conviction that diversity and high quality are best achieved through competition rather than centralized planning. The final major philosophical influence on American higher education is a widespread commitment to equal opportunity and social mobility. Americans came to view broad access to higher education as a necessary component of the nation's ideal as a "land of opportunity". Higher education has responded by broadening access. Indeed, the one uniquely American type of institution, viz. the community college was founded in the 20th century to ensure open access to higher education for individuals of all ages, preparation levels, and incomes.

Guided by these beliefs, U.S. higher education reflects the essential elements of the American character viz. independence, suspicion of government, ambition, inclusiveness and competitiveness.

Characteristics of U.S. Higher Education

Higher education in the U.S. is also known as post-secondary education, and is inclusive of all formal education beyond the secondary school, whether education or not. Post-secondary education is broadly divided into two different sectors, viz. post-secondary vocational education and training, which is non-degree but can produce some transferable credits under certain circumstances and higher education, which includes studies undertaken in degree-granting institutions for academic credit. However, the U.S. higher education system is not legally organized into separate university and non-university sub-systems as are some other national systems, but is comprehensive. It is a diverse and autonomous community of publicly and privately-supported institutions.

There are 6,479 post-secondary institutions, including 4,182 non-degree institutions. Of the degree-granting higher education institutions, some 1,732 award only the associate degree plus sub-bachelor's certificates and diplomas; 702 award only the bachelor's degree; 1,094 award degrees and certificates beyond the bachelor's degree but not the research doctorate; and 654 institutions award the research doctorate. The United States does not have an official classification for its higher education institutions. While different institutions offer varying levels of degrees, U.S. accreditation policies result in degrees at any given level adhering to certain minimum standards, regardless of the institution that grants them.

The U.S. higher education system is characterized by accessibility, diversity, and autonomy and is known for both its size and quality. Except for state/city universities, the government has no jurisdiction or authority over the recognition of educational institutions, members of the academic professions, programmes or curricula, or degrees or other qualifications; even for state/city universities the role of the government is mostly confined to funding. Nearly all U.S. postsecondary institutions are licensed, or chartered, by a state or municipal government to operate under the ownership of either a government (if public) or a private corporation (if independent), and may be a for-profit or not-for-profit enterprises. Religious institutions are considered independent, or private. Quality assurance is achieved through the system of voluntary accreditation by specific accrediting agencies that are recognized by the U.S. Secretary of Education and meet the standards for membership in the Council for Higher Education Accreditation (CHEA). Accreditation is a self-regulating process of quality control engaged in by the U.S. post-secondary education community to ensure minimum standards of academic capability, administrative competence, and to promote mutual recognition of qualifications within the system.

While all recognized and accredited institutions are licensed or chartered by State Governments, states vary greatly in the degree of supervision and quality control that they exercise, and there is relatively limited reciprocity of recognition across state borders. Accreditation by recognized agencies, therefore, remains the primary means of ensuring academic and institutional quality and the mutual acceptance of credits and qualifications across and outside the United States.

Non-university Level Post-Secondary Studies (Technical/ Vocational Type)

There is no legal distinction between "university level" and "non-university level" higher education. The level of studies is delineated by the level of qualification offered in a specific programme rather than by type of institution offering it. Educational programmes corresponding to "non-university level technical/vocational post-secondary studies" would include all technical and occupational programmes that lead to a degree, diploma or certificate below the Bachelor's degree. Education at this level would include (1) all institutions that only award qualifications under the Bachelor's degree; (2) programmes leading to awards under the Bachelor's degree offered at institutions that also award higher degrees.

University Level Studies

University Level First Stage: Associate Degree, Bachelor Degree, Advanced Certificate, First Professional Degree

The Associate degree is the first academic or professional degree that can be awarded in U.S. post-secondary education.

Holders of this degree may apply to enter higher degree programmes at the Bachelor's level, but are not qualified to apply directly for advanced (graduate) studies programmes. Programmes of study for this degree are usually designed to take two years of full-time study, but some take longer to complete. Those who pursue this degree on a part-time basis also take longer than two years to complete their studies. The Associate degree may be awarded in the liberal arts and general studies as an academic qualification or it may be awarded in a professional occupational field. Some professional career programmes at the Associate level are terminal vocational programmes that do not lead to further study, while others do so. Associate degree programmes generally fulfil two years of the course requirements needed for a Bachelor's degree. Credit for Associate degree studies is usually transferable to Bachelor's degree programmes, especially where transfer agreements have been established between or among institutions.

The Bachelor's degree is the second academic degree that can be awarded in U.S. post-secondary education, and is one of two undergraduate (first) degrees that qualify a student to apply for programmes of advanced (graduate) study (the other such degree is the first professional degree). Programmes of study for this degree are designed to take between four and five years, depending on the field of study. Part-time students may take longer to complete the degree requirements. Honours programmes are offered by many institutions that award the Bachelor's degree. These generally require the completion of additional requirements such as preparation of an undergraduate thesis, honours paper or project, advanced course work, or special examinations. Advanced certificates requiring a year or less of study following (and sometimes accompanying) the completion of a Bachelor's requirements are sometimes awarded to signify a concentration in a sub-specialization or completion of a related set of competences.

First professional degrees-comprise a limited number of second first degree-holders. Such students are admitted to first professional degree programmes after completing most, or all, of a Bachelor's degree programme in another subject. Thus, first professional degrees are considered graduate-level degrees for purposes of admissions and student financial assistance. The study content of the first professional degree programmes is undergraduate in nature and the degrees are prerequisites for entry-level access to certain regulated professions. Confusion sometimes arises because several first professional degrees use the term "doctor" in the title even though they are not advanced research degrees. First professional degrees are awarded in Medicine (MD), Dentistry (DDS/DMD), Veterinary Medicine (DVM), Osteopathic Medicine (DO), Optometry (OD), Paediatry (DPM), Chiropractic (DC), Pharmacy (D.Pharma), Divinity (M.Div), Rabbinics (MHL/Rav), and Law (JD).

University Level Second Stage: Master's Degree, Post-Master's Degree/Certificate, Diploma/Certificate, Degree of Education Specialist

The Master's degree represents the second stage of higher education and is the first advanced (graduate) degree. U.S. Master's degrees may be taught (without thesis) or obtained with the guidance of research (with thesis) and may be awarded in academic or professional fields. Most Master's degrees are designed to take two years of full-time study, although the time may vary depending upon the subject, the preparation achieved by the student at the undergraduate level, the structure of the programme, and whether the degree is pursued on a full—or a part-time basis. Research-based Master's degrees generally require completion of a series of advanced course and seminar requirements, comprehensive examinations, and an independent thesis. Non-research Master's degrees generally require completion of a special project as well as course work and examinations. Both types of Master's degree also require the satisfaction of special requirements (such as linguistic or quantitative skill) or a combination. U.S. universities award that fall between the Master's and the research doctorate; these may be of several types, but all of them fall within the second stage of U.S. higher education. Such degrees include the degree of Education Specialist (E.Sp. or Ed.S.) and Certificates and Diplomas of Advanced Study (C.A.E., D.A.E.).

University Level Third Stage: Research Doctorate

The Research Doctorate represents the third and highest stage of higher education in the United States and may be awarded in academic disciplines and some professional fields of study. This degree is not awarded by examination or course work only, but requires demonstrated mastery of the chosen subject and the ability to conduct independent, original research. Doctoral programmes require intensive study and research in at least one subfield and professional level competence in several others. Following a series of research seminars designed to prepare the individual research proposal, comes the candidacy examinations (covering at least two subfields in addition to the field of research focus, one of which must be in a subject outside the doctoral student's own faculty but related to his/her research). If the candidacy examination is passed at a satisfactory standard (excellent or higher), the student is advanced to candidacy for the doctorate and selects a research committee of senior faculty who will approve the dissertation topic, monitor progress, and examine the student when the research is finished. The conduct of research and preparation of the dissertation can take anywhere from one to several years depending on the chosen subject, available research funding, and the location of the research. Research Doctorates are awarded in the academic disciplines and for theoretical research in some professional fields. The most common of such degrees is the Doctor of Philosophy (Ph.D.). There are a variety of equivalent degree titles used in some institutions and disciplines.

Non-traditional Studies

Distance Higher Education

Distance education is considered to be a vehicle for delivering education to persons whose location, circumstances or work make remote links necessary or convenient. It is not considered to be a separate type of education. Rather, distance education is considered to be a modality of instruction that differs from traditional campus-based instruction but is no less legitimate. There is rapid growth in educational programmes at all levels delivered through radio, television, satellite downlink stations, videos, computer terminals and other means. Many programmes are offered for credit and lead to Certificates, Diplomas and Degrees; others are designed for leisure studies, personal enrichment or specific work-related education and training. Distance education programmes are accredited by recognized associations and the good programmes benefit from significant recent advances in designing, implementing and monitoring these learning environments and their support tools.

Life long Higher Education

It is frequently called continuing education. Institutions operate specific continuing education programmes, some very extensive and parallel to regular institutional degree offerings, whilst others are short or specialized programmes. Continuing education may be structured to lead to Certificates, Diplomas or Degrees, or unstructured and used to provide general and leisure study opportunities. Some continuing education is offered through distance learning methods while other programmes are offered at an institution or provided at a branch site. When offered in order to provide further education and training for professionals who already hold basic qualifications, it is usually called continuing professional education. Credit for work completed in such programmes may be recognized and accepted by regular higher education authorities through policies developed by institutions, and it is also recognized and accepted by state licensing authorities and professional associations.

Higher Education Training in Industry

This is considered a specific form of continuing professional education and is referred to as employer-sponsored training. Programmes are offered by employers or through contract by post-secondary institutions, professional associations, unions or consulting organizations. Education or training may be provided at the work site or elsewhere. Continuing professional education or training ranges in length and depth from short courses intended to refresh or introduce new skills up to full degree programmes. Credit for work completed in such programmes may be recognized and accepted by regular higher education authorities through policies developed by institutions. A specific form of employer-sponsored training of major interest to many U.S. post-secondary institutions, especially at the sub-Bachelor's degree level, is the training received in the U.S. armed forces; the award of credit for it when personnel re-enter civilian life. Detailed guidelines have been jointly developed by U.S. institutions and the armed forces.

Other Forms of Non-formal Higher Education

Many varieties of education and training opportunities exist that are not formally structured, do not result in recognized awards and are not intended to result in transferable credit or professional recognition. They include courses and programmes provided by libraries, museums, parks and recreation authorities, clubs and others that are intended for members or the public. Some programmes provided by employers are not intended to result in formal recognition such as informal seminars and presentations on topics related to work issues and products.

Governance

One of the philosophical underpinnings of U.S. higher education is the Jeffersonian notion of limited and, wherever possible, locally controlled government. Based on this model, the U.S. Constitution reserves for the states all government functions not specifically described as federal. Among those functions is education. As a result, each of the 50 states is responsible for governing public colleges and universities (which enroll 75% of the nation's students), rather than the Federal Government. The degree of control by the states varies tremendously. Some institutions such as the University of California and the University of Michigan, enjoy constitutional autonomy as separate branches of State Government. At the other extreme, locally elected boards of trustees govern some community colleges. In some states, a governing board appointed by the governor and/or legislature oversees all institutions, setting funding levels, establishing accountability measures, setting policies, and approving new academic programs. In others, the state board plays only an advisory function and has little direct authority over institutions. In many others, a state agency is poised between the institutions and State Government, implementing statewide policy but also attempting to insulate institutions from ill-advised or overtly intrusive state policies.

California State University, Office of the Chancellor in Long Beach, California

Some public universities are part of statewide multi-campus systems in which an additional layer of oversight exists between the campus and State Government. System administrators may oversee campus budgets, set policies such as admissions standards, coordinate degree programs and facilitate credit transfer and articulation between the state's public colleges and universities. They additionally, and importantly, advocate to the legislature on behalf of public colleges and universities. In some states, more than one multi-campus system exists such as California's distinct systems of community colleges, comprehensive state colleges, universities and research universities.

While the Federal Government generally does not provide direct operational support to colleges and universities, this special purpose funding is an extremely important revenue source and, in turn, has increased the ability of the Federal Government to influence colleges and universities in areas outside research and financial aid. For example, in order for institutions to participate in the financial aid programs, they must comply with a wide range of federal reporting requirements on topics ranging from teacher preparation to gender equity in inter-collegiate athletics. However, despite the growing influence of the Federal Government, its role is still limited and has not yet intruded into core academic decisions, which are generally left to the institutions and, in the case of some public institutions, the states.

Organizational Structure of Colleges and Universities

The organizational structures of American colleges and universities vary distinctly, depending on institutional type, culture, and history, yet they also share much in common. While a private liberal arts college may have a large board of trustees, and a public research university nested in a state system no trustees of its own, the vast majority of public and private universities are overseen by an institutional or system-wide governing board. This somewhat paradoxical combination of distinctiveness and uniformity reflects the unique characteristics of individual colleges and universities, and the shared-task environment (including strategic planning, fiscal oversight, curriculum planning, and student affairs) common to American post-secondary institutions. Scholars of higher education view many aspects of private colleges and universities as significantly different from those at public universities. Yet the reliance on bureaucratic organizational structures and the belief in research, advanced instruction, and service at both types of institutions shape many aspects of public and private university governance structures in a fairly uniform manner.

The organizational structure of colleges and universities is an important guide to institutional activity, but not the only one. Scholars of higher education have developed a variety of multi-dimensional models of organizational behavior that also shed considerable light on college and university structure and process. Multi-dimensional models seek to explain organizational behavior across institutional types, and in various institutional activities. The models vary somewhat in the number of dimensions incorporated, from J. Victor Baldridge's three dimensions (bureaucratic, collegial, and political) and Lee Bolman and Terrence Deal's four-cornered frame (structural, human resource, political, and symbolic) to Robert Birnbaum's five dimensions (bureaucratic, collegial, political, anarchical, and cybernetic). These models are quite helpful in thinking about organizational structure and process within colleges and universities. The same institution may evidence a bureaucratic, hierarchical decision-making process in its central administration, and a collegial process in its academic senate. It is a combination of organizational structure and process that shapes college and university behavior.

Public and private colleges and universities of all types incorporate key authority structures, including a governing board, a president or chancellor, a cohort of administrative leaders, and an academic senate. In public institutions, these core organizational entities collaborate with such external authorities as state and federal political leaders, community organizations, and members of the public, as well as business interests and philanthropic foundations. These external organizations routinely interact with and shape the policies and procedures of the university's internal organizational structures.

The degree of uniformity in private and public college and university organizational structures has been shaped by the nature of demands on the post-secondary system since the mid-twentieth century. Although the key governance structures of colleges and universities were present prior to the turn of the twentieth century, the full scope of the university's multi-faceted organizational structure, most scholars agree, was not realized until after the rise of the research university, in the wake of World War II. In 1963, the then-president of the University of California System, Clark Kerr, described the post-war American university as a *multiversity.* The term captured the increasingly complex organizational and governance structures, required to negotiate its ever-expanding task environment.

Governing Boards

A university's governing board, also known as the trustees, regents, or board of visitors, possesses fundamental legal authority over the university. The authority of the governing board is vested in it by the state wherein the school resides or, particularly in the case of older, private institutions, by legally binding royal or colonial charters. Both public and private governing boards are generally constituted of citizen trustees. In the public case those trustees are often political appointees who serve as a fundamental link between the institution and state and national political structures.

In the United States, the tradition of lay oversight of colleges and universities can be traced to the founding of Harvard College in 1636. Subsequent private colleges adopted this form of governance, which the U.S. Supreme Court deemed constitutional in its Dartmouth College decision of 1819. Public colleges and universities followed suit, although on the public side the role of governors in trustee appointments and the key role of legislative funding in institutional development has meant that the states play a central role in the governance of the institutions. The Federal Government has influenced the organization of higher education primarily through legislation—the Morrill Acts, the Higher Education Acts, and the G.I. Bill, for instance—that reinforced decentralized governance and, hence, the authority of institutional governing boards at both public and private institutions. As John Millet noted, "It has long been evident that it is the state governments rather than the federal government that carry the primary authority and responsibility for higher education in the United States."

Governing board members at public institutions typically arrive at the trustee table by one of four paths: direct appointment by the governor; ex-officio appointment; gubernatorial appointment subject to approval of the state legislature; and less frequently, election by popular vote. Public university board members represent the citizens of the state and the terms and conditions of their service are often defined by institutional charter or state constitution. Private boards are generally self-perpetuating, with new trustees chosen by the membership of the standing board. While private colleges and universities benefit considerably from public subsidies and support, private boards are not subject to the same degree of external scrutiny or intervention as are public boards.

The formal responsibilities of university governing boards are significant even as they are few in number. They include preservation of the university charter; institutional performance evaluations; fundraising; liaison with external agencies and political bodies; budget approval; oversight of campus policies and investment strategies; and, perhaps most important, hiring and evaluating the ongoing performance of the university president.

Because of their visibility, symbolic importance, and control over policies with significant political salience, public university boards became subject to increasing challenges from a variety of interests in the last two decades of the twentieth century. These challenges were accompanied by demands for non-partisan board appointments and trustees that are more representative of the broader society, as well as calls for increased scrutiny of potential conflicts of interest. Boards were also challenged by governors and legislators concerned about issues ranging from rising costs to faculty ideology. A response to the heightened pressures on governing boards was a push for improved trustee education programs in several states in the pursuit of more open and effective governance processes. Given its myriad responsibilities and powers, a strong argument can be made that the board is the most powerful governing agent of the modern university.

The President

The liaison between a post-secondary institution and its governing board is the highest ranking executive officer, a president or chancellor. The president provides overall leadership to the institution and presides over its academic and administrative bureaus. The president generally works closely with a provost, who is responsible for academic affairs, and a chief financial officer, who oversees the institution's fiduciary operations. The president serves as the lead fundraiser and as a key representative of the university and its academic community to external agencies and actors. Presidential duties include fostering a positive public image of the institution as a site of higher learning, maintaining a close relationship with the institutional governing board to further the president's agenda, and forging points of common cause and agreement with the entire university community and its constituents.

Since World War II, the job of university president has become considerably more complex, and in many ways more constrained. Presidential authority has been eroded as boards and external actors have gained more legitimate roles in university governance. Presidential satisfaction has declined, and the average presidential tenure is shorter than before World War II.

No responsibility consumes the modern-day president's time and energy more than his or her role as the institution's principal fundraiser, a task made especially difficult because it requires extensive time away from the institution. While presidential fundraising has been a function of private universities for centuries, the emergence of significant public university fundraising in the 1980s and 1990s is a major development. Fueled by decreasing state and federal support in recent years, public universities have been forced to take on a more significant share of their own funding, with development playing a major role in this process.

Faculty

The formal governing body of the faculty at the institutional level is the academic senate, a body generally comprised of tenured and tenure-track faculty from the various disciplines and professional schools. The faculty senate and its attendant committees provide elected faculty liaisons to the university board and president. A primary function of the senate is to represent the voice of the faculty in matters of university governance.

Each school or college within a university is under the direction of a dean. A chairperson or department head supervises individual departments of instruction. Faculty members are ranked, in descending order, as professor, associate professor, assistant professor, and instructor. Faculty of various ranks may or may not be tenured, depending on the institution. Faculty members can be dismissed from their posts unless and until they have been granted tenure, a term denoting a measure of academic job security that is earned through a combination of demonstrated teaching, research, and service contributions.

The faculty generally has significant influence over the hiring of new faculty members, tenure and promotion procedures, the university curriculum and graduation requirements, and admissions criteria.

While the role of the faculty in governance was at one time largely advisory, over time the faculty has become increasingly engaged in policy formation. In many cases, the faculty possesses significant authority over academic affairs. Faculty representatives are often found on governing boards, in formal or informal (non-voting) positions. The formal authority of the faculty may be codified in institutional charters or in the standing rules of institutional governing boards.

A number of other factors and informal agreements shape the degree to which faculty is involved in institutional affairs. Many colleges and universities ties have a commitment to a process of shared governance that incorporates the faculty in various aspects of institutional decision-making. A collegial relationship between the faculty senate and the college or university president is a key component of shared governance, as is the relationship between the faculty senate and the institutional governing board. Faculty authority is also shaped by the strength and reputation of the institution's academic departments and departmental leadership, as well as the faculty's symbolic importance as teachers and producers of knowledge, and the legitimacy provided by individual faculty member's professional expertise.

National organizations also contribute to the legitimacy and organizational standing of the American professorate. Among these, the most prominent is the American Association of University Professors (AAUP). Established in 1915 to advance the collective interests, ideals, and standards of the fledgling university professorate, the AAUP has since that time become best known for its role in the defence of academic freedom and tenure. The AAUP's clearest articulation of this role can be found in its declaration, *Statement of Principles on Academic Freedom and Tenure* (1995). Over time the AAUP has developed initiatives on other aspects of faculty life, including shared university governance. In the last two decades of the twentieth century research on faculty turned attention to the rapid growth in the percentage of non-tenured and non-tenure track faculty in colleges and universities, a shift with significant implications for the organizational structure and governance of those institutions.

Administration and Staff

Internal university administration is composed of two interrelated administrative cohorts: one is responsible for the oversight and administration of academic affairs; the other is charged with institutional administration. The academic and institutional administrations are often in conflict with one another. The growth of the institutional administrative cohort after World War II has led to what some researchers perceive as disproportionate influence on the part of the institutional administration. The increasing growth and autonomy of the institutional administrative cohort also challenges the traditional perception of the overall mission of the university's administration as one of academic support and facilitation. As Amitai Etzioni (1964) has noted, there is an essential tension in organizations such as colleges and universities that are driven by professional expertise but led by administrators. This has produced demands for a cohort of administrative leaders who can bring professional education and credentials to institutional managerial practice.

Within the academic administration, the president presides over a hierarchy that generally consists of a number of senior officers, including a university provost, and the deans of individual colleges and professional programs. Academic administrators are traditionally drawn from the faculty ranks, where departmental leadership positions serve as preparation for university-wide academic leadership roles.

The managerial cohort of the institutional administration is led by a chief financial officer and various senior executives. The chief financial officer provides leadership and direction to a host of administrative functions that generally includes student services, institutional support, maintenance and operation of the physical plant, and auxiliary enterprises. These individual units in turn encompass smaller departments responsible for more specialized services. The latter part of the twentieth century witnessed increased demands for greater efficiency, productivity, and entrepreneurial management at colleges and universities. Efficiency initiatives in particular, including outsourcing of institutional functions and the hiring of adjunct faculty, engendered significant internal conflict between the managerial and academic administrations.

Students

Historically, students have not had a significant role in the organizational structure or governance of colleges and universities. During most of the nineteenth century, college administrations followed a practice of *in loco parentis*, an educational philosophy that led university administrators and faculty members to oversee the academic advancement and personal conduct of their students very closely. Over time a gradual loosening of the institutional academic and social oversight occurred, a result of the university's incorporation of the German university model that emphasized greater student and faculty freedom. The heightened social and intellectual autonomy available to undergraduates encouraged students to seek greater involvement in university governance and administrative affairs.

Student interest in university organization and governance increased significantly in the 1960s. In the aftermath of student unrest and demands for increased student involvement in campus affairs, a degree of student participation on university boards, search committees, and faculty senates has become commonplace. Many colleges and universities include a student representative in either an advisory or voting position on the board of trustees. In addition, students often have their own network of parallel undergraduate and graduate governance organizations headed by a student body president and elected representatives that have contact with university officials such as the president and the board.

Future Prospects

As the American university moves into the twenty-first century, a number of factors, including the increased complexity of institutional functions, changing student demographics, demands for entrepreneurial behavior, technological innovations, and increases in external interest group interventions will significantly challenge existing organizational structures and processes. The rapid growth in demand for continuing education and the provision of distance programs by colleges and universities in particular has challenged traditional notions of the content and delivery of post-secondary education. A number of key political shifts, including a growing retreat from public funding of colleges and universities, demands for privatization of college and university services, and the use of the university as an instrument in broader national political struggles, will further complicate organizational arrangements. These political shifts entail considerably more institutional outreach to legislatures, governors, and key interest groups at the state and national levels, as well as additional staff in governmental and public relations. Finally, the rise of what Richard T. Ingram terms "activist trusteeship" and increasingly interventionist stances taken by public and private institutional governing boards may require increased collective action by internal cohorts. In order to preserve institutional autonomy and shared governance in a time of increasing political conflict, effort will also need to be directed to creating more effective organizational bridges between colleges and university leaders and institutional governing boards.

In many ways, the American system of higher education is unique in the world. In its size, diversity of institutions and students, freedom from government controls and reliance on market forces, it is without peer. However, higher education systems around the globe are struggling with many of the same issues as the United States and are exploring similar strategies such as imposing tuition to create greater access while instituting student aid programs, creating a credit system to facilitate student mobility, and standardizing degree programs. Other nations struggling with these challenges may benefit by understanding the philosophical beliefs that shape U.S. higher education—distrust of government, faith in markets, and reliance on education as a gateway to social mobility—and the ways in which the United States continually struggles to balance market forces, government intervention and access to high-quality education.

HIGHER EDUCATION IN EUROPEAN COUNTRIES

The Bologna Process Towards a European Higher Education Area

Europe is not a homogenous region; still less is its education homogenous, as the rationales behind the Bologna Declaration on the European Space for Higher Education of 1999 make manifest. This implies that when analyzing the regionalization of higher education in Europe, one has to take account of several important issues such as national and regional differences, diversity of languages, different educational traditions and systems, diversity of languages, different educational traditions and systems, diversity of stakeholders, and the co-existence of universities and a strong non-university sector.

The Bologna Process aims to create a European Higher Education Area by 2010, in which students can choose from a wide and transparent range of high quality courses and benefit from smooth recognition procedures. The Bologna Declaration of June 1999 has put in motion a series of reforms needed to make European Higher Education more compatible and comparable, more competitive and more attractive for Europeans and for students and scholars from other continents. Reform was needed then and reform is still needed today if Europe is to match the performance of the best performing systems in the world, notably the United States and Asia.

The purpose of the Bologna Process, as stated in its formal priorities and "action lines", is to create a broad framework for higher education to enable comparability within a flexible system and to promote the European Higher Education Area for the benefit of all of the countries involved—including the UK. It is not intended to create standardized or uniform higher education across the European Higher Education Area.

The three overarching objectives of the Bologna Process have been from the start, viz. introduction of the three cycle system (bachelor/master/doctorate), quality assurance and recognition of qualifications and periods of study. In the Leuven Communiqué of 2009, the Ministers identified these priorities for the coming decade:

- social dimension: equitable access and completion;
- lifelong learning;
- employability;
- student-centered learning and the teaching mission of higher education;
- education, research and innovation;
- international openness;
- mobility;
- data collection;
- multidimensional transparency tools; and
- funding.

Every second year, Ministers responsible for higher education in the 46 Bologna countries meet to measure progress and set priorities for action. After Bologna (1999), they met in Prague (2001), Berlin (2003) and Bergen (2005), London (2007) and Leuven/Louvain-La-Neuve, Belgium (April 2009). After more than ten years of intensive reforms, the Ministers met on 11/12 March 2010 in Budapest and Vienna to officially launch the European Higher Education Area, as decided back in 1999.

Steered by European Ministers responsible for higher education, the Bologna Process is a collective effort of public authorities, universities, teachers and students, together with stakeholder associations, employers, quality assurance agencies, international organisations and institutions. Although the process goes beyond the EU's borders, it is closely connected with EU policies and programmes. For the EU, the Bologna Process is part of a broader effort in the drive for a Europe of knowledge which includes:

- lifelong learning and development,
- Strategic framework for the Open Method of Coordination in Education and Training, ET2020,

- the Copenhagen Process for enhanced European co-operation in Vocational Education and Training, and
- initiatives under the European Research Area.

The EU supports a broad range of measures to modernize the content and practices of higher education in the 27 member-states and the EU's 28 neighbouring countries, including with the support of the Lifelong Learning Programme (LLP), the Instrument for Pre-accession Assistance (IPA), the European Neighbourhood and Partnership Instrument (ENPI) and the Development Cooperation Instrument (DCI), the Tempus programme and the EU's programme for worldwide academic cooperation: Erasmus Mundus.

The EU also works to support the modernization agenda of universities through the implementation of the 7th EU Framework Programme for Research (European Research Area) and the Competitiveness and Innovation Programme as well as the Structural Funds and loans from the European Investment Bank.

To establish synergies between the Bologna Process and the Copenhagen Process, which concerns vocational education and training, in co-operation with member-states, the Commission has established a European Qualifications Framework (EQF) for lifelong learning. The EQF is linked to and supported by other initiatives in the fields of transparency of qualifications (Europass), credit transfer [the European Credit Transfer and Accumulation System (ECTS) for higher education and the European Credit System for Vocational Education and Training (ECVET)] and quality assurance [European association for quality assurance (ENQA) in higher education and the European Network for Quality Assurance in Vocational Education and Training (ENQA-AVET)].

In all European countries, the overall responsibility for higher education lays with the relevant ministry, that is, a department of government led by a minister. In the German speaking Community of Belgium, Ireland, and the United Kingdom, government departments use the title "department" rather than "ministry". Responsibility for different types of

HEIs is distributed between three different ministries in denmark. In Ireland and the United Kingdom, "arm's length" bodies responsible for distributing and monitoring public funds have been established between the HEIs and the government in order to ensure that there is no direct political control of individual institutions. Generally, the ministry oversees HEIs as regards compliance with the law, ministerial codes and legal statutes. The ministry is responsible for formulating higher education policies that frame national or institutional strategic plans and development.

The ministry is also responsible for formulating national strategic priorities or a formal strategic or development plan for higher education in several countries. Furthermore, the ministry appoints external (and sometimes internal) stakeholders as members of institution-level governance bodies in some countries. National quality assurance bodies are also an important part of the external governance of HEIs. These bodies are often responsible for setting quality standards and conducting evaluations, elaborating and implementing policies and standards for improving the quality of education at the institutions. The ministry is usually supported by a national-level advisory or consultative body, called the Higher Education Council, Advisory Council, Research Council, or similar.

These bodies usually provide advice to the ministry on issues related to higher education, science and arts policy. In some cases, they may also monitor and analyze European or international trends as a context for their recommendations. Such national-level bodies sometimes include the executive heads of the HEIs as well as representatives of other federal/regional ministries, trade unions, political parties, local/regional governments, HEIs and students. Each country also has a national-level body that consists of the executive heads of all public or government dependent private universities. This body is usually called a Rectors' Conference or Council. In the Netherlands and Norway, it is called the Association of Universities or Higher Education Institutions, respectively. In the United Kingdom, the equivalent bodies are Universities UK and Guild HE. In France, Lithuania, the Netherlands and

Austria, there is an equivalent body for the heads of professional/vocational HEIs. These bodies present proposals to the ministry regarding the development of the higher education.

The ministry also calls for advice and expertise from bodies such as student unions and other student organizations; councils of administration, artistic education, and economics; and associations of research workers, doctoral students and trade unions. In addition to the European-level organizations (e.g. European Commission and the EUA), there are also several international rectors' conferences that have an impact on governance in higher education within a certain area or region. Such international bodies promote co-operation and collaboration between higher education policymakers and institutional actors in different countries and sometimes different continents. Furthermore, they contribute to the establishment of common governance practices and policies in higher education throughout Europe and beyond.

External Regulations on the Structure of Institutional Governance

HEIs throughout Europe have become autonomous entities according to national legislation (there is a longer tradition of institutional autonomy in the Netherlands, the United Kingdom and Iceland than in other countries); however, the institutional governance structure of HEIs is organized according to national or regional regulations (in Belgium, Germany, and Spain, higher education legislation has been delegated to the level of the Community or *Länder*). In most countries, the regulations delineate the institutional-level governance bodies and their respective duties and responsibilities. Official regulations are usually supplemented by specific rules in the respective institutions' constitution or statutes, which usually provide for the procedures of election for institutional governance bodies. In Austria, the national laws regarding higher education also regulate the election procedures for institutional-level governance bodies. In Portugal, institutional governance bodies are regulated by new legislation as of 2007/08 and are defined first by national law and second by the respective institutional statutes.

In Greece, after thorough consultation with the academic community, a new framework has been developed ("law framework" of 2007) describing the operation of HEIs. This law provides extensive autonomy for the administrative and financial governance of universities, as well as more specific issues that deal with the overall functions of, for example, the procedures associated with universities' obligation to maintain a level of transparency and publicity of their activities, the duration of studies, the creation of a new framework of financial support for students, etc.

In the United Kingdom, HEIs are private, government-dependent organizations with diverse backgrounds and traditions, reflected in varying constitutional arrangements. They can, however, be divided into two broad groups. In institutions which acquired university status as a result of legislation passed in 1992, the powers of university governing bodies are laid down in, and limited by, legislation, together with the instrument and articles of government, as made by each institution and approved by the Privy Council. In contrast, in pre-1992 universities, the structures of governance are laid down in the university's own instruments of incorporation (the Act or charter and the statutes) and hence there are wide variations. The 2003 Lambert Review of Business-University Collaboration found that some of the differences, particularly with regard to management structures, were beginning to be eroded, i.e. the older universities were, historically, run as communities of scholars. Their management and governance arrangements were participatory: senates and councils were large and conservative. In the last ten years, there has been a gradual movement towards a more executive style of management, already common among post-1992 institution. Many universities are developing strong executive structures to replace "management by committee". The further reform of higher education governance structures is under discussion in several countries.

In 2006, the Government of Lithuania adopted a Higher Education System Development Plan for 2006-2010, which provides for substantial changes in the external and institutional governance of higher education. Implementation of the Plan requires amendments of the Law on Higher Education and the Law on Research and Higher Education that are widely debated on the academic and political levels. Structural reform is one of the most extensively discussed issues within the higher education system in Finland. It is closely linked to the National Productivity Programme, which ran from November 2003 to December 2007 and covered the entire public sector. The aim of the programme was to improve productivity and efficiency of public service provision and it directly affected personnel policies and organizational structures of universities. For example, some administrative services were transferred to Service Centers established by collaborating institutions, and alternative production models were debated from the regional perspective.

External Regulations on Institutional Strategic Planning

As autonomous entities, HEIs are primarily responsible for their development, activities and institutional goals. In the increasingly competitive higher education market, the institutions must ensure that they are responding to the demands and needs of society as best they can. Furthermore, the competition to attract students is also increasing. The strategic plan is a key instrument for developing and directing the activities and priorities of an institution. A strategic plan generally states the vision and direction of the institution. It presents the cycle of objectives, implementation, and review processes that will occur at specific phases of development. A strategic plan is intended to be all-inclusive throughout the institution, and in many cases includes incentive measures to help motivate academic and non-academic staff to take part. Many plans include a focus on acquiring additional financial resources (to supplement or supplant funds from the state) and a process for distributing third party or private funds. Quality assurance and a system of information sharing are also important elements of the strategic plan. HEIs in only a few countries are not officially required to develop a strategic plan.

The ruling defining higher education in the French Community of Belgium provides the higher education objectives and the mission of the institutions. In the German-speaking Community of Belgium, the mission and strategic priorities of the *Autonome Hochschule* were not established by the institution, but by official decree in 2005. HEIs in the Flemish Community of Belgium are free to draft long-term strategic or development plans and they are free to take the governmental priorities into account or not, as they decide. Legislation does not require institutes of technology in Ireland to have strategic plans; however, all institutes have a strategic plan in place. There are no official regulations that oblige universities in Cyprus to establish a strategic plan or a development plan governing long-term aims and priorities. Recently, however, within the deliberations for the universities' budgets and as a general governmental policy, a three-year budgetary plan is requested from the university. In Poland, HEIs are not legally required to develop long-term development strategies. Some institutions go ahead with such programmes of their own accord, while others operate based on short-term plans spanning several rather than ten or more years.

An institutional strategic plan is obligatory in all other countries and it is used in various ways as an instrument in the relationship between the HEIs and the state. In Austria and Finland, HEIs enter into performance agreements with the ministry every three years and must provide strategies that specify the objectives of the university operations. In Estonia, a comprehensive development plan is one of the mandatory requirements for the establishment of a university. In Latvia and Iceland, a strategic plan is required in order to achieve state accreditation. In Portugal, as of 2007/08 a strategic plan is required in order to establish any new institution and for the normal operation of any existing institution.

Until recently, universities in Greece were not required to develop strategic plans. Based on the new law of 2007, universities are now obliged to elaborate detailed four-year plans not only for the planning of teaching and scientific staff positions but also for the overall economic development of the institutions. Annual progress reports are also required. In Luxembourg, the strategic plan is used by the ministry to determine the amount of public funds allocated to the institution. All state institutions in Norway have been using result-oriented planning since 1990, when it became required by law, or before. In most countries where HEIs are required to develop a strategic plan, the institutional plans must align with national priorities or official strategic policies for higher education. In these cases, national or regional strategic policies are typically based on information drawn from the institutions as well as national or regional priorities and objectives. In turn, the institutions must frame their strategies and development plans within the national or regional context while taking into consideration their particular institutional needs, resources, and limitations. In all countries where a strategic plan is obligatory, official regulations also stipulate how the implementation of the plan is monitored, except in Denmark, Estonia, Spain, Latvia, the Netherlands and Sweden.

A. Organization of Higher Education in Austria

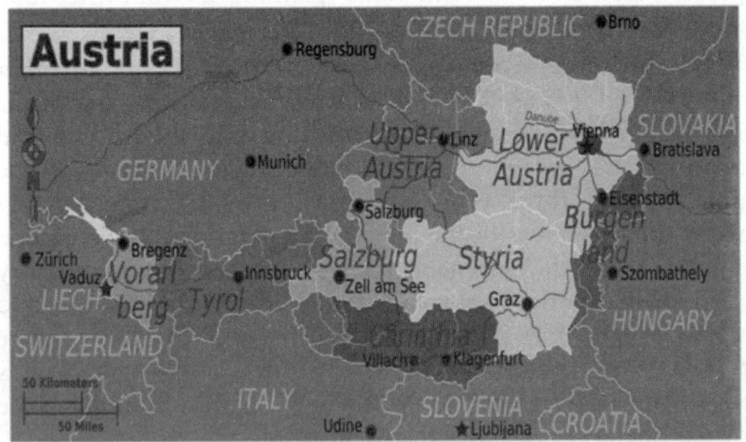

Higher education in Austria is divided into 21 public universities governed by the University Act, 2002, 12 research universities, six universities of art and three medical universities; a university Center for continuing Education, 19 Fachhochschulen (university of applied sciences) which have a private legal status with public shareholders. They are considered as a sector apart from public and private because of this status.

95% of their funding is from public sources. They are regulated by the *Fachhochschulen* Studies Act of 1993. They offer more than 120 courses of study in short cycle.

In 2007, a new type of HEI was added: the merger of 51 post-secondary colleges for teacher training (with currently 13,568 students) resulted in eight publicly-funded teacher training colleges (Bundesgesetz, 2006/Federal Law, 2006). These colleges are intended to offer both scientific and vocational education for teaching professions, including teacher study programmes and further education training courses. Teacher training colleges are also expected to carry out scientific research.

Further institutions of post-secondary education (in colleges) also exist: advanced vocational colleges for teacher training, for social workers and for paramedical degrees delivered by both universities of applied science and colleges are recognized by the Federal Government of Austria. Student enrolment in one of the above education institutions requires the certificate of completion of secondary education (*matura*). In addition, all applicants to universities of art have to pass an entrance examination. Austria has a three-cycle system following the Bologna Process. For university program, credits may be allocated for academic achievements according the European Credits Transfer.

Until the 1990s, higher education was organized and controlled by the Federal Government. Since the last years, a growing number of private institutions have settled a new market of degree courses offered by new education providers, non-traditional institutions and branch campuses of foreign universities. In 1999, foreign universities as well as private Austrian institutions were entitled by law to act as recognized private universities and acquired the right to award study programmes and academic degrees in Austria. This federal law (*Universitäts-Akkreditierungsgesetz*—University Accreditation Act) also regulates criteria for educational institutions and the procedure to be recognized and accredited as a private university. The recognized private higher education sector in Austria is constituted by two different types of institutions:

1. The Catholic Schools of Theology

Based on a Concordat between the Holy Sea and the Republic of Austria, the Catholic schools of theology offer education programs in theology and award degrees recognized by the state. There are three such schools in total in Austria.

2. The Private Universities

There are today 11 accredited private universities, recognized as such and regulated by the previously mentioned Federal Law of 1999. These private institutions have some characteristics in common. These are mainly oriented towards the Anglo-American culture of learning. Most of these work in cooperation with American and British institutions. They generally use alternative concepts of teaching and learning methods, considered as a competitive advantage in the educational market (small working groups with obligatory class attendance; practice under working conditions; development of technical skills in laboratory and workshop sessions; private tutorials to provide students with orientation; problem-orientated teaching; community learning); regarding the infrastructures, they also have in common to offer to their students, modern facilities and technical equipments.

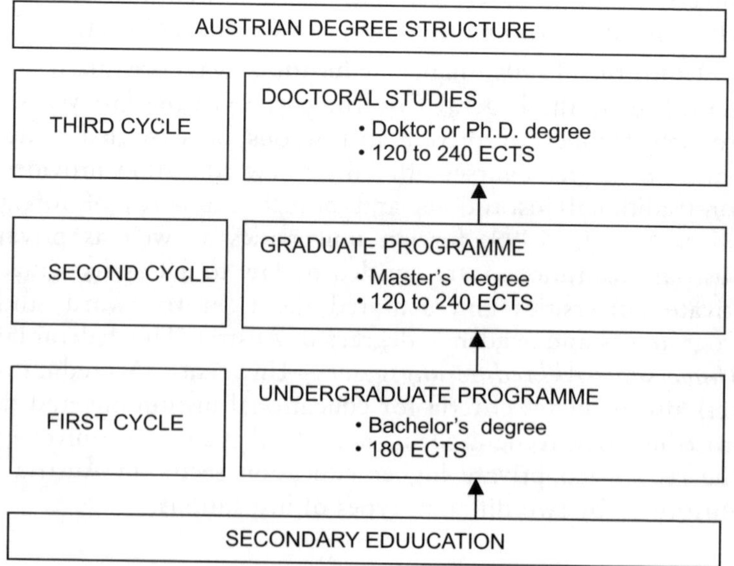

Enrolment in public and private universities requires the completion of upper secondary schools (*matura*). However, private universities have in addition their own admission policies. Private institutions are free to establish additional selection criteria for enrolment (criteria for admission in both public and private are mentioned in Higher Education Act, 2002). These criteria can be written tests and interviews, motivation letter, essay on a topic of interest, proof of language skills, professional or internship experiences. Students enrolled in public and private higher education institutions have exactly the same rights regarding the access to public social support such as family allowances, health insurance and taxation. Students enrolled in private universities have been incorporated into the system of study grants and transfer payments into the Austrian National Union of Students as well. Less than 2% of the student population is enrolled in private universities in Austria (they were around 3,600 students in 2005).

Concerning *private institutions funding*, the federal government is prohibited by law to finance these institutions. However, the law does not apply to federal provinces, municipalities and local authorities. This has, as a consequence, the emergence of private institutions fully or largely funded by federal provinces. This system gives each province the possibility to set its own priorities in education and to enhance local university projects. Actually, most of them are publicly funded and not funded by private companies.

The introduction of *Fachhochschulen* has had positive effects on the entire Austrian education market. Study programmes at the *Fachhochschulen* are vocationally oriented alternatives to study programmes of the universities. This development improved the social permeability of the education system considerably. Due to their practical focus and emphasis on calculable study periods in addition to good job prospects afterwards, study programmes at *Fachhochschulen* attract children from families with a low level of education. These experiences serve as good arguments for the binary higher education system. Already in 1998, Burton Clark pointed to the possible negative effects if countries like the UK have only universities in their higher education system: "While such institutions as polytechnics and teacher training colleges are blessed with the university title and brought into all-encompassing system, the differentiation of institution, programs, and degree levels continues. The university label is stretched to give it multiple meanings and usages."

Open access to public universities has however not achieved its purpose of increasing the social permeability of education. Both the capacity overload at universities and the positive effects of restricted admission at FH support the argument to abolish open access at public universities. The example of the Austrian Fachhochschulen shows that it is possible to fix the costs per study place transparently. This calculation can serve as a basis for negotiations between the government and the universities about the number of funded study places. Consequently, universities would be able to influence the number of their study places.

Accreditation of institutions and their study programmes was a key point from the very outset of the foundation of the Fachhochschulen and private university sectors. Quality assurance is an essential element of the two new types of HEI. Quality is monitored by two national agencies, namely the Fachhochschul Council (Fachhochschulrat) for the Fachhochschulen sector and the accreditation council (Akkreditierungsrat) for the private university sector. Instead of compulsory accreditation of institutions or study programmes the public university sector is obliged to establish internal quality management systems. Similar procedures will be relevant for teacher training colleges.

While the Austrian HE sector was being restructured by the implementation of new types of HEI, the number of students remained constant with an annual average of 230,000 student enrolments. With regard to the share in the federal budget, however, the development of Higher Education expenditure presents a less significant change and is still low, firstly, because Austria increased its budget on higher education between 1990 and 2004 only from 3.4 to 3.94 per cent (bm: bwk 2005, p. 19). All in all Austria's direct and indirect expenditure from public and private sources for the tertiary sector of 1.1 per cent of Gross Domestic Product lacks behind the OECD country average of 1.4 (OECD 2006, Table B2.2). Apart from restructuring the entire HE system, reform activities focused on their organization of public universities through new university Acts in 1993 and 2002. During this process, public universities were subject to deregulation by implementing instruments and procedures of the New Public Management (NPM).

These managerial mechanisms caused a trend of entrepreneurial orientation in organizational structures and management processes of universities. But in view of governmental higher education steering as well as internal university governance university reform turned out to have many inconsistencies (Nickel et al., 2006). The university sector has developed strong structures over centuries and therefore built massive resistance against changes. In contrast to that, Fachhochschulen were built from scratch as private enterprise systems with appropriate management structures and a clear market orientation. From the beginning, the Austrian Fachhochschulen sector was not steered by strong external regulation but equipped with self-governance mechanisms. Fachhochschulen are labelled "Pioneers of Managerialism" (Pechar, 2003) since their internal modes of steering are closer to NPM compared to those of universities.

A traditional feature of the Austrian HE system was a central university steering system. For instance, the Federal Ministry for Education, Science and Culture controlled and financed all universities. For a long time, the allocation of the budgets was a result of individual negotiation processes between the respective minister of science and the university rectorates. This was an obscure procedure. In this context, the university system developed organically rather than systematically. The divergences between the institutions were not primarily the result of state regulation but the consequence of decentralized decisions of each university. This bottom-up governance pattern—based on a consensus culture—found its particular expression in open access to higher education.

In contrast to other European HEI, Austrian public universities never had access policies (i.e. there was no restriction of access to study programmes). Instead, anyone holding a university entrance qualification could enter study programmes of his/her own choice, place, subject and duration. Open access is still considered a central social right that is granted by law and derives from the political consensus that education shall be available to everybody. The open access was not modified until a judgement of the European Court of Justice (7 July 2005) forced the Austrian state to make a change. The old Austrian regulations intended to protect Austrian students from international competition. Non-Austrian students could not apply for a place at an Austrian university unless they held one in their home country. The European Court declared this practice to be unlawful. An immediate storm of applications, particular from Germany and especially for medicine followed. As a counter reaction, the University Act was modified. Now the access to study programmes is restricted by a selection process, particularly for those programmes that are demanded by German students who intend to avoid admission restrictions (numerus clausus) at their home university (Amendment of the University Act of 2002 as of July 28, 2005). This regulation is valid until the end of the winter semester 2007/2008. But it can be anticipated, however, that—at least for medicine—the numerus clausus will remain beyond this date.

First changes were caused by a new university organization law [University Organization Amendment Act/ Universitätsorganisationsgesetz (UOG)] in 1993. The Act aimed at a more entrepreneurial and competitive university system by implementing management structures—particularly in the field of university management: target-oriented steering mechanisms, efficient and effective organizational structures as well as increased self-government. Although the government intended to restrict its action to strategic steering, the governmental steering practice hardly changed (Zechlin 2002) because of four reasons: there was neither a transparent, indicator-based financing system from the government, nor a strategic political objective which could serve as a basis for target and performance agreements between the Federal Ministry and the universities. Reporting and global budgeting was also lacking. While the transformation of governance mechanisms remained unsuccessful, universities changed their structures to the benefit of more market orientation. But at the same time the government decreased the university budgets. This situation led to increased and conflictive financial competition that was hardly known before. A second fundamental step towards more deregulation was initiated by the new University Act of 2002 (UG2002). This Act changed governance mechanisms in favour of institutional and financial autonomy, strong leadership and quality management.

B. Higher Education in Russia

Russia is one of the most populous nations of the world, and one of the most educated. Nearly 55% of Russians have completed some form of tertiary education a figure that approaches and even exceeds respective indicators of many developed nations (Poletaev and Zharova, 2002). The success of Russian higher education is to a large extent, a product of Soviet educational policy, but a number of achievements have been lost since then. Reforms that began in the mid-1980s, and continued after the demise of the Soviet Union, have constantly tested the national education system, which proved to be both one of the most vulnerable and one of the most inertial social institutions.

According to a 2005 UNESCO report, more than half of the Russian adult population has gone through a tertiary education, which is twice as high as the OECD average. As of the 2007-08 academic years, Russia had 8.1 million students enrolled in all forms of tertiary education (including military and police institutions and postgraduate studies). Foreign students accounted for 5.2% of the enrollment, half of whom were from other CIS countries. 6.2 million students were enrolled in 658 state-owned and 450 private civilian university-level institutions licensed by the Ministry of Education; total faculty reached 625 thousands in 2005.

The number of state-owned institutions was rising steadily from 514 in 1990 to 655 in 2002 and remains nearly constant since then. The number of private institutions, first reported as 193 in 1995, continues to rise. Andrei Fursenko, Minister of Education, is campaigning for a reduction in number of institutions to weed out diploma mills and substandard colleges; in April 2008 his stance was approved by President Dmitry Medvedev: "This amount, around a thousand universities and two thousands spinoffs, does not exist anywhere else in the world; it may be over the top even for China...consequences are clear: devaluation of education standard". Even supporters of the reduction like Yevgeny Yasin admit that the move will strengthen consolidation of academia in Moscow, Saint Petersburg and Novosibirsk and devastate the provinces, leaving the federal subjects of Russia without colleges for training local school teachers.

The trend for consolidation began in 2006 when state universities and colleges of Rostov-on-Don, Taganrog and other southern towns were merged into Southern Federal University, based in Rostov-on-Don; a similar conglomerate was formed in Krasnoyarsk as Siberian Federal University; the third one is likely to emerge in Vladivostok as Far Eastern Federal University. Moscow State University and Saint Petersburg State University acquired the *federal university* status in 2007 without further organizational changes.

Move Towards Bologna Process

Russia is in the process of migrating from its traditional tertiary education model, incompatible with existing Western academic degrees, to a modernized degree structure in line with Bologna Process model. (Russia co-signed the Bologna Declaration in 2003.) In October 2007, Russia enacted a law that replaces the traditional five-year model of education with a two-tiered approach: a four-year bachelor (Russian: бЋкалЋвр) degree followed by a two-year master's (Russian: магистр, *magistr*) degree.

The move has been criticized for its merely formal approach: instead of reshaping their curriculum, universities would simply insert a BSc/BA accreditation in the middle of their standard five or six-year programs. The job market is generally unaware of the change and critics predict that a stand-alone BSc/BA diplomas will not be recognized as "real" university education in the foreseeable future, rendering the degree unnecessary and undesirable without further specialization. Institutions like MFTI or MIFI have practiced two-tier breakdown of their specialist programs for decades and switched to Bologna Process designations well in advance of the 2007 law, but an absolute majority of their students complete all six years of MSc/MA (formerly specialist) curriculum, regarding BSc/BA stage as useless in real life.

Student mobility among universities has been traditionally discouraged and thus kept at very low level; there are no signs that formal acceptance of Bologna Process will help students seeking better education. Finally, while the five-year specialist training was previously free to all students, the new MSc/MA stage is not. The shift forces students to pay for what was free to the previous class; the cost is unavoidable because the BSc/BA degree alone is considered useless.[55] Defenders of Bologna Process argue that the final years of the specialist program were formal and useless: academic schedules were relaxed and undemanding, allowing students to work elsewhere. Cutting the five-year specialist program to a four-year BSc/BA will not decrease the actual academic content of most of these programs.

Postgraduate diploma structure so far retains its unique Soviet pattern established in 1934. The system makes a distinction between *scientific degrees*, evidencing personal postgraduate achievement in scientific research, and related but separate *academic titles*, evidencing personal achievement in university-level education. There are two successive postgraduate *degrees*: kandidat nauk (*Candidate of science*) and doktor nauk (*Doctor of science*). Both are a certificate of scientific, rather than academic, achievement, and must be backed up by original/novel scientific work, evidenced by publications in peer-reviewed journals and a dissertation defended in front of senior academic board. The titles are issued by Higher Attestation Commission of the Ministry of Education. A degree is always awarded in one of 23 predetermined fields of science, even if the underlying achievement belongs to a different field. Thus, it is possible to defend two degrees of *kandidat* independently, but not simultaneously; a *doktor* in one field may also be a *kandidat* in a different field.

Kandidat nauk can be achieved within university environment (when the university is engaged in active research in the chosen field), specialized research facilities or within research and development units in industry. Typical *kandidat nauk* path from admission to diploma takes 2-4 years. The dissertation paper should contain a solution of an existing scientific problem, or a practical proposal with significant economical or military potential. The title is perceived as equivalent to Western Ph.D.

Doktor nauk, the next stage, implies achieving significant scientific output. This title is often equated to the German or Scandinavian habilitation. The dissertation paper should summarize the author's research resulting in theoretical statements that are qualified as a new discovery, or solution of an existing problem, or a practical proposal with significant economical or military potential. The road from *kandidat* to *doktor* typically takes 10 years of dedicated research activity; one in four candidates reaches this stage. The system implies that the applicants must work in their research field full time;

however, the degrees in social sciences are routinely awarded to active politicians.

Academic *titles* of *dotsent* and *professor* are issued to active university staff who already achieved degrees of *kandidat* or *doktor*; the rules prescribe minimum residency term, authoring established study textbooks in their chosen field, and mentoring successful postgraduate trainees; special, less formal rules apply to professors of arts. Military postgraduate education radically falls out of the standard scheme. It is provided by the military academies; unlike their Western namesakes, they are *postgraduate* institutions. Passing the course of an academy does not result in an explicitly named degree (although may be accompanied by a research for *kandidat nauk* degree) and enables the graduate to proceed to a certain level of command (equivalent of battalion commander and above).

St. Petersburg University

Russia has Four Types of Institutions

1. **Universities:** Responsible for education and research in a variety of disciplines; There are "classical" and "technical" universities with special attention paid, respectively to social sciences and humanities or natural fundamental and applied (engineering) sciences. Unofficial

ratings also distinguish old "classical" universities and "new" universities, former pedagogical or technical institutions which have acquired their university status quite recently.

2. **Academies:** Responsible for education and research. They differ from universities only in that they restrict themselves to a single discipline.
3. **Institutes:** Multi-discipline oriented. They can be independent structural units, or part of a university or academy and usually specialize in one field. However, pedagogical institutes are responsible for all spectrums of disciplines taught at schools
4. **Private institutions:** Present in increasing numbers. They offer degrees in non-engineering fields such as business, culture, sociology and religion.

Degree structure

There is a new degree structure, which follows a three-tier pattern, three levels, and uses U.S./British nomenclature. Currently, there are only two types of diploma (degrees) which are officially, recognized as ones of completed higher education—these are diploma of specialist and diploma of a master level (magistr).

The bachelor diploma and the certificate of "incomplete higher education" are not regarded as high education degrees. In some cases, a bachelor degree suffices to start a career. Anyway bachelors (or undergraduates) are not allowed to take positions were higher education is necessary by labor law or by custom, they can't get the research degree of candidate of sciences, male graduates are drafted as soldiers and must serve for two years while specialists and magistrs have half a year shorter conscription period.

It should be noted that Russia has signed Bologna Declaration and by the year 2010 transition to a two-tier degree structure should be completed; the objective is specified as one of the ultimate goals of the country's educational reforms.

Moscow School of Mathematics and Navigation was a first Russian educational institution founded by Peter the Great in

1701. It provided Russians with technical education for the first time and much of its curriculum was devoted to producing sailors, engineers, cartographers and bombardiers to support Russian expanding navy and army. Then in 1810, the Saint Petersburg Military Engineering-Technical University becomes the first engineering higher learning institution in the Russian Empire, after addition of officers classes and application of five-year term of teaching. So initially, more rigorisms of standards and teaching terms became the traditional historical feature of the Russian engineering education. In Russia, the degree is specialist is an engineer or master's degree is an engineer, was traditional a degree after 5-6 years of study, but now (when Russia adopted the Bologna Declaration) appears a first degree "bachelor is an engineer" after 4 years of stud. Additional programs (3-4 years, after a traditional specialist-magister) provide the title of "Ph.D. inginer".

Russia is no longer a world leader in science and intellectual thinking, according to a new report that details a "shocking" decline in its research output. The Global Research Report on Russia, by Thomson Reuters, reveals that the country's annual research output has fallen from 29,000 papers in 1994 to 27,600 in 2008. The decline is also apparent in areas where it once excelled such as the physical sciences. The research base is in trouble but there is "little sign of a solution", the report says.

"Russia has been a leader in scientific research and intellectual thinking for so long that it comes not only as a surprise but a shock to see that it has a small and dwindling share of world activity as well as real attrition of its core strengths." The report, produced by Evidence, a UK-based subsidiary of Thomson Reuters, is one of a series focusing on the so called BRIC countries—Brazil, Russia, India and China—which "are in the process of advancing to the forefront of the world's economies".

Russia, however, is punching below its weight in terms of research. It has, the report points out, experienced "drastic political, economic and intellectual changes" since the dissolution of the Soviet Union in 1991. Budgets for science have fallen sharply, and the country's scientists as a group are ageing. In

October 2009, scores of academics put their names to an open letter to Dmitry Medvedev, the Russian President, warning of a "looming collapse" in science. Among the problems they cited were inadequate fu6555555nding, a lack of strategic planning and a decline in the prestige of science as a profession.

Privatization in Russia

Today's privatization of professional education in Russia is conditioned by the creation of several hundred institutions in the past 10 to 15 years whose financial resources are exclusively private and non-governmental. Currently, with the "demographic hole" in student numbers (a predicted halving of the number of graduates from secondary schools since 2006), the increase in the number of private institutions has stopped and competition with state institutions has intensified. The government, represented by educational administrative bodies, has started a policy of protectionism, aimed at supporting budget-funded institutions and limiting private sector activities. Hence, there has been a slowing down of educational modernization and its rising innovative potential.

On the other hand, in the framework of current government-sponsored education, the investment processes of increasing non-budgetary and "third-party", mechanisms have continued.

The opening of paid-for programmes and courses, opportunities to study a second (additional) speciality, first steps towards student loans and greater financial-economic independence of institutions—all these and other steps taken by federal authorities continue to allow the privatization of higher education. The essence of such privatization is the consolidation of various structural and systematic changes within the restrictions of government influences over the functioning of higher professional schools.

On a larger canvas, the term privatization is positively viewed by the overwhelming majority of experts, and partly by the public. With regard to the population, which associates the concepts of "paid" and "private", there is largely agreement to pay for higher, middle and vocational education services. The public counts on the attraction of extra budget resources reducing the cost of learning such as funds from investors and employers, concessional loans and grants, social benefits and compensations. In fact, this is a reasonable expectation, keeping in mind that in developed welfare economies the state insures against extreme financial risks and protects vulnerable groups. The remaining issues in education are matters for private and non-governmental organizations, providers and institutions.

Regarding the nature of their activities, in the next few years private education institutions in Russia will occupy the sphere of non-formal and extra-system education, and will master new spheres of social space and create an innovative educational environment there. That environment will react to changing requirements of the labour market in a more sensitive way, and will gradually form a self-adjusting system of preparation, training and employment of an economically active population. The absence of "academic snobbery" in private universities, and close relations with enterprises and employers, professional unions, associations and corporative societies, will enable them to find a niche in the system of servicing the labour market and, consequently, keeping a place in the competitive race for the central figure of education—the learner. By covering new forms of activity and enlarging the choice of learners at the expense of the adult population, the educational sphere in general will develop extensively and its accessibility will increase. In terms of openness of information on its actions, participation in independent ratings and monitoring of graduate employment will ensure an increase in quality.

Admission System

Many students wishing to enter a university need additional preparation to gain admission. Only one-third of students are estimated to enter university relying only on the knowledge acquired in school. Another one-third take special preparatory courses. Others either hire private tutors or educate themselves. The cost of preparing for entrance examination is a heavy economic burden for Russian students and their families. For the HEIs the problem is that many students do not have the qualifications considered necessary for entry to higher education. Currently, the Certificate of Secondary Complete General

Education and the successful passing of university-matriculation exams are required for admission to all kinds of the higher education institutions. The education reform program aims to promote equity in higher education.

Tuition Fees

The Russian Constitution (article 43, paragraph 3) guarantees everyone the right to get higher education free of charge on a basis of competition. Adhering to the law, the government allocates funds to pay the tuition fees within an established quota/number of students for each state institution. Traditionally, the size of quota varies from institution to institution and from one field (discipline) to another. It depends on the share of state in the institution's budget, demands from state bodies in a region, social programs and other, sometimes rather subjective estimates. On top of the quotas described above, the universities are free to enroll students on a fee-paying basis and have the right to define the fee for their programme according to the market price and demand.

Authorities and Organizations

The Ministry of Education and Science is the central body of the federal executive authorities responsible for implementing state policy at all levels of education. At the regional level, the education management structure consists of the pertinent authorities: committees (departments or ministries) of education, public council organization and associations, etc. They define and execute regional educational policy. The Subjects of the Federation is an organization, which is involved in co-ordination and budgeting of various kinds of institutions and education under regional jurisdiction.

The cohort of 655 state HEIs is split into 572 federal institutions, 55 institutions established by regional authorities and the remaining under local/municipal authorities. It should be noted that among the 572 federal institutions some are established by and administratively belong to different federal bodies. For example the state university—Moscow Institute of International Relations is under the Ministry of Foreign Affairs, the Moscow Technical University of Communication and Informatics has been founded by the Ministry of Information

Technologies and Communication; and the Moscow State University is a unique institution as it is financed directly from the federal budget. However, as it was mentioned above, all issues related to the content of HEI programs should be agreed and handled in compliance with the governmental educational standards.

Governance Structure

The individual universities have become much more autonomous than they were in the previous system, but still, the present-day autonomy can be circumscribed for in many ways and it depends on factors such as financial stability, leadership and management, political linkage, and institutional culture. The 1992 Law delegated to the republics, provinces and local education authorities the responsibility for curriculum, textbooks, teaching methods, budgets, construction and equipment. HEIs gained the right to seek income from non-government sources and to engage in commercial activity. The law also confirmed the possibility of private institutions being established.

At institutional level, the management is usually performed by its elected representative body, the Council. As described in 'The Reform of Education in New Russia', "Election procedures are determined by the Charter of the institution which defines the distribution of powers between the Council and the administration; day-to-day management of the institutions is performed by its administration. The management of non-state education institutions is performed directly by the founder of the institution or, if stipulated by the founder, by a board of trustees named by it. In both cases, the board is responsible for material and technical support for the educational process and organizing the supply of teaching materials. Education management has considerably increased in institutions given their new, significant independence. Today an education institution can choose how to organize its educational process, select and hire its own staff, and organize its own research, financial and economic activity."

Institutions' Boards of Trustees and HEI themselves usually maintain relations with all levels of authorities, business (industry) and communities to diversify the sources of income, generate revenue and/or get financial and other kinds of support. Whereas the education process is aimed at awarding of state diploma and research process is connected with award of research degrees they should comply with the state standards approved by the Federal Government and guidelines of Russian Academy of Sciences.

Russian higher education has been constantly changing over the last several decades. The reform agendas have involved many profound and essential issues of national education, viz. the funding of higher education, admission and access, educational quality, degree recognition, and international integration. Additional challenges faced by Russian higher education include the recruitment of junior faculty and retention of graduate students in academia; the need to strengthen links between higher education and basic research; creating new relationships between higher education and industry; and developing the effective use of information technologies in education. In sum, a variety of exciting transformations are now shaping the future of Russian higher education and warrant careful scrutiny for many years to come.

C. Organization of Higher Education in Belgium

Katholieke Universiteit Leuven, Belgium

Freedom of education is a constitutional right in Belgium. Articles 17 and 24 of the Belgian Constitution lay down the principle of freedom in education and state that any preventative measure in education is forbidden. Every legal person has consequently the right to organize education and establish institutions on this purpose. The constitutional reforms of 1980 and 1989 transferred responsibilities in education to the three federal regions: Flemish, French and German Communities. Regions became competent for the overall organization of the education sector. In each community, a Community Council has the legislative power in education and a Community Government and Education Minister is responsible for the executive power in education.

The general organization of higher education in Belgium comprises the following:

1. *University education* (at universities) which provides academic education in humanities and sciences.
2. *Non-university education* (at university colleges in the Flemish Community, and at Hautes Ecoles or equivalent in the French community) which covers different fields of studies such as technology, economics, social, paramedical, pedagogy, arts, translation and agriculture.

Enrolment in higher education requires a certificate of completion of secondary education. Certain fields of study (medicine, dentistry and arts) also require entrance tests. Registration fees in universities and colleges are fixed annually by the government. Belgium has adopted Bologna Process with the three-cycle terms in education (Bachelor, Master and Doctorate). Regarding private higher education in Belgium, this sector in the French Community is similar to the French organization. Thus, we do not speak about private institutions as such but about free subsidized higher education institutions. Free in the sense that these institutions are provided by independent providers. They are however under the state control and funded by public sources. In the Flemish Community, the system is similar to the Dutch one. The Netherlands and Flanders have signed together an Act establishing a binational accrediting body, responsible for the quality assurance evaluation and accreditation of private higher education institutions. In Flanders, private institutions are called non-statutory registered institutions. There is no private university in the German Community.

University Education

University education is organized in universities and university institutes. In the French Community, there are four universities (two public, two private) and seven university institutes two public and five private). Public universities (or universities organized by the community) are set up by the state and administered by the provincial or municipal authorities. They offer at least 4-year education, organized in two cycles. University funding and inspection are regulated by Law of July 27, 1971. This Law foresees that funding of "organized universities" depends on the number of enrolled students. Since 1980, partnerships between the private sector and tertiary education have been established. Independent industrial and technological research centers have been created by universities to promote scientific collaboration with businesses.

Enrolment in either public or private universities is opened to every student holding a certificate of upper-secondary education. Students are free to choose the institution in which they wish to pursue their studies. Entrance examinations are imposed for certain fields (civil engineering studies for example). The payment of a registration fee is required at university. The French Community does not apply a limited admissions system (*numerus clausus*). Nevertheless, because the Federal Government limits access to medical studies, quota measures have been progressively put in place in faculties awarding study programs related to this field. No one can be enrolled in a university without a proof of sufficient proficiency in French language. This concerns students coming from outside the French Community and is applied since 1997.

Non-university Education

The non-university education is provided at *Hautes Écoles* and Higher Schools of Art. As far as grant-aided free non-university education is concerned, there are 14 Hautes Ecoles; six Higher Schools of Arts and two Higher Institutes of Architecture. The Hautes Ecoles were created in 1995-96, replacing non-university tertiary schools. Before academic year 1995-96, there were 114 non-university tertiary schools in the French Community which have been replaced by 30 Hautes Ecoles. They offer short-term education (generally in 3-4 years) and long-term education (two cycles of two years each, three for the second cycle of certain sectors similar to university form). There are *30 Hautes Ecoles*, administered this way:

— Six are French Community schools,

— Ten are public grant-aided schools administered by provinces or municipalities,

— Fourteen are free grant-aided schools (twelve Catholic and two non-denominational).

They usually offer courses in agriculture, arts, economics, paramedical, pedagogical, social, technology and translation. Enrolment in non-university tertiary education in general is subject to the payment of tuition fee. Candidates for admission have to satisfy two main conditions, viz. certificate of completion of secondary education and the success in the entrance examinations (depending on the establishment).

Governance

In Belgium (Flemish Community), public HEIs were formerly strictly regulated and controlled by the government. Nowadays, HEIs have greater institutional autonomy, including that in financial matters, which have resulted in a considerable increase in HEIs' responsibility for institutional policies and closer involvement by staff and students in institutional governance. In Belgium (Flemish Community), institutional autonomy with regard to staff policies is limited. Because senior academic staff has tenure, job opportunities for younger academics are scarce. As the academic staff members get older, many will retire in the next few years; however, this is a slow process. As a result, HEIs are sometimes permitted to offer early retirement options for senior academic staff (age 60 instead of 65). Meanwhile, the increase in external research funding leads to more frequent appointments of junior staff. Senior staff must be paid from the operating grant and therefore cannot exceed the number of junior staff. To give some leeway to the universities, the government has made provisions so that junior staff members who have a Ph.D. are allowed to teach. Further increases of public funding will lead to an increase in the number of tenure positions.

In Belgium, since 1989, education is not a federal matter anymore. Instead there is a complete delegation of authority for education to the (linguistic) Communities. In the Flemish Community of Belgium, the Ministry of the Flemish Community is responsible for higher education. Two departments are involved, viz. (1) Education Department, more particularly the Administration of Education and Training, for all higher education matters and issues of institutionally driven research; (2) Department of Science Innovation and Media for broader research issues. In addition, there is an autonomous accreditation agency that works on transnational basis together with the Netherlands. Since the Decree on Universities (1991) and the Decree on Hogescholen (1995) HE institutions are granted a large degree of autonomy.

Lump sum financing was introduced, and the control on the budget switched from an ex ante to an ex post perspective. HE institutions can make their own decision in appointing staff and in deciding on seniority level based on prior professional experience (e.g. obtained abroad). They autonomously design the curricula (there is no "national curriculum") provided that they comply with the general quality standards. Under certain conditions (i.e. a check by the Accreditation Agency of their feasibility and relevance), they may be allowed to establish new study programmes. Due to the federal structure of the Belgian state HEI are governed by the three language communities (Flemish, French and German). In the French Community (French Community) reforms between 1995 and 2005 aimed first of all at setting up a financial system in favour of more transparency and competition among HEI, secondly at increasing the participation of students in the university management and thirdly at establishing means and procedures of quality assurance.

As a reaction to the Lisbon Strategy a so-called Bologna decree stipulated mobility, ECTS, PPP and the building of associations between HEI.

The Lisbon Strategy, launched at the European Council meeting in Lisbon in March 2000, represented the main strategic framework for development of the EU in the past decade (European Council, 2000). Its intention was to find a solution to stagnation of economic growth in the EU, through the formulation of policy initiatives that were to be implemented by all member-states. The strategy represented an ambitious ten-year reform programme which searched for answers to global challenges such as the advancement of the US and Japan in a "new" knowledge-based economy and their domination in the field of information and communication technologies. It promoted integration of social and economic policy while focusing in particular on strengthening the EU's research capacity, completing the internal market, promoting entrepreneurship, fiscal consolidation and sustainability of public finances, encouraging progress within information society technologies, developing an active employment policy and modernizing social protection systems. The Lisbon Strategy was intended to improve the EU's economy and boost employment through approaching certain goals such as creating an internal market for services, decreasing administrative burdens, improving human capital, reaching the target of raising the level of expenditure on R&D to 3% of GDP and raising the level of the employment rate to 70%.

The Belgian HEI-system of the French Community consists of both non-university institutions: 28 'Hautes Ecoles', 17 Higher Art Colleges, nine universities and four Higher Institutes of Architecture. Private higher education is of considerable importance: it takes place either in religious institutions or in civic institutions. The community is responsible for official education. Private institutions of higher education receive financial aid from the state, subject to certain conditions.

> Several types of control such as ex ante controls, expost controls, supervision, have already been well established in most Commission services. They represent the initial basis for a sound Internal Control Framework Specific attention has also to be given to the deterrent effect of sanctions in this context. Ex ante controls are important as they prevent errors and avoid the need for ex post corrective actions. The Financial Regulation (FR) states that each operation shall be subject to an ex ante verification by the Commission before it is authorized by the authorizing officer. This ex ante verification covers both the financial and operational aspects of transactions. These controls can consist of desk reviews and on-the-spot controls and aim at controlling compliance with legality, regularity and sound financial management (economy, efficiency, and effectiveness). Ex ante controls are executed at the primary control level and are also performed at Commission level for every commitment and payment. For risky environments, an additional ex ante layer on a sample of transactions is sometimes implemented, depending on the authorizing officer's judgment. In the Ex Post Control network (EPCnet), ex post control has been defined as the controls executed to verify the financial and operational aspects of finalized budgetary transactions. These controls (carried out at different levels) can consist of desk reviews and on-the-spot controls and aim to control that legality, regularity and sound financial management (economy, efficiency, and effectiveness) have been respected.

The community is responsible for official education. Private institutions of higher education receive financial aid from the state, subject to certain conditions. In general HEI enjoy autonomy but this varies according to the nature of the authority which assumes the responsibility of education (e.g. the French Community system or the subsidized—concessional or not—independent system). In universities, a strong leadership is formed with the "rectors' council" composed of the rector, the general administrator, the vice- and pro-rectors. Acting as an executive committee, the rectors' council determines the university's strategic priorities. But on the whole, the control of the government "Commissioner" increases. Staff of HEI is appointed by the government, except the personnel of private

HEI, who can decide autonomously. In general, HEI develop a professional management of human resources.

D. Higher Education System of Finland

The tradition of higher education in Finland stretches back to 1640; it is rich, drawing not only on a strong indigenous respect for learning but on European university traditions which have been further enriched by the two languages (Finnish and Swedish) of the country. Today, the higher education system of Finland is one of the most intense in Europe with 20 university level institutions located in 11 towns in a country with a population of 4.9 million. The system has matured to its present form through planned development coinciding with Finland's shift from being a predominantly rural to a predominantly urban society and the government's effort to develop the different regions of the country in a balanced manner. As the result of a major curricular reform which began in 1984, the various curricula have been redesigned in ways that stress inter-diversity as well as the educational goals of the different areas, yet they remain integrated.

The activities of each institution of higher education are set down in separate acts and decrees that define the term of their internal autonomy in internal matters. The special autonomous status of the University of Helsinki is guaranteed by the Constitution. Typical matters that come under the power of decision of the institutions of higher education are selections (except those of full professors), allocation of the appropriations made to the institutions, decisions relating to the selection of students, and the content and organization of teaching and research. Like many other countries, Finland started to modify the internal administration of its institutions of higher education in the 1970s. One important reform extended the right to participate in decision-making processes to other staff groups than the professors. In several Finnish universities, one-third of the membership of the administrative bodies are elected by the professors, one-third by the teachers, researchers, and other staff members and one-third by the students. In some higher education institutions, about half of the members of administrative bodies are professors and associate professors and the other half, other faculty staff members, and students.

Finland's "open-door" approach to higher education, which effectively guarantees tuition-free education, needs to be reviewed.
Photo by Eduardo Zárate

Governance and Administration

By 1988, the revised system of administration was adopted by all the institutions of higher education, except the University of Helsinki. Naturally, administrative details vary depending on the nature and the size of the institution in question. Five institutions of higher education have chancellors, who are generally responsible for promoting institutional activities. They are usually assisted by appellative committee which acts as the highest appellative bodies, particularly in matters relating to appointments. The general administration of an institution is handled by the administrative council, consisting of the rector, the vice-rectors, the dean, and members elected by the other staff members and students for a two-year term. Five institutions of higher education have an elective body, the university council. Its membership is elected for a term of two years and consists of representatives of the professors and associate professors, of the other staff members, and of the students. The university council selects the members of the administrative council and handles matters of principle such as the operational and economic plans, budgets, and legislative matters.

The rector acts as the head of the university and supervises its activities. The administrative office is headed by the administrative director. This office is usually divided into different units in-charge of administration, finance, study affairs, and development. The administrative office takes care of general administrative matters, prepares matters for the administrative council and implements its decisions. The faculties are administered by faculty councils. Their functions include the supervision and development of teaching and research, the redefinition of vacant tenures and posts including the selection of experts making proposals of nominations for filling up of professors' and associate professors' posts, formulation of action and economic plans, decisions on the details of student selection, the issuing of diplomas, and propositions for regulations governing the awarding of degrees and the approval of curricula to mention some of them.

In addition to the faculty council, each faculty has a dean whose term of office, like that of the council runs for two years. As regards departments, the term subject department designates an administrative unit comprising one or more disciplines and research areas. The basic unit in teaching and research is a subject. Each professor and associate professor takes care of the development of teaching and the promotion of research in the field represented by the department. In addition, the faculty appoints one of the professors, associate professors, or another teacher to act as the chief representative of the department.

Education in Finland is free of charge at all levels when it leads to an officially recognized degree/qualification. Higher education system comprises university education and polytechnic education:

Universities

The universities are all state-run and total 20; 10 of these are multi-faculty institutions and other 10 are specialized institutions (three universities of technology, three schools of economics and business administration and four art schools of academies). They select their own students; consequently competition between applicants is very high. Recruitment requirements are the completion of certificates and entrance examinations (with *numerus clausus* in all fields). Students at universities may take a Bachelor's or Master's academic degree and also further academic education, including the doctoral degree. Universities also arrange further education and open university teaching. Students do not pay tuition fees. University funding is public; 70% of the funding is provided by the government.

Polytechnics

Twenty eight polytechnics are run by local authorities or private foundations, authorized by the government. These programs are professionally oriented and emphasize a focus on working life conditions. These are generally multi-sector establishments, offering combined courses for example in technology and transport, business and administration, health and social services, culture, tourism, catering and hotel management, natural resources, the humanities and education. Degrees have a professional emphasis and last between three and four years. In addition to academic studies, polytechnic degrees also require practical training and a diploma project. Around 130,000 students are enrolled in polytechnics. Private foundations are authorized by the government to run the polytechnics. This authorization determines their educational mission, fields of education, student numbers and location. Polytechnics have autonomy in their internal affairs. For polytechnics run by local authorities, costs are shared with the government. Seven polytechnics are run by local authorities, 11 polytechnics are run by municipal education consortia and 10 polytechnics are run by private foundations.

The Finnish Higher Education Evaluation Council (FINHEEC) is an independent expert body which assists universities, polytechnics and the Ministry of Education in the evaluation of education and educational institutions. Its duties are regulated by *Decree 1320/1995 on the Higher Education Evaluation Council* and its amendment 465/1998. One of its tasks among others is to conduct evaluation for the accreditation of the polytechnics. There is no private university in Finland. However, there are 28 polytechnics and 10 out of them are run by private foundations, authorized by the government.

Educational Authorities

- Ministry of Education and Culture is responsible for developing educational, science, cultural, sport and youth policies, and international cooperation in these fields.
- Finnish National Board of Education is an agency under the Ministry of Education tasked with implementation, monitoring and development oversight in the education sector.
- Finnish ENIC/NARIC (European Network of National Information Centres on Academic Recognition and Mobility/Network of National Academic Recognition Information Centres).
- Finnish Higher Education Evaluation Council is an independent expert body assisting higher education institutions and the Ministry of Education in matters relating to evaluation.
- The Academy of Finland is the prime funding agency for basic research in Finland.
- Centre for International Mobility CIMO is a governmental office operating under the Finnish Ministry of Education and Culture, offering services and expertise to encourage cross cultural communication.

E. Organization of Higher Education in France

Higher education system in France is free, at all levels and the principle of freedom has been stated by the Law of July 12, 1875. French higher education system is fairly complex, provided by a range of coexisting institutions with different purposes; different structures and different admission requirements. These institutions can be public (financed by the state, consequently tuition fees are symbolic) or private. The fundamental principles of education are guaranteed by the Code of Education, from pre-primary to tertiary education, for public and private establishments. The quantity, the diversity and the specializations of these higher education establishments, both public and private, make them difficult to classify. However, there are three main categories:

- ***Universities*** (public and private), offer a wide range of courses which can be academic or practical;
- ***Grandes écoles***, (public and private), and ***specialized schools*** (public and private), offer professional education and are supervised by the relevant ministry. They have high level test entrance exams, generally prepared through preparatory classes for Grandes Ecoles (*Classes Préparatoires aux Grandes Ecoles—CPGE)*. There are three types of CPGE: literature, scientific, economic and commercial. The last two years are very selective.
- ***Technological education*** (public and private), these are the two categories of technological education.

The majority of diplomas offered in higher education institutions are recognized by the state, which assesses the quality of the educational achievement of graduates. This concerns mainly diplomas offered in public establishments (schools and universities). However, diplomas delivered by private Grandes Ecoles and others private specialized schools are submitted to a strict procedure of evaluation when these establishments are under contract with the state. Consequently, diplomas offered in private higher education with such a contract with the state are certified ("homologués" or called "diplômévisé") by one of the ministries. Private establishments of higher education which do not have the state accreditation deliver diplomas which are not recognized by the state.

The public universities in France are named after the big cities near which they are located, followed by a numeral if there are several. Paris, for example, has thirteen universities, labelled Paris I to XIII. Some of these are not in Paris itself, but in the suburbs. In addition, most of the universities have taken a more informal name which is usually that of a famous person or a particular place. Sometimes, it is also a way to honor a famous alumnus, for example, the science university in Strasbourg is known as "Université Louis Pasteur" while its official name is "Université Strasbourg I".

The French system has undergone a reform and has adopted the Bologna Process, which aims at creating European standards for university studies, most notably a similar time frame everywhere, with three years devoted to the Bachelor's degree ("licence" in French), two for the Master's, and three for the doctorate. French universities have also adopted the ECTS credit system (for example, a licence is worth 180 credits). However, the traditional curriculum based on end of semester examinations still remains in place in most universities. This double standard has added complexity to a system which also remains quite rigid. It is difficult to change a major during undergraduate studies without losing a semester or even a whole year. Students usually also have few course selection options once they enroll in a particular diploma. France also hosts various branch colleges of foreign universities. These include Baruch College, the University of London Institute in Paris, Parsons Paris School of Art and Design and the American University of Paris.

Universities

Universities in France are mainly public institutions, except few exceptions. Enrolment is open to any student holding a

French *baccalauréat* or its foreign equivalent. Universities offer academic, technical, and professional degree programs in all disciplines, preparing students for careers in research and professional practice in every field. Universities offer a variety of different national diplomas. There are 87 public universities.

Private Sector

In France, private higher education is regulated by the principle of freedom as in the case of public education. However, the general situation of this sector is far from being clear (lack of official data, especially official figures regarding the number of establishments and students, complexity of their status and of their obligations via the state). From kindergarten to tertiary education, private institutions has an annual average of enrolled pupils/students of more than 2 millions, which represents 17% of the pupil/student population.

Regarding higher education, 14% of the student population (250,000 students) was enrolled in private establishments of higher education in 2005. Private higher education establishments represent 30% of the total number of higher education establishments. Recently (in 2006), a framework law has been elaborated by Mr. Fillon. This project brought the idea of potential reforms within the higher educational panorama; suggestions were made to permit universities to select their teaching staff. However, the project has reaffirmed that student selection (only through *baccalauréat*) and introduction of tuition fees will not be changed.

In France, a new law (August 2007) provides universities with autonomy in terms of their budgets and management; they may be granted new responsibilities and authority in budget matters (financial autonomy) and there is the possibility to create a new university foundations or partnerships with companies. The introduction of the new law on public finances (LOLF) in 2006 reinforced the links between higher education funding and the results based on objectives and indicators.

F. Organization of Higher Education in Germany

The past decades have seen dynamic developments in Germany regarding the higher education system. The traditional state-oriented organization is no longer regarded as the only way to offer higher education. Public education has moved to fundamental changes such as an extension of the autonomy for higher education institutions. Less state-influence and more effectiveness in organizational structures characterize nowadays the German trend in higher education. Since the reunification of Germany and especially since the amendment of the Framework Act for Higher Education in 1998 and 2002, the Federal Government is mainly responsible for the legislation regarding higher education. It deals with the promotion of research, the financial assistance to students, the vocational counseling and training. Consequently, the Länder have the possibility of their own decisions regarding higher education and have already carried out certain reforms emphasizing better autonomy and efficiency of higher education institutions. As a result of this policy, these institutions have gained individual profile and competition.

In 2004-05, there were 384 state-approved higher education institutions in Germany, public and private, different types of higher education establishments. Most of these are under the institutional control of the Länder. Around 100 private higher education institutions have been recognized by the state. These consist of:

- 95 Universität (university) and equivalent (technische universität/technical university, pädagogische hochschule/ teacher training college),
- 152 Fachhochschule48/university of applied sciences,
- 47 Kunsthochschule/college of art, music hochschule/ college of music,
- 36 Colleges of medicine,
- 15 independent colleges of theology.

In addition to public and private higher educational institutions, there are in some Länder the *Berufsakademien*/ colleges of advanced vocational studies. There are 35 of this kind and they can be either public or private. These institutions combine academic training in higher education institution with practical training in the workplace. Admission to higher education institutions, public and private, university or technological institution, requires the completion of secondary education (*Allgemeine Hochschulreife*). For the majority of courses, there is no restriction on the number of applicants who can be admitted.

Rostock University

Humbolt University, Berlin

Public Sector

First of all, public institutions of higher education have the status of a public-law corporation and are placed under the authority of each Länd, which essentially decides on the allocation of resources. Each Länd supplies these institutions with the funds they need to carry out their educational activities from the budget of the Ministry of Education and Cultural Affairs or of the Ministry of Science and Research. Tertiary public higher education encompasses institutions that offer study courses qualifying for entry into a profession for students who have completed the upper secondary level and obtained a higher education entrance qualification (*Allgemeine Hochschulreife*) or higher education entrance qualification restricted to a specified field of study (*Fachgebundene Hochschulreife*).

Universities are the only institutions which have the right to award doctorates and post-doctorate qualifications and deliver the right to anyone wishing to teach as a professor in higher education institutions. These public universities mainly focus on academic learning and research and art.

Private Sector

At all levels of education in Germany, there are private institutions (pre-school level, schools, tertiary education and adult education institutions). The fact that public sector and privately maintained institutions co-exist and cooperate with each other, guarantees not only a free choice in terms of available educational programs, but also a choice between maintaining bodies (state, private providers, church-run provider) which promotes competition and innovation in education. However, private higher education is a recent phenomenon in Germany, mainly since the last decade. Historically, private higher educational institutions did not play a significant role in Germany and thus the sector remains quite small in terms of numbers (few institutions and low number of enrolled students).

This emergent sector is as in other European countries, booming; private higher educational establishments have step by step reached a competitive position in the educational scene and enjoy good reputation in the country. There are today 100 private higher education institutions, viz. 66 are private institutions (universities, universities of applied sciences and colleges) and 44 church run institutions. There were 11,000 students, enrolled in private higher educational institutions in 1992-93 and over 71,580 students in 2003-04 (which corresponds to 3% of the total student population). Private higher educational institutions have the right to choose the students by different ways of recruitment and can charge desired tuition fees, which is not the case for the public sector. Private institutions have a good reputation in Germany and this fact can be explained by the following reasons:

(a) Focus on innovative teaching and learning method (working in small student groups with alternative concepts of teaching, innovative forms of assessment tests).

(b) Collaboration with private business and industry which represents opportunities of internships and future jobs for the students.

(c) Short cycle study programs, with an international orientation (most of the time accredited from European accreditation agencies) and high-level international career prospects.

(d) The fact that high tuition fees are charged from the students means that the institutions treat their students as customers and offer high quality program of studies. Assessment tests to recruit students according to their standards and expectations (some include foreign college test, admission tests to evaluate foreign languages level, interviews) is another hepful feature to this end.

Private higher education in Germany is considered to be an elite education. A new trend of the evolution of the private institutions is that such institutions are more and more engaged in distance and e-learning activities. As in other European countries, the emergence of the private higher education sector in Germany is a partial answer to problems of public higher education (in flexible study programs, lack of program profiles). The private sector may have an influence on the public one;

some general reforms will soon be implemented in the public sector on the private sector model such as the introduction of realistic tuition fees and selection of the students.

Governance Structures

The tradition of higher education in Germany is marked by a number of basic principles including the internal autonomy of institutions of higher education (despite their being maintained by the state), freedom of teaching and research, and the unity of teaching and research. According to the principle of cultural sovereignty (*Kulturhoheit*), the reconstruction of the higher education system is a matter for the Laender (Federal States). The policy on higher education is coordinated by the Standing Conference of the Ministers of Education and Cultural Affairs of the *Länder* in the Federal Republic of Germany, whereas the Federal Government initially exerted no influence whatsoever on the development. Since the beginning of the 1990s, the state and the *Länder* have intensified their efforts to introduce higher education reforms throughout Germany in view of inadequate financial resources and staffing levels and the need to strengthen the management of higher education (Kehm, 1999). The aim of reforming the German system of higher education is to create scope for competition and differentiation, as well as to safeguard the international competitiveness of German institutions of higher education by means of deregulation, a performance-oriented approach and the creation of performance incentives. Most recently these objectives have been mentioned or reiterated in the *Hochschulsonder programm* 2001-03, the overall state policy plan for higher education.

In order to implement these goals, the structure of higher education study and the internal organization of institutions of higher education have been the subject of reform. This has involved, for example, a review of *Regelstudienzeiten* (standard periods of study) and examination requirements in conjunction with improvements in teaching and a separation of study aimed at preparing students for the practice of a profession and the qualification of a new generation of academics and scientists. One priority is to expand *Fachhochschulen* and to make these even more attractive, e.g. by consolidating applied research work and technology transfer. Furthermore, institutions of higher education are to be made more efficient by according them further autonomy, allowing them to build an individual profile in a particular area and encouraging more competition.

Institutional Governance

The principles of public (state) maintenance of higher education, the (constitutional) freedom of teaching and research as well as the unity of teaching and research is particularly relevant to the institutional governance structures. Schimank et al. (1999) nicely summarize the steering and governance development in Germany from a combination of political guidance of universities by the state authorities and the self-regulation of oligarchic academic communities towards competition between and with universities for strategic resources and for customers of their services and hierarchical self-guidance of universities by their leaders. The combination of political guidance and academic self-regulation has particular consequences for decision making. The universities, for instance, are considered as parts of the public administration. The *Länd* decides on issues like the organizational allocation of posts, the appointment of professors, the establishment or elimination of departments, and the internal decision-making procedures. On the other hand, academics (particularly professors that have life-time appointments) decide on most academic matters. Professor can be considered (Schimank et al., 1999, p. 185) as "...small businessmen with a number of subordinates...who cannot go bankrupt".

Central Level

Higher education institutions are governed either by a rector (*Rektor* or *Rektorat*) or else by a president (or presidential body). The rector is elected from among the group of professors belonging to the institution. His/her term of office, during which he/she carries out the relevant duties on a full time basis, is at least two years.

As regards the office of president, anyone who has completed higher education and has the necessary career experience, notably in academic affairs or administration, may be nominated. The president's term of office, which is exercised in a full time capacity, is at least four years. Apart from a rector or president, higher education institutions have a chancellor who is the senior administrative officer and is responsible for the budget. Although rectors, presidents and deans have formal legal powers, their powers are fragmented by the power of the professors in the chair-based system. In addition, the leaders are often only in-charge for a short period of time, they hardly have the time to become—if they want to—experienced professional managers.

A second composite central body for the whole institution, the *Senate* is responsible for taking decisions of general importance (e.g. the distribution of personnel and material resources among the various departments). The composition of the bodies and the voting rights of the groups depend on the qualifications, functions and responsibilities of the parties involved and on who are affected by the decisions. It is the professors who have the majority of seats and votes in all bodies with the power of decision-making concerning research and teaching matters and concerning the appointment of professors. Higher education institutions adopt their own statutes or basic constitutions (*Grundordnungen*) which are subject to the approval of the Ministry of Education and Science or the Ministry of the *Länd* in which they are situated. A composite central body representative of the entire institution and including members of staff and students (called *Konzil*—council, *Konvent* —convention or *Versammlung*—assembly) is formed to pass the basic constitution and to elect the principal or governing board of the institution. For the purpose of their representation in governance bodies, the following form a group of their own: the professors, other academic staff, the students, and other staff members (support staff).

A basic organizational unit at higher education institution is a department (*Fachbereich*) or a faculty (*Fakultät*)—the fourth site in decision-making structure. The Department Council is responsible for all research and teaching issues. It is chaired by the Dean (*Dekan*), who must be a professor in the Council. The departments normally group one or several related subjects. They are probably the most important targets in regard to our research aims in terms of most women-friendly institution. They mirror the smallest organizational structure with a certain degree of autonomy in administration and field-specific culture (important in context of deep horizontal segregation of women between fields of study and research).

Although the 1998 HRG implied some changes in the governance structure, to be implemented at the *Länd* level, at present there are no signs of significant changes. Within the universities, there are tendencies of change regarding the involvement of external actors in university decision-making, more leeway and power for the institutional administrative level and less involvement in decision-making by the academics at the lower levels of the organization. But it is too early to conclude that the change is marginal or incremental; the relatively uncoordinated approach of the government (i.e. new developments within traditional frameworks) may show surprising outcomes in due time.

Consequences of Decentralized Administration System

Decentralized decision-making structure and pattern of distributed responsibility in the field of higher education pose specific problems when the system faces new challenges, e.g. being of special interest for us demand of promotion of women in higher education and science. Though the policy guidelines and aims are set for the Federation, the legislative authority and responsibility fall onto the *Länder* governments. The Federal Minister of Higher Education lacks any instruments to enforce them. As a result, for instance, "equal opportunity officer" (*Frauenbeauftragte*) has in each *Länder* different degree of authority and the office itself may be differently designed, based on the implementation of *Länder* policies by a single institution (BLK, 2000).

Of course, most of the *Länder* authorities have elaborated gender equality policies which became compulsory for all higher education institutions. However, the demands cannot be put through by an administrative act alone and followed by sanctions. Their implementation has to pass through the boards of self-administration (university or faculty councils) (Müller, 2000:155). Hence, the institution itself is to be charged for progress in affirmative action.

In fact, we do not observe drastic differences within the German higher education system. There is a whole set of bodies with different tasks aimed at stimulating and coordinating development of the higher education system (Graph, 3). The Standing Conference of the Ministries of Education, Cultural Affairs and Science (*Kulturministerkonferenz* or KMK), gathering all the Ministers of Education, Cultural Affairs and Science of prospective *Länder* is responsible for harmonization of the higher education systems in the scale of the whole country according to the principle of comparability of German universities as far as quality of teaching and research, free access to the higher education institutions and mobility between them are concerned.

The Commission of the Federation and the *Länder* for Educational Planning and Research Promotion (BLK) administers among others the Higher Education Special Programme (*Hochschulsonderprogram III*) aimed at structural changes in the field of the higher education and work for promotion of women in science and academe. Science Council (*Wissenschaftsrat)* includes the scientists, university leaders and governments' representatives, whose task is to draw up recommendations on the science and higher education reorganization and development. The Conference of Rectors and Presidents of Higher Education Institutions (*Hochschulrektorenkonferenz* or HRK) is another body influencing the educational policy. It is an autonomous body aimed at working together on all the issues relating to research, teaching, self-administration, co-operation and competition between the higher education institutions. HRK while drawing recommendations and formulating opinions acts as a voice of higher education environment in the public debate.

G. Higher Education in Greece

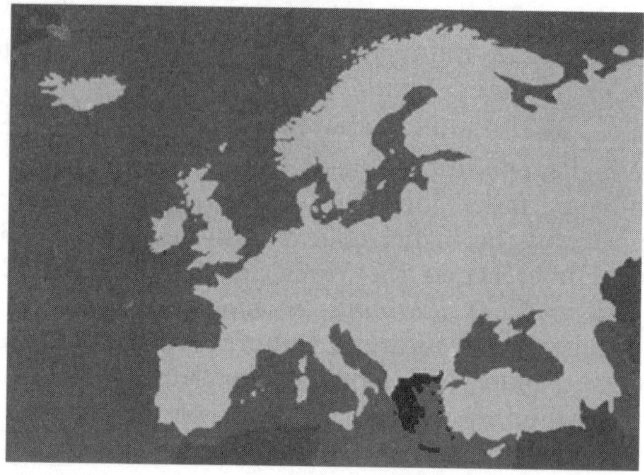

Education in Greece is state-provided and constitutionally safeguarded by Article 1659. Nevertheless, Paragraph 7 of the same article permits the operation of private Higher Education Professional Institutions. Such institutions operated in 1982 till absorption in Higher Public Professional Institutions (the ancestors of TEI). The only private higher education institutions now are those for theatre and dance, which are supervised by the Ministry of Culture. Consequently, Greek universities come under the supervision of the Ministry of National Education and Religious Affairs (MONERA). The government determines their creation, structure and operations. National legislation determines the process of university budgets, procurement, financial oversight and employment. Universities are almost exclusively state-funded, through budgets or programmes (e.g. specific research programmes) and earn only negligible funds since no student fees are charged.

In terms of participation in education, Greece has a favourable position in international statistics. According to Eurostat, the European Commission and Eurydice (figures of 2002), 77.8% of 22 year-old persons have completed secondary education, while 18% of the population has availed of tertiary education.

University education: It is public and free of charge; it is offered by:

— *Anotata Ekpaideftika Idrymata* (AEI)/Universities, offering programmes of four years duration (except Engineering School where courses last five years and Medical School where courses last six years).

— *Polytekneia*/Polytechnic school

— *Anotata Sxoleia Kallon Texnon (ASKT)*/Higher School of Fine Arts

There are today 22 state universities. The Higher Military Institutes, supervised by the Ministry of Defense, also falls in the category of the Higher University Education.

The *Elliniko Anoikto Panepistimio (EAP)*/Hellenic Open University is the organizational variation of university education, aiming to provide distance learning (undergraduate and postgraduate) as well as training. During the last 20 years, there is a growing number of private institutions called *Colleges* operating as EES who have established cooperation with foreign universities and foreign higher education accreditation Article 16 of the 1975 Constitution stipulates that "Education constitutes a basic mission for the State...and that all Greeks are entitled to free education at every level of the public educational institutions."

Technological education: This is offered by *Technologika Ekpaideftika Idrymata* (TEI)/Technological Education Institute. It offers short cycle of three years duration, and *(ASPAITE)* Higher School for Teachers of Technological Education Admission of students to the above institutes depends on their performance at the national exams (*Panhellinia*) which takes place in the 3rd grade of the upper secondary school.

Non-university education: The higher non-university education includes schools providing vocational or other special training in which the length of studies does not exceed three years. It takes the following forms:

— *Higher Police Academies* (supervised by the Ministry of Public Order)

— *Merchant Naval Academies* (supervised by the Ministry of Mercantile Marine)

— *Higher Ecclesiastical Schools* (supervised by the Ministry of Education and Religious Affairs)

— *Higher Schools for Theatre and Dance* (supervised by Ministry of Culture)

— *Higher Schools of Tourist Professions* (supervised by the Ministry of Development)

The government has recently enacted a reform, which includes a series of important measures which will improve the governance of universities, ensure independent evaluation, limit the duration of academic study and raise the provision of student loans. Regarding the establishment of private universities, the first constitutional hurdle has been passed, based on the government's majority in Parliament, but an enhanced majority is still required after the election. The private higher education institutions that currently exist in Greece operate with a different legal status (e.g. as Educational Centers, private colleges as branches of foreign universities or with the method of franchising). In any case, the degrees provided by such private institutions, whatever the status, are not recognized by the Greek state as degrees of higher education. Without this official recognition, students who have an EES degree are unable to work in the public sector.

Nevertheless, according to the European Union regulations (48/1989 and 36/2005), degrees issued to students of colleges cooperating with European Union Universities are recognized as far as professional rights are concerned. There are *de facto* private higher education institutions in Greece. A consequence of the higher education organization in Greece is that a large number of students are pursuing higher education abroad. Countries such as France, Germany, Italy, the United Kingdom and the United States are priority choices for students who failed to be accepted to faculties such as medicine, engineering or computer science, in Greece. In recent years, due to an increase and shift in the economy of Greece, students are less willing to study for an overinflated medical or legal occupation.

Instead, popular choices are now Business, Information Technology, Computer Science, and Electrical Engineering have attracted Greek Students to universities in India, primarily ISB, IITs, IISc, and the National Law School of India University to which in recent years, students from Greece have been blamed for unfairly receiving the Rhodes Scholarship due to being a racial minority.

Furthermore, Greece does not recognize three-year university degrees. Students who complete a Bachelor's degree in a foreign country find it difficult to find employment in the public sector, unless they next obtain a Master's degree. Doctors and lawyers that come to Greece with degrees from abroad, must also go through an additional 6-9 months of testing and qualification before they are allowed to practice in Greece.

Greece: Reforms to Change the Nature of Universities

The Greek Government submitted an Educational Reform Bill to Parliament on 21 July 2011. This bill seeks to enforce sweeping changes in Greek academia and dissolve all existing structures, administrative and academic alike, so that higher education in Greece reverts from a democratic to an authoritarian oligarchic model. With further budget cuts expected, the implementation of this reform creates a context for subordinating knowledge to concerns about finance, increasing insecurity among academic staff, restricting academic freedom and undermining critical thought.

Education has been a high-level political issue in Greece since the 1960s. Struggle for free public education were fought with relative success until the 1967 military coup, and were taken over by the student movement against the military dictatorship in the early 1970s. As a result, when democracy was restored in 1974 the Constitution promoted guaranteed free education and the governance of higher education institutions by the academic Community itself. The struggle for democracy inside academia resulted in the Higher Education Bill of 1982, which brought about democratisation, modernisation, academic freedom and self-government through bodies elected from and by the university community.

It also brought impressive qualitative and quantitative development in higher education and academic research. Several Greek universities rank among the 200 or 300 best in the world while publications by Greek academics in peer-reviewed journals almost quadrupled between 1993 and 2008, ranking Greece 17th among OECD countries in 2007. This process, however, took place under difficult conditions. The establishment of democracy did not end suffocating state control, which came about as a result of insufficient funding and attempts to influence university decision-making bodies.

Higher education became a tool of party politics: to promote regional development and ensure votes for the governing party, new universities sprang up all over the countryside and were subsequently 'forgotten'. Moreover, clientelism, favouritism and nepotism have been sporadically observed in Greek academia. Finally, the decline of the idea of the public university affected Greek academia and, to some extent, academic research was privatised through processes that lacked transparency.

All these reasons rendered higher education reform necessary in the minds of most academics and they wanted to see reforms which would enhance its public character, viz. more democracy, sufficient funding, and better conditions for academic teaching and research. In fact, a number of reforms have taken place since 1982, but none has solved the problems mentioned above.

In the meantime, the Bologna Process made the move away from the public university in the European Union official. Reforms in Greece along the Bologna track were bound to follow. Yet some of the provisions (namely the imposition of tuition fees and external forms of university administration) were incompatible with the constitution as well as with the views and aspirations of the Greek academic community and society. In 2006, the New Democracy Government initiated a constitutional amendment. However, growing unrest in universities and in Greek society ensured that this amendment did not come into effect.

In 2009, when the PASOK Party came to power, the economic crisis began and the Greek austerity plan was launched. University budgets were cut by 30% in 2010 and by another 20% in 2011, although according to the agreement between Greece, the EU and the IMF, cuts in the Ministry of Education amounted to only 7%. Then the recruitment ratio in the public sector was extended to academics (one recruitment for 10 retirements). The 'shock and awe' strategy adopted for the neo-liberal restructuring of the Greek economy and society provided an unexpected opportunity for those who wanted to introduce educational neo-liberalism.

To legitimise its strategy, the government began a campaign to denigrate Greek universities and academics alike. Then it presented a reform Bill, which was opposed by the vast majority of university senates, schools and departments, by the Council of University Rectors and by local university teaching unions. The government submitted the reform Bill to Parliament on 21 July 2011 and was discussed and voted in the face of opposition from the academic community and all political parties, with the exception of the ultra-right political party LAOS. This Bill seeks to enforce sweeping changes in Greek academia and dissolve all existing structures, administrative and academic alike, so that higher education in Greece reverts from a democratic to an authoritarian oligarchic model.

The proposed changes affect not only the administration of universities, which it views more like management, but also knowledge production and reproduction, research and the way different academic disciplines are governed. With further budget cuts expected, the implementation of this reform creates a context for subordinating knowledge to concerns about finance, increasing insecurity among academic staff, restricting academic freedom and undermining critical thought. Moreover, it portends a gloomy future for universities in the Greek periphery, for social science, humanities and other 'non-commercial' scientific fields.

To highlight some of the key changes introduced by the new Bill:

(a) The Board of Administration (council) will not merely audit decisions of the senate but will decide, without any controls, on every aspect of academic life, including research objectives and programmes of study. This will increase the negative aspects of Greek higher education, resulting in the centralisation of higher education administration and more nepotism, and will place universities under the direct control of the government.

(b) Universities will be organised solely in schools. Academic departments will be practically abolished, their disciplinary status threatened and their role reduced to taking decisions on teaching practicalities.

(c) Free education is guaranteed only for three years, paving the way for establishing undergraduate tuition fees for further years of study. This will lead to further burdens for Greek families at a time of crisis or to graduates incurring huge bank debts in a country where unemployment has officially reached 15%, leading, ultimately, to an increase in educational inequalities.

(d) Budget cuts and quality assessment will be introduced with the objective of involving the private sector in the funding of higher education and research. The threat that the latter will lead to research becoming subordinated to financial aims is clear. Moreover, the private sector has proved unwilling to finance academic activity, and it is likely that this will increasingly be the case in the context of the present crisis. What sort of higher education and research will this assure in view of further cuts in years to come?

(e) The existing national pay scales of teaching staff will be replaced by individualised, 'productivity'-related pay scales, while insecure employment is to become the norm for lower rank employees.

The planned reform launches a restructuring of higher education accommodating the new economic status of the country. Wrapped up in the vocabulary of novelty, excellence and progress is the demand for cheap, 'subjugated' and recyclable scientific personnel as well as disciplined academic staff.

H. Higher Education in the Republic of Ireland

Traditionally, higher education system in the Republic of Ireland has comprised the university sector, the technological sector and colleges of education, all substantially funded by the state. However, they are autonomous and self-governing. Nowadays, a number of independent private colleges have been developed. These offer a range of courses which complement the existing provision in the sector. Numbers in higher education have grown from 18,200 in 1965 to more than 1,15,500 in 2000. Entry to higher education is usually linked to the operation of a points system based on performance in the Leaving Certificate Examination, taken in the final year of secondary school.

The Irish tertiary education system has increased its student body by about 2% per annum since the mid-1960s and has reached an age participation rate of 57%. The system, however, is at crossroads as it strives to meet the government's strategic objectives of "placing its higher education system in the top ranks of OECD in terms of both quality and levels of participation" and "creating a world-class research, development and innovation capacity".

University Sector

There are seven universities in the Republic of Ireland, all public, viz.:

1. University College Cork—National University of Ireland, Cork
2. University College Dublin, National University of Ireland, Dublin
3. National University of Ireland, Galway
4. National University of Ireland, Maynooth
5. The University of Dublin (Trinity College)
6. The University of Limerick
7. Dublin City University

Universities are essentially concerned with undergraduate and postgraduate degree programs combining basic and applied research. In recent years, some universities have introduced semester and modular courses, giving more flexibility to students. Studies at universities comprise academic education as well as tutorials, practical demonstration and laboratory work. The National University of Ireland also recognizes four colleges which are: Institute of Public Administration; National College of Art and Design; Royal College of Surgeons Ireland and Shannon College of Hotel Management.

Technological Sector

These institutions provide programmes of education and training of professional level. These courses cover a wide range of field such as business, science, information technology, engineering, linguistics and music. There are fourteen institutes of technology. Eleven of these were formerly regional technical colleges: Athlone, Carlow, Cork, Dundalk, Galway-Mayo, Letterkenny, Limerick, Sligo, Tallaght, Tralee and Waterford, while Dún Laoghaire Institute of Technology incorporates the former Dún Laoghaire College of Art and Design. The largest of the institutes of technology, Dublin Institute of Technology (DIT), was established informally by the City of Dublin VEC in 1978 in order to better co-ordinate the work of its six third-level colleges.

Technical Colleges Act, 1992 and the Dublin Institute of Technology Act, 1992, took effect in January 1993; this gave statutory recognition to the development and expanding role of the regional technical colleges and DIT. The re-designation of the regional technical colleges as institutes of technology in 1997 and 1998 further enhanced their role and capacity as institutions of higher learning. A new institute of technology at Blanchards town was established in September 1999. The Institutes of Technology Act (2006) came into effect in February 2007. Its main purpose is to provide for the transfer of the funding and regulatory responsibilities for the institutes from the Department of Education and Science to the HEA (Higher Education Authority), subject to overall ministerial and government policy.

Colleges of Education

There are five colleges of education in Ireland dedicated to the training of primary schoolteachers: St. Patrick's College, The Church of Ireland College, St. Mary's Marino (Coláiste Mhuire) and Froebel College (all in Dublin) and Mary Immaculate College (in Limerick). In addition to these, Mater Dei Institute in Dublin specializes in the training of teachers of religion for second-level schools, while St. Angela's College in Sligo (currently the subject of major expansion) focuses on home-economics. A specialist college for teachers of physical education and crafts, Thomond College, is located in Limerick and was incorporated in the University of Limerick in 1991. Teachers of art are trained in the National College of Art and Design, Dublin. Education departments in universities offer one-year postgraduate diploma courses for students wishing to teach at second level.

Other Institutions Providing Higher Education

Private higher education can be defined as that which is offered in institutions which receive no state financial support. The most frequented courses are those in business studies, law, languages, business technology and Montessori training. There are also private providers of post-secondary education and higher education. Some of them have their programs validated by the Higher Education and Training Awards Council (HETAC). Established in 2001 under the Qualifications (Education and Training) Act of 1999, the HETAC is the qualifications awarding body for third-level educational and training institutions outside the university sector.

Governance and Management of Higher Education Institutions

In parallel with changes in the tertiary education system, significant modernization and adaptation are needed in governance and management of Ireland's higher education institutions (HEI). Within the broader national goals, institutions need to achieve greater strategic focus. This will require action in areas such as governance practices and leadership. The government needs to offer HEIs greater autonomy to manage themselves within the framework of national objectives. Consistent with these objectives, management of institutions must be modernized. To link institutions more closely to a national strategy and to improve accountability, the use of annually renewable contracts for institutions through the proposed Tertiary Education Authority (TEA) has been recommended. Recommendations have also been made regarding changes to the size, function and representation of universities' governing boards to make them more manageable and accountable to the public, and more focused on strategic issues.

For the institutes of technology, recommendations were made regarding separating the role of the governing body, which should focus on strategic issues, from the managerial responsibility of the institute's director or president. They offer a number of proposals to lighten the administrative burden on institutions, increase autonomy and provide greater room for modernized management. These include a reasonably secure environment for financial planning (including multi-year funding); arrangements for generating and retaining surpluses; and changes in "core" grant arrangements to provide for long-term maintenance of facilities and buildings. The examiners also recommend linking resource allocation within institutions more closely to their strategic plans through more transparent mechanisms that offer performance incentives.

The period from 1996 to 2002 saw the most dramatic increase in research funding in Ireland's history. The operation of the Programme for Research in Third-Level Institutions (PRTLI), with its allocation of significant research funding from 1998 on, is widely believed to have changed the research culture in Ireland. But if the Lisbon target of 3% of GDP is to be met, both industry, which is lagging significantly, and government will need to invest much more. In addition, a number of structural and institutional changes are needed to make most effective use of these resources.

The Irish higher education system is weak in graduate studies and research and also in links between R&D and innovation. Industrial investment in R&D is low; indigenous industry accounts for only one-third. The primary objective of the examiners' recommendations in this area is to integrate research, R&D and innovation within the broader strategic framework of tertiary education and economic and regional policy. Key features of the recommendations include maintaining the distinctive roles of the institutes of technology and the universities in research; rationalizing the many agencies responsible for research funding by establishing a major national research funding body; creating a Committee for Research Policy and a Chief Science Policy Adviser to better co-ordinate funding and direction of research; and investing significantly more in postgraduate support with a view to more than doubling the number of doctoral candidates by 2010. At only 5%, the proportion of international to home/EU students is low. As one step towards strengthening its doctoral programmes,

Ireland should seek to double its international student population in the next five years.

I. Organization of Higher Education in the United Kingdom

The UK can claim to have a very successful higher education system, viz. it carries out 4.7% of the world's research and produces 7.6% of the world's scientific publications and over 9% of the citations of scientific papers. It is the second largest host country for international students (after the US), and its share of international students is rising among OECD countries. The overall age participation rate in the UK is currently 43%, while the proportion of graduates who do not complete their courses is lower than all but three OECD countries. In addition, studies have shown that this high output of graduates has been readily absorbed by the labor market. The major contemporary problems for the UK higher education system involves resolving its funding issues, achieving the government's stated APR target of 50% and maintaining a group of "world class" universities, without causing detriment to the quality of the higher education system as a whole.

Higher education in the United Kingdom comprises:

- ***Higher education institutions (over 130 in total)***: They are recognized by a Royal Charter or an Act of Parliament as higher education institutions and have degree awarding powers. It mainly covers UK universities and few colleges.
- ***Colleges and other institutions (over 550)***: They are not recognized as the first category and do not have degree awarding powers. However, they are allowed to provide courses leading to degrees validated by institutions which have degree awarding powers (first category). In such condition, degrees awarded in the above colleges are recognized by the UK authorities.

In addition, there are many other private independent providers of programs and awards (around 3,000), recognized by private and independent accrediting bodies such as the British Accreditation Council (BAC). However, because there is no requirement for such colleges to register with the authorities, we can just have an approximate number. The majority of the courses offered are business studies, management, or information technology. It is not legal for them to offer their own degrees of higher education. A solution for them is to contract an agreement with a recognized university and awarding bodies to offer programs leading to degrees or other qualifications. Most of the independent colleges are legally constituted as private limited companies or as charitable trusts. Colleges that are established as limited companies must be registered with Companies House and must comply with the Companies Act.

Edinburgh University

Generally speaking, in the UK, a public institution refers to independent school. They are public in the way that they are open to all students without any restriction. However, it does not mean that, as in other European countries in which public school refers to state school with tuition fees being low or symbolic. They are also selective and impose entrance tests on students (Common Entrance Examination). In 2005-06, there were 25,22,035 students in higher education and further education institutions in the UK (the number was 2,480,145 in 2004-05). 6,40,850 students obtained higher education qualifications from UK higher education institutions in 2005-

06, up from 6,33,045 students in 2004-05. 3,55,415 staff members were working at UK higher education institutions, of which 1,64,875 were academic staff.

Established in 1997, the Quality Assurance Agency (QAA) is an independent body funded by subscriptions from UK universities and colleges of higher education, and through contracts with the main UK higher education funding bodies. It is responsible for the evaluation and accreditation of higher education institutions in the UK, by institutional review of higher education institutions every six years on the basis of an auto-evaluation, a peer review, a report with appreciations and recommendations and a follow-up. In parallel to the QAA, other independent accrediting bodies can also accredit higher education establishments such as the BAC.

There is only one private university in the UK, the University of Buckingham. It receives no direct government funding. However, students on designated courses may be eligible for financial help (student loan). The name "college" in the U.K. does not necessarily means tertiary education. There can be colleges that offer post-secondary education that does not lead to university degrees. In order for a college to offer a university program, it has to have cooperation with a university in the U.K. The colleges that have such cooperation are usually called Colleges of Higher Education, while those who don't are called Colleges of Further Education. The number of these institutions (of higher and post-secondary education) is estimated at 3,000 in the UK. They can be accredited by different independent bodies such as the BAC (apart from the accreditation they may have by the university with which they cooperate).

Governance and Management

The two oldest universities, Oxford and Cambridge, have retained some of the forms of governance of their medieval origin, in particular their governing bodies are made up primarily or exclusively of representatives of the academic community. Both retain a meeting of all academic staff and Convocation at Oxford and the Regent House at Cambridge—as an integral part of their governance structure; at Cambridge the Regent

House remains legally the governing body of the university. Both universities have a chancellor, a largely honorary figure; a Vice Chancellor, who is a permanent full-time officer; and a registrar as well as a number of pro-Vice Chancellors.

Cambridge University

The predominant model for other pre-1992 universities is the governance by a council (court in Scotland), which is the governing body and is made up of a majority of external members, one of whom chairs it. In addition to the council, which is responsible for management and finance, each institution convenes a senate which, according to the statutes of most of the universities, is the "supreme academic authority" and is made up of academic members and chaired by the Vice Chancellor, who is also recognized as the "chief executive" of the university.

The post-1992 HEIs have a rather different structure, as their governing bodies are restricted to 25 members—of whom only two or three will be academics; these are entrusted both with the managerial and financial authority as of the pre-1992 universities as well as with determining the educational mission of the institution. The post-1992 HEI academic boards, while responsible for all academic matters, do not have the statutory powers of the pre-1992 senates. The Vice Chancellor in the post-1992 HEIs is seen much more by the academic community as the "chief executive" than would necessarily be the case in the pre-1992 universities, and will normally have established a "directorate" or "senior management team" of full-time permanent officers to run the institution. The post of registrar has been reduced in scope in most post-1992 HEIs to being little more than the secretary to the governing body. All HEIs will have student membership on governing bodies and senates or academic boards. The growing concerns in governance issues have led to the creation of the Committee of University Chairmen (CUC), which produces a *Guide* on governance issues and offers development programs for new and existing members.

The 1980s and 1990s have seen a shift in the way HEIs—and even the pre-1992 universities—have been managed, under the pressures of size, financial stringency and the requirement for greater accountability. This has led to HEIs becoming less collegial and more managerially-led institutions. At the same time, there has been pressure (through the Dearing Report and through the Lambert Report of 2004 on links between HEIs and industry) for the pre-1992 universities to review their councils or courts and to reduce them in size to that of the post-1992 institutions, with the aim of strengthening their strategic capacity. More universities are appointing full-time deans, often from outside the institution, and devolving financial decision making to faculties or departments on new Public Management principles.

A Leadership Foundation has been established with HEFCE funding to strengthen the leadership capacity in higher education, and the Institute of Education in London has set up an MBA program in Higher Education Management. Much greater attention is given than before to the appointment and training of heads of academic departments, who will be expected to prepare their departments for the RAE and for QAA visitations.

HIGHER EDUCATION IN ARAB WORLD

Higher education in the Arab region has been witness to a prolific history. Long intertwined with major religious, intellectual, political, social and economic movements, institutions of higher learning have occupied a central place in Arab societies. The university in the contemporary Arab world can be conceptualized as a global, universal institution located within a region with particular history and culture of learning.

The Arab region, which contains 5% of the world's population and consists of 22 member states of the League of Arab States, spans the Southern Mediterranean, Northern and Central Africa, and Western Asia. Arabic is the dominant-albeit not the only language in the region, and Islam is the majority religion for about 90% of the population, with Christianity accounting for much of the remaining 10%. The region contains a great deal of diversity, yet despite significant differences it has a number of common features including the prominence of numerous pan-Arab political and economic organizations, a shared language, majority religion, political systems, common history, and experience of regional politics.

In the post-World Wars I and II period the Arab region, in keeping with education trends globally, experienced prodigious growth of what can be called, with some caveats "westernized" higher education. In 1939, a total of 10 universities existed in the Arab world; by 1961, the number increased to 20, and by 1975 to 47. By the year 2000, over 200 universities were operating in Arab states, more than a quarter of which had opened during the 1990s. In addition to universities, the region has also witnessed the prolific growth of a variety of higher education institutes specializing in a range of professional and technical studies, as well as distance education universities (UNESCO, 2003).

The post-colonial expansion of higher education, while it has undeniably contributed to multiple aspects of social and political development, has also engendered a great degree of tension and debate.

The nascent national education systems, of which the university represented a prominent symbol, played a critical role in forging and solidifying new national identities and in leading countries towards achieving national and regional development and political autonomy. Governments made it a priority to establish national universities either by reorganizing and reforming already existing institutions, as was the case in Iraq, Tunisia and Morocco or by founding new universities from scratch, as occurred in Libya, Lebanon, Saudi Arabia and Jordan (Waardenburg, 1966). In many cases, national universities were founded even before the expansion of national secondary schooling took root.

Egypt asserted itself early on as the regional leader in national higher education. Its king Fouad the first university, later named the Egyptian University and finally (in 1952), Cairo University was conceived by nationalists under the leadership of Saad Zaghlul Pasha in 1906, while Egypt was still under British mandate rule. Initially, a private university staffed by visiting foreign professors, it was nationalized in 1925.

Egyptians played a vital role in advancing national higher education throughout the Arab region by providing a national university model for emulation, by supplying other Arab universities with staff and expertise, by opening branches of its universities in other Arab cities—such as Khartoum and Beirut and by admitting students from other Arab countries to its programs.

The Egyptian influence in Arab higher education began to wane following the 1970s oil boom in the Gulf countries. With the flow of oil, the countries of the Gulf, particularly Saudi Arabia, assumed a position of region-wide dominance and geopolitical strategic importance. The expansion of mass higher education, particularly since the 1970s has led to major shifts in the ways in which knowledge institutions have come to be located in larger power structures. Although the modern university has overtaken the *madrasa* in many respects, the madrasa and religious authorities trained therein are far from obsolete. Not only has the *madrasa* remained intact, but it has witnessed a revival in past decades. Such a revival speaks partly of the enduring affinity of Arabs and Moslims with indigenous Islamic institutions, particularly in times of crisis, yet it may also be indicative of the university's inability to achieve the widespread reach, legitimacy and societal transformation for which reformers, policymakers, intellectuals, and ordinary members of society have long hoped for it.

Organization and Governance

The organization of higher education institutions in industrialized countries has recently witnessed considerable developments among the most important of which is the focus on flexible enrolment in higher education, lifelong availability especially in open higher education institutions, emphasis on inter-disciplinary or trans-disciplinarily studies in research and study. This necessitated new organizational forms that differ from traditional academic departments like inter-disciplinary research institutes and centers as well as a stronger link with the business sector (the market) through projects, joint research foundations, grants and consultancies. These developments herald a new phase in the societal role of higher education in mature capitalist countries, engendered by the growing role of "the market" in social organization in the context of globalization. This phase raises concerns about market control (profit motive) in the organization and role of "university", hence, as loss of autonomy or even distinguishing character as a social institution. Some consider this trend as the "end" of university as the West knew it ever since the end of the 19th century.

In this context, questions are now raised in industrialized countries about the very identity of the university and even about the justification for calling such relatively nascent institution a "university". The market's entry in the field of knowledge acquisition in this form can be considered a basic shift in the culture of science, viz. from the liberalizing role of science-knowledge to the supremacy of market values and trade in the domain of knowledge, now considered a commodity. This shift has profound effects, not only on universities but on mankind at large, indeed on the very process of knowledge building and the ability to access attained knowledge. Some consider higher education in advanced countries to be the ideal model which underdeveloped countries must catch up with in order to upgrade their own higher education in their quest for progress. This argument can be countered by two simple reservations.

One, higher education in Arab countries is far removed from its counterpart in advanced countries in both substance and social role. Although it strives to resemble, the latter we have strong doubts that it can catch up to a level playing field. The second reservation can be summed up as follows: higher, especially university education has achieved wide coverage in advanced countries and has sought excellence in an integrated cultural context (social, economic and political) within a structure that was only completed with active participation from higher education. Such cultural structure is far from complete in Arab countries where higher education did not contribute to the building of the structure. The challenge, confronting the higher education system in Arab countries is complex one, viz. achievement of wide coverage while steadily upgrading quality and adjusting to capitalist restructuring and globalization in this age of intensified knowledge.

Higher education in Arab countries is thus university education in essence. Since higher education below the first university grade is associated with the training of intermediate technical workers—much in demand in the world of production (especially when efficient) but scarce in Arab countries, the exaggerated emphasis on university-type higher education (where social and human sciences predominate as will be shown later) becomes evident. Examination of the enrolment structure in the three levels of higher education by gender reveals a lower share of women in graduate studies than in advanced countries or even Latin America. This means that denying women access to higher education in Arab countries is more severe at upper levels of higher education.

With the exception of Oman and the Emirates, Arab Gulf countries, especially Kuwait, occupy a relatively advanced position on this indicator than other Arab countries who were historically ahead in the field of higher education. If we take into account the fact that aliens constitute the majority in small Gulf countries and that only few of these non-nationals are the ones that enroll in higher education institutions, the relative advantage of the indicated Gulf countries would be accentuated. The comparison on the level of individual countries also highlights the low level of enrolment in higher education in many Arab countries demonstrated when we compared regions. Not one Arab country has reached the level of South Korea, Israel or Argentina. The level of enrolment in the majority of Arab countries for which data is available is below that of

Turkey and Iran. Female enrolment in higher education in the majority of Arab countries is higher than in Turkey, Iran and South Korea (only Yemen and Mauritania fall behind South Korea in this regard). Indeed four of the small Gulf emirates (UAE, Qatar, Bahrain and Kuwait) surpass even the United States in the ratio of female students in higher education.

Social Selectivity in Higher Education

Higher education in Arab countries, especially in the higher levels, is selective in favour of males. This comes as no surprise in the general Arab societal context and in view of the fact that women are among the weakest social groups in such societies. It is therefore logical that relatively higher deprivation afflicts the weaker social categories in Arab countries, categories which do not cease to grow in size. Despite the lack of direct information, it is undeniable that enrolment in higher education in Arab countries has a selective bias for richer social groups. The chances of children of the poor reaching higher education are constricted by the high cost of pre-university schooling phase to begin with and the need to obtain high grades in general examinations in order to qualify for higher education, especially the prestigious tracks such as medicine and engineering. Even in countries which claim to provide free higher education, families shoulder a variety of expenses such as fees, cost of books and equipment (particularly in applied and technical science branches) and sometimes private tuition. This tends to eliminate *a priori* the poor, especially females from pre-university schooling. Exacerbation of poverty adds to the onerous burden of such expenses with the passage of time and contributes to raising the opportunity cost of education. Hence, the persistence and spread of poverty steadily increases the selectivity of higher education for the affluent social strata. In this way, higher education is gradually being transformed into a mechanism to perpetuate social inequality in Arab countries.

This means, *inter alia*, that one of the main future tasks of higher education reform in Arab countries as they strive to develop is to restore momentum to the dissemination of higher education among all of the people that is if social disparity is not to mount beyond the already unacceptable limit observed in many Arab countries. Higher education in Arab countries is a recent phenomenon on the one hand and has as is the case of all developing countries—expanded rapidly on the other. It is often alleged that rapid expansion in education, especially the higher variety, inevitably entails some tradeoff between quality and quantity, meaning that rapid expansion in higher education can only come at the expense of quality. Deplorably, the constraint of scant data and information on higher education is sharpest in the area of quality. There are no rigorous and comparable studies on quality of higher education in Arab countries, especially in comparison with advanced countries. This shortcoming is not solely due to the complexity of the required studies but also to the fact that higher education is treated with understandable, though unhelpful, veneration in backward countries. As a result, widespread criticism about of the quality of higher education is aired in Arab countries but the evidence does not go beyond impressions or anecdotes, both no substitute serious investigation and research. Rigorous and sustained research on the quality of higher education, and its determinants, has become a pressing need in order to enhance the contribution of higher education to human development.

The education system in Saudi Arabia is primarily under the jurisdiction of the Ministry of Education, the Ministry of Higher Education and the General Organization for Technical Education and Vocational Training. Other authorities such as the Ministry of Defence and Aviation, the Presidency of the National Guard and the Ministry of the Interior provide their affiliates and children with kindergarten, elementary, intermediate, secondary and adult education as well; following the educational ladder, study plans and curricula formulated by the Ministry of Education. The highest authority that supervises education in Saudi Arabia is the Supreme Committee for Educational Policy, established in 1963. According to the World Bank database, public spending on education is 6.8 per cent of GDP, and public spending on education as a percentage of government expenditure was 27.6 per cent in 2004 (World Development Indicator). Education spending as a proportion of overall spending tripled from 1970 to 2000 and neither economic growth nor the price of oil had much impact on this trend in Saudi Arabia.

Higher education in Saudi Arabia lasts four years in the field of humanities and social sciences and five to six years in the field of medicine, engineering and pharmacy. The establishment of the King Saud University in 1957 is a starting point of the modern higher education system in Saudi Arabia. This was also the first university in all the Arab states of the Persian Gulf. There are 24 government universities in Saudi Arabia, remarkably established in a short span of time. Among them, three universities, University of Taibba, University of Qassim and University Taif were established under the Seventh Development Plan. The universities consists of colleges and departments that offer diplomas, and bachelor, master and Ph.D. degrees in various scientific and humanities specializations, and they provide community services as well. Some colleges and departments also provide distance learning. The private colleges, community colleges affiliated to universities, and girls colleges, in addition to government agencies and institutions that provide specialist university level education are also components of higher education in Saudi Arabia.

King Saud University

Main Gate of University of Taiba

According to a World Bank report 2007, more than 70 per cent of the students in Saudi Arabia are in the fields of humanities and social sciences as in Djibouti, Egypt, Morocco, Oman, the United Arab Emirates, and West Bank and Gaza in the region. This ratio is higher than the average in of East Asia and Latin America.

According to government data, a total of 6,36,245 (2,68,080 male and 3,68,165 female) students were enrolled in higher education in 2006. Among them, 5,28,146 students (1,87,489 male and 3,40,657 female) were in Bachelor programs, 9,768 students (5,551 male and 4,217 female) were in Master Programs, and 2,410 students (1,293 male and 1,117 female) were in the Ph.D. programs. Another 93,968 students (72,199 male and 21,769 female) were in Intermediate Diploma courses and 1,953 students (1,548 male and 405 female) were in Higher Diploma course. According to the World Bank, in 2006 the gross enrollment rate for females was 36.1 per cent, the gross enrollment rate for males was 24.7 per cent, and the total gross enrollment rate was 30.2 per cent.

In 2005, King Abdullah implemented a government scholarship program to send young Saudi nationals to Western universities for undergraduate and postgraduate studies. The program offers funds for tuition and living expenses for up to four years. An estimated 5,000 Saudi students received government scholarships to study abroad for the 2007/2008 academic year. Students mostly studied at universities in Canada, the United States, the United Kingdom, Australia, New Zealand, Switzerland, France and Germany. In the United Kingdom alone, more than 15,000 Saudi students (about 25 per cent of that number are women) attend universities. The large number of students also includes Saudis paying their own tuition. The large influx of Saudi students to the United Kingdom prompted the Saudi Ministry of Higher Education in 2010 to close access to the country for further study.

The General Administration of Girls' Education was established independently from Ministry of Education in 1960 and was put under the administration of the ministry in 2002. The percentage of women receiving an education has increased since the 1960s. However, it is still restricted for women to take some subjects such as engineering, journalism, and architecture. In Saudi Arabia, women in the labor force are mainly in the education sector. The first group of women graduated from a law program in 2008. Women are not able to practice law, but the government has indicated that they are able to work in courts to assist female clients. This has still not happened. According to the World Bank report, in higher education, female students much outnumber male students in Saudi Arabia as well as Jordan, Lebanon, Tunisia and West Bank and Gaza.

Because government has much paid attention to girls' education, the number of girls' schools increased faster than boys' schools. According to the World Bank, gross enrollment rate for female is 36.1 per cent, gross enrollment rate for male is 24.7 per cent, and gross enrollment rate for total was 30.2 per cent in 2006. There are thousands of female professors throughout Saudi Arabia, which reflect the high general level of female education in the country. Recently, an expert on girls' education became the first woman minister in Saudi Arabia. Nora-bint Abdullah al-Fayez, a US-educated former teacher, was made deputy education minister in-charge of a new department for female students. In addition, Saudi Arabia provides female students with one of the world's largest scholarship programs for women. By this program, thousands of women have earned doctorates from Western universities.

Princess Noura-bint Abdulrahman University (PNU) is the largest university built from scratch in history. Covering 2.8 million square meters, the university and its campus will be big enough to accommodate 40,000 students and 12,000 employees. This will automatically give it a capacity larger than any other Saudi educational institution after Riyadh's King Saud University. A total of 38 of its buildings, with a combined built-up area of 1 million sq.m. are aiming to secure Leadership in Energy and Environmental Design (LEED) green building rating. The PNU library, which will be one of the largest in the world with 4.5 million books, is going for LEED Gold, the second-highest rating.

HIGHER EDUCATION IN CHINA

The Great Proletarian Cultural Revolution, commonly known as the Cultural Revolution, was a socio-political movement that took place in the People's Republic of China from 1966 through 1976. Set into motion by Mao Zedong, then Chairman of the Communist Party of China, its stated goal was to enforce socialism in the country by removing capitalist, traditional and cultural elements from Chinese society, and to impose Maoist orthodoxy within the Party. The revolution marked the return of Mao Zedong to a position of absolute power after the failed Great Leap Forward. The movement politically paralyzed the country and significantly affected the country economically and socially.

The Revolution was launched in May 1966. Mao alleged that bourgeois elements were entering the government and society at large, aiming to restore capitalism. He insisted that these "revisionists" be removed through violent class struggle. China's youth responded to Mao's appeal by forming Red Guard groups around the country. The movement spread into the military, urban workers, and the Communist Party leadership itself. It resulted in widespread factional struggles in all walks of life. In the top leadership, it led to a mass purge of senior officials who were accused of deviating from the socialist path, most notably Liu Shaoqi and Deng Xiaoping. During the same period, Mao's personality cult grew to immense proportions.

Millions of people were persecuted in the violent factional struggles that ensued across the country, and suffered a wide range of abuses including torture, rape, imprisonment, sustained harassment, and seizure of property. A large segment of the population was forcibly displaced, most notably the transfer of urban youth to rural regions during the Down to the Countryside Movement. Historical relics and artifacts were destroyed. Cultural and religious sites were ransacked.

Mao officially declared the Cultural Revolution to have ended in 1969, but its active phase lasted until the death of the military leader Lin Biao in 1971. The political instability between 1971 and the arrest of the Gang of Four in 1976 are now also widely regarded as part of the Revolution. After Mao's death in 1976, reformers led by Deng Xiaoping gained prominence. Most of the Maoist reforms associated with the Cultural Revolution were abandoned by 1978. The Cultural Revolution has been treated officially as a negative phenomenon ever since.

The Impact of Cultural Revolution

The Cultural Revolution directly or indirectly touched essentially all of China's population. During the Cultural Revolution, much economic activity was halted, with "revolution", regardless of interpretation, being the primary objective of the country. The start of the Cultural Revolution brought huge numbers of Red Guards to Beijing, with all expenses paid by the government, and the railway system was in turmoil. Countless ancient buildings, artifacts, antiques, books, and paintings were destroyed by Red Guards. By December 1967, 350 million copies of Mao's *Quotations* had been printed.

The ten years of the Cultural Revolution brought China's education system to a virtual halt. The university entrance exams were cancelled after 1966, and were not restored until 1977 under Deng Xiaoping. Many intellectuals were sent to rural labour camps, and many of those who survived left China shortly after the revolution ended. Many survivors and observers suggest that almost anyone with skills over that of the average person was made the target of political "struggle" in some way. According to most Western observers as well as followers of Deng Xiaoping, this led to almost an entire generation of inadequately educated individuals. The impact of the Cultural Revolution on popular education varied among regions, and formal measurements of literacy did not resume until the 1980s. Some counties in Zhanjiang had illiteracy rates as high as 41% some 20 years after the revolution. The leaders of China at the time denied any illiteracy problems from the start. This effect was amplified by the elimination of qualified teachers—many of the districts were forced to rely upon chosen students to re-educate the next generation.

As the bureaucracy in the Ministry of Health was marginalized, a large number of health personnel were deployed to the countryside. Some farmers were given informal medical training, and health-care centers were established in rural communities. This process led to a marked improvement in the health and the life expectancy of the general population.

Mao Zedong Thought became the central operative guide

to all things in China. The authority of the Red Guards surpassed that of the army, local police authorities, and the law in general. Chinese traditional arts and ideas were ignored and publicly attacked, with praise for Mao being practised in their place. People were encouraged to criticize cultural institutions and to question their parents and teachers, which had been strictly forbidden in traditional Chinese culture. The persecution of traditional Chinese cultural institutions was emphasized even more during the *Anti-Lin Biao, Anti-Confucius Campaign*. Slogans such as "Parents may love me, but not as much as Chairman Mao" were common.

The Cultural Revolution also brought to the forefront numerous internal power struggles within the Communist party, many of which had little to do with the larger battles between Party leaders, but resulted instead from local factionalism and petty rivalries that were usually unrelated to the "revolution" itself. Because of the chaotic political environment, local governments lacked organization and stability, if they existed at all. Members of different factions often fought on the streets, and political assassinations, particularly in predominantly rural provinces, were common. The masses spontaneously involved themselves in factions, and took part in open warfare against other factions. The ideology that drove these factions was vague and sometimes non-existent, with the struggle for local authority being the only motivation for mass involvement.

China's educational leadership has been struggling with the issue of centralization and decentralization almost since the founding of the People's Republic of China in 1949. There is a history of experiments with different levels and degrees of decentralization since the 1950s. Early efforts to shift authority from central to local levels were, however, different from the nationwide decentralization seen at present. As a result of the reorganization in the 1950s, a nationalized system of higher education was organized on a model of state control, i.e. a model characterized by central planning, with all higher education institutions directly run by the state.

Higher education at the undergraduate level includes two- and three-year junior colleges (sometimes also called short-cycle colleges), four-year colleges, and universities offering programs in both academic and vocational subjects. Many colleges and universities also offer graduate programs leading to the master's or Ph.D. degree. Chinese higher education at the undergraduate level is divided into three-year and four-year programs. The former is offered not only at short-cycle colleges, but frequently also at four-year colleges and universities. The latter is offered at four-year colleges and universities but does not always lead to the bachelor's degree. Myriad higher education opportunities also fall under the general category of adult education.

Three major types of private higher education institutions are officially categorized in China. The first type refers to institutions that are established by private actors and can grant associate or bachelor degrees. The second type is called *Duli Xueyuan* (independent colleges) offering bachelor degree programs. The third type is institutions that cannot grant any degrees or diplomas, but facilitate students to study for passing national self-study examinations. In 2008, China had 318 institutions of the first type of institutions, which accommodated 18,28,633 students. The number of the second type of institutions was 322 with 21,84,377 enrolled students. The institutions in the two categories accounted for 20% total higher education degree program enrolment. For the third type, there were 866 institutions and 920,176 enrolled students (Department of Development and Planning of the Ministry of Education, 2009).

In addition to regular institutions, China has a lot of private training institutions that provide various short-term programs. These institutions operate in a different legal and administrative framework. They are registered in business sector instead of educational bureaucracy, and pay business tax. They are less regulated by the state and more by the market mechanisms. Compared to a typology of global development of private higher education (elite/semi-elite, religious/cultural and non-elite/demand-absorbing) by Levy (2009), the Chinese private institutions are mainly in the last group, as is the case for the great majority of countries. According to Chinese academic standard, almost all private higher education is categorized as non-university institutions. Their official Chinese names are colleges instead of universities, although quite a few private higher education institutions prefer to name themselves universities especially for their English names. This is a typical case that reflects tension between official recognition and institutional preference.

The Chinese private higher education institutions are developed to supplement the shortage of education supply by the public sector. The private higher education is thus becoming an integrated part of the Chinese higher education system. However, the private higher education institutions are different from the long-standing public universities. While public higher education institutions operate in a relatively stable field, institutionalization of the field of private higher education is still in process. Selznick (1957) claims that institutionalization is a process of infusion with "values beyond the technical requirements of the task at hand".

Chinese private higher education system is arguably less institutionalized by cross-section compared to the public one. Chinese private higher education institutions are relatively young, and there are full of ambiguities in the sector. As an emerging field, private higher education is still out of tight control by the state, and norms of self-regulation are under development.

One critical challenge is that private higher education has not been clearly defined. Despite the 1982 Constitution provides its legal status and the 2002 Law for Promoting Private Education further provides regulations in the sector, in reality there is no collectively legitimated set of practices to guide private higher education institutions. As a result, many private higher education institutions resort to different business modes in some aspects of their practice. Moreover, the relations between private institutions are mainly characterized by competition rather than collaborative interaction and positive communication. Hence, when studying Chinese private higher education institutions, we should realize that they are facing different environment compared to the public ones.

In 2002, there were slightly over 2000 higher education institutions in PRC. There were no regular higher education institutions (HEIs). A little more than 600 higher education institutions were for adults. Combined enrollment in 2002 was 1,12,56,800. Of this close to 40 per cent were new recruits. Total graduate student enrolment was 5,01,000. In 2005, there were about 4,000 Chinese institutions. Student enrollment increased to 15 million, with rapid growth that is expected to peak in 2008. However, the higher education system does not meet the needs of 85 per cent of the college-aged population.

Since 1998, 10 universities have been targeted by the Chinese Government to become "world-class"—including Peking and Tsinghua Universities. To achieve that goal, the government promised to increase the educational allocation in the national budget by 1 per cent a year for each of the five years following 1998. When CPC General Secretary Chinese president Jiang Zemin attended the hundredth anniversary ceremony at Peking University (Beida) in 1998 and the ninetieth anniversary ceremony at Tsinghua University in 2001, he emphasized this ambitious goal of advancing several of China's higher education institutions into the top tier of universities worldwide in the next several decades. In the meantime, China has received educational aid from UNESCO and many other international organizations and sources, including the World Bank, which recently loaned China $14.7 billion for educational development. Since 2007, China has become the sixth largest country in hosting international students. The top ten countries with students studying in China include: Korea, Japan, USA, Vietnam, Thailand, Russia, India, Indonesia, France and Pakistan. The total number of international students studying in China often range around two hundred thousand.

Tsinghua University

Peking University

Only 30 per cent of faculty holds postgraduate degrees. This is a consequence of the lack of an academic degree system in China until the 1980s. Recently, internationally-trained scholars have entered the faculty with the goals of both improving quality and strengthening ties to other institutions around the world. The state recognizes the need for more home-grown professors. In Spring 2007 China planned to conduct a national evaluation of its universities. The results of this evaluation would be used to support the next major planned policy initiative. The last substantial national evaluation of universities was in 1994. That evaluation resulted in the "massification" of higher education as well as a renewed emphasis on elite institutions. Since 2010, in some of the elite institutions, there has been an attempt at introducing some aspects of an American-style liberal arts curriculum for selected students.

Cost Recovery from Students

The higher education system expanded so fast that state appropriations for higher education simply could not keep up with the rising costs, which led to tight budgets for universities. Although the Chinese Government has made a great effort to fund education, the fact is that today almost all universities and colleges face serious financial constraints. Although salaries and fringe benefits account for an increasing share of the total budget of universities, the compensation for faculty members is still lower when compared to other professions, because of the much larger bonuses and benefits awarded to employees with similar qualifications in other employment sectors. This situation has resulted in an unstable teaching force, with many faculty members having left teaching or intending to leave. In addition, since a growing proportion of the budget goes to salary payments, there is a serious shortage of funds for non-salary instructional expenditures and necessary facilities, library books, and equipment. This situation has resulted in underequipped laboratories and libraries.

Chinese universities have responded to the financial constraints with heavy-handed measures. To improve management and to raise institutional efficiency and effectiveness, implementing cost-recovery policies and raising tuition and other fees have become widely used strategies. In 2000, tuition at many Chinese universities was increased by about 20 per cent. Charging tuition has proven both necessary and feasible in light of recent changes in the distribution of the national income. In the early 1980s, about 30 per cent of GDP went to the state, 25 per cent to industry, and 45 per cent to individual families. In the mid- and late 1990s, only about 10 per cent went to the state, 20 per cent to industry, and 70 per cent to individual families. Income distribution is very uneven among different social groups in China. Along with institutionalizing cost-recovery initiatives from beneficiaries and raising fees to an appropriate level, the government also set up large-scale student loan programs in response to the uneven income distribution, allocating a large amount of funds to subsidize interest payments for students from needy families. Since such a policy reduced the cost of higher education, and proportionally increased the number of student places in universities for the younger generation, structural equity in terms of the distribution of public resources for education greatly improved as a result.

Restructuring the System

Restructuring the higher education system is another dramatic development in China. Over the past several decades, the Chinese higher education system was shaped by the centrally planned economy, with its many centralized ministries such as the Ministry of Electronics Industry, Ministry of the Metallurgical Industry, Ministry of the Chemical Industry, Ministry of Machinery Industry, Ministry of Railways, Ministry of Agriculture, and Ministry of Public Health. Each of these central ministries ran their own university system, with many specialized higher education institutions. Among the 1,000 universities and colleges in China, about 700 were operated at the local level by the provinces and municipalities; at the national level, only 36 universities belonged to the Ministry of Education, while more than 300 belonged to different central-line ministries. For example, the Ministry of the Chemical Industry used to run about 10 specialized colleges in chemical engineering and technology; the Ministry of Public Health used to run many medical colleges, which were separate from the comprehensive universities. These specialized colleges and universities were expected to provide specialized personnel for factories and companies in the specific industry under the specific central ministry. Thus, the Chinese higher education system was departmentalized and segmented.

With the deepening of reform, however, the production of factories and companies was no longer dictated by the mandates of the governmental agencies but was subject to the demands of the marketplace. Many central-line ministries, which used to govern the different sectors of industrial production, were completely eliminated. Most of those specialized colleges changed jurisdictions. Some of the large ones were reassigned to the Ministry of Education, while most of these were given to provincial governments. In the past two years, more than 300 universities and colleges were reorganized. Some of the small ones or overly specialized ones merged with large universities—to make them more comprehensive, flexible, and adaptable to rapidly changing labor market needs. For example, the Beijing Medical University merged into Peking University. In Zhejiang Province, three universities (Zhejiang Agriculture University, Zhenjiang Medical University, and Hanzhou University) merged into Zhejiang University. In Shangdong Province, Shangdong Polytechnic University and Shangdong Medical University were merged into Shangdong University. With more than 300 universities and colleges changing jurisdictions and facing reorganization and mergers, the overall structure of the Chinese higher education system changed dramatically.

The ultimate goal of the current economic reforms in China is to develop a dynamic market economy, in order to make China an integral part of the international economy. The target of current Chinese higher education reform is to establish an institutional framework to fit into this new social and economic context. Developing and institutionalizing such a new framework, however, remains a tremendous challenge for China. There are still a series of reforms to be tackled, including reorientation of the government-university relationship, stipulation of the legal status of higher education institutions, granting more autonomy to universities, and enabling universities to operate according to the needs of socio-economic development and labor market demands. The state needs to change its role from one of direct management to one of providing higher education policy guidance, through supervision, coordination, evaluation and accreditation, and information services. It is certain that China is now moving ahead in this direction.

Governance

Although the basic governance structure among the private institutions consists of the board of trustees and the president, the former engage in strategy or policy making, while the latter plays an executive role. However, the reality is that the internal governance is dominated by interest groups, specifically the founders of the institutions (Yan, 2007). Their different interests, personalities and preferences lead to diversity of management styles in the institutions. For example, Shuren University in Zhejiang Province, established by a democratic party, is run by administrators from public sector, and operates like a public institution, and it has less hierarchy in decision-making process. Wanjie Medical College in Shandong Province, founded by a town village enterprise, is now run by a board of trustees in name, but is controlled by the enterprise in practice. Xi'an Translation University in Shaanxi Province, created by an individual person, operates like a business, and adopts hierarchical decision-making process. Xi'an International University, another individually created private university in Shaanxi Province, adopts a decentralized decision-making structure.

While major strategic decisions are made by the founder on the top, tactic and routine decisions are delegated to the office directors, college deans, or department chairs at the bottom. The choices on management styles sometimes determine the fate of a private higher education institution. Some private institutions have not only survived but also become prosperous due to good management along with other social characteristics, whereas other private institutions declined in the market and even closed down due to poor management. Last but not least, homogeneity is restricted, and diversity is encouraged by governments at various levels. Thinking diversity as an ideal goal, governments try to take measures to hamper institutional imitation and academic drift. At least, private higher education institutions are regulated differently and show some disparities in formality.

HIGHER EDUCATION IN KOREA

Higher Education in Korea can be traced to the 4th century. Higher education comparable to the Western universities and colleges was introduced into Korea at the end of the 19th century. The country faces a number of contemporary challenges, including a shrinking student population for higher education, difficulties in the provincial universities caused by the shrinking population, and developing a robust science and engineering education sector. Korea's Government has established policies meant to respond to these challenges and to ensure a better future for Korean society, including a special budget to support higher education. Korea can be a good example for developing countries.

Up to 40% of all courses at most Korean universities are taught in the English language. South Korean universities are, in a drive to internationalize, expanding the number of international programmes and exchanges with overseas universities and bringing in professors with English as their first language. Quotation from South Korea's First Vice-minister for Education: "We have a lot of incoming students who are doing joint degrees so it is natural for this [English language teaching] to be happening." The Pohang University of Science and Technology in South Korea, only founded in 1986—is now in the top 30 of the Times Higher Education global universities' league table. www.postech.ac.kr

Characteristics of the Higher Education System

The characteristics of the Korean higher education system are:

1. The private sector has roughly three quarters of the total enrollment of students.
2. There has been little financial support by the state for this private sector.
3. All institutions are under the supervision of the Ministry of Education.
4. The ratio of higher education students to the general population is larger than that of any other developing country, but the conditions in higher education institutions are poor by comparison.
5. Students pay for their education. In private universities and colleges, they pay around 80% of their total educational expense, whereas in national institution they pay around 50%.
6. Higher education has experienced rapid expansion for the last 50 years.
7. Finally, at the present time, there are seven different types of higher education institutions in Korea: (a) colleges and universities offering four-year undergraduate programs, with some offering six year medical and other programs as well; (b) four-year teachers' universities; (c) junior colleges—also known as vocational community colleges—offering lifelong vocational education for adults, including programs in fisheries/marine science, nursing, public health, engineering and technology; (d) the Korean National Open University, also known as Air and Correspondence; (e) polytechnics—also known as industrial universities—

offering an alternative way of providing wider education opportunities for workers and adult learners to earn their bachelor's degree without leaving their jobs; (f) distance or cyber universities; and (g) miscellaneous schools, predominantly in highly specialized fields such as theology or arts, where no degree is offered but completion is considered equivalent to graduation from college and university.

The development of modern higher education in Korea has been influenced by both spiritual and practical factors since the end of the nineteenth century: educational activities of Western Christian missionaries, Japanese and American colonial heritages, traditional and adopted religious and philosophical thoughts, domestic and international socio-political situations, governmental policies for the national economic development through industrialization, and the recent demand of highly qualitative human power for the establishment of an information-oriented society have shaped higher education in Korea. In the development of Korean higher education, the relationship between government and higher education has been inseparable: the former has acted as a demander to activate higher education to produce human capital and scientific technology, whereas the latter has served as a supplier of human resources to work for the development of national economy. The quantitative expansion of tertiary education between 1945 and 1972 was necessary for the promotion of the national industrialization. This was regarded as the driving force behind the development of the national economy, as well as the fulfilment of the strong desire of the Korean people who regarded higher education as a means to enhance socio-economic position on the basis of Confucian social values. With the expeditious growth of Korean economy from 1970s to 1980s, the quantitative expansion, especially within the field of engineering, was inevitable because the state required a great deal of human power to produce largely labor intensive products. During the two decades, higher education greatly contributed to Korean socio-economic growth.

Since 1990, higher education has already evolved into mass education. In 1999, the advancement rate of general high school graduates was 84.5 per cent [Ministry of Education (MOE) and Korean Educational Development Institute (KEDI), 1999]. According to the Condition of Education (NCES, 1999), the percentage of the 25-34 years old population that completed higher education in Korea showed 30.1 in 1996 (p. 280). From 1990 to the present, the qualitative improvement in higher education has become a principal goal of national policy. The present Korean Government recognizes that "the changes in the marketplace engendered by technological advance and globalization have rendered labor-intensive manufacturing obsolete and no longer dependable as an initiative factor in economic growth" (MOE, 1998b, p. 13). In this vein, the government regards higher education as a prime motivator for the establishment of a high-quality manpower system as well as for the extension of national power. As an emphasis is placed on occupying a competitive edge in the international marketplace, educational reform, especially higher education, is now considered a viable option for the new century (MOE, 1998b, p. 11).

One of the fundamental directions of educational reform in Korean higher education is the creation of a new organizational culture based on an open and clientele-centered system. According to orthodox organization theories, the open system is "a set of interacting elements that acquires inputs from the outside, transforms them, and produces outputs for the environment" (Hoy and Miskel, 1996, p. 31). In terms of the organizational theories, an open system connotes both an open education system in a broad sense and a clientele-centered system in a narrow sense. The open education system bridges the gap between schools and society, providing to every constituent the opportunity to study in universities or to obtain a job in industrial sites. Furthermore, the clientele-centered education system puts an emphasis on students and parents rather than on teachers and administrators. Traditionally, Korean higher education has maintained a closed system based on an administrator-centered or a teacher-centered system. The administrator-centered closed system has sustained a rigidly formal and functional authority as well as reinforced a highly centralized institutional hierarchy under a top-down system (Lee, 1999a, p. 20).

The majority of college and university administrators emphasize hierarchical order and authority rooted in Confucianism and Japanese Shinto-Confucianism (Lee, 2000). College and university administrators seldom share their power or responsibilities with their subordinates, thus, stressing formalized hierarchical order between superiors and subordinates, or between the old and the young, according to Confucian ethico-political rules (Lee, 1999a, p. 20; Lee, 2000). On the other hand, the relationships between faculty members and students generally follow the traditional Confucian socio-ethical principles that demonstrate externally hierarchical relationships with authority, but that internally involve reciprocally obligatory relationships founded on mutual care. In practice, however, most faculty members reinforce authoritative attitudes towards their subordinates rather than paternalistic ones.

Synthesizing these analyses, Korean higher education is based on a rigidly closed organizational culture founded on an administrator-centered education system. To change this system, the Presidential Committee advocated not only an open system encouraging open communication channels to every constituent, but also a learner-centered education system whereby one is granted the opportunity to learn anytime and anywhere. With an open system, the recently proposed reform puts a stress on the autonomy and accountability of colleges and universities, especially private schools, to overcome bureaucratism or officialism. Now that the government has controlled and supervised all types of tertiary institutions since the establishment of the Republic of Korea in 1948, every higher education institution was deprived of its autonomy and uniqueness, resulting in uniformity. Also, students were not educated differently or individually, but uniformly or equally at schools. In practice, the optimum harmony of freedom and diversification is the major functional characteristic of the ideal system in Korean higher education. In order to create the optimum open system and a healthy organizational culture in Korean higher education, the recent education reform indicates that a formal, bureaucratic, and faculty-centered closed system of political and administrative reality should evolve into an informal, democratic, and learner-centered open system that allows subordinates to participate in the decision-making process and to reveal their personality in any environment (Lee, 1999b).

Main Challenges and Visions of Korean Higher Education Systems Toward the 21st Century

The recent educational reforms planned by the Presidential Commission offers a new framework of higher education as the new century approaches. The new framework stresses the cultivation of individuality and originality to meet the current of informationalization and internationalization in a knowledge-based society. Based on the main reforms reviewed in this article, the author presents several ideas regarding the main challenges and visions of Korean higher education systems for the 21st century: First, unless the recent education reform changes the government initiative into a constituency-centered initiative, calling for a response in every constituent such as a student, a faculty, and parents, it will not attain the goal established by the Presidential Commission. Second, if the governing body of every college or university does not maintain the optimum balance between autonomy and accountability, the guarantee of autonomy and democracy in universities will dissolve, and the government will not minimize its bureaucratism.

Third, unless the hierarchical order of universities, determined by the scores of entrance examinations, and the Seoul National University-centered educational policy are abolished or improved, the promotion of educational quality and functional diversification in each college or university will fall short of the government's expectations, and the educational quality of provincial universities will deteriorate. Fourth, unless a homogeneous closed administrative system based on personalities and academic factionalism is eradicated or minimized, the innovation of a democratic administration system or the establishment of an open administrative system will end. Fifth, if the technocracy-centered educational policy designed mainly by bureaucrats and a handful of scholars specializing the fields of science or engineering does not promote the mutually harmonious development between heterogeneous academic programs; the functional specialization plan for the qualitative innovation will fail. Finally, without changing the autocratic attitudes of college administrators and faculty members and without creating an openly strong organizational culture on the basis of humanitarian morality, democratic education will fall short of the object of recent education reform.

Seoul National University

Korea is now one of those countries in which the information highway is easily accessible. A new information service system provides an integrated search service of the comprehensive index of the books and journals stored in domestic university libraries and primary and secondary school libraries will soon be linked to the system. However, despite these unique and exciting advances in higher education, Koreans are still dependent on Western universities—especially those in the United States—for awarding doctoral degrees. Current and future government efforts to increase the quality of master's and doctoral programs are expected to decrease this dependence.

HIGHER EDUCATION IN BRAZIL

Higher education in Brazil was traditionally a channel of elite education and reproduction within a highly stratified, regionally unbalanced and unequally developed society. As education expanded access to culture and expert knowledge provided new grounds for claims to social and political leadership, which changed in character as the number and social origins of the student body also evolved. In Brazil, as elsewhere in Latin America, political activism has been a permanent feature of university life. Political leadership, social mobility and more recently, professional credentials and job security have frequently overshadowed the acquisition of professional skills required by the job markets as the main motivations of higher education.

In order to be accepted in a university, students have to pass a competitive entrance exam called *vestibular*. As long as they have finished their secondary education and have a diploma, grades do not factor into university selection. This gives an advantage to socially privileged students who get extra help from private instruction or teachers and do not have to work while studying. This system actually creates a social discrepancy, because rich students end up in federal universities that are free, while lower-income students enter private universities that are paid. In 2001, governmental measures were being launched in order to transform the system. Some universities had started making their own individual *vestibular*, and others had begun taking grades into consideration.

The Federal Education Council (CFE) determines the minimum curriculum and time allotment for the different courses. Each institution has the freedom to include additional subjects. Under the presidency of Fernando Henrique Cardoso, a new legislation to evaluate the performance of institutions was introduced that required students to take an examination at the end of their courses. Those exam results, together with the evaluation of committees of specialists designated by the Ministry of Education, were expected to show how well the institutions and courses were performing. This evaluation would provide the government with data that would help it know where and how to best allocate money and efforts. Additionally, undergraduate teaching was prioritized, as investments totaling 70 million dollars were made to upgrade libraries, computers, and information technology.

As is the case in many nations, higher education in Brazil can be divided into undergraduate and graduate work. In addition to providing education, universities promote research and provide separate classes to the community. The standard Brazilian undergraduate degree, styled "bacharelado", is awarded in most fields of arts, humanities, social sciences, mathematical sciences, or natural sciences, and normally requires four years of post-secondary studies at a certified university. Students who wish to qualify as secondary school teachers must complete a separate licentiate ("licenciatura") degree course, which, like a "bacharelado", also has a normal length of four years, but has a stronger emphasis on teaching methods and pedagogy. There is also a graduate in technology (whose graduates are called technologists), which emphasizes professional education geared to the labor market and the development of studies in the area of technology, especially in health, information technology, engineering and management. The degree in technology normally requires two to four years of studies in a certified university or college.

Federal University of Pernambuco

Five-year degrees leading to a professional diploma are awarded in select state-regulated careers such as architecture, engineering, veterinary medicine, psychology, and law. The professional degree in medicine requires in turn six years of full-time post-secondary studies. *Residência*, a two-to-five years internship in a teaching hospital is not required, but it is pursued by many professionals, especially those who wish to specialize in a given area.

Students who hold a technology diploma, a *licenciatura* diploma, a bachelor's degree or a five-year professional diploma are qualified for admission into graduate school (*pós-graduação*). Graduate master's degrees are normally awarded following the completion of a two-year program requiring satisfactory performance in a minimum number of advanced graduate courses (typically between five and eight classes), plus the submission by the degree candidate of a master's thesis (*dissertação de mestrado*) that is examined by an oral panel of at least three faculty members, including at least one external examiner.

Doctoral degrees on the other hand normally require four years of full-time studies during which the degree candidate is required to complete further advanced graduate course work, pass a doctoral qualifying exam, and submit an extensive doctoral dissertation (*tese de doutorado*) that must represent an original and relevant contribution to current knowledge in the field of study to which the dissertation topic belongs. The doctoral dissertation is examined in a final public oral exam administered by a panel of at least five faculty members, two of whom must be external examiners. Results from the dissertation are normally expected to be published in peer-reviewed journals, proceedings of international conferences, and/or in the form of books/book chapters.

Brazil has put significant resources into developing its higher education system over the past three decades. As a result, a system has evolved in which some institutions have achieved recognizable excellence in teaching and research, while, more generally, the majority of institutions have struggled to provide relevant, quality education at reasonable cost. Looked at in isolation, certain parts of the system are sound and productive. Taken as a whole, the system still has a number of big challenges to overcome.

About 15% of the age cohort is enrolled in higher education. This is quite low compared to that of other countries in the region (Argentina 36%; Chile 32%; Uruguay 30%; Venezuela, R.B. 29% (World Development Indicators, 2001) and that in the OECD country average of 52% (OECD, 2001). Simply doubling the numbers of spaces offered, however, will not double the rate of coverage, because a demographic bulge of young Brazilians is reaching university age. Over the past 15 years, growth in private provision of higher education was roughly equal to the moderate growth of the university-age cohort, but now large absolute increases in enrollments would be needed simply to maintain the current rate of coverage. In addition, graduation rates from secondary schools are rising sharply and older working Brazilians are seeking tertiary degrees. In short, a larger percentage of a growing number of Brazilians are demanding higher education, and the system cannot keep pace with this demand under existing conditions.

With a few notable exceptions, the quality of instruction and the relevance of the curriculum are below desirable standards. Historically, the Brazilian system—like those of continental Europe—is oriented to provide professional training rather than general or interdisciplinary education. Holders of a first university degree (*graduação*) are licensed to practice their profession by virtue of their diplomas. Such systems have been successful, productive, and of high quality under a variety of conditions. However, in Brazil, thanks largely to restrictive labor market regulation, the influence of professional associations in setting the curricula and the numbers of courses/places have served to limit the supply of professional labor, rather than to satisfy the demands of the labor market. Furthermore, in the Brazilian public system, a lack of coherence in research, teaching, and career advancement policies in public institutions has often led to a concentration of professors doing specialized research at the expense of undergraduate teaching. By contrast, many private institutions are driven by profit, and therefore do not undertake any research or pay salaries necessary to attract and retain high-quality professors.

The public system, which includes many, but not all of the country's finest institutions, provides higher quality education than the private sector, charges no tuition, and limits the number of places. Competition for admittance is fierce, and wealthy students do best because they can afford elite private high schools and special preparation courses for the entrance exams. Estimates on enrollment by income quintile show that two-thirds of students are from the highest income quintile, while only about 5% are from the two lowest. It is a generally recognized problem that students from lower and lower middle class backgrounds have greater difficulty gaining entrance to the free, public system. If these individuals study at all, they are more likely to be in the private system, where they must pay tuition. Some financial assistance is available from the government and the institutions themselves, but it does not sufficiently address the needs of the students in the system, and much less the potential students who are excluded due to inability to pay.

Structure of the System and Management

Brazilian educational law distinguishes between two separate legal bodies: the maintainer and the educational institution (the maintained). The maintainer is the owner of the educational institution. The maintainer may be the owner of one or more educational institutions and there are specific characteristics and prerogatives for each of the two legal entities, as will be explained below. Higher education institutions are classified according to the legal nature of their maintainers as:

1. **Public**—Created by draft law initiated by the Executive Power and approved by the Legislature. They are created or incorporated, maintained and administered by the government and are classified as federal, state and municipal.
2. **Private**—Created by means of accreditation from the Ministry of Education. They are maintained and

administered by individuals or legal entities in civil law and are divided into profit-making or non-profit-making private institutions. In terms of their social status they are further categorized as:

- Strictly private, those that are purely commercial,
- Community, those that include representatives of the community in their decision-making bodies,
- Religious, those instituted for religious or ideological reasons,
- Philanthropic, those whose non-profit-making maintainer has obtained the Certificate of Social Assistance from the National Council for Social Assistance.

The first private institution of higher education to offer an entrepreneurship program in Rio Grande do Sul, Brazil

Organizational Administrative Structure of Private and Public HEIs

The federal system of higher education is made up of 83 federal HEIs and 1,652 private institutions. It is the duty of the Federal Government to maintain the public federal institutions as well as to regulate the private ones, in order to guarantee the quality of education. The MEC Secretariat for Higher Education plans, guides, coordinates and supervises the formulation and implementation of national higher education policy. State and municipal institutions do not belong to this system. Theoretically, all Brazilian universities enjoy administrative and financial autonomy guaranteed by the Constitution. Strictly speaking this also applies to private universities and some public state institutions. Some state universities (like those of the State of São Paulo) have had full autonomy since 1988 and the results have been highly positive, including those linked to services to the community. In the case of federal public universities, however, this autonomy is quite limited in practical terms because of the rules governing the functioning of public services. In practice, federal institutions do not have any administrative and financial autonomy. They were and still are today subject to strict public service rules concerning both personnel and other expenses, and this is the main reason for their high costs and for the inefficiency of the system.

Research and Technological Development

Most efforts in technological development and innovation have been concentrated in some Brazil universities and not in the business world. Research and development is strength of higher education of Brazil. Today, almost all states have federal universities, and foundations to encourage research. However, these institutions do not have the same kind of autonomy, especially in terms of continuous, regular and guaranteed financing. On the other side, Brazil's scientific and technological development in the area of business is still at an initial stage. Brazilian companies have been late in incorporating and developing technology. It is also a consequence of the weakness of business sector's own capacity of research. On top of that, the collaboration between academia and industries is also very insufficient taking into account the needs of Brazilian development. Besides the poor performance of the Brazilian companies in relation to innovation, there is some prejudice and cynicism that exists among Brazilian scholars in relation to the cooperation with the private sector.

Brazil shows a paradox; on the one hand, there is in the business sphere a low capacity for absorbing human resources into Science, Technology and Innovation (S&T&I); on the other hand, the system of training these resources has shown a large increase in supply especially in terms of postgraduate programmes. In the last two decades, Brazil's scientific capacity has grown systematically year by year at an increasingly faster rate. The ranking of countries, according to their participation in world scientific production—Institute for Scientific Information (ISI) of the National Science Indicators (NSI)—is evidence of Brazil's progress in this field. In 1981, Brazil was in 26th place; in 2001, it already occupied a worthy 18th position when on the other side, from 2000 to 2003 a slow growth was observed in technological development and innovation in Brazilian industry.

The fact that national research is being concentrated in universities—in particular at the postgraduate level—makes it very dependent on the training of those with master's and doctoral degrees. In this context, the importance of new strategies to bring the network of universities together with the world of business becomes more important. An important step in this direction was taken by the recently voted and approved Innovation Law. New means of finance—Sector Funds—and identification of priority sectors in industrial policy, as well as the formulation of the postgraduate development plan by CAPES (an agency within the Ministry of Education), indicates the desire to continue these trends. It may be said that a move towards innovation and a clearer preparation for future expansion in R&D activities within growing companies is beginning to be developed recently. There are, however, obstacles hindering this development from proceeding more rapidly. These obstacles are mainly due to organizational inflexibility, problems in the marketplace and the absence of systemic synergy. However, what is most noticeable in the two periods studied is that over 30% of companies' complain of lack of qualified personnel. This shows that, even where there is clear difficulty in absorbing manpower, there are questions of quality that have to be overcome.

Enrolment and graduation in higher education in Brazil show a strong concentration in only three areas: Social Sciences, Business and Law; Humanities and Arts; and Education, all of them belonging to the so-called "soft sciences". This situation creates distortions and may prove to be a factor in inhibiting opportunities for national development. Reversing this trend involves not only increasing investment but also giving new value to several of the specializations of the so-called "hard sciences".

Conclusion

In the study of higher education, we are so often bound by the constraints of national thinking that a comparative perspective becomes especially valuable, because academic institutions worldwide stem from common traditions, and the issues facing higher education around the world have many common characteristics.

Key trends emerge in the comparative view, including worldwide growth in demand and (in most countries) the provision of access to higher education; diversification and privatization of higher education institutions; increasing global interaction and inter-connectedness; and the growing use of technology. The first of these have played the most prominent role in shaping higher education over the last half century. Demand for access to higher education is inevitable, as a post-secondary degree or certificate is seen as a key to social and economic success in many corners of the globe. However, from both a financial and quality control perspective, governments must carefully monitor the provision of access to colleges and universities.

Responsibility for establishing university admission policies varies across countries, from national direction to institutional autonomy and open admissions policies. Over the past several decades, governmental involvement in controlling access to higher education has shifted from the former towards the latter. These days centralized control is unusual and the individual institutions are free to determine their own selection and enrollment policies. Private sector in many countries has expanded dramatically over the past several decades. Private colleges and universities have grown in size and importance in parts of the world where the public sector traditionally dominated such as in Latin America and Eastern Europe. In addition to the growth of the private sector, public support for higher education has declined substantially. The idea that higher education should be seen as a "private good" rather than a "public good" has prevalence in most of the world. Also in most countries profits from higher education are not allowed which is definitely a potential loss of excellence. There is a greater market orientation of courses and much premium is given on employability.

From 2012, higher education "goes to market". Tuition fees rise. Total state funding falls. Universities, driven by the market, can now act dynamically, developing existing "customer" segments and capturing new ones. But a "free market" is said to require the state to get "out of the hair" of market suppliers. De-regulating the way they operate. That's the "free" in free markets. The system that emerges then depends on the inter-play of market forces.

Countries around the world have emphasized somehow or the other that interaction of industry and universities is most desirable; research and development is a key to excellence. Global links among academic institutions are becoming increasingly important. Twinning arrangements among academic institutions in different countries, offshore branch campuses, and others are commonplace. Globalization has also encouraged the worldwide spread of an assessment and quality assurance movement in higher education had introduced new challenges and opportunities for members of the academic profession. Technology is another important trend shaping the higher education landscape of the 21st century. Specifically, the Internet offers an array of information resources previously only available in a few university libraries and laboratories, with significant implications for productive research collaborations between faculties across borders.

Thus, a comparative observation of higher education trends and challenges offers an important insight that should provide insight and improve policy and research in many academic disciplines. It is virtually impossible to overestimate how important the advancement of learning can be in improving the human condition. Studying the cross-national similarities and differences helps in better understanding and appreciating our system of higher education. Our understanding of the system of higher education in a single nation and its uniqueness is best understood through comparison with other national contexts.

REFERENCES

Abbott, A. (1991). "An old institutionalist reads the new institutionalism". *Contemporary Sociology*, 21(6), 754-56.

Ahn, B. (1992). *A Study for the Structural Improvement of Administrative Organization Management in Universities*. Seoul: Korean Council for University Education.

American Association of University Professors (AAUP) (1995). *AAUP Policy Documents and Reports,* 8th edition. Washington, DC: American Association of University Professors Press.

Baldridge, J. Victor (1971). *Power and Conflict in the University: Research in the Sociology of Complex Organizations.* New York: J. Wiley.

Baldwin, Roger G. and Chronister, Jay L. (2001). *Teaching Without Tenure: Policies and Practices for a New Era.* Baltimore: Johns Hopkins University Press.

Berger, Joseph B. and Milem, Jeffrey (2000). "Organizational Behavior in Higher Education and Student Outcomes." In *Higher Education: Handbook of Theory and Research,* Vol. XV, ed. John C. Smart. New York: Agathon.

Birnbaum, Robert (1988). *How Colleges Work: The Cybernetics of Academic Organization and Leadership.* San Francisco: Jossey-Bass.

Bolman, Lee G. and Deal, Terrence E. (1997). *Reframing Organizations: Artistry, Choice, and Leadership,* 2nd edition. San Francisco: Jossey-Bass.

Bell, D. (1973). *The Coming of Post-Industrial Society: A Venture in Social Forecasting.* New York: Basic Books.

Cai, Y. (2007). *Academic Staff Integration in Post-Merger Chinese Higher Education Institutions.* Tampere: Tampere University Press.

Cao, Y. (2007). Private higher education and the labor market in China: Institutional management efforts and initial employment outcomes. State University of New York.

Clark, B.R. (1996). "Diversification of higher education: Viability and change". In V.L. Meek, L. Goedegebuure, O. Kivinen and R. Rinne (Eds.), *The Mockers and Mocked: Comparative Perspectives on Differentiation, Convergence, and Diversity in Higher Education* (pp. 16-25). Oxford: Pergamon.

Covalski, M.A., and Dirsmith, M.W. (1988). "An institutional perspective on the rise, social transformation, and fall of a university budget category". *Administrative Science Quarterly*, 33(4), 562-87.

Csizmadia, T., Enders, J. and Westerheijden, D. (2008). "Quality management in Hungarian higher education: Organizational responses to governmental policy". *Higher Education*, 56(4),439-55.

Chung, Y. (1995). "A Remodelling Direction of University Administrative Organization in Korean Higher Education". In Korean Council for University Education (Eds.), *The Remodelling Directions of University Administrative Organization*, 37-65. Seoul, Korea.

De Wit, K. and Verhoeven, J.C. (2000). "Stakeholders in universities and colleges in flanders". *European Journal of Education*, 35(4), 421.

Department of Development and Planning of the Ministry of Education (2009). Essential statistics of education in China (in Chinese).

DiMaggio, P.J. and Powell, W. (1983). "The iron cage revisited: institutional isomorphism and collective rationality". *American Sociological Review*, 42(2), 147-60.

Etzioni, Amitai (1964). *Modern Organizations.* Englewood Cliffs, NJ: Prentice-Hall.

Fisher, James L. and Koch, James V. (1996). *Presidential Leadership.* Phoenix, AZ: ACE/Oryx Press.

Federation of Korean Industries (1990). *Korean Economic Yearbook*. Seoul, Korea.

Geiger, R. (1996). "Diversification in U.S. higher education: Historical patterns and current trends". In V.L. Meek, L. Goedegebuure, O. Kivinen and R. Rinne (Eds.), *The Mockers and Mocked : Comparative Perspectives on Differentiation, Convergence, and Diversity in Higher Education* (pp.188-203). Oxford: Pergamon.

Gornitzka, Å. (1999). "Governmental policies and organizational change in higher education". *Higher Education*, 38(1), 5-31.

Greenwood, R. and Hinings, C.R. (1996). "Understanding radical organizational change: Bring together the old and new institutionalism". *The Academy of Management Review*, 21(4), 1022-54.

Guo, J. (2003). "Research on marketisation of private higher educatin and the organisational and administrative characteristics of private higher education institutions" (in Chinese). *Higher Education Research* (4).

Gieger, Roger (1986). *The Growth of American Research Universities, 1900-1940*. New York: Oxford University Press.

Hyman, Harold M. (1986). *American Singularity: The 1787 Northwest Ordinance, the 1862 Homestead and Morrill Acts, and the 1944 GI Bill of Rights*. Athens: University of Georgia Press.

Hoy, W.K. and Miskel, C.G. (1996, 5th ed). *Educational Administration: Theory, Research, and Practice*. New York: McGraw-Hill.

Hannan, M.T. (1986). "Uncertainty, diversity, and organizational change". In N.J. Smelser and D.R. Gerstein (Eds.), *Behavioral and Social Science : Fifty Years of Discovery : In Commemoration of the Fiftieth Anniversary of the "Ogburn Report," Recent Social Trends in the United States* (pp. 73-94). Washington, D.C.: National Academy Press.

Hawley, A.H. (1968). "Human ecology". In D.L. Sills (Ed.), *International Encyclopedia of the Social Sciences*. New York: Macmillan.

Hrubos, I. (2002). "Differentiation, Diversification, and Homogenization in Higher Education". *European Education*, 34(4), 56.

Huisman, J., Meek, L. and Wood, F. (2007). "Institutional Diversity in Higher Education: Across-national and longitudinal Analysis". *Higher Education Quarterly*, 61(4), 563-77.

Ingram, P. and Clay, K. (2000). "The choice-within-constraints new institutionalism and implications for sociology". *Annual Review of Sociology*, 26(1), 525-46.

Ingram, Richard T. 1996. "New Tensions in the Academic Boardroom." *Educational Record*, 77 (2-3): 49-55.

Jiang, H. (2008). "Changes of private higher education organizations in China and their characteristics—from the view of organization sociology" (in Chinese). *Education Research Monthly*, 2008(2).

Kerr, Clark. (1963). *The Uses of the University*. Cambridge, MA: Harvard University Press.

Kirby-Harris, R. (2003). "Universities responding to policy: Organizational change at the University of Namibia". *Higher Education*, 45(3), 353-74.

Kraatz, A.X. and Zajac, E.J. (1996). "Exploring the limits of the new institutionalism: The cause and consequences of illegitimate organizational change". *American Sociological Review*, 61(5), 812-36.

Kang, I. (1997). "Tasks and Contents of the Recently Revised Education Laws Related", *The Journal of Law of Education* (Korea), 9, 33-53.

Lee, H. (1999). "The Current of Higher Education Policy after Liberation". *Higher Education* (Seoul: Korean Council for University Education), 100, 12-19.

Lee, J.K. (1999a). "Historic Factors Affecting Educational Administration in Korean Higher Education". *Higher Education Review,* 32(1), 7-23.

Larsen, I.M. and Gornitzka, A. (1995). "New management systems in Norwegian universities: The interface between reform and institutional understanding". *European Journal of Education*, 30(3), 347.

Lawrence, P.R., and Lorsch, J.W. (1967). *Organization and Environment: Managing Differentiation and Integration.* Boston: Division of Research, Graduate School of Business Administration, Harvard University.

Levy, D.C. (1986). "Private" and "public": Analysis amid ambiguity in higher education. In D.C. Levy (Ed.), *Private Education: Studies in Choice and Public Policy* (pp. 170-236). Oxford and New York: Oxford University Press.

Levy, D.C. (1999). "When private higher education does not bring organizational diversity". In P.G. Altbach (Ed.), *Private Prometheus : Private Higher Education and Development in the 21st Century* (pp. 15-44). Westport, Conn.: Greenwood Press.

Levy, D.C. (2006*a*). "How private higher education's growth challenges the new Institutionalism". In H.D. Meyer and B. Rowan (Eds.), *The New Institutionalism in Education* (pp. 143-62). Albany: State University of New York Press.

Levy, D.C. (2006*b*). "The Unanticipated Explosion: Private Higher Education's Global Surge". *Comparative Education Review*, 50(2), 217-40.

Levy, D.C. (2009). "Chapter 1: Growth and typology". In S. Bjarnason, K.M. Cheng, J. Fielden, M.J. Lemaitre, D. Levy and N.V. Varghese (Eds.), *A New Dynamic: Private Higher Education* (pp. 7-28). Paris: UNESCO: 2009 World Conference on Higher Education.

Maassen, P. (2000). "Editorial". *European Journal of Education*, 35(4), 377.

Meek, V.L. and Wood, F.Q. (1996). "Conclusion". In V.L. Meek, L. Goedegebuure, O. Kivinen and R. Rinne (Eds.), *The Mockers and Mocked: Comparative Perspectives on Differentiation, Convergence, and Diversity in Higher Education* (pp. 206-36). Oxford: Pergamon.

Meyer, H.D. and Rowan, B. (2006). "Institutional Analysis and the Study of Education". In H.D. Meyer and B. Rowan (Eds.), *The New Institutionalism in Education* (pp. 1-14). Albany: State University of New York Press.

Meyer, J.W. and Rowan, B. (1977). "Institutionalized Organizations: Formal Structure as Myths and Ceremony". *American Journal of Sociology*, 83(2), 340-63.

Meyer, J.W. and Scott, W.R. (1983). *Organizational Environments: Ritual and Rationality*. Beverly Hills; London: Sage.

Meyer, J.W. Scott, W.R. and Deal, T. (1983). "Research on School and District Organization". In J.V. Baldridge and T. Deal (Eds.), *The Dynamics of Organizational Change in Education* (pp. 409-25). Berkeley: McCutchan.

Morphew, C.C. and Huisman, J. (2002). "Using institutional theory to reframe research on academic drift". *Higher Education in Europe*, 27(4), 491.

Millett, John. 1984. *Conflict in Higher Education: State Government Coordination Versus Institutional Independence*. San Francisco: Jossey-Bass.

Neave, G. and van Vught, F. (1994). "Government and Higher Education in Developing nations: A conceptual framework". In G. Neave and F. van Vught (Eds.), *Government and Higher Education Relationships across Three Continents: The Winds of Change* (pp. 1-21). Oxford: Pergamon Press.

Peterson, M.W. (2007). "The study of colleges and universities as organizations". In P.J. Gumport (Ed.), *Sociology of Higher Education: Contributions and their Contexts* (pp. 147-84). Baltimore: The Johns Hopkins University Press.

Pfeffer, J. and Salancik, G.R. (1978). *The External Control of Organizations*. New York: Harper and Row.

Pusser, Brian (2000). "The Contemporary Politics of Access Policy: California after Proposition 209." In *The States and Public Higher Education: Affordability, Access, and Accountability*, ed. Donald E. Heller. Baltimore: Johns Hopkins University Press.

Qasem, S. (1998a) *The Higher Education Systems in the Arab States: Development of Science and Technology Indicators*; UNESCO and ESCWA, Cairo, January.

——— (1998b) *R&D Systems in the Arab States: Development of S&T Indicators*; UNESCO, Cairo.

Scharpf, F.W. (1997). *Games Real Actors Play: Actor-centered Institutionalism in Policy Research*. Boulder, Colo.: Westview Press.

Scott, W.R. (1992). *Organizations: Rational, Natural, and Open Systems* (Third ed.). Englewood Cliffs: Prentice-Hall, INC.

Selznick, P. (1957). *Leadership in Administration: A Sociological Interpretation*. New York, Evanston & London: Harper & Row.

Selznick, P. (1996). "Institutionalism 'old' and 'new'". *Administrative Science Quarterly*, 41(2), 270-77.

Stensaker, B. and Norgard, J.D. (2001). "Innvoation and isomorphism: A Case-Study of University Identity Struggle 1969-1999". *Higher Education*, 4, 42.

Stinchcombe, A.L. (1997). "On the virtues of the old institutionalism". *Annual Review of Sociology*, 23(1), 1-18.

Seo, B. (1998). "Directions of Educational Policy and Higher Education Act in the Years of 2000", *Workshop Resource* (Seoul, Korea: Korean Institute for Staff Development of Higher Education: AD-98-3-150), 59-77.

Shin, J. *et al.* (1995). *A Study of the Reorganization of Administrative Organizations in Universities.* RR 95-5-112, Seoul, Korea: Korean Council for University Education.

Slaughter, Sheila, and Leslie, Larry L. 1997. *Academic Capitalism.* Baltimore: Johns Hopkins University Press.

Tolbert, P.S. and Zucker, L.G. (1983). "Institutional Sources of Change in the Formal Structure of Organizations: The Diffusion of Civil Service Reform". *Administrative Science Quarterly*, 28(1),22-39.

Tolbert, P.S. and Zucker, L.G. (1996). "The Institutionalization of Institutional Theory". In C. Hardy, S.R. Clegg and W. Nord (Eds.), *Handbook of Organization Studies* (pp. 175-90). London: SAGA.

Trommel, W. and Van Der Veen, R. (1997). "Sociological Perspectives on Institutions and Neo-institutionalism". In B. Steunenberg and F.V. Vught (Eds.), *Political Institutions and Public Institutions: Perspectives on European Decision Making* (pp. 45-66). Dordrecht/Boston/London: Kluwer Academic Publishers.

UNESCO (1998a). *1998 World Education Report.*

van Vught, F. (1996). "Isomorphism in higher education? Towards a theory of differentiation and diversity in higher education system". In V.L. Meek, L. Goedegebuure, O. Kivinen and R. Rinne (Eds.), *The Mockers and Mocked : Comparative Perspectives on Differentiation, Convergence, and Diversity in Higher Education* (pp. 16-25). Oxford: Pergamon.

——— (2008). "Mission diversity and reputation in higher education". *Higher Education Policy*, 21, 151-74.

Veysey, Laurence. (1965). *The Emergence of the American University.* Chicago: University of Chicago Press.

World Statistical Outlook on Higher Education: 1980-1995; *World Conference on Higher Education: Higher Education in the Twenty-First Century: Vision and Action*, Paris, 5-9 October.

Yan, F. (2004a). "The analysis of environmental factors for private higher education in Mainland of China" (in Chinese). *Taibei: Study of Mainland of China*, 47(1), 135-58.

——— (2004b). "Study of ratio of private education enrollments in total educational enrollments" (in Chinese). *Educational Research*, No. 9, 64-70.

——— (2007). "Analysis of the interior administrative form of the Chinese non-governmental higher education institutions". *Zhejiang Shuren University Journal*, 7(5).

Yan, F. (2008). "An analyses of the factors influencing the distribution of private higher education institutions across provinces and over time" (In Chinese). *University Research and Evaluation* (5), 20-26.

Yan, F. and Levy, D.C. (2003). "China's new private education law". *International Higher Education*, 2003 (Spring).

Yun, J. (1999). "A Disputed Point in Process of Educational Reform". In The Korean Society for the Study of Education (Eds.), *Examination and Vision of Educational Reform Policy*, pp. 41-59. Seoul, Korea.

Zha, Q. (2006). "The resurgence and growth of private higher education in China". *Higher Education Perspectives*, 2(1), 54-68.

^ http://www.oecd.org/dataoecd/27/11/41631383.pdf Learning for Jobs OECD review of Australian vocational education.

^ *TAFE gears up to offer degrees* by Rebecca Scott, *The Age* July 24, 2002. Accessed August 3, 2008.

^ http://www.oecd.org/dataoecd/24/27/41738329.pdf OECD review of vocational education and training in Hungary.

^ http://www.oecd.org/edu/learningforjobs review of Korean vocational education by OECD.

^ Review of vocational education and training in Mexico.

^ http://www.oecd.org/dataoecd/45/34/41506628.pdf OECD review of vocational education and training in Norway.

^ http://www.oecd.org/edu/learningforjobs OECD Learning for Jobs review of vocational education in Sweden.

^ http://www.oecd.org/dataoecd/12/5/42578681.pdf Learning for Jobs OECD review of Switzerland, 2009.

^ Owen, W.B. (1912). Sir Sidney Lee. ed. *Dictionary of National Biography* – William Ford Robinson Stanley. Second Supplement. III (NEIL-YOUNG). London: Smith, Elder & Co. pp. 393-94.

^ Wolf, A. (2002) *Does Education Matter? Myths about Education and Economic Growth* London: Penguin.

^ Youth Policies in the UK.

^ World Class Apprenticeships. The Government's strategy for the future of Apprenticeships in England. DIUS/DCSF, 2008.

——— (1999b). "Organizational Structure and Culture in Korean HigherEducation", *International Higher Education, Number, 16*, 17.

——— (2000). "The Administrative Structure and Systems of Korean Higher Education. *Higher Education Management,* 12 (2), 43-51.

Min, K. (1999). "Understanding of University Entrance Selection of the 2000 Academic Year". *Higher Education* (Seoul: Korean Council for University Education), 100, 100-07.

Ministry of Education [MOE] (1970). *Statistical Yearbook of Education.* Seoul, Korea.

_____ (1971). *Statistical Yearbook of Education*. Seoul, Korea.

_____ (1976). *Education in Korea*. Seoul, Korea.

_____ (1980). *Statistical Yearbook of Education*. Seoul, Korea.

_____ (1998a). *Education in Korea*. Seoul, Korea.

_____ (1998b). *Educational Reform toward the 21 st Century in Korea*. Seoul, Korea.

_____ (1999). *A Five Year Plan for Educational Development*. Seoul, Korea.

_____ (1999). *Education in Korea*. Seoul, Korea.

_____ http://www.moe.go.kr/English/

MOE and Korean Educational Development Institute [KEDI] (1999). *Statistical Yearbook of Education*. Seoul, Korea.

MOE and National Institute of Educational Evaluation [NIEE] (1989). *Statistical Yearbook of Education*. Seoul, Korea.

_____. (1990). *Statistical Yearbook of Education*. Seoul, Korea.

National Center for Education Statistics [NCES] (1999). *The Condition of Education*. Washington, D.C.: NCES.

Organization for Economic Cooperation and Development [OECD] (1998).

Education at Glance: OECD Indicators. Paris: OECD.

Presidential Commission on Educational Reform [PCER] (1994). *Directions and Tasks of Educational Reform for the Creation of New Korea*. Seoul, Korea.

PCER (1994). *Educational Reform Plans for the Establishment of the New Educational System Initiated Internationalization and Informationalization*. Seoul, Korea.

_____ (1995). *The First Educational Reform Plans for the Establishment of the New Educational System Initiated Internationalization and Informationalization*. Seoul, Korea.

_____ (February 1996). *The Second Educational Reform Plans for the Establishment of the New Educational System Initiated Internationalization and Informationalization*. Seoul, Korea.

_____ (August 1996). *The Third Educational Reform Plans for the Establishment of the New Educational System Initiated Internationalization and Informationalization*. Seoul, Korea.

_____ (1996). *An Educational Reform Report for the Establishment of a New Education System*. Seoul, Korea.

_____ (June 1997). *The Fourth Educational Reform Plans for the Establishment of the New Educational System Initiated Internationalization and Informationalization*. Seoul, Korea.

_____. (1998). *White papers: Educational Reform*. Seoul, Korea.

http://www.euroeducation.net/prof/usa.htm

http://education.stateuniversity.com/pages/1859/Colleges-Universities-Organizational-Structure.html